CRYSTAL CONNECTIONS

A GUIDE TO CRYSTALS
AND HOW TO USE THEM

NEW EDITION – REVISED AND EXPANDED

CRYSTAL CONNECTIONS

A GUIDE TO CRYSTALS AND HOW TO USE THEM

NEW EDITION – REVISED AND EXPANDED

ADAM BARRALET

Animal Dreaming Publishing
www.AnimalDreamingPublishing.com

Crystal Connections
Revised and Expanded

ANIMAL DREAMING PUBLISHING
PO Box 5203 East Lismore NSW 2480
AUSTRALIA
Phone +61 2 6622 6147
www.AnimalDreamingPublishing.com
Email: Publish@AnimalDreamingPublishing.com
www.facebook.com/AnimalDreamingPublishing

First edition published 2014
Second edition published 2017
Reprinted 2018

A special thanks to Kelly Wale and Crystal Universe Perth, Australia for supplying many of the specimens for the photos. Other crystals are from the author's personal working collection.

ISBN 978-0-9953642-3-3

This book is intended for spiritual and emotional guidance only.
It is not intended to replace medical assistance or treatment.

Designed by Animal Dreaming Publishing

Disclaimer
All information in this book is offered for educational purposes only. Please consider and consult professionals in the relevant field to make an educated decision as to whether each suggestion in this book is right for you.
Adam Barralet 2017

SPECIAL THANKS

My gratitude goes to J Lynn for showing me the door, Scott for opening it, and Trudy for guiding me through the doorway of birthing this book.

Thank you to Shanta, Kelly, Denise, Rebecca, Vicki, Linda, Lyn, Peta, Emma and Sarah for your hours of dedication and reading. Also thank you to Strez for your support, Tamara for your teachings and Wes for reinforcing my faith in my work.

To nature, its crystals, animals and plants as well as the astrological bodies that orbit around us. Thank you for whispering in my ear, speaking to my soul and making my heart race so that I may know and be inspired to share your wisdom. May this book help to inspire other children of Mother Earth to protect and preserve her so that future generations, including my godson Taj, can also experience the magic and beauty of Gaia.

And with all my love I thank my late father who told me to keep my feet on the ground, my mother who tells me to reach for the stars, and Jonathan, who holds my hand as I fly in-between.

Contents

INTRODUCTION

Crystals have been used around the world for thousands of years to attract love, promote luck, banish evil, ensure protection and restore health. Now you can learn how to easily access the power of crystals too.

The structure, chemical make up, colour, shape and place of origin all affect a crystal's energy and its beneficial properties. Some crystals will lead you to new and exciting adventures, while others will protect and build upon what you already possess. One thing is for sure though, there is a crystal perfect for every hope and dream you hold.

This book is a comprehensive guide that will enable you to discover what each crystal does and how you can utilise its powers. It will allow you to discover new crystals and further enhance your connection with your current favourites. Crystals are a gift from Mother Earth and are waiting to work with you towards creating a happier, healthier, loving, safe, free, and powerful you on a greener, fairer, and more harmonious planet. Enjoy the journey!

CHOOSING YOUR CRYSTALS

Use this book as a guide to identify the crystal energetically closest to what you would like to work towards. There are plenty of retail and online stores where you can buy your crystals. When choosing, hold your intention in your mind and choose the crystal that you are most drawn to. Don't think about it too much. You may not choose the prettiest crystal of the lot, but energetically this will be the one for you.

While shopping, also consider where your crystal was sourced from and whether it was obtained in an ethical manner. Unfortunately, in some places around the world, employees are forced to risk their lives in dangerous mines and are paid next to nothing, while some mines totally destroy the natural environment surrounding them all for others to have cheap crystals. However, there are other crystal suppliers who ensure all their crystals come from a source where employees are treated well and paid appropriately and that the environment is protected.

Some crystal books will include the use of ivory, bone, coral and other animal products. If you are gifted by Great Spirit to find the remains of an animal from which you can acquire these parts then it is a great blessing to help you connect with this animal. However, buying these products is often supporting illegal trades that usually lead to the extinction of the species, and thus should be avoided.

Crystals are a finite resource and in most cases you only need one of each crystal for most crystal works. The exception may be collecting eleven Clear Quartz points or several tumbled stones for grids. If a crystal comes into your life that you already have, consider thanking the old one for its service and returning it to the earth or passing it on to another.

WORKING WITH YOUR CRYSTALS

Crystals are a gift from the Earth, an integral part of the web of life. They have their own energy and consciousness and are a tool to help you improve life on this planet. It's not quite accurate to say you own a crystal, for as you work with them more, you will start to realise that they have their own personality and free spirit just like you and I. Rather, they come to us so that we may be their guardian, their temporary companion until they will one day be passed on and eventually return to the earth as we all do when our work here is done.

Crystals are a creation of nature and although they can assist us in living in our modern, urban world we must meet them half way. We must take steps to reconnect with the natural world from where they come. We must understand their origins, their make up, and their energy—just like a good friend—in order to get the most out of our relationship with them. Through your work with crystals, allow yourself to step back to nature, even if that just means standing outside your back door. Cleanse them on the bare earth in the cold rain. Sit with them on your porch, rather than in your living room. Or better still, head far, far away into the bush or forest. Venture far away from all other people. Here in the depths of nature your crystals won't just speak to you, they will sing to you, for they are glad to be home again.

Working with crystals and including them in your life can be as simple or as complex as you like. There are three simple steps to working with crystals: Cleanse – Connect – Combine. These three steps can be done in a matter of minutes or you can make the cleansing and meditation as elaborate as you please. Let's explore these now:

STEP 1 – CLEANSE

The first step to working with a crystal is cleansing it. Crystals, like everything else in our material world, are a solidified form of energy. They are made up of atoms and molecules just as we are. They have a vibration and, thus being an energetic being, have a consciousness. Like us, crystals are sentient creatures but because their vibration is different to ours, this may be hard to recognise at first. This means that crystals are affected by their immediate surroundings, just as we are. People, emotions, sounds, radiation, toxins, and temperature all affect a crystal's energetic balance. Cleansing a crystal simply means giving it a chance to rebalance, just as you may take a walk to relax after a stressful day.

The best way to cleanse any crystal is to take it back to nature. Nature is always working to return to a state of balanced equilibrium and here your crystal can do the same. You may already be familiar with some of these cleansing techniques such as putting your crystals out under the full moon or running them under water. When choosing how to cleanse each crystal you should use a natural element that either has a similar energy to your crystal or has a desirable energy you'd like your crystal to adopt. Just as different people find different activities relaxing and rebalancing, so do crystals.

Placing a Sunstone or Ruby under the soft, nurturing energy of the full moon to cleanse is not energetically compatible with these fiery crystals and will not allow the crystals to cleanse to their full potential.

As well as cleansing your crystals, it is important to cleanse yourself in preparation. You can't clean a house wearing dirty shoes, so you can't optimise your connection with crystals if you don't cleanse, balance and harmonise yourself with the energies that resonate with your crystal.

There are six main ways to cleanse yourself and your crystals, incorporating the four magical elements plus the two major astrological bodies that influence our planet.

Fire: This is the element of energy, action and quick transformation. Crystals that harmonise with fire often bring you energy and passion. To cleanse a crystal with fire you can place it near a campfire or fireplace, ensuring it doesn't get too hot to affect the crystal physically. Otherwise, you can carefully pass it through a candle flame, ensuring you don't burn yourself. Again make sure the crystal doesn't get too hot. Visualise any unwanted energies singeing away and returning the crystal to its lively self. Sit by the fire or candle and feel the warmth of the flame cleanse you.

Air: This is the element of insight, intellect and freedom. Crystals that harmonise with air aid mental and intellectual pursuits and bring you great new ideas. To cleanse a crystal with air, leave it outside where the wind can blow across it, carrying unhelpful energies away. You can sit outside for a while and allow the wind to carry away all your worries. Another air cleansing technique is to pass your crystal through incense or smudge smoke. Choose a cleansing incense such as white sage, cedar and palo santo or the incense of the plant that harmonises with each crystal. Let the smoke pass over you as a cleansing too.

Earth: This is the element of strength, solidarity and comfort. Crystals that harmonise with earth may offer grounding and protection or promote healthy growth in your life. Ideally bury crystals that harmonise with earth in the natural earth. Otherwise, place them on top of the earth or in a container with salt, which is the purest form of earth. Be sure to know a little bit about your crystal as burying some in wet soil or putting them with salt may affect their appearance. Take some time to sit or walk upon the earth with bare feet to cleanse yourself. This will help you feel grounded and can improve your health.

Water: This is the element of feelings, intuition and love. Crystals that harmonise with water will help to draw love into your life, allow you to relax and balance your emotions. Cleanse these crystals in a natural source of water. Place them in a stream, let the ocean's waves wash over them or leave them out during a rainstorm. If this is not possible, place them in filtered or purified water. Don't let your crystal have all the fun! Jump in the water with them or take a cleansing shower or bath.

The Sun: This is the major energy source for all life on Earth. Without the Sun, life would not start, nor continue to grow. The Sun is connected to masculine energy, which is active, projective, warming, dominant and yang. Crystals that harmonise with the Sun will help you achieve goals, ignite change and gain you recognition. Cleanse these crystals by leaving them in the sunlight. Take a few minutes to sit in the sun too.

The Moon: The moon affects our planet in gentler ways. It rules the ocean's tides and since we are largely made up of water, the moon has an impact on our wellbeing. The moon offers an energy that is restful, magnetic, cooling, introspective and yin. Crystals that harmonise with the moon allow you to improve your intuition and learn the mysteries of the world. The waxing and full moon give an energy that nurtures loving growth, while the waning, dark and new moon allow you to step back and tune in to the lessons life has for you. Cleanse crystals by the moon by leaving them outside in direct moonlight overnight. Take the time to bathe in the moon's glow that night too.

Other Techniques: Certain crystals have been found to resonate with other aspects of nature such as lightning, meteor showers, rainbows, flower petals and rice. These techniques are discussed in the chapter of the relevant crystals.

STEP 2 – CONNECT

Once your crystal is cleansed, it's time to connect with it. This involves two steps. Firstly, allow yourself to tune in to its energy, and once you've gotten to know it, program your crystal.

The best way to connect with a crystal is through meditation. When you meditate you simply slow down enough and allow yourself to listen to the crystal. Crystals are a product of nature and thus to understand the wisdom of crystals you must understand and connect with nature. In each chapter the recommended meditation will start with the phrase "Go to… (a forest, hill, lake)." Again these are an aspect of nature that harmonise with your crystal's energy or lessons. Ideally explore the natural surroundings near your home and discover exciting and wild places to dedicate as your personal sanctuaries. However, if you can't go to a place because of geographical, weather or other reasons that doesn't render the task fruitless. Simply 'go' there in your mind. You could utilise some soundscape music or a beautiful photograph to help transport you there. The Crystal Connections guided meditation range was created as a way of meditating and connecting with your crystal. Each meditation includes relaxing music in the resonating chakra key, corresponding planetary frequencies and potent symbology and imagery to further facilitate a powerful relationship with your crystal.

Once you are ready to meditate, give yourself some time to enjoy the natural setting and feel yourself find a state of natural equilibrium. When you are ready, pick up your crystal and hold it in your receptive hand, the one you do not write with. Allow yourself to sense the energy or messages from the crystal. This can happen in different ways. You may hear or see something in your mind's eye, an idea may pop into your head as an inspired thought or your body may start to feel different. Just relax, stay aware and allow.

Once your crystal has spoken, it is your turn. This is called programming your crystal and involves clearly communicating your intent of how you need the crystal to assist you. Choose a few simple words or a precise image and share this with your crystal. First feel the essence of what you want within you. Visualise in your mind the successful business you want to start. See the masses of people, hear the sounds, smell the smells and most important feel how you will feel when it comes true. Then, holding your crystal in your projective hand, the one you write with, send those images into the crystal as though you are storing that energy within the crystal. Seal it with a kiss and your crystal is programmed.

This step may seem lengthy but it can be done within a minute if you are clear on what you want. A more elaborate practice will allow you to raise more energy and intent, benefiting the process. Taking time to get to know each crystal intimately will prevent "crystal speed dating". There are so many great crystals available on the market today, each with beautiful colours, unique shapes and amazing properties. When you love crystals, it's easy to want to dive amongst them and immerse yourself in all their possibilities. However, taking the time to get to know each crystal as an individual will lead to a more intimate and powerful connection. Wearing and working with one crystal at a time is the best way to master using their energy, so allow yourself to experience "crystal monogamy" for a while.

STEP 3 – COMBINE

This is a key step that many people neglect. Crystals are not magical tools that will transform your life as you sit there. Rose Quartz will not bring you love if you sit at home by yourself every night, nor will Blue Apatite help you achieve the perfect body if you don't maintain a healthy lifestyle. Crystals are vehicles for change but you must drive them. As you change your thoughts and actions to mirror what you want, your crystals will affect the energy around you and allow opportunities and guidance to arise in unexpected and magical ways. Working with crystals is a partnership, not a quick fix for the lazy or uninspired. There are many different ways to implement crystals into your everyday living. Here are a few:

Jewellery and tumbled stones: By carrying or wearing a crystal, you keep its energy with you throughout the day. Pendants, rings, bracelets and other beautiful jewellery are available to suit any budget. Otherwise a tumbled stone can be placed in your pocket, bra or bag. A crystal doesn't necessarily have to be touching your skin, as it is affecting your energy field, which expands beyond your physical body. Wearing a crystal near a relevant chakra can be ideal as this is where the centre of a particular energy resides in your body.

Medicine bags: Create a medicine bag by adding crystals with parts of plants such as leaves, twigs or flowers into a small fabric pouch. You can add symbols and small tokens that correspond with your intent. Your medicine bag can then be worn or carried. They are a powerful tool as they not only use crystal power but also combine the corresponding elements of other natural and magical items for increased energy.

Grids: Combining crystals in a formation so they work together in harmony towards a common goal is a powerful way of using crystals. Grids can be categorised into three groups: personal, space and power grids.

A personal grid is often used by crystal healers and involves the placement of chosen crystals on specific points along your body. You may place certain crystals on chakras or on a site of pain in the body. You can combine this with Reiki, massage, aromatherapy or colour therapy to achieve amazing results. You can perform this by yourself, with another, or visit a professional practitioner.

Space grids require you to place a series of crystals around your home, office, outdoor area or any space to create a web of energy. A simple space grid can be created by placing a set of the same crystals around an area's perimeter to fill the space with the programmed energy of that crystal. As you gain experience and confidence, try combinations including crystal points and carved shapes. Incorporating Feng Shui with crystals is an effective practice.

Power grids are a formation of crystals set up on an altar, in a meditation room or another specified place. A power grid placed in a special part of your home works as a constant reminder of something important in your life that you are devoting energy to. They are great focus points for absent or distance healing, a form of healing sending energy to someone or somewhere you cannot attend physically. Used in meditation groups, power grids help collect and direct the intentions of the collective. A power grid usually has a power crystal in the middle. The power crystal encompasses the energy of the primary focus such as a Citrine for happiness or an Angelite for peace. You can add other items that symbolise the intention such as a photo of the person to receive the healing, a coloured candle or a statue. Surround your power crystal with a series of points. Clear Quartz is most commonly used for this purpose as it amplifies and purifies energy and focuses white healing light where directed. Face these points inwards toward the power crystal to attract energy, outwards to send energy, clockwise to raise energy or anti-clockwise to diminish energy. Around the edge of the grid you can add supporting crystals to contribute to the intention. For example, you may want to add Sunstone to a healing grid for extra vitality or Tugtupite to add passion to a conservation grid. There are plenty of layouts available on the internet for free but feel free to rely on your own creativity. A power grid created purely with your own imagination and flair will contain a lot more effective energy than something you download and mechanically set up.

Elixirs and essences: These are liquid solutions, mainly water that contain the energy of the crystal. They are ingested to bring the crystalline energy into your body. Direct elixirs involve placing a crystal into water for a period of time. This requires significant caution and some research. Tumbled stones are often covered in a lacquer or varnish that can leech into the water. Alternatively, using some raw crystals can be dangerous as they contain toxins or carcinogens such as aluminium, Copper, sulphur, asbestos or other harmful elements that can make you quite ill. In these cases make an indirect elixir by placing your crystal near the water for several hours before drinking it. Gem essences are generally a combination of water and whisky and have been created by exposing crystal to water in various ways so that the water holds the crystalline vibration. Crystal essences can be taken as drops, placed in baths or sprayed as room mists.

Scrying: This is a form of open-eyed meditation that involves gazing into the reflective shine of a crystal. It is a great technique for those who find they get too distracted by their thoughts when their eyes are closed. Scrying helps you block out distractive thoughts and allows you to access your subconscious mind. To scry, sit in a darkened room with a lit candle. Stare at the reflection in the crystal, allowing your eyes to relax. Let your focus soften as you look deeper into the crystal. Simply relax and messages will flow to you once you are ready to receive them.

Carved shapes: Crystals are carved into a variety of shapes. The geometry of the shape affects the way the crystal's energy is directed. Point, wands and generators send energy in the direction the point is facing. Obelisks attract and draw energies while a pyramid will bring energy to a specific point. Spheres send energy equally in all direction making them great to place in the centre of the room while eggs confine and shape energy in order to birth an intention. Skulls allow us to access innate wisdom while carved animals encompass the power of that creature's medicine or energy.

CORRESPONDENCES – WAYS TO ENHANCE THE POWER OF YOUR CRYSTALS

Using crystal correspondences is a way to enhance your crystal workings. By combining crystals with other items that possess a similar and compatible energy, you generate a mass of energy where the sum of the whole is greater than all the parts used separately. When all these energies combine in harmony you raise a lot more energy to direct toward your intention. If you were creating a romantic dinner at home for a partner, you wouldn't just light a red candle and expect that to create a romantic atmosphere or energy. You'd dim the lights, light candles, diffuse romantic scents like jasmine and ylang ylang, play sensual music and prepare a meal of delicious foods with loving intentions. By combining crystals with animal guides, plants, astrological influences and certain days of the week you align yourself with a vibration that matches your intention and all these elements work together to manifest it for you.

Throughout this book are suggestions on how to combine these correspondences with crystals. These are just examples to get your imagination flowing. Incorporate these correspondences in as many ways as your creativity can conceive.

ANIMALS

Every animal on this planet has a unique skill set that allows it to live and survive each day. Anyone who considers humans to be a superior species should consider how they'd survive in the middle of the Amazon jungle during a thunderstorm or through an Antarctic winter. Many other species would fare far better than we would. Humans may have impressive intellectual abilities but we can never hope to have the strength of Ant, the speed of Cheetah or the endurance of Camel. When you open yourself up to each animal on this planet, you are accessing teachings that are commonly referred to as animal medicine. You are connected to all other animals on this planet and when you wish to, you can invite the spiritual essence, or guide, of any animal to connect with you.

You can learn about the animal by watching it in nature, visiting zoos or wildlife parks and watching documentaries. Take time to read articles and search for conservation organisations when the animal is endangered. As you see how each animal lives, plays and interacts to ensure its survival and wellbeing, you'll see how its wisdom can help you too. Surround yourself with the animal's energy however you can. When you are ready to make a spiritual connection with the animal, sit peacefully in meditation holding the corresponding crystal. Visualise before you a natural setting like that of the habitat of the animal you wish to connect with. Invite your animal guide to join you in this space. As they join you, allow yourself to interact with your animal guide however you feel appropriate. You may want to ask a specific question, ask for general guidance or request they help you through an upcoming time in your life. Your crystal can then serve as a physical talisman that connects you to your animal guide.

PLANTS

Plants play an integral part in our everyday lives. They help fulfil our daily need for oxygen, food and shelter. Plants are used to nourish and heal our bodies. Plants are also sentient beings like crystals and us, and each plant has its own spirit or energy. When working with a particular crystal find innovative ways to include its corresponding plant into your daily life. Using the plant in the form of food and drink, incense, essential oil, flower essence and other products will all strengthen the crystal's working.

ASTROLOGICAL INFLUENCES

The effects of the Sun, Moon and other planets are still being unveiled to us at this time. Perhaps the effect of our closest companion, the Moon, is best known for its effects on the tides, as well as our mental state of mind. The ancient study of astrology dates back thousands of years and is still referred to by countless people. An accurate astrological reading can give you clear indications about your personality and the direction of your life.

As celestial bodies are discovered, their energies are interpreted and their influences become part of the general knowledge, also known as the global consciousness. For example, Mercury rules communications while Saturn regulates structure. Each planet, dwarf planet and asteroid in our solar system has a unique energy and impacts us in subtle way.

Tune in to the energy of the astrological body that harmonises with your crystal and draw its influence into your crystal work. Understanding its influence in your astrological chart will give you guidance on your personal relationship with the body. Another powerful technique is to sit outside at night facing the direction of the planet, dwarf planet or asteroid even if you cannot see it with your naked eye. Tune in to its energy and as you connect and develop your relationship with the planet, you'll start to feel its energetic pull. Feel, interpret and understand its influence and combine this with your crystal work. Breathe in the astrological body's energy and project it into your crystal when cleansing and programming it, include its symbol in your medicine bags and grids and choose the best times to implement crystal work based on your astrologer's advice.

POWER DAYS

Centuries ago, the days of the week were named after the seven celestial bodies that were known at the time. The Sun, Moon, Mercury, Venus, Mars, Jupiter and Saturn each hold a specific energy and this is carried into the day they rule over. Have you ever noticed how you don't feel like working on a Monday, the day ruled by the Moon's lunar energy of rest and reflection? Is Saturday, ruled by organised Saturn your day of chores, while Sunday, day of the vibrant sun, is a recreational and fun day? This is the impact of the global consciousness connecting with certain energies of the planets and tuning into them on certain days.

Each crystal has at least one Power Day; a day the unique planetary energy most corresponds with that crystal. By doing your crystal work on that particular day, you are adding an extra energetic element to your efforts.

OTHER CORRESPONDENCES

CHAKRAS

The chakras are energy centres located around the body. They govern different organs, glands and systems of your body and each regulates different aspects of your life. As centres of energy, they can be underactive and require stimulating, overactive and require soothing, or balanced and simply need nurturing. This can be measured intuitively, with kinesiology or a pendulum or through special photographic techniques. Each crystal corresponds to and affects certain chakras in different ways. Some soothe while others stimulate, and when combined with other techniques such as visualisation and deliberate conscious energy movement you can balance each chakra so that they are all equally vibrant and flowing. The seven main chakras that exist along your spine are acknowledged in many traditions. They correspond with the seven colours of the rainbow. They are:

Base: Your first chakra is located at the base of your spine and resonates with the colour red. The base chakra is connected to your primal instincts of survival and your sense of security and stability. It governs your legs, feet, kidneys and bladder. Healing this chakra alleviates tiredness, fear, aggression or materialism. When balanced you feel grounded, settled and able to adapt within this changing world. You have a sense that you have all you need.

Sacral: You can sense the energy of this chakra when you are sexual aroused. It is located below your navel and resonates with the colour orange. This chakra governs your ability to create and manifest and is concerned with the relationships in your life. The sacral chakra is associated with your sexual and reproductive systems. Healing this chakra removes feelings of arrogance, indifference and repression. When your sacral chakra is balanced you feel sociable, connected and ready to share with others. You passionately welcome the pleasures of life and have a healthy sex drive.

Solar Plexus: You feel your solar plexus chakra react when you get a sudden fright. This chakra vibrates to the colour yellow. This is the centre of emotional stability and personal power. Healing this chakra allows you to release any frustration, anxiety, nervousness, guilt and emotion baggage that you still hold. Your solar plexus affects your digestive system. When balanced you feel harmonious and emotionally content. You are ready to work with others to create a peaceful, harmonious world.

Heart: Your heart chakra resides within the centre of your chest level with your physical heart. It harmonises with green but pink can also be used when dealing with love. It is concerned with your ability to give and receive and when balanced ensures you do both freely and equally. A healthy heart chakra ensures efficient functioning of the circulatory and immune systems as well as strong arms and hands. Healing this chakra removes jealousy, selfishness and insecurity. When your heart chakra is balanced you show love to others by giving them freedom to explore life and be themselves. You feel love for the world, and feel loved by the world.

Throat: This chakra resonates with blue and can be felt when you are choked up and unable to speak. It is concerned with communication and self-expression. Your throat chakra governs your respiratory system plus your mouth, tongue, teeth, ears and thyroid. Healing the throat chakra allows the release of stubbornness as well as domineering and critical behaviours. When balanced you embrace opportunities to hear others speak. You happily share your ideas, thoughts and feelings. You are able to express yourself and be understood by the world. You speak with truth and integrity.

Third Eye: This chakra is at the point in the centre of your forehead. It vibrates to the colour indigo and is your psychic centre, allowing you to receive intuitive and telepathic messages. It ensures the health of your eyes, pituitary gland and lower brain. Healing this energy centre releases forgetfulness, confusion, deep-seated doubts and disbeliefs that weaken your intuition. When balanced you can think clearly and have a strong intuition. You think for yourself and do not need to rely on authority figures. You have an accurate understanding what is happening in the world.

Crown: At the centre of your head is your crown chakra that harmonises with the colour violet. It governs your spiritual connection to the world and universe. It governs the pineal gland and upper brain. Healing this chakra removes any sense of being uninspired or lost and the need to intellectualise everything. When balanced you are in tune with the cycles of your body, nature and the universe. You are in alignment with your true self and each day discover more about your path of service in the world. You know how to share your gifts and contribute to your community. You are beautiful and see beauty in all things.

Beyond the seven main chakras, others are also recognised. Intuitive sources believe that as humankind evolves, chakras concerned with higher vibrational, spiritual, and more universal pursuits are coming into existence. The first two to explore should be the Earth star and soul star chakras. These two chakras work in harmony and balance each other. They assert that you cannot go higher than you dig deep.

Earth Star: This chakra is located about 15 centimetres below your feet. It resonates with a brown or infrared colour. Whereas your base chakra is associated with your personal connection to your physical environment, the Earth star goes deeper, establishing a bond between you and the whole planet. It connects you to the collective consciousness of every animal, plant and mineral. As the Earth star gets stronger in each person, we will become more conscious of the needs of the planet and help the Earth to heal itself.

Soul Star: This chakra is positioned about 15 centimetres above your head. This chakra resonates to the colour of magenta or ultraviolet. It is essential that you purify your body to open this chakra. Drugs and other chemicals found in food and beverages lessen our ability to access the knowledge channelled through this chakra. It connects you to the collective consciousness and wisdom of this world. It allows us to access all possibilities available in the world and use them as guidance on your path of service. When you tune in to this chakra you can connect energetically to everyone in the world.

As a rule, the colour of a crystal will harmonise with the matching colour chakra. This crystal will have some impact on that energy centre, especially when worn or held nearby. Within this book, certain chapters will further explore how you can use various crystals to heal or balance a chosen chakra. Refer to the glossary at the back of this book to determine the recommended crystals for each chakra.

DIVINE BEINGS

Past cultures and religions have celebrated a multitude of gods, goddesses, angels and mythological beings and some of these are discussed in this book. There are many ways of viewing divine beings. If everything is merely energy, then divine beings are simply personifications of a type of energy or an aspect of life. By personifying this energy, it allows the human mind to categorise, interpret and understand this ethereal vibration more easily. The inclusion of spiritual beings in this book is not intended to encourage you to alter your religious or spiritual belief. Rather it offers you an archetypal energy that resonates with a particular crystal and can aid in deepening your connection with your favourite crystal.

COMMONLY USED TERMS IN THIS BOOK

A few terms appear constantly in this book. Here is a definition of each to avoid confusion later.

Projective and Receptive Hand: Energy is constantly flowing in and out of us via our chakras, crown, lungs, skin, feet and hands. Generally speaking, energy flows in one hand and out the other. Your projective hand is the hand you write with. It is the hand you produce and give to the world with. The other hand is your receptive hand as this is the hand that receives energy. This hand is often stronger at feeling crystal energy.

Greater Good: All thoughts, feelings and actions can have positive and negative effects. Some cause suffering whereas others promote growth and improvement. To do something for the greater good means it will benefit the many, rather than the few.

Path of Service: We all are on a life purpose or destiny upon Earth. We are here to contribute some role towards the greater good. Once you are clear on your skills and passions and are driven to devote your life to harnessing your gifts to your full potential, you have found your path of service.

Great Spirit: The term used in this book to refer to God, the Source, the One, the Universal Energy or any other term referring to the cumulative spiritual energy.

True Self: This is the purest part of yourself. It may be referred to as the soul and is experienced as the seer, the observer, the one that simply experiences life and your reactions to it. It is your constant self, remaining the same and unchanged, deeper than your thoughts and attitudes. If any opinion, belief or aspect of you changes in life, this is part of your outer being rather than an aspect of your true self.

AGATE, BLUE LACE
Peace / Throat Chakra / Motherhood

Blue Lace Agate is a crystal of gentleness and tranquility with waves of soft blues that resemble the thawing ice of winter. Blue Lace Agate guides you towards a simpler and more peaceful life. It works best when you need to slow down your pace of life and give yourself time to relax, recoup and recover. It is a crystal of communication, ensuring you speak your truth while also listening to others.

Animal: Deer
Plant: Chamomile
Astrological Correspondence: Neptune
Power Day: Monday
Cleanse with: Cool water

Your Crystal Alignment Meditation

Go to a forest where you can walk and get away from all human contact and other distractions of the modern world. If it is not possible to visit one, visualise a forest in your mind. Take a few breaths to relax yourself. Make a conscious effort to turn your awareness away from your thoughts to what is happening in your surroundings. Just sit there and watch, then allow your other senses to start to heighten. What can you hear, smell, feel? Feel and hear a gentle breeze blowing through the trees. Listen to any animal calls. See if you can observe the gentle pace at which much of nature moves. Connect with the gentleness of the forest and feel that sensation start to assimilate within you. When you feel that inner peace resides within you, connect with your crystal.

Peace

Blue Lace Agate brings you peace whenever you are feeling stressed or out of balance. Keep a crystal on your desk if you become tense at work. Place a sphere or bowl of Blue Lace Agate in the centre of the home to promote peacefulness and settle screaming children, barking dogs or screeching cats. Snoring, possibly being a physical manifestation of a refusal to let go of old patterns, can be quelled with a Blue Lace Agate in the pillowcase.

If you feel your stress levels are constantly high, make a daily ritual of sitting outside in the silence, drinking a cup of chamomile tea and holding your Blue Lace Agate in your receptive hand. You may want to read a comforting poem such as *Desiderata* or just focus on taking deep breaths. After a few days you should notice a difference in how you feel throughout the day as well as sleeping better at night.

Blue Lace Agate is used to promote world peace and to send pacifying energy to war-torn areas. Hold your Blue Lace Agate in your projective hand and visualise covering the area in a soft, calming blue mist. See and feel the people in the area changing, thanks to your energy. You can also create a power grid with Blue Lace Agate as your power crystal place on top of a map or picture of the area you are working with.

Throat Chakra

Blue Lace Agate helps to ease fear or anxieties associated with talking or communicating. It also soothes an overactive throat chakra, symptomised by tendencies to be critical, swearing, talking over people, yelling unnecessarily, over-opinionated and abusive. Blue Lace Agate will help you pause before you talk. Take time each day to lay down, place your Blue Lace Agate on your throat chakra and visualise a soft blue ball of light slowly spinning at the energy centre. Back this up by wearing the crystal near your throat chakra for the rest of the day. A Blue Lace Agate elixir will also be beneficial.

If you suspect you have an oncoming argument or confrontation, bring Blue Lace Agate along. It will encourage active listening and gentle language between all parties. Simply place it in a bowl in the middle of the discussion area and allow it to do its magic. If this is not possible or too obvious, place a piece near your feet. You can also use either of these techniques when required to speak in public.

Motherhood

Blue Lace Agate is connected to the Virgin Mary and thus offers support to mothers. Place a tumbled stone in your bra for encouragement and support. Its circular, flowing energy calms, uplifts and elevates. A piece in the nursery can ease a crying baby and when given to a young child can reduce whining or clinginess. Use Blue Lace Agate to ease tensions with your own mother. Place a stone and a light blue candle near a photo of her and each time you look at the picture affirm, "My mother does the best she can".

AGATE, BOTSWANA

Centring / Reducing Sensitivity / Habits

Waves of volcanic activity in southern Africa millions of years ago created the stunning Botswana Agate. These brown and pink hued crystals, banded with fine, parallel lines, of white, are considered some of the most beautiful Agates in the world. Like all Agates, Botswana Agate works to lead you back to a state of inner balance and harmony. This aids you to release hindering habits and patterns, leading to a healthier, happier lifestyle.

Animal: Warthog
Plant: Cassia
Astrological Correspondence: Mercury
Power Day: Wednesday
Cleanse by: Ideally, place it on the ground near volcanic activity to cleanse and charge it with both the elements of fire and earth. Otherwise, cleanse with fire to connect with its more determined energy or earth for its settling energy.

Your Crystal Alignment Meditation

Go to where you can touch the earth. Become aware of the ground beneath you. Notice the parts of your body in contact with the earth. Tune in to rhythms of nature around you and see if you can sense the energy of the land upon which you are resting. You may feel a pulsing, vibration or an emotion come across you. Perhaps the land has a message for you today. Just relax and allow your bond with the land to grow. Feel the energy reach out and kiss you. Once you are feeling centred, connect with your crystal.

Centring

Botswana Agate leads you to a state of inner stability, composure, and maturity. It helps you deal with change, allowing you to see the positive and to understand the cyclic nature of the universe. Nicknamed the "sunset stone", it retains sunlight and comforts people through dark, lonely nights. Whenever you are feeling fragile or uncertain hold or wear Botswana Agate near the centre of your body. It also ensures safety as when you are balanced it prevents you from taking reckless risks. Team Botswana Agate with cassia essential oil. Diffuse it around your space or inhale it during meditations. Cassia, with its comforting, warming scent similar to cinnamon, promotes self-assurance and confidence in yourself and your abilities.

Three to four times each year Mercury goes into retrograde for a period of about three weeks. During this time the planet Mercury appears to go backwards in the sky. This is simply an optical illusion as no planet can orbit backwards and is a result of the interplay between the orbit of the Earth, Mercury and the Sun. When Mercury, the planet of communication, is in retrograde motion, many people become unbalanced. This is a time when plans can go awry, electronics can break down, agreements should not be signed and unnecessary spending or travelling should be avoided. However, this is an excellent time to reflect on the past, when your intuition is stronger, and extraordinary coincidences occur more often. Botswana Agate will help you take advantage of these times rather than spinning out of control. Throughout the day carry two crystals, one in each pocket. For further balance sit before a yellow candle with the symbol of Mercury (☿) inscribed on it. Anoint it with cassia oil, inhaling its grounding scent then hold a crystal in each hand and focus on your breath until you feel relaxed and centred while watching the candle burn.

Reducing Sensitivity

Botswana Agate works to reduce the sensitivity of people who are often upset or offended by other people's words. It's an ideal crystal for children or teenagers who are easily hurt by teasing or pressure, and can assist them in finding more like-minded friends. Botswana Agate also supports spiritually minded adults whose partner does not share their spiritual beliefs. By wearing the crystal over the chest, it will allow you to focus on your partner's virtues rather than determining who is right or wrong.

Habits

Botswana Agate is great to use to release habits that counter a healthy lifestyle. If you have an addiction to smoking, alcohol, drugs (prescription or recreational), an eating disorder or any other habit you are prepared to break, work with Botswana Agate. Use this crystal to awaken the inner-nurturer within you.

Each day take time to sit in a quiet place, holding Botswana Agate in your receptive hand and focus on your breath. Take a long, deep breath through your nose, mouth closed, until your ribcage and chest are fully expanded with air. Hold your breath and affirm in your mind, "I honour my body" and then exhale through your mouth, all at once, allowing your chest to relax. Before taking the next breath affirm, "...and I choose good health". Continue this activity every day for at least 28 days. For further support wear Botswana Agate over your solar plexus and make a crystal elixir. Adopt the teachings of your Warthog guide for further determination.

AGATE, FIRE
Fire / Advancement / Safety

This is a spectacular variety of Agate containing inclusions of goethite or limonite, producing an iridescent effect or 'fire'. Use Fire Agate to develop your relationship with the magical element of fire, which governs change, will, radiance, passion, activity and courage. Also use this crystal to facilitate a connection with fire deities such as the Hindu god, Agni, or Greek god, Hephaestus. However, being an Agate this crystal's intensity and vibration is slower ensuring you remain grounded while bringing about change in your life. Fire Agate is associated with the spiritual flame of absolute perfection. Gaze into the depth of the crystal and allow the flames to show you their secrets.

Animal: Salamander
Plant: Nettle
Astrological Correspondences: Mars and Kaali
Power Day: Tuesday
Cleanse with: Fire

Your Crystal Alignment Meditation

Go and sit before a fire. It may be a candle flame, fireplace or campfire. Sit close enough to feel the flames' warmth. Watch the flames dance and see them change whatever they touch. Connect with the essence of the fire and allow it to energetically burn away all stresses and tension. Allow all physical discomfort and mental disharmony to be replaced by a warm, comforted feeling. When ready, connect with your crystal.

Fire

Fire Agate allows you to bring the essence of fire into your life. It awakens the base, sacral and solar plexus chakras stimulating your sexuality and creative abilities. It works to boost your energy levels, increasing stamina and circulation, and is helpful in treating sexual imbalances, including impotence or fear of sexual intimacy. Carry Fire Agate in your pocket each day and at night combine this with lighting red and orange candles around your home to awaken your inner fire. Placing a piece where air circulates will help warm a space in winter.

Advancement

Fire Agate's affinity with fire allows you to burn away addictions, habits and destructive desires, making room for new growth in your life. If worn near the throat, Fire Agate helps burn away artistic blocks, allowing full expression of your creativity. This also encourages timid adults and shy children to speak up and not be ignored or bullied. When feeling stuck in your life, sit quietly with a nettle tea and your Fire Agate. The nettle tea will release limited thinking while the Fire Agate awakens your inner knowledge, allowing the emergence of a solution. Once you are clear on what you want, pass Fire Agate through a candle flame four times and make a wish. If you require help from others, work with your Salamander guide to help you recruit others' involvement. This is especially powerful for activists.

Safety

To ensure safety on all levels, hold your Fire Agate in your projective hand each morning and visualise yourself engulfed in protective flames. Keep the crystal close to your chest to maintain this fiery protection all day. Fire Agate offers a unique form of protection. Like other iridescent crystals, it reflects unwanted or unhelpful energies back to the source. However, it first transmutes it so the sender can become aware of the harm they are causing.

Fire Agate gives you a healthy respect and understanding around fire. Electricians and others working near electricity should wear or carry Fire Agate to avoid electrocution. Firefighters benefit from carrying this crystal as it will guide them on what is a safe risk to take. Place four pieces of Fire Agate with some nettle around your house if you live in an area susceptible to bushfires. If you or your house is ever threatened by fire, hold a piece in your receptive hand to guide you to safety.

Incorporate Fire Agate into your life if you tend to work primarily with high vibration or spiritual crystals. Fire Agate reminds you why you came here to Earth at this time and the physical experiences your soul is seeking. Use Fire Agate with your other crystals to keep you physically grounded and energised, particularly if you feel lethargic or spaced out after doing spiritual work.

AGATE, MOSS

Beginnings / Plants / Nature

Imagine the sunshine gently peeking through the canopy of a forest of trees and dotting the forest floor with its soft light. This gentle scene encompasses the gentle energy of Moss Agate. This crystal helps you attune to the spirits of the trees and the knowledge of Mother Earth. Listen to the whispers and find new ways to grow a fruitful life filled with friendship, peace and abundance. Moss Agate refreshes the soul and awakens your vision to the beauty in all that surrounds you.

Animal: Tortoise
Plant: Oak moss
Astrological Correspondences: Ceres and Earth
Power Day: Friday
Cleanse with: Earth, ideally placed on a patch of moss

Your Crystal Alignment Meditation

Go to where you can touch the earth. Immerse your hands into the earth. Feel its temperature, texture and moisture. Tune in to its energy. How does the earth feel? Just relax and allow your bond with the earth to grow. Feel the energy reach out and kiss you. Once you are feeling centred, connect with your crystal.

Beginnings

Moss Agate is a crystal of new beginnings, and allows the manifestation of abundance and success in all areas of your life. It supports steady and stable growth and development. It works perfectly in line with the lessons of Tortoise, who reminds you that if you just put one foot in front of the other and keep moving, you are bound to reach your desired destination. Tortoise encourages you to set ambitious, even seemingly impossible goals, for with patience and tenacity, you can accomplish anything you set out to do, if only you keep going and never quit. Wear or carry Moss Agate each day, while drawing on the resolve of Tortoise and day by day you'll notice improvements in your life.

Moss Agate can be really supportive for any child who is shy, especially when they're starting at a new school or to help them grow friendships. Moss Agate will also help children bond with young animals. Add Moss Agate to water for a fertility promoting elixir. Midwives should wear a piece to assist with smooth deliveries.

Plants

When worn around the neck, Moss Agate improves your ability to talk with and connect to plants and trees. This ability to understand plants that has given Moss Agate the nickname 'gardener's stone'. One of the best ways to connect with nature is to get into the garden. Use Moss Agate in conjunction with starting a garden or growing fruits, vegetables and herbs. Soon you will be enjoying the bounty of Mother Earth. Botanists, horticulturist and avid gardeners should wear Moss Agate daily.

Moss Agate supports large-scale growth of plants too. To promote an abundant crop, grid eight pieces of Moss Agate around a farm. Use a similar technique to strengthen efforts to rehabilitate a drought-ridden area, but bury each Moss Agate with a Red Jasper to attract rain and pour in a little water. Any meditations to support your efforts should be done facing the dwarf planet Ceres, as it governs fertility, growth and gardening. Moss Agate offers you support in eating organic and local food while avoiding GMO foods. A charged crystal should be carried to give you guidance when food shopping.

Nature

When worn over the heart, Moss Agate reminds you to slow down and listen to Mother Earth. Like the teachings of Tortoise, much benefit can be gained when we take time each day to pause, pull inwards and contemplate where we are heading. Both Moss Agate and Tortoise will show you that when you slow down, the real treasures of life will be revealed. If you are feeling overwhelmed, hold your Moss Agate in your receptive hand and focus on your breath. It will give you guidance on how regain your confidence and inner peace amidst a life of extreme or excessive duties. Use the crystal in harmony with oak moss essential oil. The combination will ground you while also awakening an erotic and wild sensuality that urges you to immerse yourself in the ways of the wild. As your connection with nature deepens, Moss Agate reduces adverse reactions you may have towards weather conditions or environmental pollutants. Use Moss Agate to receive guidance from nature's deities such as Gaia, Pachamama, Pan and the Green Man.

AMAZONITE

Soothing Illness / Deportment / Harmony

Amazonite has a long history, as far back as the Neolithic era. Its uses around the world are extensive where it has been used as an amulet in ancient Egypt, jewellery in Ecuador and discovered in artefacts in northern India. The soft green-blue shades of Amazonite give this crystal a soothing and harmonious energy. However, this softness should never be mistaken for meekness. As bold as the legendary women warriors with which it shares its name, Amazonite imbues you with great strength. Like the Amazon River, Amazonite allows you to navigate around any obstacle, not with force but with grace and love. It helps you clearly and confidently express what you want and take the lead to make it happen. This is a crystal to work with over the long term rather than summoning its energy for a quick burst.

Animals: Alpaca and Llama
Plant: Cajeput
Astrological Correspondences: Venus and the asteroids Lilith and Pallas Athena
Power Day: Friday
Cleanse with: Earth or Water

Your Crystal Alignment Meditation

Go to a large tree, ideally one with healing properties such as a cajeput or eucalyptus. Take a few moments to study the features of the tree. Notice its leaves as they dance in the wind. Does this tree have flowers? Can you smell any scent? Reach out and feel the bark. Each tree has its own energy and spirit. Allow yourself to connect to its beauty and magic. Now sit with your back against the tree. Nature is always seeking to regain balance so ask the tree to help you regain your own personal balance. Hear the tree creak as it absorbs your ills and hear its leaves flutter as it sends them far away upon the healing winds. Sense any tiredness, aching, pain, sickness, discomfort or disease leaving your body and being absorbed by the tree. Once you are enjoying a sense of wellbeing, connect with your Amazonite.

Soothing Illness

Whereas other crystals fire up the body's immune system, Amazonite offers a more soothing option. It can be used for any part of the body or the body as a whole to assist in healing ailments caused by stress, inflammation or allergic reaction. Take your crystal and state that your intention is to soothe the body then hold or wear it near the site of illness. For overall wellbeing, wear it over your heart and with every beat it will pulse its soothing energy around the body. Amplify your crystal's effect by inhaling the scent of cajeput essential oil; an oil renowned for its purifying effects. Cajeput can also be used to support you in breaking of compulsive, unhealthy habits by focusing your mind and willpower.

The calming energy of Amazonite can be beneficial for those operating on a lot of nervous tension. Anyone heading towards a nervous breakdown should wear this crystal over their heart. It's important to set aside time each day to sit with someone you love and trust to discuss how you are feeling. If you are experiencing upper back problems caused by a sense of lack of emotional support, also try Amazonite. It reminds you that not only is the universe supporting you in your journey but that you have much inner strength to handle challenges that cross your path. Massage the affected area with a tumbled stone and some cajeput essential oil in a carrier oil/ cream. This will help your muscles relax and improve respiration.

Deportment

Amazonite improves the way you conduct and hold yourself. It promotes confidence and self-respect leading to improved posture, grace and eloquence. It helps you behave in a manner of truthfulness, honour, open communication, integrity and trust. Lie down and place one piece at your head and one at your feet. Feel them lengthening your spine, and visualise yourself interacting with others in a way you desire. Then carry one in each pocket every day.

As a green crystal, Amazonite works with the heart chakra to bring your heart's yearning into consciousness. It also awakens a determination to do good in the world. Amazonite brings fears to the surface so that you can become consciously aware of what is holding you back. It then supports you in overcoming these fears and heading towards fulfilling your dreams.

This crystal is great for getting rid of victim mentalities and encourages you to take charge of your life. Amazonite instils an energy like that of a female warrior, keeping you calm and composed while giving unwavering determination to have control of the direction you want your life to take. It ensures that once you are clear on what you want, you then take the lead in expressing your desires with confidence, grace and love. As a crystal of the Goddess, use Amazonite to connect and align with the energy of the Divine Feminine, and to summon support and strength from the universe to help you along your path of service.

Amazonite will also help you deal with where others are holding you back. Astrologically Amazonite can be linked to the asteroid Lilith. The energy of this asteroid encourages you to boldly be who you want to be, and explore what calls to you. Lilith confronts issues of repression and discrimination, especially sexism aimed at women. To gain insight on where and how the world tries to suppress your divine nature, explore this asteroid's position in your birth chart. With this knowledge, sit outside at night with your Amazonite, facing the direction of Lilith and contemplate what changes to make.

Connecting with your Alpaca or Llama guide will help you adopt the graceful frequency of Amazonite. Alpaca and Llama show you how to walk steadily along your path, even at the rockiest of times. They help you slowly and safely climb towards the peak of your success. These two South American camelids will also give you the gusto to stand up for yourself when others threaten your integrity or wellbeing.

Harmony

Amazonite strongly works to promote harmony between people. Use it in meditation and grids to send a message of peace to areas of unrest. It also evokes from others a willingness to help and contribute. It encourages you and others to keep a space clean and tidy. If you feel you need more help around the home either place a small stone in each corner of the family area of the house or a large specimen in the centre. Alternatively you can bury some small stones in the soil of an indoor plant (one for each family member). Just make sure everyone takes turns to water the plant! By placing Amazonite around the home it also encourages kids to get outside and play as well as encourages teenagers and young adults to participate in life and make a significant contribution. Team your use of Amazonite with diffusing cajeput essential oil as the aroma helps cleanse away lethargic and apathetic attitudes.

Amazonite also encourages people to live harmoniously with the natural environment and nature. It encourages recycling, using natural products and conservation, especially of forest areas. Bury programmed pieces of Amazonite in an area you wish to defend from logging or destruction. If you cannot get to the area, bury the programmed crystals in a pot plant and surround them with Clear Quartz points to send your intentions out into the world. Amazonite can be held during meditation to connect with animal guides and totems as well as earth and water spirits to receive their guidance on the best steps to take to live in harmony with the environment, and to enhance your personal connection with nature.

As a green crystal, Amazonite can be used for luck, especially in competitions. The bonus with using this crystal as a lucky charm is because it creates harmonious scenarios it ensures your luck doesn't come through the misfortune of others but rather in a way that it serves the greater good of everyone involved. Take a Turquoise coloured candle and hold it in both hands while visualising luck coming your way. Light the candle and say,

"With the power of the flame, good fortune I am ready to claim." Place either a piece of Amazonite jewellery or three small crystals in a green bag next to the candle. If you are choosing the bag option, include some herbs associated with luck such as nutmeg seed, thyme or chamomile. Once the candle has burned down, your Amazonite is ready to be carried for luck. Gridding around a space or sitting within a circle of nine Amazonites will support luck in business.

AMBER

Detox and Soothe / Sacral Chakra / Life Force / Resourcefulness

Amber is not just dried tree resin. True Amber has taken hundreds of thousands, if not millions of years to polymerise, making it less soluble in common, organic solvents and will not become sticky if wet with alcohol, acetone or gasoline. It ranges in colour from light yellow to deep orange similar to the colour spectrum of the sun's rays from dawn to dusk and can sometimes have small insects or plant matter captured inside from when they became trapped in the tree's resin as it was secreted. It is possibly the oldest substance used by humans for adornment, with beads and pendants being found in gravesites dating back to 8,000 BC. Much myth surrounds Amber. One legend tells of Amber being formed by the rays of the setting sun. Another says Amber is the tears of Freyja, the Norse goddess of love and beauty.

Animal: Crocodile
Plant: Orange
Astrological Correspondence: Sun
Power Day: Sunday
Cleanse with: Sun

Your Crystal Alignment Meditation

Go to a swamp during the day or visualise one in your mind. Consider how this moist environment is a place of great life as well as great decay. Great trees and animals prosper in this harsh habitat whereas the weak will eventually dissolve and die. Know that great work will echo into infinity whereas the insignificant soon dissolves into nothingness. Remember that we are only here momentarily. Contemplate your time, how you spend each day and whether you are spending it wisely, contributing to great things rather than chasing petty desires. Now connect with your Amber. It too was once part of a living being and has found a way to preserve itself. Feel its warming energies of longevity and survival.

Detox and Soothe

Amber is a natural analgesic, which has been popular in Europe for centuries due to its reputation for boosting the immune system, reducing inflammation and accelerating the healing of wounds. Mothers will swear by its ability to soothe teething babies. Professionally strung Amber necklaces and bracelets are available for infants that, if broken, do not become a choking hazard. However it's not just for children. Wearing Amber against the skin can soothe any inflammations from arthritis to eczema. Amber is also reputed to help its wearer remove toxins from within their body. Place Amber around your home or any space that you feel needs cleansing. Amber is perfect for helping animals (particularly older animals) self-heal. Simply place a small piece on their collar or where they sleep.

Sacral Chakra

Amber is the perfect choice for soothing an overactive sacral chakra. Symptoms of an overactive sacral chakra include a tendency to be a drama queen or crisis junkie, or being over emotional on a regular basis. You may form unhealthy emotional attachments to people with poor boundaries and often become overly dependent. You may show obsessive behaviour relying on other people or sources (food, drink, drugs etc.) for pleasure. Severe imbalances result in hysterical outbursts and bipolar behaviour. Imbalance may also result in sexual addiction where you view people as mere sexual objects, behaving in an overly sexual manner and using seductive manipulation to try to fulfil your needs. Allow Amber to help you rebalance this chakra. Take at least ten minutes each day laying down with the Amber over your sacral chakra, focusing on your breathing and feeling balanced. Visualise a soft orange ball of light slowly spinning at the energy centre. Then carry the Amber with you in a pocket throughout the day, massaging it in your hands when you start to feel anxious or unbalanced.

Life Force

Amber possesses a gentle, warming glow, often linked to the sun's energy. The Chinese believed it contained the powerful souls of tigers. Amber has the ability to rebalance and replenish your life force giving you a youthful glow. It aids women with fertility and men with potency. Stand outside in the sunshine, hold the Amber against your solar plexus and take several deep breaths for a quick energy burst. To create invigorating massage oil, take a carrier oil such as macadamia or coconut oil and add a few drops of orange essential oil. Add a piece of Amber to the oil for at least 30 minutes so its energies can infuse into the oil. A firm massage with quick movements using the oil will have you feeling lively within minutes. You can use the same recipe as an anointing oil, as orange increases the available bioelectrical energy in your body to be directed towards your intent in creative visualisation or magical work. Combining Amber and orange is perfect for any undertaking aimed at turning sadness to joy or manifesting a more abundant life.

Resourcefulness

The warm, nourishing energy of Amber allows you to release your petty desires and wants, focusing on important needs. It is an ideal shopping companion if you tend to overspend. Simply keep it in your handbag or pocket with your purse or wallet and reach for it when wondering whether to make a purchase, roll it in your hand and ask if the purchase is a want or a need. Taking a few drops of orange flower essence can help release buried emotional yearnings that cause you to want to buy things in order to feel better. This flower essence is great when you become obsessed with obtaining a material item with the belief it will make you happier.

Simplicity is a key to spiritual success and fulfilment, for the more you have, the more worries you generate. Amber teaches you to be resourceful with what you have and encourages you to reduce, reuse, recycle and refuse. Place a piece in the kitchen surrounded by four Clear Quartz points pointing outwards to encourage resourceful behaviour at home. Gain further guidance from your Crocodile guide who has survived on Earth since prehistoric times. He knows how to conserve his energy for only that which is essential for wellbeing. Ask Crocodile to help you only spend energy and money on what is necessary. Ask him to shred away your superfluous wants and desires so that in the long run you will prosper.

AMETHYST

Bliss / Spiritual Wisdom / Sleep / Crown Chakra / Sobriety

For many people, Amethyst is one of the first crystals they add to their collection for it is perfect for those commencing their spiritual journey. It has a soothing and healing energy that encourages you to step away from the chaos of modern life and take a few minutes for yourself supporting blissful relaxation and restful sleep. Once you give way to the peace and harmony, Amethyst opens your connection to Great Spirit. This is when the path to true wisdom begins.

Animal: Owl
Plants: Lavender and Mulberry
Astrological Correspondences: Jupiter, Polaris (Northern Star) and the asteroid Pallas Athena
Power Day: Thursday
Cleanse with: Full Moon or Water

Your Crystal Alignment Meditation

Go to a quiet place outside in nature, ideally at night. Ideally find where Polaris or Pallas Athena are in the sky and sit facing that direction. Settle into your surroundings. Let your mind still and allow all thoughts to drift away. Listen to the world around you, what can you hear amongst the silence? When you are ready, connect with your Amethyst.

Bliss

Amethyst is the perfect crystal to help you explore greater depths of relaxation. Take some time to contemplate what you find relaxing. Is it listening to music, receiving a massage or getting out in nature? Find some time to dedicate to relaxing and have your Amethyst accompany you. Then wear it near the top of your body to keep the feelings of bliss long after you are back in action. Combine Amethyst with lavender. Inhale the essential oil or flowers through diffusing or rubbing it in your hands and inhaling. Allow it to enhance your experience with Amethyst by inducing deep relaxation and melting away stress and irritation.

Set up an Amethyst power grid in your home to create a tranquil space. Use a small cluster or sphere as the power crystal and add Clear Quartz points facing in a clockwise direction to generate waves of peace. You may want to use supporting crystals such as Black Tourmaline to transform unwanted and unhelpful thoughts or Sugilite to attract compassion and universal love into your space. Pop some lavender in the grid too, or better still create a similar grid outside with lavender plants.

Spiritual Wisdom

Amethyst supports the pursuit of wisdom. Its soothing energies will calm any irritation and anxiety and quietens your mind from unnecessary chatter. Once you have found peace within the silence, it allows you to tune in to your psychic abilities so information and answers will flow to you. This lovely violet crystal is one of the stones connected with the violet flame, a healing light brought to us by the ascended master, St Germain. Visualise yourself surrounded by a violet light descending from above as you relax with the crystal. You may also want to invite your Owl guide, your spirit guides or Athena, the Greek goddess of wisdom with some simple words to bless you with their guidance.

If you have a particular question you need answered, hold the Amethyst up to your mouth and whisper your query. It will bring you the answer as soon as you are ready to hear it. You may want to try placing a few drops of mulberry flower essence under your tongue too. This essence works to return to you to a state of love and balance. It will awaken your sense of purpose and allow you to find the correct course of action.

If you use a form of divination such as tarot cards, runes, I Ching coins or a pendulum, keep them with an Amethyst. This will not only increase their 'powers' but also enable you to interpret their messages with greater understanding and wisdom.

Sleep

Amethyst has a sedative effect and will aid in getting a peaceful night's sleep. It is a strong crystal for ensuring the optimum functioning of the pineal gland. This gland secretes the hormone melatonin, which regulates our circadian rhythms or internal body clock, controlling wake/sleep cycles as well as seasonal functions. This makes Amethyst useful for shift workers, those with jet lag or anyone trying to get a good night's sleep. Place a tumbled stone in your pillow case or grid four pieces on the four points of your bed or bedroom. Just before getting into bed, place a few drops of lavender essential oil on your hands, rub them together, rub it all over your pillow and sheets and then cup your hands over your nose and inhale deeply. The serene scent of lavender will work with Amethyst to give you a sound night's sleep.

If you find yourself lying in bed at night thinking and unable to sleep use Amethyst as a worry stone. Simply tell it your worries before you go to bed then cleanse the crystal with water and slip it in your pillowslip. Pay attention to your dreams as Amethyst can bring you solutions as you sleep.

For babies, place an Amethyst near their cradle. It will work to make them feel more secure and protected. Double it with a leaf or piece of wood from a mulberry tree, which has long been used to protect sleeping babies and children. Tradition states the leaf should be picked just before the sun sets.

Crown Chakra

Use Amethyst to stimulate your crown chakra. If you have coordination difficulties, poor balance or are clumsy this can be symptomatic of an underactive crown chakra. Behaviours such as an attempt to stop yourself and others exploring new thoughts or a general lack of interest and exploration in spirituality suggest this chakra needs to be given more attention. Place Amethyst above your head and visualise a vibrantly glowing violet sphere of light resonating at your crown and stretching out to the universe. Complete this visualisation each day and carry or wear Amethyst until you sense this chakra is more balanced. Filling your life with purple and violet foods, clothes and decorations will also help.

Sobriety

A popular myth about the origin of Amethyst comes from the Greeks. Dionysus, the god of wine, celebration, intoxication and joviality, was drunkenly pursuing a mortal woman named Amethyste (alternative versions of her name are Amethystas, Amethystos and Amethyst). Since she was not keen on this god, who was known for his virility, she prayed to the virgin goddess Artemis. The goddess, taking pity on Amethyste who wished to keep her chastity, turned her into stone. Dionysus, seeing that the girl of his affections was now a statue of Quartz Crystal wept tears of wine over her, which turned the stone purple.

Thus the name 'Amethyst' comes from the Greek meaning 'not drunken' and Amethyst has long been considered to be a strong antidote against drunkenness. Wine goblets were often carved from it, and the gemstone still symbolises sobriety to this day. If you wish to keep your dignity and a level head while drinking, wear an Amethyst pendant or carry a small piece in your pocket. It is also the perfect empowerment talisman for alcoholics.

In fact, one of the greatest spiritual lessons of Amethyst is to avoid obsession or addition to any physical thing. Amethyst supports you to not become overly fixated on anything whether it be obtain the affection of another, alcohol or another substance, new shoes or a car, et cetera. When you place the solution for your happiness outside yourself, it is bound to end unsatisfactorily. Again, Amethyst reminds you to slow down and find that inner joy and peace within, rather than from around you.

AMETRINE
Balance / Tolerance / Obsessive-Compulsive Disorder

Ametrine is a powerful combination of Citrine and Amethyst. It possesses the radiant energies of Citrine, with the calming effects of Amethyst. Rather than a blend of the two energies, Ametrine helps you find balance between the two polarities of active and passive, work and play, yin and yang. Much of today's Ametrine comes from Bolivia and therefore is sometimes known as bolivianite.

Animals: Hummingbird and Owl
Plant: Plum
Astrological Correspondences: Moon and Sun
Power Days: Monday and Sunday
Cleanse by: Moon when wanting a calmer energy or sun when wanting a more motivating energy.

Your Crystal Alignment Meditation

Go to a quiet place outside in nature, ideally when the sun is shining. Settle into your surroundings and become silent. Feel the warmth of the sunshine on your skin. Let your mind still and allow all thoughts to drift away. Listen to the world around you. What can you hear when you are silent? Once you are feeling a sense of vibrant bliss, connect with your Ametrine.

Balance

The uplifting energy of Citrine dances with the peaceful energy of Amethyst within Ametrine to create a crystal ideal for bringing balance in your life, whether you need more time to relax and recoup or a kick to get you out and about. Use it if you are studying, working from home or self-employed to help you manage your schedule ensuring you commit necessary time to your academic/work commitments as well as having personal time for yourself and those you love. You can call upon the lessons of your Owl or Hummingbird guide on how to find balance. Owl can guide you in slowing down and spiritual affairs, while Hummingbird will support you in the social, financial and motivational aspects of your life. A beautiful meditation to try while holding your Ametrine is to sense them each sitting on your shoulder and have them advise you on where you need balance. After meditating with your Ametrine, sit down and allot your time for the week, making sure you have enough time for you, others and your work. Then place your Ametrine on top of the schedule. You can also place a sphere, generator or two tumbled stones on your desk to remind you when it's time to switch off the computer and step away from the "office".

The balancing effect of Ametrine also makes it great for supporting any ecosystem that may have been damaged through development, pollution or exploitation. Grid eight pieces of Ametrine that have been programmed with your intent around the edge of the area as well as a single Clear Quartz point buried in the centre, point down. This will encourage both animals and plants to be safe to follow their instincts and find a natural balance in the area.

Tolerance

If you are experiencing unrest amongst your family due to your relationship or lifestyle choices, Ametrine can help build understanding and tolerance. It is great for when there is tension amongst family members because of inter-racial, inter-religious or homosexual relationships.

Create a power grid with Ametrine as the power crystal. Under the crystal place photos of all the people you wish to get along harmoniously. If you have one photo of everyone together, this is ideal. Then have Clear Quartz points surrounding the photo pointing outward in the direction of the family members' home(s). Use supporting crystals such as Morganite for equality, Dioptase for acceptance and Black Tourmaline for shifting unhelpful attitudes.

If you are nervous about an upcoming event when the family is together, create a space grid around the room with alternating Ametrine and a blue crystals such as Aqua Aura Quartz, Angelite and/or Blue Lace Agate. Hold this combination in your hand if you need to make a phone call you fear may be uncomfortable. The Ametrine will promote harmony while the blue crystal will aid open and honest communication. You can add some plum flower essence to a jug of water to share as it promotes realignment of unbalanced attitudes.

Obsessive-Compulsive Disorder

Consider using Ametrine for obsessive-compulsive disorder (OCD). The Amethyst aspect calms, soothes and gives a sense of inner peace while Citrine offers clarity and stability that is important because often these ritualised behaviours are performed in the effort to seek solidity. Ideally, wear the Ametrine daily to give constant support. Otherwise, place a crystal in some water in the sunshine for a few hours to make an elixir and drink daily.

ANGELITE

Customer Service / Listening / Angels / Peace

Angelite, or Blue Anhydrite, is new to the crystal world, only discovered in 1987 in Peru. As the name implies, its tender nature helps you make contact with the angelic realms. Angelite is perfect for those beginning their spiritual journey or taking the first steps to connect with their angels. With its gentle manner, this crystal slows and quietens you down to allow the perception of the angels around you. Angelite is said to open a stairway of light to the heavens for you and the angels to travel between.

Animal: Hawk
Plant: Lemon
Astrological Correspondence: Moon
Power Day: Monday
Cleanse with: Air

Your Crystal Alignment Meditation

Go to a place in nature where you can be alone and undisturbed. You may even like to make it your sacred sanctuary where you go often to find peace and serenity. Find a comfortable position here and sit still and silently. Allow your sanctuary to talk to you. Once you are feeling relaxed and focused, connect with your Angelite.

Customer Service

Angelite is a great support stone if you work in customer service. It helps you deal with rude or unpleasant people, awakening the realisation that their behaviour is based on their own sufferance and has little to do with you. Angelite gives you wings to allow you to rise above petty concerns, even helping you find ways to turn negative situations into memorable, positive ones. Each day for work wear Angelite close to your throat. As you put it on affirm to yourself that you have many opportunities today to improve others' day. Angelite will open up new levels of listening ability so you can uniquely.

identify what each customer needs. If you become offended or upset at work take as few minutes to step away, hold Angelite in your receptive hand and remind yourself of the higher purpose in your role. Today is your day to be an angel.

Listening

Angelite allows you to shift your vibration in tune with the angelic realms, improving your ability to hear and receive the loving guidance of the angels and your spirit guides. Before doing any work to communicate with the angelic realms, drink a glass of lemon water to cleanse and purify your body, mind and soul. There are many ways to work with your Angelite to enhance contact. You can simply hold your Angelite in your hands during prayer or meditation. If you have an Angelite skull, scry into its eyes and as your mind stills, messages of wisdom will be unveiled to you. To increase your connection with the angels throughout the day wear Angelite earrings. This can improve clairaudience, the ability to hear divine messages and angelic whisperings. At night, create a space grid by placing four stones at the corners of your bed or bedroom and a fifth above you in the centre to create a pyramid. This will invite the angels to watch over you as you sleep. If you have a message you would like to send to the angels, communicate with your Hawk guide and ask him to deliver it.

Angels

Using Angelite allows you to receive the loving guidance of the angels and your spirit guides. Wearing Angelite shifts your vibration in tune with the angelic realms. Before doing any work to communicate with the angelic realms, drink a glass of lemon water to cleanse and purify your body, mind and soul. Then try one of the following:

1. Use an Angelite skull and scry into its eyes. As your mind stills, messages of wisdom will be unveiled to you.
2. Hold a piece of Angelite carved into shape of an angel in both hands as you pray.
3. If you have a message you would like to send to the angels, communicate with your Eagle guide and ask him to deliver it.

To increase your connection with the angels throughout the day wear Angelite earrings. This can improve clairaudience, the ability to hear divine messages and angelic whisperings. At night, create a space grid by placing four stones at the corners of your bed or bedroom and a fifth above you in the centre to create a pyramid. This will invite the angels to watch over you as you sleep.

When you bury a much-loved pet, you may like to perform this simple yet beautiful ritual. Thank the pet for all the love and memories it has shared with you. Then place an Angelite crystal beside it and ask the angels to lead your animal friend to the other side. Once you have covered your pet, place a light blue candle on top of the mound and let it burn to the ground as a beacon to the angels to come and take your friend until you are reunited in the next life.

Peace

Angelite promotes peace and brotherhood, both locally and globally. It helps the insensitive become more compassionate and teaches acceptance of that which cannot be changed. If you are dealing with anyone towards whom you feel any anger or negative feelings, keep a piece of Angelite on you to help you to feel calmer when you are talking with them. It encourages forgiveness and reminds you that everyone is doing what they believe to be the best they can at any given time.

Angelite is a strong choice for working towards world peace. It encourages people in volatile areas to communicate honestly and prompts leaders to consider the wellbeing of their people. In a grid, it can be used to send strength to people living under intolerant political or religious regimes. Create your power grid with an Angelite placed upon a photo or picture of the place you wish to send peaceful energy towards. Surround it with an even number of Clear Quartz points facing outwards from the centre. Add other supporting crystals around the perimeter of the grid such as Purpurite for compromise and Morganite for equality.

APACHE TEARS
Grief / New Ventures / Protection

Apache Tears are formed when small balls of molten lava are thrown up into the air then cool and solidify before hitting the ground. Their name comes from a Native American legend that tells the story of members of the Apache tribe being pursued by the cavalry and although they fought bravely, they were outnumbered. Rather than be captured they jumped off the cliff to their deaths. The distraught women of the tribe cried dark tears of grief that fell to the earth. The tears formed into these dark crystals and it is said they not only cried for their loss, but for yours too.

Animal: Penguin
Plants: Coconut and Cypress
Astrological Correspondences: Chiron and Pluto
Power Day: Saturday
Cleanse by: Ideally near a volcano to allow it to cleanse and reconnect with its fiery place of origin. When this is not possible, use fire.

Your Crystal Alignment Meditation

Go to a place in nature considered sacred to the native or first people of your land. If you cannot locate somewhere nearby, visualise a place in your mind. Sit quietly and reflect on the history of the land. Tune in to the heartbeat of the land. Feel the joys and the sorrows, the triumphs and the downfalls that have soaked into the environment through history. Once you feel you have connected to the land shift your attention to connecting with your Apache Tear.

Grief

When you have experienced great loss such as bankruptcy, divorce or death of a loved one, Apache Tear facilitates the mourning process, allows healing tears to flow and guides you towards eventual acceptance. It also is great for helping you finally lay to rest any long held grudge, fixations with the past or anything that has been suppressed. Keep an Apache Tear on you through the challenging period. At times of quietness, take the Apache Tear out and roll the black crystal around in your hand and feel it soothe your soul. Also offer them to friends or family who are suffering. Diffuse or inhale cypress essential oil as this tree is renowned to help guide you through the grief process. It is emotionally healing for both the individual and groups, especially when incorporated with song and dance.

Penguin is a great guide when you are taking an emotional battering. Penguin can help guide you through the harshest time, lending you resilience during the greatest struggles of life. He reminds you that step-by-step eventually you will make it to the edge of your suffering and be able to again dive into life's waters. Bird guides teach us how to find freedom and while most birds are free to fly through the air, Penguin flies freely through the sea. Water is the realm of the emotions and thus Penguin teaches us that the time will come when your emotions lift so that you may fly again.

New Ventures

If you are starting a new project, undertaking any new venture or moving to a new city, work with Apache Tear until you feel comfortable in your new lifestyle. The black energy of Apache Tear will absorb all dangers and help you see only helpful opportunities. Due to its fiery creation this form of Obsidian will suck away the impacts of any of the rocky or aggressive energies so that your path is smooth sailing. Keep a natural Apache Tear in your pocket. Here it works with your base chakra to keep you feeling safe, secure and grounded.

To further enhance your success, take a purple candle and engrave it with the astrological symbol of Chiron (⚷). In astrology, Chiron helps you rise above your feelings of inadequacy and low self-worth to see how you can use your unique set of skills and experiences to succeed. Sit in front of the lit candle, hold your Apache Tear in your receptive hand and visualise yourself succeeding. When you are confronted with an obstacle, relax, breathe and allow the energy of Apache Tear to guide you on how to remove this barrier.

Protection

Apache Tear can be used for various forms of protection. It helps you to stay safe, especially when walking alone at night. Hold the Apache Tear in your projective hand and visualise yourself surrounded in a black cape. It will lower your vibration making you less obvious to others. Legend has it that if you perfect this practice you can master the ability to become invisible.

Psychic attack can be anything from someone looking at you with malice, speaking ill of you or going as far as wishing for or taking spiritual actions to promote your downfall. This negative energy can cause you to feel unbalanced and create problematic events to arise in your life. If you fear that you are being psychically attacked, Apache Tear is an asset. First take a bath and add some coconut to the water. Magically, coconut is used for purification and protection. As you bathe, focus on purification and feel all mental, emotional and spiritual impurities soaking away. For further effect, you can burn coconut incense for purifying areas and warding off evil. After the bath, wear an Apache Tear close to the centre of the body. As you place it on you state, "By the power of this Apache Tear, others' ill wishes have no effect here."

For protection for yourself and your house, cut a coconut in half, drain its juice and then fill it with protective herbs and an Apache Tear before sealing it and burying it at the front of your house. For further protection, place four more Apache Tears around the border of your house.

Apache Tear helps to preserve and regenerate indigenous spirituality. If you are studying a native belief system, keep an Apache Tear near your receptive side, as either a raw stone or ring. This will help you comprehend the new content without your preconceived beliefs blurring your studies. To protect a native sacred site, bury eight Apache Tears around the perimeter of the space.

APATITE, BLUE
Weight Control / Old Patterns / Vision

Found throughout the world, Apatite occurs in a variety of colours, including purple and yellow, however the most readily available colour is blue. Blue Apatite allows you to express yourself openly and honestly. It facilitates the release of long-buried emotions that can have harmful effects on your physical and emotional wellbeing. As you improve your ability to express yourself, your words become powerful tools. They carry great energy, which help to create your future. Work with Blue Apatite to ensure the words you speak are optimistic, loving and share a vision of the future you wish to see for yourself and the world. Blue Apatite ensures your self-expression is not for the purpose of gaining attention or showing off, but rather to shine as the glorious individual you truly are. Look around in nature and see how the plants and animals share their own beauty. The birds serenade the world with song and the plants flower, flooding the earth with colour. Blue Apatite will help you discover your way to dazzle the world through the expression of your natural essence.

Animal: Giraffe
Plant: Acacia especially Wattle and Mimosa
Astrological Correspondences: Mercury and Neptune
Power Days: Wednesday and Thursday
Cleanse with: Blue Apatite harmonises with the elements of air and water. To cleanse this crystal ideally place in a bubbling spring where the two elements are combined. Otherwise, place Blue Apatite in running water and then dry it in the wind. Also use both elements to cleanse yourself before starting to work with Blue Apatite.

Your Crystal Alignment Meditation

Go to a grassland and sit in the middle of the open area, or visualise this scene in your mind. Start by focusing on the space directly in front of you. Then start to expand your attention out further in front of you, then around you, behind you and above you. How far can you expand your attention? What do you notice? What stands out to you? Perhaps this has some meaning or lesson for you. Once you are ready, pick up your Blue Apatite and connect with it.

Self Expression

Blue Apatite helps you find balance in your throat chakra, supporting you to communicate and express yourself in a manner that is honest and easily understood by others. Start your day holding your crystal against your throat chakra and repeat nine times, "I communicate from my heart and mind, clearly and effortlessly today." End your day by resting your Blue Apatite on your throat chakra for a few minutes as you close your eyes and visualise the most perfect blue sphere of light radiating from your throat, clearing away any energetic blockages. Continue to carry your Blue Apatite with you all day and keep it near you as you sleep. Other activities that will support balancing your throat chakra include wearing the colour blue and practicing the fish, cobra and plough yoga positions.

Weight Control

Although its name resembles the word appetite, this blue crystal gained its name from the Greek word *apate* meaning "deception" since it is often mistaken for other crystals such as Fluorite and Aquamarine. However, Blue Apatite can affect your appetite and works to help you maintain a healthy weight. Blue Apatite works from the inside out, helping you release emotional issues that lead to eating issues. It does that by maintaining balance of the throat chakra, ensuring you find effective ways to communicate and express upsets and pain rather than repressing or burying them. Wear Blue Apatite near your throat daily, and when combined with physical activity and healthy food choices, you'll work towards the body you want. Also place a piece near the fridge to remind you of your health goals and deter emotional or binge eating.

Creative visualisations can further enhance you achieving your goal. Charge Blue Apatite and then place it in your body wash container or with your soap in the shower. Each day as you wash, feel and visualise unwanted fat washing off you and down the drain, being replaced by strong, toned muscle.

Old Patterns

Blue Apatite is linked to Ketu, the lunar south node in Vedic astrology, an aspect in our astrological birth charts. Ketu, along with Rahu (north node) are not planetary bodies, but rather points that take into account the relationship between the Sun, Moon, and Earth at the time of our birth. The position of Ketu relates to our overdeveloped character traits that are easy for us to fall back on, but can undermine our lives if we hold on to these traits for security. They are karmic lessons we have brought back from past lifetimes that we are yet to learn or complete.

Working with Blue Apatite can help you understand these traits or old patterns and how we can balance them. What is your default behaviour? What do you already know how to do? Have you nothing to learn except what you need to let go of? What do you "always do" that prevents you from exploring new paths? Ask yourself these questions and write down whatever comes to mind on a piece of paper. Then look back over what you have written and soon you'll start to see old patterns that no longer serve you. Light a blue candle and (safely) light the piece of paper until it all burns away, symbolically removing these patterns and behaviours from your life. Take a new piece of paper and start to write down the new ways of being you wish to explore. Each day read the piece of paper and then put it into your pocket with the Blue Apatite. You will notice changes happening in your life in the coming weeks.

Vision

Blue Apatite is known as the "Crystal of the Future." Firstly, by facilitating effective communication and interaction with the world, helping to clear your mind of distractions or issues that you may have difficulty letting go of. Then, as you develop your relationship with Blue Apatite, it will connect you to higher levels of spiritual contact, opening up opportunities for you to receive higher visions. If you foresee any challenges in the future, there is no need to worry as Blue Apatite also has the ability to enhance your creativity and help you innovatively find solutions. It is through your throat chakra that you create your future, expressing the desires of the heart and third eye chakras and sending the energy out into the world to manifest. So hold your Blue Apatite and announce your vision for the world that you wish to see manifest. Burn acacia resin while working with Blue Apatite to draw out your visionary skills. Diffusing mimosa or wattle essential oil will add a happy and harmonious energy to your future. You may also like to work with your Giraffe guide. He can teach you to look beyond your own nose and to be prepared for the future. Then you may "stick out your neck" and take calculated risks.

AQUAMARINE
Health / Water / Mermaids

Aquamarine is the blue member of the beryl family along with bixbite, Emerald, Morganite, Heliodor and Goshenite. These crystals all work with you to lead you towards changes for the better, with the various colours affecting different aspects of your life. Aquamarine's name originates from the old Greek name *aqua marinus*, meaning water of the sea because of its aquatic colouring. Linked to water, Aquamarine helps you move towards all associated with this realm including cleansing, tranquillity and emotional balance.

Animal: Fish
Plant: Seaweed
Astrological Correspondence: Neptune
Power Day: Friday
Cleanse with: Water

Your Crystal Alignment Meditation

Go to a waterway, either one that is nearby or visualise one in your mind. It can be a gentle stream, a gushing lake, a vast lake or the great ocean. Place your hands or feet in the water and feel its flow, both physically and energetically. Let the water wash away all stresses and tension. Slowly let relaxation flow within you, allow the natural ebb and flow of the world return you to a state of balance. Once you feel ready, connect with your Aquamarine.

Health

Aquamarine is one of the great crystals for helping you flow towards optimum health and wellbeing. It soothes the body, especially parts governed by the throat chakra including the mouth, tongue, teeth, ears, throat, lungs and thyroid. Aquamarine helps you balance the water levels in your own body so it is great to work with for issues of dehydration or water retention. When you are feeling emotionally congested this can manifest as a cold or hay fever. Allow Aquamarine to wash away the effects of viruses, pollens and allergens as well as emotional issues that are overwhelming you.

Wear Aquamarine near your throat on a daily basis until you no longer need its support. Also place a natural piece in a glass of filtered water before you go to bed at night. In the morning, add the juice of a fresh squeezed lemon and drink.

Water

Aquamarine teaches you to understand and respect the water. It helps you understand the power of the river and the ebb and flow of the ocean. To know and be in tune with the water helps to keep you safe when in its presence. It also helps those who have a fear of the water to feel comfortable.

Place four pieces of Aquamarine around a family swimming pool including one at the gate to guard against drowning. Anyone travelling on the water should wear or carry a piece to keep them safe. It is also a great ally to anyone working with the oceans from sailors to marine biologists. It allows them to connect and understand the ways of the oceans.

Aquamarine is especially useful for helping to protect or cleanse a polluted waterway and the animals and plants that call the water home. Charge a piece of Aquamarine with this intent and toss it into the ocean, ideally on a Friday. If there is a particular place or species you wish to work with, build a power grid with Aquamarine as the power crystal. Have eight Clear Quartz points spirally clockwise and use supporting crystals such as Larimar when concerned with oceans, Selenite for cleansing, or Blue Tiger's Eye (Hawk's Eye) for protection. You may like to add pictures and Silver or light blue candles to lend their added energy and help you focus on your intention.

Whenever working with Aquamarine and water you may wish to summon the king of the depths, Poseidon, also known as Neptune. As you set up your grid or charge your crystal sprinkle some sea salt and say, "Poseidon, Almighty God of the Seas, I call upon your power and will to aid my noble work. With the powers of the ocean at your command, at this time I ask you ..."

Mermaids

Seafarers around the world have caught glimpses of mermaids as they journeyed across the oceans. Legend has it that some are so beautiful sailors have jumped overboard in pursuit of them, never to return. Where did they go? Who knows if they perished or now happily live in a mysterious wonderland sharing the wisdom and treasures of the oceans and the mer-people.

If you would like to attract a mermaid or merman, take your Aquamarine (ideally one that is shiny or sparkly as this appeals more to the mer-people) to a quiet, watery place such as a river or cove at the beach. Hold your Aquamarine in your hands and whisper your request to the crystal. Ask it to bring you in contact with a mermaid or merman. Then set it before you as you sit by the water. You may choose to close your eyes and feel their presence near you even if you cannot see them. The mer-people can offer you their wisdom without you having to lay eyes upon them. Allow the mermaids to teach you to wash away your doubts and to allow the universe's abundance to drift in your direction.

AVENTURINE, GREEN

Creation / Fertility / Luck

Aventurine is a variety of Quartz often containing glistening fragments, usually mica. It is found in a range of colours including red, blue, yellow, and most commonly green, caused by the inclusion of the crystal fuchsite. Green Aventurine is the variety we will explore here. Most green crystals are associated with the element of earth, however Aventurine is connected to the element of air, the realm of insight, inspiration, thought, knowledge, mental capacities and ideas. Working with this crystal awakens new ideas and inspired thinking, allowing you to dream up ways to progress along your path swiftly.

Animal: Ibis
Plants: Arborvitae, Ash and Hazel
Astrological Correspondences: Ceres and Mercury
Power Day: Wednesday
Cleanse with: Air

Your Crystal Alignment Meditation

Go and sit beside or within a pyramid, either physically or by visualising the pyramid in your mind. It may be the great pyramids of Egypt, a similar structure built by another civilisation or one you create yourself. Take a few breaths, relax and clear your mind. Contemplate the great knowledge dedicated to the design of the pyramid. Open yourself up and allow yourself to connect to the global consciousness where all the great knowledge of the world exists. You may want to ask a particular question or simply, "What is it that I need to know right now?" Don't necessarily expect to hear a voice reply but the more you quieten your mind, the greater the chance that a profound thought or idea may come to you. Once you are ready, connect with your Aventurine.

Creation

Aventurine combines the insightful energy of the air element with the fruitful energy of the colour green, making it a crystal for sprouting new ideas. The more you work with Aventurine, the more you will come to realise that your abilities and the possibilities in life are limitless. Aventurine frees you from self-imposed restrictions, allowing you to bring forth new creations into your life. Learn to be comfortable sitting in the centre of your universe and to summon everything to you. There is no need to chase anything. Aventurine guides you to nurture the seeds of your desires and when the time is right, they will grow. Wear Aventurine over the centre of your chest each day when you need to manifest something. Enhance your ability to create by working with your Ibis guide. He will unveil the bigger picture that lies before you and teach you the mysterious inner workings of the world. Connecting with the Ibis-headed god Thoth can reveal how you can change and create the life you want by simply using the power of precise words and language.

Each winter contemplate what you would like to manifest for the coming year. Program an Aventurine with this desire (if you have several, use one crystal per desire) and plant it with a seed, ideally an ash or hazel. After you have covered the seed with soil, use your finger to draw the symbol of the dwarf planet Ceres (⚳). Ceres governs fertility, nurturing and gardening and will add its celestial energy to your working. Caring for the plant each day as it grows will add energy to the manifestation of your goal.

Aventurine is an academic stone helping anyone starting school or university. It helps children to take more care with their schoolwork and to improve handwriting. It will give the student the ability to comprehend new concepts and help them rise to be a leader within their class. Aventurine also helps improve writing, typing and computer skills for both children and adults. Place a small stone in a child's pencil case or place a piece on your desk or next to your computer on your receptive side.

There are two trees that work in harmony with Aventurine and by including them in your life, they will enhance your work with the crystal. When you are in the stages of planning a new creation, start with the hazel tree, which has a carefree and playful energy. Aligning with this energy promotes insight and helps you determine the best path towards your goals. Include hazelnuts in your diet and sit by a hazel tree or wear a crown of intertwined hazel branches during times of meditation or contemplation to increase your ability to conceive fresh ideas.

Once you have your initial concept switch to working with the ash tree. The energy of the ash tree is similar to that of an effeminate male. It promotes wit, intelligence, communication, knowledge and curiosity making it ideal for the scholar, the writer or anyone who needs words to freely flow. Wrap your Aventurine in an ash leaf and carry it with you whenever you need to draw on these traits.

Fertility

One common use of Aventurine's creation energy is in helping women fall pregnant. If you are trying to start a family, both partners should keep Aventurine in their pockets each day. Also create a triangular grid around the bed with a Carnelian for virility on the top corner where the man sleeps, a Moonstone for promoting a healthy moon cycle on the woman's side of the bed and an Aventurine (ideally in the shape of an egg) for overall luck and fertility at the bottom middle of the bed.

Another traditional method of increasing fertility involves burying an Aventurine crystal with an egg in the garden outside your bedroom window whilst visualising your desire. Aventurine promotes healthy growth of children from birth to age seven. Once the child is born, the Aventurine can be kept in the nursery and then worn by the child when they are old enough.

Aventurine's fertile energy can also help you in the garden. Bury a small piece with each seed or seedling you plant. If a plant is struggling and just needs a little bit of a helping hand, place a stone on top of the soil until the new growth has established itself. If you have too many plants, such as a vegetable patch or field, bury an Aventurine and a Quartz point facing towards the centre of the field at the four corners of the area.

Luck

Aventurine is a stone of chance or luck. It enhances your perception and allows you to seize favourable new opportunities as they arise. Aventurine helps you at times when you need to take a gamble or risk in life. Never buy a lotto ticket or sit down at a poker table without your Aventurine. When money is tight, it will help you know where to spend your money and attention. Aventurine will help you generate new sources of income. It is great to ensure a favourable job interview or business meeting.

Keep Aventurine with your other lucky charms or keep it on the receptive side of your body such as in your pocket so that you draw lucky vibes into your energy field. You can also create a power grid to attract new income. Place an Aventurine in the centre of a one hundred dollar note. Use four Citrine points facing inwards to draw prosperity from all directions. Add supportive crystals such as such as Jet for preventing over spending and Turquoise or Chalcopyrite for allowing the free flow of money.

Sometimes a particularly unlucky time can be Mercury retrograde. Communication breakdowns and electronic malfunctions can make you feel like the world is against you. However by wearing or carrying Green Aventurine during this time, it will bless you with the Mercurial sharp mind and tongue and allow you to keep yourself ahead of the game. The Mica in the Aventurine keeps you stable and its green colour brings an abundance of insight. Add the scent of arborvitae to your space for extra support. This woody essential oil from the massive red cedar will keep your roots firmly planted in the ground.

AZURITE
Rebirth / Psychic Awareness / Indigo Children

Azurite is a powerful evolutionary crystal. It assists personal growth by protecting what you have acquired and learned while pushing you to change, grow and accumulate new skills. Azurite is known as the "Stone of Heaven" for its ability to elevate you spiritually, allowing you to become a better version of yourself. It promotes a healthy re-evaluation of your life and helps you to uncover hidden skills and dormant talents. Let Azurite boost your creativity, inspiration and intuition as well as increase confidence, enabling you to find ways to rid yourself of old, unwanted habits and change for the better. Due to Azurite's ability to have such profound effects, it is best to use it just when you have special need or a certain intent.

Animal: Bat
Plant: Apple
Astrological Correspondence: Jupiter
Power Day: Thursday
Cleanse by: Azurite harmonises with the element of water however as Azurite is quite soft it may crumble if immersed in liquids, unless it is tumbled and sealed. Simply leaving raw Azurite by a pond, creek or stream will allow it to cleanse and harmonise with the transient energy of the nearby water. Otherwise, leave it outside on the night of the new moon for a dose of 'new beginnings' energy.

Your Crystal Alignment Meditation

Sit outside and watch the sunset. Take in the beautiful array of colours that sprawl across the sky as the sun vanishes below the horizon. As the day comes to an end, contemplate the great circle of life. Know that although everything must finally cease and die, as one door closes another is opened. As the day ends, it reveals a beautiful star-filled sky, which will later vanish at the emergence of a brand new day. You exist within this circle and all that currently exists for you will one day pass. As you become aware of the ever-changing cycles of the world, connect with your Azurite.

Rebirth

Rebirth is a process whereby you reinvent or revive an aspect of your life. It can be as simple as a conscious decision to release worries and stresses of the past and reaffirm to seek only happy and positive experiences from here on. A rebirth can also be as significant as leaving a whole life behind and adopting a new one such as quitting a job, breaking up with a partner or moving to a new city. Azurite offers you support during any rebirth process. Create a small ritual whereby you write a list of what you are leaving behind and then burn or bury it. As the smoke rises, visualise the new life you desire while holding your Azurite in your projective hand. Keep the Azurite with you each day as a constant reminder and support of your decision to change.

When using Azurite for rebirthing in your life, also connect with your Bat guide. Bat shows you how to fly easily through life's important transitions. She teaches you how to effectively adapt, transform and rebirth oneself in order to thrive in life. Let Bat guide you into the cave of darkness where you can quietly evaluate your current situation and, once ready, fly with you into the light of a new stage of your life.

Azurite is often available with Malachite. This is a perfect combination for those wanting to move forward as Malachite will allow you to let go of anything that is holding you back from your rebirth. Also include apple flower essence for psychological cleansing. It helps you release mental attachments to past difficulties and find new pathways to a better life. This flower essence brings to the consciousness those things immediately necessary for spiritual growth.

If you are currently working in a job you don't enjoy you have two options: stay or leave. If leaving is not viable then Azurite can help you learn to find enjoyment at work. Sit down with your Azurite by you and reflect on the positive aspects about your job. On a piece of paper list at least ten positive things and ensure you connect with what you are writing, allowing yourself to start to feel a sense of gratitude. Then carry your Azurite with you each day as you travel to work and have it sit at your desk or workstation throughout the day. Azurite will help you uncover a new passion for your role.

Azurite can not only assist you but also animals who need a fresh burst of life. Use Azurite to give old animals more energy by placing a piece in their bed. Assist animals being relocated by placing a piece in their transport cage and gridding the crystal around their new home. Protect long-living animals such as elephants, whales and tortoises by placing it in their habitat or creating a power grid with Azurite as your power crystal with an image of the animal in the centre. Surround these with four Clear Quartz point pointing outwards and use supporting crystals such as Black Obsidian for protection from aggression and Aventurine or Unakite to promote breeding.

Psychic Awareness

Azurite is linked to Atlantis and ancient Egypt where the crystal's powerful properties were often restricted to be used by only high priests and priestesses. Azurite has the potential to bring you massive insight and clarity. With this wisdom it is possible to bring about great transformation and manifestations. An example of its effects are shown in the story of renowned channel Edgar Cayce spending time in Azurite mines in the Arizona, USA and Mexico to help him realign with his life purpose and receive guidance following a challenging period in his life.

As you work with Azurite to release old patterns, thoughts, behaviours and attitudes, you'll clear the way towards stimulating the third eye chakra and improving your intuition. This crystal helps you release thoughts and behaviours that no longer serve you, creating fresh space for new information. It helps you to side-step your conscious mind and move into deeper levels of consciousness, allowing better communication with other realms of consciousness. Once this is achieved, Azurite assists you to integrate the knowledge you receive into everyday life. To work with Azurite, surround yourself with several white candles. Still your mind and breathe deeply. Once relaxed take the Azurite and hold it in your receptive hand, sensing its energy. Contemplate a specific question you wish answered. Once ready, open your eyes and gaze at the crystal. Allow a message or answer to come to you. Wear Azurite high on your body each day to open yourself up to continued intuitive awareness. When worn over a period of time it works to improve your memory (especially photographic) and your attention to detail. Azurite when held or worn also nurtures communication with babies in the womb.

Indigo Children

Nancy Ann Tappe, a teacher and counsellor, studied the human auric field and started to notice that about eighty percent of the children born after 1980 had a new, deep-blue coloured auric field. She referred to this new colour 'indigo' and thus the term Indigo Children was born. These children tend to display certain characteristics such as a belief they are special and their needs must be met. They have high confidence, feel uncomfortable with absolute authority and rules that are given without creative thought.

They offer insight beyond that expected for their age or experience as well as feel lost or misunderstood by others who simply comply with the status quo. These children have high energy levels and strong psychic abilities. Often they are diagnosed as having ADD or ADHD and once prescribed medication can start to lose these abilities.

Azurite helps Indigo Children nurture their psychic skills while balancing and focusing their energy levels. It will help them assimilate with others and find effective ways to communicate their messages. During the day have the child wear or carry Azurite and at night place a piece in their pillowslip.

You can also place pieces around their bedroom and the home. Due to their intuitive nature, it is best to allow the child to choose their own pieces of Azurite and position them as they see fit. Parenting an Indigo Child can be challenging at times but Azurite teaches compassion and patience. If you are having a rough time with an Indigo Child, take time to sit quietly for a few minutes outside with your Azurite. Breathe deeply and centre yourself. Once relaxed contemplate the troubles you are facing and as you gaze at the crystal, allow inspirational solutions to come to you.

Further Crystal Connections — Azurite-Malachite

Although Azurite and Malachite are both crystals in their own right, they can be found growing intertwined. When this happens, they create a powerful synergy of energies which unite the heart and third eye chakras. When the heart and mind are both awakened, you will find you are truly guided in the right direction. It is great to use when you are feeling torn between your head and heart, allowing you to overcome disunity or inner conflict. Azurite-Malachite allows you to listen to your feelings, put them into words and find a positive outcome.

Azurite-Malachite allows you to clearly comprehend your soul's goals as well as giving you motivation and courage to turn them into a reality. When you are looking for direction in life, use Azurite-Malachite in meditation to receive clear direction and new perspectives. It can reveal deeply hidden negative emotional thought patterns that are holding you back, and can guide you on the steps needed to release them. This stone is ideal for those involved in the arts — visionary artists, writers, musicians, dancers and actors — as it will allow you to both intellectualise and empathise with your work and audience. For creatives, when you are feeling blocked, stand outside and hold Azurite-Malachite either against your heart or forehead while taking some deep breaths.

Since the green of Malachite lends its loving energies to Azurite, when the two crystals are combined it will add great love to your work, especially in healing, meditation, clairvoyance or working with animals and nature. This stone will ensure that there is no room in your life for arrogance, conceit, vanity and fear. A loving connection to a higher state of being will replace the deceptive state of living via the ego.

You'll also notice an increase in perception when working with Azurite-Malachite. This stone encourages you to take more interest in your surroundings and others, making it great for counteracting selfishness or narrow-mindedness. It encourages open, honest and helpful behaviours, leading to more fulfilling interactions for everyone. Use Azurite-Malachite in conjunction with any work aimed at increasing the public's awareness of an important environmental, social or health issue.

The rich blue of Azurite combined with the vibrant green of Malachite creates a stone that resembles planet Earth. Therefore use this stone in any working involving healing the Earth as a whole. Create a healing grid surrounding a piece of Azurite-Malachite with crystals that possess the energies you want to send to the planet. Alternatively charge the stone with your own healing energies for the planet, then leave it outside on the earth overnight for the energies to be absorbs into the land. Azurite-Malachite is also great for promoting harmony between nations.

BLOODSTONE
Health / Victory / Bullying

Bloodstone, also known as Heliotrope, is a powerful crystal that empowers and supports you upon your path of service. Legend has it that Bloodstone was originally just a green Chalcedony and when Jesus Christ was crucified his blood spilt upon the crystal, creating the red spots while imbuing it with his heavenly traits of altruism; the strength against overwhelming adversity and the ability to heal the body of any illness. Since then, Bloodstone has been used as a crystal for communing with Christ and invoking Christ Consciousness into your life. It is also a crystal of the Sun and Mars, giving its guardian determination, clout and the ability to succeed.

Animal: Koala
Plant: Eucalyptus
Astrological Correspondence: Mars
Power Day: Tuesday
Cleanse with: Earth and Sun

Your Crystal Alignment Meditation

Wander amongst the trees, ideally eucalyptus. Choose one tree and take a few moments to study its features. Notice the leaves as they dance in the wind. Does this tree have flowers? Can you smell any scents? Reach out and feel the bark. Each tree has its own energy and spirit. Allow yourself to connect to its beauty and magic. Understand why the tree has grown to be the way it is. Once you have formed a connection with the tree, you are now ready to connect with your Bloodstone.

Health

Bloodstone has a long history of being used in healing, dating as far back to Mesopotamia around five thousand years ago. It is most powerful in rectifying imbalances of the blood, heart, blood vessels or circulatory system and for detoxification of your organs. Place your Bloodstone in the sun for a short period and then wear it against your skin to improve circulation or speed up the healing of a wound. Place the crystal with your hot water bottle to keep warmth moving around your body on cold nights. Bloodstone dipped in cold water and applied to an afflicted area is highly beneficial in staunching blood flow, particularly nosebleeds. Keep the crystal wet and re-dip as necessary. A Bloodstone elixir can be applied to varicose veins, haemorrhoids or insect bites.

For general crystal healing, as Bloodstone has a very yang energy, it is best used as an overall health crystal when the body needs firing up. An excellent stimulator of the immune system, use Bloodstone to ward off colds, flu, or infections. Use it to get back on your feet and return to optimum energy levels after illness, injury, or physical exhaustion. If you feel the body needs more soothing, for example due to inflammation, tension or stress, then opt for a crystal with a more pacifying yin energy such as Amazonite or Amber.

When working with Bloodstone explore the ways of Koala who reminds you of the importance of good food, sufficient sleep and spending time in nature, with the trees and in solitude. According to Aboriginal legend, she's the keeper of the waterways because she never seems to need to drink, and the trees she prefers are those that grow along riverbanks. Thus, she reminds you that everyone needs water, not only physically but also emotionally, to cleanse and purify. Koala also helps you cleanse and remove toxic situations from your life. Diffusing eucalyptus essential oil will further support the cleansing and healing of your body promoted with Bloodstone.

Bloodstone is beneficial for pregnant or nursing mothers and animals. It stimulates nutrient-rich blood and hormonal balance, and is used to help prevent miscarriages. Bloodstone assists in easing the birthing process, providing strength during labour and creating supportive vibrations so the infant travels easily through the birth canal. Combine with Epidote, Rainbow Moonstone or Unakite which all support healthy and ongoing growth of the young. Following birth, Bloodstone can be used in assisting both human and animal mothers in the bonding process, especially if the process was traumatic or mother and baby were separated for a significant amount of time. You can also use Bloodstone to alleviate symptoms of PMS and menstrual disorders, especially when used with Hemimorphite or Larimar. Along with Emerald, Eudialyte, Mahogany Obsidian and Morganite, Bloodstone helps with the challenges of menopause by stabilising hormones.

Bullying

Bloodstone is a great stone to call upon if you or another is being bullied. It guides you on how to handle the situation and gives you the wisdom to know when it is appropriate to withdraw and the courage to confront when needed. Hold the Bloodstone in your projective hand and say over and over, "Away from me, set me free" until you feel a sense of strength. Then wrap the crystal in an ivy leaf for protection and place in a pouch or medicine bag. Wear this bag around your neck or keep it in your pocket. Repeat every Tuesday until the bullying stops.

Bloodstone, as a green crystal, awakens the heart chakra, increasing your compassion for the bully. It allows you to shift from a state of being intimidated to one of understanding, encouraging you to empathise and comprehend why the bully chooses to resort to intimidating behaviours. Perhaps they have a volatile or loveless home life or that due to fear or life circumstances they have learned that this is the best way for them to survive and fulfil their needs in the world. Just as Jesus said as he was crucified, "Father, forgive them, for they do not know what they are doing" (Luke 23:34). As you shift your approach to the situation, from disempowerment to empowered kindness, you'll often find the bullying stops. Keep Bloodstone by you through this process and take time to sit in contemplation with your crystal each day to advance your forgiveness. It is a wonderful companion for prayer and meditation, and brings a stable and centring vibration into your life. In doing so, this helps you establish a greater union with Great Spirit. Bloodstone also helps alleviate feelings of isolation or loneliness that your mind may create when you are being bullied.

Victory

Bloodstone harmonises with the energies of Mars, the planet of strength and victory. Wear or carry your crystal to increase mental clarity and to aid in decision making. It provides a mental boost when motivation is lacking, and can revitalise your body if you are exhausted. If you have a tendency to lose motivation for a project over time, the green, prosperous energy of Bloodstone will help you develop an idea through to actualisation.

While meditating, sit facing the direction of Mars. Visualise a victory you need assistance with. See yourself winning, hearing the sounds, smelling the scents and feeing the emotions. Then say either in your head or out loud the following or something similar, "Mighty Mars, I summon your strength. Merge with me, come with me. Awaken within me my energy and passion. Walk with me through the fires of challenge and lead me upon the path of victory." Know that victory is yours as long as you maintain a strength of belief greater than your opponent's. Keep the Bloodstone near you until completion and then cleanse the crystal to reuse it again. Bloodstone is ideal for athletes as it supports both their physical wellbeing and is a good luck charm for sports competitions and matches.

Not only does Bloodstone maintain personal wellbeing, it is also reputed to bring its guardian respect, good fortune, riches and fame. It can be used to guard you from deception, overcome those with ill intentions, and to secure victory in court and legal matters. Bloodstone facilitates connection with nature and fosters a working relationship with the elements and elemental beings. When in dire need, ask Bloodstone to help you avert lightning, to conjure storms or summon rain. Remember that to work most effectively with crystals and nature you should work in harmony with its cycles rather than try to interrupt them for personal gain. Beautiful rituals to perform with your Bloodstone are with the winds to bring change or clarity, or with the rains to wash away emotional pain and suffering.

One of the greatest victories you can have is to live a long life and Bloodstone is renowned for that. With the combination of its health promoting, open-hearted and good fortune traits, Bloodstone surrounds its guardian in an energy of longevity. In your younger years, hold Bloodstone in meditation and visualise yourself in old age, energetic and happy. When older, wear or carry Bloodstone whenever you need a renewing burst of energy, especially after a run of poor health or bad luck.

BRONZITE

Manners / Kindness / Decisiveness

Working with Bronzite facilitates the acquisition of knowledge enabling you to gain clarity by coercing you towards simplicity and allowing you to regain balance in your life. It helps you identify situations that hold no benefit to you and guides you on how to remove it in a respectful manner, enabling you to be direct and confident in your dealing with others. However, this crystal is more concerned with benefiting the greater good rather than simply achieving your own goals. Bronzite enables you to develop healthy respect for beauty in the world and urges you to act in ways to preserve and protect it.

Animal: Seahorse
Plant: Strawberry
Astrological Correspondence: Venus
Power Day: Friday
Cleanse with: Earth

Your Crystal Alignment Meditation

Go to some woodlands near your home or visualise yourself there in your mind. Woodlands are a habitat that is both home and protection for countless animals and plants. Here, when uninterrupted, life flows harmoniously with each species fulfilling its role in the circle of life. To humanity, the woods have often been a place of mystery, for this is where the hidden lie undiscovered, both the beautiful and the frightful. Find a sacred place to call your own here. Sit and take in the surroundings. Breathe in the fresh air. Focus on one item in the woods, such as a single tree, a rock, maybe an insect. Change your energy so that you are like the object. Feel the power of the tree, the strength of the stone or the resolve of the insect. Feel your connection and then try the same activity with another object. Eventually you want to start to sense the overall connectedness you feel with the woods, and thus the Earth. You are now ready to connect with your Bronzite.

Manners

Bronzite is a crystal of social success. It enables you to feel settled and comfortable in any situation. Bronzite brings you back to the basics of polite and sensible human interaction by promoting awareness of those around you and encouraging courtesy and manners. Concierge staff or restaurant hosts should wear a Bronzite pendant. Likewise, when you are on a first date it will ensure you don't forget your chivalrous behaviour. Place a piece at the dining table to encourage good table manners in children. Bronzite will help you remember correct etiquette so take it to formal events and make it your travel companion when overseas. Meditate on the wisdom of your Seahorse guide when working with Bronzite. Ask Seahorse to awaken a sense of kindness, and compassion encouraging you to perform noble and selfless acts.

Kindness

Greek philosophers believed that what you did was more important than what you knew. Being kind and generous not only gives a beneficial lift to the recipient, but also as the giver you'll find it improves your mood and self-worth. If you are ever feeling down or sad, focus on doing a kind deed for another and see how it raises your spirits. Bronzite encourages you to be kind to all you come into contact with; those you love, those you don't know, the unfortunate as well as the blessed. It gives you the courage and the guidance to make this world a more pleasant place. Carry Bronzite in your pocket and adopt a challenge in a course of kindness. Each day tally up how many acts of kindness you performed and week after week keep attempting to increase your number. Know that your kindness will come back to you and the more you give, the more you'll receive.

If you are trying to attract a new lover, Bronzite can help inspire you to take actions to show you care. Wear it near your heart so it can resonate with your heart's desire. Strawberries are a fruit of love and by eating them, enjoying strawberry teas and using strawberry incense and oils each day, in conjunction with using Bronzite, you'll shift your way of being to radiate an energy of love.

Decisiveness

Bronzite eliminates doubt and indecisiveness. It gives you the courage to take action, share your gifts with the world and find ways to return things back to their natural state of balance and harmony. If something needs to be removed or ended, Bronzite give resolution to make that call. If you need to make a major decision, prepare and drink a Bronzite elixir. Then sit holding your Bronzite in your receptive hand and ask yourself three questions:
1. Which option will I regret more if I don't do?
2. What would a wise person do?
3. Which option better serves the greater good?

Don't think too hard but rather pay attention to your emotional responses and how your body feels. Bronzite will guide you in the right direction. The Bronzite elixir is great to drink every Friday if you are constantly indecisive.

CALCITE, BLUE

Throat Chakra / Reconciliation / Major Events / Future Generations

Calcite tends to have a gentler energy than other crystals but this should not be mistaken as a weaker energy. Sometimes subtle, slow change is the most beneficial. Calcite allows you to clear baggage from the past and guides you to look at improving the future. Blue Calcite works with the throat chakra and heals all forms of communication. It promotes empathy and understanding and the discovery of new peaceful ways of interaction.

Animals: Dugong and Manatee
Plant: Bluebell
Astrological Correspondence: Venus
Power Day: Friday
Cleanse with: Water

Your Crystal Alignment Meditation

Go to a still body of water such as a pond or lake or visualise one in your mind. Gaze into the water and look upon your reflection. Place your hands or feet in the water and feel the cool and soothing energy. Notice each time you touch the water the ripples you send out. Gift yourself some time just to connect with the calming energy. Once ready, connect with your Calcite.

Throat Chakra

All Calcites are great for cleansing and clearing energy. Use them in healing when you sense there is a blockage or to help the energy move freely around the body and via the meridians. If there is an emotional issue, habit or mental script that is keeping you stuck, use Calcite. When it comes to chakra balancing, Calcite is used to soothe overactive chakras. This can be done by using the corresponding coloured Calcite for that chakra i.e. Honey Calcite for the Earth star chakra, Red Calcite for the base, Orange Calcite for the sacral and so on. Blue Calcite is ideal for soothing an overactive throat chakra. If you have a tendency to talk loudly, rudely or a lot, talk out of turn or over people, swear, gossip and criticise, then your throat chakra may need some soothing. Wear or carry your Blue Calcite each day, ideally near your throat chakra. Find time, to meditate with your Blue Calcite on your throat while drawing its soft blue colour into the energy centre. Singing can also be beneficial.

Reconciliation

Blue Calcite releases emotional grudges and welcome forgiveness. It clears the way for a more peaceful future and truthful communication. It is a great crystal for crime prevention officers, mediators, negotiators, priests, race and equality workers. Is there someone you'd like to mend a rift with but are finding them resistant? Place a piece of Blue Calcite and a photo of them between two light blue candles and look at the photo each day and wish them well. When the time is right you will have a chance to mend the bridge.

Blue Calcite is a crystal of fairness. To ensure legal proceedings, negotiations or peace-keeping efforts are reasonable and just, bring a piece of Blue Calcite to the meeting. A vase of bluebells in the room will also encourage truthfulness. If you have adopted the attitude that life is not fair, wearing Calcite near your throat can help rectify this belief. Combine this with a positive affirmation such as, "I speak my truth with peace and love and receive fair treatment in return" that you recite daily.

Major Events

Blue Calcite keeps you calm during major events, especially when you are the centre of attention. Keep a piece in your pocket if you are giving a speech, presentation or performance. It is the perfect "something blue" to give to a bride on her wedding day. Also slipping a bluebell flower into your shoe will give you extra luck.

Future Generations

There is a Greek proverb that says, "A society grows great when old men plant trees whose shade they know they shall never sit in." This proverb resonates perfectly with the energy of Blue Calcite. This crystal inspires you to consider the wellbeing of future generations and take actions today that will improve tomorrow. Wear or carry a piece often as a reminder that your actions affect future generations. You can work with your Dugong or Manatee guide to remember the virtues of slow, steady action and walking gently upon the Earth. Hold a Blue Calcite in your projective hand and send supportive energy to politicians and leaders. Alternatively write them a letter requesting they look beyond the limited years of their leadership and include a Blue Calcite sphere as a gift.

CALCITE, MANGANO

Love Issues / Emotional Security / Loving Life

The soft pink vibration of Mangano Calcite helps you eliminate the cumbersome and mundane so you can live the life you love. It allows you to reconnect with the pleasures of life and reminds you that life should never be all work and no play. Gentle Mangano Calcite cleanses away all past hurts and pain, opening the way for closer relationships with family and friends.

Animal: Flamingo
Plants: Alder and Raspberry
Astrological Correspondence: Venus
Power Day: Friday
Cleanse with: Water

Your Crystal Alignment Meditation

Go to a peaceful place in nature. Close your eyes, and run your hands over your surroundings. Tune in to your sense of touch. Keeping your eyes closed, take some deep breaths and see what you can smell. Open your mouth to see if you can taste anything and then stop and simply listen. Finally open your eyes and look around. Once you've tuned in to each sense individually, allow all five to flood you with sensory pleasure. Form a connection with your environment through all five senses. Once you are feeling at one with your surroundings, connect with your Mangano Calcite.

Love Issues

Mangano Calcite clears away emotional hurt. It will allow you to forgive others, making way for the release of long-standing emotional baggage. It will soften a hardened heart, letting you feel comfortable to give and receive love again. Make a charm bag with a Mangano Calcite and a piece of alder bark. Carry it near your heart each day during periods in your life when you are working to release an emotional issue. Reiki and Seichim practitioners can benefit from using a Mangano Calcite wand or having a piece in their room to help clients release emotional blockages.

Mangano Calcite allows you to release any guilt that you are still carrying from past events. Guilt that is not dealt with can manifest in middle back pain or large intestine issues. For healing, rest with Mangano Calcite on you site of the pain each day until it clears. For further support, wear the crystal over your heart to allow you to forgive yourself.

Emotional Security

Mangano Calcite promotes emotional bonding, especially between family members. Give a piece to each family member or grid ten pieces around the house to improve parent-child bonds. Hold the crystal in your hand, examining its soft pink colour to ease post-natal depression. When placed in enclosures Mangano Calcite encourages animals to look after their young.

The tender nature of Mangano Calcite is perfect for first-love spells. It will attract someone who will be gentle with your heart and patient in their ways, allowing you to feel safe. Mangano Calcite restores a sense of security after a crisis in the home or when a property has been vandalised or robbed. Cleanse the household with a smudge stick then place a Mangano Calcite at each window or door to ensure only love enters the house from now on. A Mangano Calcite sphere in the centre of the house will bring more love to the space and a raspberry branch hung over the front door works to prevent any negative reoccurrence.

Loving Life

As you release emotional issues from the past, Mangano Calcite opens you up to the pleasures of life. It allows you to relish in a cup of tea, celebrate beautiful music and thoroughly enjoy a blissful massage. Create a home of sensuality by adding Mangano Calcite to your mop water. As you clean your floors, you will spread this energy into every room. Discover more ways to find pleasure in life by developing a relationship with your Flamingo guide. She shows us how to filter all that life has to offer and keep only that which is beneficial. Flamingo reminds us of the importance of nourishing ourselves so that we become a radiant beacon of love.

CARNELIAN
Sacral Chakra / Sensuality / Creation

Carnelian is a red-orange variety of chalcedony found around the world. It has been known since antiquity and is referred to as sardius in the Bible and allocated as one of the twelve gemstones upon the breastplate of the high priest Aaron. This fiery orange crystal encourages you to seek a life of pleasure for yourself and others. The ancient Egyptians associated Carnelian with the fertile menstrual blood of the powerful fertility goddess Isis. Thus, Carnelian is a crystal that brings forth new births, both as newborn children and exciting new life opportunities. Work with Carnelian to awaken your sexuality, reignite passion and allow yourself to enjoy the pleasures of life.

Animal: Rabbit
Plants: Cacao and Carrot
Astrological Correspondence: Sun
Power Day: Sunday
Cleanse with: Fire or Sun

Your Crystal Alignment Meditation

Go to a meadow, either near you or visualise one in your mind. Find a spot to sit or lie down. Feel the sun on your skin. Take in the beautiful colours of any wildflowers and enjoy the floral scent in the air. Watch birds and other animals go about their day. Allow the gentle energy of the environment to nurture you. Let your body and mind slowly move towards feelings of relaxation and peace. Allow any anxiety, frustration, anger or sadness dissolve from you and sink deep into the earth below. Once you feel relaxed, connect with your Carnelian.

Sacral Chakra

Carnelian works on increasing the amount of energy at your sacral chakra. If you deny yourself enjoyment, lack creativity, feel unmotivated to interact, have a low sex drive or have physical problems with your sex organs, you may need to devote some more attention to your sacral chakra. Each day, sit or lie down with your Carnelian near the chakra. Hold your hands cupped in front of the chakra as you start to visualise and sense energy building within them. Once you feel you have generated significant energy in your hands, direct this energy into the chakra by moving your hands to place them on your skin over the navel. Continue this activity until you feel fully energised. Keep your Carnelian with you throughout the day. Filling your life with orange foods, clothes and decorations will also bring the healing colour of orange in your life and will help stimulate your sacral chakra.

Sensuality

Carnelian resonates with passion, pleasure and sensuality. If you lack sexual confidence or your sex life needs a helping hand bring Carnelian into the bedroom. Grid crystals around the bed or place some pieces around a pair of red candles. Combine with a drink made from raw, organic, super-food cacao to increase energy, joy and fertility. For couples trying to conceive, place an egg-shaped Carnelian in the bedroom. This crystal ignites a man's virility so have him carry a piece in his pocket or wear a Carnelian belt buckle each day as well. Connect with your Rabbit guide to unveil obstacles to falling pregnant. Later on, place pink-hued Carnelian in the centre of the home to help adjust to parenthood.

Carnelian shouldn't be restricted to the bedroom. Carnelian brings awareness of the importance in allowing daily pleasure and sensuality. Wear Carnelian over the centre of your body to maximise the enjoyment of a cup of tea, a pleasing song, and warm hug or a piece of art. Carnelian increases your ability to connect with the Egyptian goddess Isis, who helps to awaken your own inner goddess or feminine side. Create an altar devoted to your inner goddess with images of Isis, her crystals of Carnelian and Lapis Lazuli, as well as other items that honour your sacred self and take time to meditate before it each day.

Creation

Carnelian ignites a passion for life that can be channelled into constructive pursuits. For those wanting a pay rise or promotion, take Carnelian to work. It will give you the eloquence to influence others and overcome resistance. If you are looking for a change in career, Carnelian allows you to conceive new ideas on how to make a living.

Carnelian creates luck and safety when worn. Add the crystal to a tank or pond with orange fish to draw prosperity your way. The proverb says, "No man who wore a Carnelian was ever found in a collapsed house or beneath a fallen wall." Tradespeople can carry Carnelian to protect them from workplace injuries. To create a safety net that will preserve a sacred or ancient site, charge five Carnelian crystals with this intent and bury them around the site's perimeter. If you can't get to the site, simply meditate while holding Carnelian and visualise the site surrounded by a protective white light or fire.

If you are feeling lethargic, slip Carnelian into your pocket or keep it with your fresh fruits and vegetables to increase their effectiveness. Diffusing carrot seed essential oil at home also will inspire you into action. Otherwise, combine the two by making an invigorating massage oil by adding a Carnelian and some carrot seed essential oil to your base oil. (NB. Carrot seed oil is not recommended for use during pregnancy).

CELESTITE

Beauty / Inspired Communication / Minimalism

Celestite, also known as Celestine, with its soft baby-blue vibration is a true gift for the modern world. Amidst the frantic chaos of everyday life, it promotes peace, calmness and slowing down. Celestite stops you drowning in a world dominated by materialism and guides us to seek higher ideals. Working with Celestite will reconnect you with the joy, beauty and the power available to you from the universe. As you deepen your relationship with this heavenly crystal it will facilitate connection with your guides and angels.

Animal: Swan
Plants: Cherry and Cherry Blossom
Astrological Correspondences: Pleiades and Venus
Power Day: Friday
Cleanse with: Water

Your Crystal Alignment Meditation

Go to a swing set and sit down. Allow a childish joy to fill you as you start to swing. Swing so high you feel as though you are reaching into the heavens. Feel as if you are become part of this celestial realm, touching it with your aura of beauty. Enjoy this experience of being carefree. Awaken your inner child. You are now ready to connect with your Celestite.

Beauty

Working with Celestite will open your eyes and allow you to notice all that is beautiful in the world. Furthermore, it awakens your radiant inner beauty and allows it to shine for all to see. Working with energies of the constellation Pleiades, deities Aphrodite or Adonis, or Archangel Jophiel can bring you guidance on how to restore your own sense of beauty. Keep a cluster of Celestite near your skincare products to increase their ability to make you glow. Each morning pick up a piece of Celestite and hold it against your chest. See and feel a dazzling aura of beauty surrounding you and affirm, "I am beautiful." Start to visualise yourself going about your day projecting beauty. See other people attracted by your beauty and paying you the attention you deserve and desire, and with this deserved attention, you feel compassion and comfortable around others. Keep the Celestite with you all day. To keep you in this uplifted mood, include cherries in your diet as their magical properties remind you of the sweetness of life and they promote vibrant and magnetic energies within you. You can also try taking the flower essence of the sweet or wild cherry which increase vitality, cheerfulness and give you a more optimistic outlook.

Celestite helps you remain composed in stressful situations. Hold it in your receptive hand and take eight deep breaths when you need to calm down. You may want to call upon your Swan guide who calmly glides across the water, while below the surface her legs are frantically working. She will offer you her wisdom on how to keep your cool no matter how disordered or demanding your circumstances are.

If you continue to carry old patterns from your mother or grandmother that you would like to release, create a power grid with a photo of the matriarch and a piece of Celestite in the middle honouring the positive they gave you. Surround this by nine Quartz Crystals, five pointing in and four pointing out. Add supporting crystals of Jet and Black Tourmaline to absorb and transmute the behaviours and attitudes that no longer serve you now. You can also add cherry blossoms and an image of the goddess, Tara, who guides us to love, appreciate and nurture yourself and others.

Inspired Communication

Celestite reminds us that, "Life is not measured by the number of breaths we take but by the moments that take our breath away." Working with Celestite reminds you that petty insignificances often prevent a life of amazing experiences. Miscommunications, bickering, judgement and grudges separate people rather than bring us together. Celestite helps you actually hear what is being said, rather than what you think is being said. Wear Celestite near your throat and allow it to banish communication barriers so that understanding and compassion flourish in all your relationships. Pairing Celestite with a small twig of cherry wood in your pocket helps conquer conflict, see clearly what is true and act rationally rather than emotionally. If you must go to bed with an unresolved issue with someone, hold your Celestite and tell it your worries. Place it by your bedside and it will work to alleviate worrisome thoughts.

Celestite, if worn or carried, gifts you with eloquence, grace and compassion for others, the Earth and our fellow creatures. It is also a great crystal for actors and singers, or other onstage performers as it will bring out their best performance. It helps artists produce works that inspire humanity to reach for the heavens and the greater good.

Minimalism

Celestite motivates you to aim for higher ideals. It has the ability to awaken an understanding of the downfalls of capitalism and consumerism, teaching that an accumulation of possessions doesn't bring inner happiness. It combats desperation by giving you the foresight to wait and allow what you need to come to you rather than chasing something unnecessarily. Celestite brings you happiness with what you already have while quelling any hunger to constantly acquire superfluous possessions. Furthermore, it brings to light that having less gives you freedom to have more time, energy and money to devote to that which you truly love and serves the greater good. By placing Celestite on your desk or keeping it in your pocket, purse or handbag this crystal prevents greed or unnecessary purchasing. By meditating with the crystal each Friday while contemplating what you can reduce, to enable you to have more of what you really seek can have profound results. Find a cherry or cherry blossom tree to sit under with your Celestite and allow its wisdom to soak into your consciousness. Cherry trees remind you when life is feeling too complicated, that it is simple pleasures that often bring you the most joy.

Another effective activity involves taking a walk in nature whenever you feel something is lacking in your life. Hold your Celestite in your receptive hand and allow your crystal to show you the beautiful perfection of the natural world that has sustained humanity for millions of years. This will help to rebalance you and help you realise that you already have everything you truly need. As you give yourself time to contemplate in the fresh air, you may realise that you are receiving, just not in the form you expected.

CHAROITE

Life Purpose / Overcoming Personal Challenges / ADHD

Charoite is linked to the sixth spiritual ray of service, peace and brotherhood and its vibration encourages you to give of yourself to others. It is also a highly protective crystal and will prevent others taking advantage of your generosity. This makes Charoite a supportive crystal for healers, carers, charity workers and volunteers. Charoite is only found in one place in the world, by the Chara River in Russia. In the past, this area was an area where political prisoners were kept so the crystal holds some energy of this time making it great for endurance and comfort during adversity. It is often found alongside a golden crystal, Tinaksite. These two are a perfect pairing. Tinaksite shields you from the effects of the past and helps you release any prior karma so that you may move forward with Charoite.

Animal: Dog
Plant: Mandarin
Astrological Correspondences: Chiron and Pluto
Power Day: Monday
Cleanse with: Full Moon

Your Crystal Alignment Meditation

Go to a forest or woodlands that you have not visited before, either one nearby or if that is not possible, visualise one in your mind. Find a path and set along the way. As you come to forks along the path pause and listen to your inner guidance on which of the two options to take. Pay attention to what is affecting your decision. Does the path you prefer look easier or quicker? Maybe it looks more mysterious or beautiful. Then contemplate whether you always choose the easiest, quickest, mysterious or more beautiful way in life. Does this work for you or would it be worth trying another approach in your everyday life? Allow any realisations to arise. After walking for a while, find a place that feels special to you to sit and rest and, when ready, connect with your Charoite.

Life Purpose

Charoite is great for helping you discover your path of service. When your life is feeling directionless and pointless, work with Charoite. It will help awaken awareness of your true calling and allow you to see how you can use your unique set of talents to contribute to the world. Take your time and listen to your intuition when choosing your Charoite as this is one crystal that will strongly draw its guardian to it.

Once you have cleansed your Charoite, find a quiet place where you will not be disturbed. Light a purple candle and invite your spiritual guides to join you. Take a piece of paper or your diary and write the following questions:

1. What makes me happy?
2. What activities make me lose track of time?
3. What do people say I am good at? What is my gift?
4. If I could give one message to the world, what would it be?
5. Who would I like to help most?

Contemplate the answers to these questions while holding your Charoite in your receptive hand. Slowly, you will start to gain clarity about what drives and inspires you and where an opportunity exists for you to use your talents. If answers don't come immediately, be open to receiving signs in the coming days. During this period, keep Charoite near you all day. At night, place it in your pillowslip and note dreams that may offer answers. As you start to gain clarity on your path of service a great guide to work with is Dog. Man's best friend teaches us the great rewards of loyalty and service to those we love. By connecting with his energy you can experience a greater opening of the heart and discover newfound value in other's close companionship.

Overcoming Personal Challenges

Often the challenges that prevent us from moving forward are constructs of our own thoughts. It is you who believes you cannot be fitter, richer, funnier, in a relationship or successful. Often you create excuses or justifications such as a lack of time, money, resources or traits that stop you. However, many great success stories often tell of how an individual overcame great odds to succeed. You are no different and when you focus on ways to succeed rather than why you can't succeed, you are taking positive steps to writing your own story of success.

Create a power grid to help you find solutions to challenges. This power grid is different to the structure of the format described in the introduction. Place a double-terminated Amethyst or Clear Quartz point in the centre. Have one end pointing in the direction in the sky at Chiron (an internet search should be able to answer this for you or there are smart phone apps that tell you the current positions of all the planets, asteroids, etc.) Chiron possesses energies of wisdom and patience and can help you see that your wounds and pitfalls are gifts when looked at from a different angle. Chiron offers a great energy to find solutions to personal challenges.

Around the crystal point place seven (the number associated with Chiron) Charoites in a circle. You can then add a second circle of supporting crystals including Black Tourmaline for transmuting unwanted energies, Covellite for understanding the shadow self, Labradorite for awakening a sense of adventure or Mahogany Obsidian for removing external barriers.

Each day sit with your grid between you and Chiron. Feel its influence transferring via the crystal point. Say, "Hear my words, Chiron. I am ready to move forward. Help me see the way. I am ready to move forward." Sit and allow guidance to flow to you in the silence. Carry a different one of the seven Charoites with you each day of the week.

ADHD

If you or your child has been diagnosed with ADHD, Charoite can help bring focus, direction and a calming energy into your lives. Have the person with ADHD choose seven Charoite crystals and place them around their room. One in the pillowslip is always a good choice as by being close to them it'll align with their energy field and help them while they sleep. Wearing a simple pendant or bracelet at all times will also be beneficial.

To enhance the effects of the Charoite, diffuse mandarin essential oil or add it to a spray bottle with purified water and spritz it around the home. The uplifting scent of mandarin will promote a more harmonious environment.

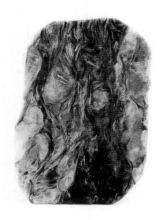

CHRYSOCOLLA

Tolerance / Emotional Healing / Self-Expression / Mother Nature

Chrysocolla is a vibrant blue Copper-rich crystal found around the world. It supports emotional healing so that past baggage has no impact on future interactions and relationships. Chrysocolla encourages you to speak from the heart and helps you to have open and honest conversations with others, especially with people you have found unhelpful, rude or abusive. Chrysocolla possesses a gentle, motherly energy that helps you let go of anger and frustration. Sitting with Chrysocolla in a natural environment will help you develop a bond with and receive guidance from Mother Nature.

Animal: Squirrel
Plants: Grape
Astrological Correspondence: Venus
Power Day: Friday
Cleanse by: Water

Your Crystal Alignment Meditation

Go to a tree hollow and sit inside it. If you cannot find one nearby, visualise one in your mind. Feel the energy of the tree surround you and nurture you. Let the tree embrace you with its energy and dissolve the pain and suffering inflicted by the past. Trust that as you release these hurts, the future is safe, Affirm to yourself "I flow with ease through my day". Once you are feeling balanced, connect with your Chrysocolla.

Tolerance

Chrysocolla promotes patience and teaches us the virtues of silence and listening. Wearing Chrysocolla allows you to open your heart and mind to others, and to understand their perspective. In ancient Egypt, Chrysocolla was called the "wise stone" as those who wore it generally came up with clever compromises when it seemed impossible to find a solution in negotiations or disagreements.

Lore also says that Chrysocolla makes violent people more sensitive and tolerant, which is why Cleopatra carried the crystal with her everywhere she went. When you get angry or frustrated by another, hold Chrysocolla in your receptive hand and take ten deep breaths. Chrysocolla's ability to enhance your sense of ease and willingness to adapt can have positive effects on your physical health, namely your lymphatic system. Thymus issues can arise if you're paranoid or feel singled out. To counteract this keep Chrysocolla against your chest, near your thymus, and constantly affirm, "I am accepted, loved and safe". Chrysocolla can also help with other areas of your lymphatic system that arise if you tend to be resistant to those around you and become unwilling to go with the flow. If this is the case, add two more pieces of Chrysocolla to your pockets and repeat to yourself throughout the day, "Go with the flow." Combining the use of Chrysocolla with any form of sound healing can yield powerful results.

Emotional Healing

The Copper (the metal of Venus and love) content of Chrysocolla make this crystal a wise choice for those who are hurting. It inspires you to be gentleness and nurturing towards yourself, encouraging you to pause and rest to regain your strength. Wear or carry Chrysocolla constantly throughout any challenging time and take time to sit outside and meditate with it each day, focusing on listening to your emotions. If someone else has played a role in your pain, Chrysocolla prompts you to remain generous and kind to him or her. Hurting another simply adds more pain to the world. Grid Chrysocolla around your home or space following a burglary, mugging or any physical abuse to bring a protective, nurturing energy back into your life. It also soothes physical pain and is ideal for a woman to hold during childbirth.

When combined with Chrysoprase, the two crystals synergise as a nurturing emotional healing yin yang couplet that enable you to deal with any childhood hurt. Chrysocolla nurtures the feminine inner child while Chrysoprase awakens the masculine inner child to feel comfortable to play. They help you to connect and talk through meditation with the child version of yourself from the past, offering the child love and support so the hurts are released and no longer plague you in the present. Following this practice eat some grapes, take a few drops of grape flower essence or enjoy some wine as a recognition that you wish to celebrate the future, one full of joy and love. Continue to carry the two crystals with you as a support for your inner child. To extend this practice you may like to honour your inner child on your altar with a couple of meaningful items.

Chrysocolla helps facilitate the release of past baggage so it doesn't impact future interactions and relationships. During times of great emotional healing, explore the wisdom of Squirrel. Squirrel is aware that change is an inevitable part of life and prepares himself accordingly. In preparing yourself for changes in the future, Squirrel also teaches you to lighten your load if you have gathered too much. Are you collecting too many possessions, thoughts or engagements? Lighten your load to enable you to remain alert and nimble. Squirrel also reminds you of the importance being playful has in your life.

Self-expression

The greens and blues in Chrysocolla allows it to connect two chakras, the heart and throat. When these two energies centres harmonise together it allows you to speak from the heart. Carry or wear Chrysocolla near these chakras when you want to be more empathetic in your communication. It is a great crystal to have with you when you have to have a difficult discussion such as a break-up, redundancy or delivering upsetting news. It helps you communicate to someone that their behaviours make you feel uncomfortable. Chrysocolla will help you express how you feel in a caring and compassionate way. It allows you to speak the truth. It is nurturing to the thymus and thyroid, ensuring you always feel heard and valued when worn near the glands. You can also place it next to some purified water for 24 hours to make an elixir for consumption.

Chrysocolla supports singers, actors, coaches and speakers to delve into the depths of their emotional being and express this in their communication or performance. Anyone wishing to inspire or touch others should wear Chrysocolla during rehearsing and then again when they are performing. Chrysocolla also has a reputation of working well with music. It encourages children to appreciate music. Musicians will also benefit from working with this crystal, as will anyone performing or receiving any type of sound healing. Have it near you when learning a new musical instrument or joining a choir, orchestra or theatre group. It will also give you confidence when it is time to perform in public.

Mother Nature

Chrysocolla has a very yin or feminine energy and thus is great as a tool to forge a stronger connection to the Goddess. Sit outside in silence, holding your crystal, allowing yourself to observe and sense the gentle aspects of nature that surround you. If you wish to create an altar at home to honour the Divine Feminine, make sure you include a piece of Chrysocolla, and hold it when working with your feminine side. If you are casting a magical circle, place a piece of Chrysocolla in the west (or the direction dedicated to water) to represent the emotional aspect of life.

Chrysocolla encourages you to find comfort in the quietness and solitude, a valuable asset in a world full of busyness and noise. Since antiquity it was used to support those choosing to spend time alone. It helps you take time to explore your relationship with yourself, your spirituality and Great Spirit. It is a crystal for monks, hermits and prisoners, diminishing the anxiety and depression that often accompanies seclusion. Due to Chrysocolla's musical links, chanting while holding your crystal can achieve great results. Those who tend to have a tendency to never sit still can benefit from working with Chrysocolla.

If you wish to spend time in nature, take Chrysocolla. It helps you attune to the energies around you and connect and communicate with its spiritual forces. Those wishing to help the planet heal can use Chrysocolla to receive guidance on what actions are most beneficial. Include Chrysocolla in Earth healing grids to gently nurture the planet back to its natural state of balance. Also use Chrysocolla to help care for the earth's creatures. It is very supportive of pregnant animals, especially first time mothers.

Further Crystal Connections – Gem Silica

Gem Silica is the name given to highly silicated Chrysocolla. In other words, under certain geological conditions, Chrysocolla can undergo chemical changes and forms amidst Quartz. This process causes the colour to often be more intensely blue, whereas Chrysocolla is quite opaque, Gem Silica is more translucent and gemmy. Since Quartz is an amplifier of other crystals this leads to Gem Silica being a higher and more powerful form of Chrysocolla.

Gem Silica can be used in all the ways discussed above for Chrysocolla but is definitely worth working with if past emotional pain is severely affecting your current progress. It helps you get in touch with your deepest and most repressed feelings. Its energy resonates with Archangel Raphael (governs healing) and Archangel Gabriel (governs communication and the emotional element of water), so call on their assistance. In meditation Gem Silica will help you discover your truth and align your life to resonate with it. Use this crystal alongside the scent of cognac essential oil (derived from grapes). Cognac essential oil has a serene effect that relaxes and relieves emotional tension and drama through inhalation. It also stimulates the imagination and creative impulses, encouraging you to get your life back on track and start exploring new possibilities.

In communication, Gem Silica adds eloquence as you speak. This high-vibration crystal can assist with communicating with others not on the physical plain such as angels, ancestors and elemental or nature beings. It is extremely harmonious with either classical or spiritual music. If you are writing, performing or producing music designed to touch the hearts and souls of humanity, Gem Silica is a valuable amulet to have with you not only when you are working but at all times, to facilitate divine inspiration. If you are attending a musical attendance, wear or carry Gem Silica to maximise the benefits of your experience. Those who chant, sing or use mantras will benefit greatly from Gem Silica.

The combination of the nurturing and peaceful Chrysocolla with the amplification properties of Quartz allows you to use Gem Silica for creating greater peace. When there is a major attack or fight in the world, use Gem Silica in grids designed to send waves of peace to an area. Wear or carry the crystal to start spreading waves of peaceful and compassionate energy that will send ripples across the world. These techniques can also be applied to create harmony when there are hostilities in your own life.

CHRYSOPRASE

Childhood / Playfulness / Nature

Chrysoprase is a variety of Chalcedony found in a range of greens depending on the amount of Nickel content. It has a long history, being mentioned in the New Testament, and was popularly used in the 13th century, where it was engraved with the image of a bull and worn for protection. As a crystal of Venus, Chrysoprase promotes love, but not merely for another person, more so as a passion for exploring and understanding the world. As a crystal that instils patience, it allows us to find happiness even if we only comprehend a minute amount of truth about the universe. Chrysoprase reminds you that the joy is in the discoveries, not in the final answers. Chrysoprase awakens your spirit and allows you to notice the synchronicities around you as spiritual guidance. It also promotes a greater appreciation of aesthetics, beauty and the arts.

Animal: Quokka
Plant: Lemon-scented gum
Astrological Correspondences: Venus and asteroid Eunomia
Power Day: Friday
Cleanse by: Earth

Your Crystal Alignment Meditation

Go and sit in nature. Your garden or a park will suffice, or you can venture out into the wilderness. Examine the plants near you, whether it be the grass you sit upon or a nearby tree. Look at the ease at which they go about their day. Each day the plants grow, but they never struggle. Can you see any animals? See the ease at which they go about their efforts. Are regrets and past baggage weighing them down or are they totally in the moment? Nature shows us that what is before us is never a struggle. Contemplate this and when ready meditate with your Chrysoprase.

Childhood

Chrysoprase has a childlike feel about it and thus helps children keep their joyous and curious spirit. It gently stimulates their heart chakra allowing them to open up to the love in the world. Troubled children will benefit greatly from having a piece of Chrysoprase as a constant companion. It rebuilds trust when appropriate and allows them to have the confidence to explore the world, learn lessons and make new friends. At night leave a piece near their bed if they are suffering recurring nightmares. Our skin is associated with our sense of security so if a child is suffering from skin problems create an elixir placing a piece of Smokey Quartz (for grounding and comfort) in a glass of natural water and surround the glass with pieces of Chrysoprase. Leave it in the sunlight for a few hours. Spritz this water on problem areas as well as have them drink a small amount each morning and night.

When combined, Chrysocolla and Chrysoprase synergise as a nurturing emotional healing yin yang couplet that enable you to deal with any childhood hurt. Chrysocolla nurtures the feminine inner child while Chrysoprase awakens the masculine inner child to feel comfortable to play. They work together to release all emotional pains and baggage from the past. These crystals promote forgiveness and allow you to detach from any emotional ties you still have to someone who has hurt you. They are the perfect combination for anyone who has suffered abuse.

Find a photo of yourself when you were a child, place it before you. Diffuse lemon-scented gum essential oil to purify the space. Hold your Chrysocolla in your receptive hand and your Chrysoprase in the other. Gaze into the eyes of your younger self and allow yourself to connect. You may find emotions or words bubble up. If so, allow yourself to express them. Once you have said all you need to say, finish by saying, "You are safe, loved and cared for and everything is going to be okay."

You may need to repeat this activity several times to get the full benefit. Continue to carry the two crystals with you as a support for your inner child. To extend this practice you may like to honour your inner child on your altar with a couple of meaningful items. Once you have found closure with the past, the two crystals lead you into the future with a refreshed sense of spritely optimism and hope.

Playfulness

Chrysoprase encourages you to approach life with a sense of reckless abandon, like that of an innocent young child ready to explore the world. Its uplifting vibration helps you maintain a youthful spirit, remain aware and alert and attract kindred spirits to play with. Use Chrysoprase to banish greed, envy and selfishness. To bring a playful energy to your house, make a crystal elixir to spray around the house. Soak a Chrysoprase in water for a couple of hours then pour the water and a few drops of lemon-scented gum essential oil into a spray bottle. Spritz the elixir around the house and enjoy the difference it makes to your space. This is ideal if you offer healing at home or are going through a period of healing yourself.

Chrysoprase gives an optimistic approach to starting any new project or seeking new employment, and with its green colour, it also helps you make choices that will aid your abundance. Rub it over any applications or hold it over the computer before sending off resumes or loan applications. When you have work, keep Chrysoprase at your desk or work area for inspiration and innovative ideas.

If poor health is dampening your spirits then keep Chrysoprase within your energy field to encourage detoxification. It is a good choice of crystal support if you are taking heavy medications. Gaze at the crystal and hold its colour in your energy field as you meditate, allowing the vibration to return you back to balance. When placed near the liver it strengthens this organ through the release of anger which can be stored here. Due to the youthful spirit of Chrysoprase, place it with your skin care products to encourage younger looking skin. Attune to the abilities of your Quokka guide when working with Chrysoprase as this Australian mammal increases your awareness and sensitivity to your environment. He can help you gain insight into nutritional issues and deficiencies and the cause of allergies, especially caused by pollutants in your surroundings.

Chrysoprase opens you to new love, whether that be starting a new relationship or reinvigorating your current one. Once you've found the love of your life, try using an old Greek tradition to ensure a happy marriage by cleansing and programming a Chrysoprase under the half waxing moon. To assist healing heartbreak, wear this cheery crystal over your heart for a full lunar cycle (28 days) it over your heart each day for a full lunar cycle (28 days).

Nature

With its youthful energy, Chrysoprase allows you to remember the magic you once saw in the world when you were young. It supports a reality where angels, guides and the spirit world are not in conflict with rational or logical thinking. With its impish energy, Chrysoprase is ideal for connecting with elemental beings out in nature, even as close as in your own garden. Use Chrysoprase to commune with fairies, elves, gnomes and other garden sprites. Place Chrysoprase around your garden and then take time each day to sit holding a piece. Speak to the elementals, telling them you are open to hearing their whisperings.

Use Chrysoprase for strengthening your relationship with small creatures around you. Chrysoprase is used to improve communication with reptiles. You can also place Chrysoprase in animals' beds, enclosures or environment to help them endure a long, cold winter.

CITRINE

Happiness / Prosperity / Solar Plexus Chakra / Digestion

Citrine is a variety of Quartz whose colour ranges from a pale yellow to brown due to its Iron content. Natural Citrines are generally quite light in colour, whereas the most readily available bright-yellow Citrines are heat-treated Amethysts or Smokey Quartzes. Regardless of being natural or heat-treated, both varieties possess the same structure, chemical composition and colouring so they have very similar energies.

Citrine is like sunshine in a crystal. Its radiant and jubilant energy encourages you to lighten up and enjoy your journey through life. It's joie de vivre vibration helps you feel better about yourself, increasing your self-confidence and sociability. Citrine also cultivates optimism regarding your financial position. By releasing restrictive and pessimistic beliefs, it helps bring the constant flow of prosperity into your life. As you deepen your relationship with Citrine you may feel inspired to expand your horizons and travel to new places.

Animal: Hummingbird
Plant: Bergamot (heat-treated Citrine) and Citron (natural Citrine)
Astrological Correspondence: Sun
Power Day: Sunday
Cleansing: Most people find Citrine does not need cleansing due to its vibrantly strong, joyous energy, however, if you sense your crystal needs an energy boost, simply leave your Citrine in the sunlight for a while.

Your Crystal Alignment Meditation

Go to a waterfall or visualise one in your mind. Immerse yourself in the water and as it falls over you allow it to wash all unhelpful and unwanted feelings, thoughts and energies. Then sit in the sunshine enjoying the warmth on your skin. Let this warmth fill your body. Allow yourself to feel happy. Feel a smile on your face. You are now ready to connect with your Citrine.

Happiness

If you are having a down day use Citrine to lift you back to feeling happy and optimistic by wearing it close to your solar plexus. Meditate with your Citrine and visualise yourself going about your day happy and smiling. See how your happiness changes your day and your interactions with others. While meditating, call upon your Hummingbird guide. She will teach you how to "lighten up" and that you are allowed to be happy, laugh and have fun. Hummingbird can also teach you the value of going after what makes you happy. To add an extra happiness boost to a home or workplace, place a Citrine cluster in the centre of the room. This also works to deter ghosts and paranormal activity from the space. Program another Citrine with your desire for happiness and place it in your honey pot. Add some honey to your breakfast or tea each morning as another way to increase your happiness levels.

Prosperity

Whenever you notice there is a blockage stopping the flow of money in your life increase your contact with Citrine. Team it with visualisation and affirmations about money flowing to you and gratitude for the money you already have to revive your stream of cash. If you are feeling stuck on how to find new income or make ends meet allow Citrine to unlock your imagination and creativity to find solutions to difficult problems. Keep Citrine in a cash register or wherever you keep cash to promote the flow of money into your hands. Anoint a one hundred dollar note with bergamot and sit it with a charged Citrine in the sun for a day. If you keep this note in your purse or wallet and never spend it, you will always have enough money for what you need. Every time you open your wallet, you see you have money. This starts to change your thought patterns from "I have no money" to "I always have money available" and this positive attitude will change your relationship with money. If you are selling a house, it is said that by placing six Citrine crystals along the front of the house will attract the right buyer. Place Citrine near your computer if you're installing new programs or applying for finance online. If you are looking for jewellery to attract prosperity, a ring worn on your receptive hand is perfect.

Solar Plexus Chakra

The solar plexus chakra governs personal power and when it is underactive there is a tendency to allow others to assert their power on you. You may find it hard to say "No" and start becoming distrustful and resentful of others because you feel life is not fair. Those with an underactive solar plexus chakra can exhibit a lack of joy, depression and emotional numbness.

The joyous energy of Citrine adds joy and confidence to this energy chakra. If you want a vibrant energy, use heat-treated Citrine or for a more content energy, choose natural Citrine. Take a few minutes each day to hold the appropriate Citrine against your solar plexus chakra while visualising a bright yellow ball of energy in the area. Continue wearing your crystal over the chakra throughout the day to help stimulate the changes needed to balance this chakra. Diffusing citron or bergamot essential oil will also help.

Digestion

Citrine not only helps improve the flow of energy in our lives but can also improve the flow within different systems of our bodies. Colon ailments, poor digestion and constipation can be physical manifestations of an unwillingness to let go of an issue. Place a Citrine in a glass of water and leave it in the sun for a few hours before drinking it each day to improve digestive issues. If you have abdominal pain, roll a tumbled stone or wand over your belly in a clockwise direction for a few minutes.

COVELLITE

Shadow Self / Senses / Dreams Become Reality

Covellite is a fascinating and powerful crystal. It consists of equal parts Copper, a metal of movement, transition and healing, and Sulphur, for energy and upliftment. However, this is not a crystal for the fainthearted or those seeking quick happiness. Covellite is a crystal of darkness and its message is this: in order to balance the light you must face your dark. It leads you to face the unknown and embrace the discoveries it unveils.

Animal: Howler Monkey
Plant: Star Anise
Astrological Correspondence: The asteroid Lilith
Power Day: Saturday
Cleanse by: Placing outside in nature on the new or dark moon or during a lightning storm.

Your Crystal Alignment Meditation

Sit outside amongst the wilderness at midnight. Connect with the stillness. If you feel scared, contemplate that this is simply because you cannot see as far as when there is light. To fear is to not trust that the universe will provide you with what you need and keep you safe. Calm yourself until you feel at ease, then connect with your Covellite.

Shadow Self

Carl G. Jung coined the term "shadow" to describe the repressed or denied part of the self. As infants, we expressed the full breadth of our human nature, without editing or censoring. However, as we grow up and have experiences we start to believe that certain parts of our self are unacceptable to the people around us. Maybe we were shamed for crying or punished for being angry. Maybe we were ridiculed for wanting attention or feeling proud of ourselves. We learned to repress these aspects of our self; the aspects that got us hurt. However, repressing these is to deny our self and the world of the full expression of who you truly are. These decisions, which you probably made as a child, may still be carried with you as an adult. Covellite enables you to explore ways to start unveiling these aspects in a way that is safe for yourself and all others. By finding aspects of yourself you've "swept under the rug" you can discover new abilities that can benefit you upon your path. Covellite also helps you face any "demons" from the past that arise from abuse or neglect. Repressing emotions or feelings can consume momentous energy so as you work more with Covellite you may find your physical energy levels increase.

Covellite encourages you to deal with your shadow self. Listen to the call of your Howler Monkey guide, a strong harmonic of Covellite. He summons you to look deep into your past, to appreciate where you came from, and honour your primordial and shadow self. Howler monkey can evoke the Artist, the Musician, the Diviner, the Trickster, the Actor, the Scribe and the Storyteller lying dormant within you. This guide and crystal both help artists delve deep into their psyche and express themselves in a way that connects with the core of the human spirit.

When you are ready to explore your shadow self, sit outside at night. Place a bandana or head scarf around your head to hold your Covellite against your third eye chakra. Ideally face the direction of the asteroid Lilith, named after the biblical figure who was Adam's first wife (before Eve). This asteroid will help trigger suppressed feelings and thoughts if you connect to its energy. You may want to invoke the goddess of mystery, Hecate, with a simple chant such as, "Dark Hecate who has always been, reveal to me all that's unseen." Scrying into a cauldron of water can be beneficial, otherwise simply close your eyes.

Senses

Wearing Covellite every day will start to heighten all your five senses as well as heal any related sensory disorders. It can also help you find the hidden root cause of your sickness. Lay on the ground with Covellite resting on your third eye. State, "I am ready now to understand the root cause of my sickness. I allow the reason to be revealed to me so that I may enable my complete healing." Then simply rest and allow Covellite to draw what you need to the surface. It may be a past memory that you need to let go of or you may receive an inspired idea of what you need to explore. This is also a powerful practice for fighting cancer when used in conjunction with medical treatment.

Covellite also heightens your sixth sense, or intuition. It helps you maintain a balanced third eye chakra. Its ability to awaken the virtues lying dormant within your shadow side helps you tap into your inner guidance rather than ignoring uncomfortable thoughts or feelings that arise. Hold your Covellite in your receptive hand or against your forehead during meditation, scrying or divination. When not in use, keep the crystal with your tarot cards or runes. Diffusing star anise essential oil will allow you to relax and reach other levels of consciousness when working with your Covellite. A dried star anise fruit with a piece of cotton or string tied around it makes a simple, cheap, yet effective pendulum. As you become more connected and in tune with your senses, this can help to alleviate any fear of the darkness. If a child gets scared at night, place Covellite near their bed.

Dreams Become Reality

As you work with Covellite more, you'll increase your ability to turn your dreams into a reality. By strengthening your senses and intuition, you increase awareness of opportunities that exist around you as well as being able to easily navigate around obstacles. Knowing your own darkness is the best method for dealing with the darkness of other people. This will prevent other people's wayward behaviour swaying you from your path. Covellite eliminates vanity, which prevents self-reflection and analysis, traits essential for advancing your plans. Wear or carry Covellite each day for ongoing support in fulfilling your dreams. Also carry a carry a star anise and you'll increase your luck.

DIAMOND
Expanding Success / Unity / Archangel Uriel

Ancient Greeks named Diamond *adamas,* meaning invincible or indestructible since there is no harder crystal in the world, nor one that boasts more purity. Diamond is simply compressed carbon, the chemical element that is fundamental to all life, making it an adaptable crystal for strength, health, protection or whatever you need. If you are not in the position to acquire a high-grade, sparkling gem, a low-grade piece will still be effective. Worthy substitutes are a Herkimer Diamond or Clear Zircon. These two may be better if you are working with animals or children as the intensity of Diamond can be too overwhelming.

Animal: Any
Plant: Ginger
Astrological Correspondence: Sun
Power Day: Sunday
Cleanse with: Fire

Your Crystal Alignment Meditation

Go to the top of a mountain or visualise one in your mind. Take a few deep breaths and inhale the fresh mountainous air. Observe everything around you and take in the diversity of the surroundings from every direction. Then become aware of the sky above you. See it stretching to the horizon. Consider that beyond the Earth's atmosphere expands a universe beyond measure. Tune in to the vastness of the world. Acknowledge the limitlessness of this place. Diamond also encompasses these limitless possibilities, and once this has soaked into your consciousness, connect with your Diamond.

Expanding Success

Diamond enables you to grow upon what you already have in your life. Whether you want to strengthen a relationship, have a more vibrant social life, increase your income, speed up healing or expand your knowledge,

Diamond can help. However, Diamond requires clarity so think clearly about what you ask for, as Diamond is powerful and you may get exactly what you asked for, but not what you expected.

Diamond exists in a cubic crystal structure so to connect with its power, hold the Diamond in your projective hand and visualise yourself and your desire in a white cube of light. Start to see the cube rotating, slowly gaining speed, and as it does, it sends energy to your goal. When working with Diamond incorporate ginger into your life by including the root in your diet, diffusing ginger essential oil or any other way your creativity can conceive. This will enhance your own personal power and thus the effectiveness of your work.

Due to its hardness, Diamond bestows the power upon you of invincibility, preventing anything from standing in your way. Throughout history Diamond has been used to protect against fire, water, snakes, thieves, illnesses, predatory animals, sorcery and poison. Ideally wear a Diamond faceted in a six-sided cut as this allows the reflective nature of the crystal to bounce destructive energies away from you back to their source. Diamond is capable of driving away your own personal fears and preventing negative thinking and behaviour.

Unity

Just as white light is a unification of all colours, Diamond works to bring groups together to work towards the greater good. It encourages people to get off their smart phones and other electronic devices and start interacting. As a crystal of clarity, it can help you to understand the needs of other people. It'll ensure your charitable and altruistic efforts are truly benefiting the recipients. Since Diamond brings clarity of mind and stimulates the imagination, carry it to help you find the right present for a loved one.

Diamond can be programmed by several people all working on the same project. Either take turns working with the crystal or place it in the centre of a group meditation. Then keep the Diamond at a general meeting place or central point to maintain group focus and cohesiveness.

Obviously, Diamond is a popular crystal for engagement and wedding rings. Be sure to program your Diamond ring with your intention of unity with your partner. If you are ever struggling with how to keep a partnership or group unified, try scrying with a faceted Diamond in soft candle light. The exquisite colour and light will open you up to endless possibilities and can even take you to the point of finding nirvana or euphoria.

Archangel Uriel

Archangel Uriel is the guardian of the element of earth and governs the arts, magic, ideas, astrology and protection. Uriel is one of the wisest archangels, offering intellectual information, practical solutions and creative insight. He has an intense energy and having Diamond with you will help you harmonise with his energy. Uriel is adept at transforming your emotions, such as anger, fear and despair into more proactive feelings that will enable growth and success. When you need change, call upon Uriel by whispering his name as you hold your Diamond. Ask him to come to you for inspiration, spiritual guidance and discovering your own true potential. However, do not necessarily expect a mighty angel to appear. You may not even realise he has answered your prayer until you've suddenly come up with a brilliant new idea. Uriel is also known for warning of and rebuilding after natural disasters.

DUMORTIERITE

Third Eye Chakra / Organisation / Learning

Whereas many dark blue and indigo crystals work to increase your intuitive abilities, Dumortierite has the opposite effect. It removes distractions and extraneous stimuli, rebalances you and allows you to isolate your focus to the task at hand. It is a stone of the intellect, enabling you to clarify, classify and comprehend. Dumortierite ensures that while you expand your life, you do not neglect your responsibilities.

Animals: Meerkat, Monkey and Mouse
Plant: Almond
Astrological Correspondences: Saturn and Uranus
Power Day: Saturday
Cleanse with: Air when wanting to become more organised and water when wanting to focus on guidance or intuition.

Your Crystal Alignment Meditation

Go to an open place outside in nature where you can be alone. Firstly start to relax, focusing on the air flowing in and out of your lungs. Once you feel present and a sense of peace inside start to feel the air move across your face and body. It may be a soft breeze or a powerful wind. Close your eyes and let your other senses take over. Can you hear the wind as it passes your ears or blows through tree branches and your surroundings? Listen carefully and allow yourself to hear any messages riding on the wind. Once enough time has passed, thank the wind and connect with your Dumortierite.

Third Eye Chakra

Your third eye chakra may be overactive if you find you often experience confusion, mental fogginess or information overload. This may lead to mental exhaustion and can make it difficult for you to be effective in your life, due to an inability to focus your mind. A severely overactive third eye chakra can lead to nightmares, headache in the forehead or temples, or mental disease. Dumortierite helps to soothe the energy and allows you to regain control.

Take time to rest with your crystal upon your forehead. Meanwhile visualise a soft glowing ball of indigo light radiating in the area. Continue to carry your crystal with you until you find this chakra is staying balanced.

Organisation

Wearing Dumortierite settles your mind making it great for overcoming stage fright, shyness, stress, phobias, insomnia, panic, fear and depression. Dumortierite harmonises with two planets of very different energies. The energy of Saturn is structured and controlled while Uranus is spontaneous and chaotic. Sit outside facing the direction exactly between the two planets and feel their energies both mingling within you as you hold your Dumortierite. By harmonising with these two energies and finding a balance between them, you'll remain organised in the craziest of situations. Dumortierite is an ideal crystal for people who work with crisis and trauma on a daily basis, giving them the ability to concentrate on the task at hand. Grid Dumortierite around disaster zones to help everyone cope with the stress and bring hope to those who have given up. If you cannot get to the area, meditate with the crystal and send them the needed energies or construct a power grid. It also calms overly excited or barking dogs if you place a piece on their collar.

Dumortierite is a great stone for the modern world as it encourages organisation, tidiness and discipline. Use Dumortierite to bring your life into order and get all your ducks in a row. It helps you find a neat and tidy place for all the things in your home so they can be easily found when you are frantically busy. Tidy your desk, clearing lots of space for working, and place Dumortierite there to ensure you remain organised. Place Dumortierite around your home or in children's bedroom to encourage others to keep the whole house tidy. Start the habit of writing lists and keep your notepad and Dumortierite together on you. Crossing tasks off as you go not only keeps you on task but also gives a sense of achievement.

Learning

As you work with Dumortierite to remove physical clutter from your life, you will find it helps to clear your own mental clutter too. This clarity of mind that comes from strengthen your relationship with your crystal will allow you to enjoy more inner peace and an increased ability to deal with change. With a more focused mind you'll avoid misunderstandings. Dumortierite is especially beneficial when speaking foreign languages so keep a piece in your pocket when travelling to make sure nothing gets lost in translation.

Dumortierite facilitates accelerated learning, enabling you to focus, understand guidance and reflect on what you're offered. Several animal guides harmonise with Dumortierite and can help you when in a period of learning. Meerkat teaches you about attention, Monkey shows curiosity and Mouse governs detail. It is possible that one of these three will stand out to you. Make this the lesson you focus on. Almonds harmonise with Dumortierite and eating them is renowned for attracting wisdom and can further your efforts with Dumortierite.

EMERALD

Wisdom / Growth / Gnomes / Archangel Raphael

Emerald brings you the qualities of a sharp memory, eloquence and patience. Working with Emerald will enable what you desire to manifest around you. Initially it allows you to resonate from within what you want and then your external environment will begin to reflect this. Emerald helps you unveil the truth to any situation and, when you are ready, will present you with the teacher you need. Emerald is best used at times of need rather than making it a constant companion.

Animals: Green Parrot or Ostrich
Plants: Date Palm or Dill
Astrological Correspondences: Mercury and Venus
Power Days: Wednesday and Friday
Cleanse with: Air or Earth

Your Crystal Alignment Meditation

Go to a peaceful place in nature. Close your eyes, ensure your spine is straight and place your hands on your heart. Tune in to the beating of your own heart for a few minutes, allowing all other noises to slip away. Now start to see a glowing green light, emanating from your heart centre. With each beat, it grows stronger and more radiant. Allow it to spread over your body. This green light balances and heals your body, mind and spirit. Now spread this green light beyond yourself offering healing to your surroundings. Spread this out further, affecting your whole country, then the whole planet and out to the universe. Finally connect with the healing, balancing nature of all that is. When you are ready, connect with your Emerald.

Wisdom

Emerald has long been associated with the pursuits of the mind and truth. Hermes Trismegistus carved on an Emerald tablet the cornerstone key of magic, stating, "as above, so below". Emerald helps bring awareness of the unknown to conscious recognition, imparting reason and wisdom. It strengthens memory and promotes clarity of thought enabling discernment, the ability to find the truth and a trust in your own inner knowing. Working with Emerald in conjunction with your Ostrich guide can keep you grounded while expanding your mind. The Ostrich feather also connects you to Ma'at, the Egyptian goddess of truth. Hold Emerald for five minutes a day to bring on rapid recall of facts. To receive spiritual advice, place it on a holy book such as the Bible, Koran, or a simple affirmations book for five minutes and then open up to a page. That page, especially the first sentence, offers the wisdom you need.

Growth

Emerald is a stone of abundance and helps you realise that you can freely give without fearing that there will not be enough for yourself. Place an Emerald with a bowl of dates in your house, offering them to guests when they visit. The date palm is a tree of fertility and by sharing their energy you are spreading abundance with your friends. The more freely you give, the more you shall receive. Use Emerald to bring you whatever your heart desires. Wearing it over your heart will enable it to tune in to what you truly want and lead you there. Emerald will guide you to a loyal lover and when placed around the home, brings domestic bliss. Emerald dissolves tension, reveals cheating partners and allows you to escape any abuse at home. An Emerald on the desk or near the phone supports social workers, counsellors and life coaches in aiding their clients to grow.

Emerald offers special support to women especially when undergoing any life stage of physical transition. It alleviates fear or discomfort a woman may experience during puberty, pregnancy, labour and menopause. Furthermore, it assists with fears of ageing or times when a woman may feel uncomfortable with her body. For this, keep an Emerald in the bathroom and each day look into the mirror and say, "I love myself, and my body" four times. Couple this with a course of date palm flower essence as it can help with the body's distribution of life force and reduce the effects of ageing, helping you feel more vibrant.

Gnomes

Have you ever walked through a park or through the woods and felt a sudden sense of peace, minimising all your problems after a discouraging day? It is possible you were just visited by some elementals of the earth element. Like mermaids of the watery realm, dragons and salamanders of fire and fairies and sylphs of the air, gnomes teach us the mysteries of the earthly realm. They encourage us to be kind to nature, teach how to live in harmony with the environment and how to heal yourself naturally. They are very helpful to those who have established a connection with them through prior acts of kindness, bringing a wealth of wisdom and treasures.

If you would like to connect with the gnomes take a hike into the woods or anywhere else abundant with trees and plants. Take your Emerald with you and whisper your request to the crystal. Ask it to bring you in contact with the gnomes. Then set it before you as you sit on the earth. Even though you may not see them you can close your eyes and feel their presence near you. They can offer you their wisdom without you having to lay eyes upon them. Simply listen with your heart and hear their words echo within you.

Archangel Raphael

Raphael is the archangel that supervises healers and healing for all on Earth. Hold your Emerald (a crystal he harmonises with) between your hands and ask Raphael for help when you are in any kind of pain, whether it is physical, emotional romantic, intellectual or spiritual. Raphael can offer you healing in subtle or obvious ways. He may lead you to find a book, documentary or other sign that points you towards a solution. While resting you may experience sudden inspiration, heat, tingling, an angelic sense of peace or even sense a green sparkling light around you. You may like to connect with any green Parrot guide to help you find out more about healing.

Raphael coaches and motivates healers, whispering instructions into the ears of doctors, surgeons, psychologists, nurses and other caregivers. His intervention helps scientists in making breakthroughs in medical cures. If you are working in one of these fields, devote an Emerald to Raphael and carry it with you each day at work.

Raphael is also in charge of the element of air, and thus the archangel that governs travel. As you check in at the airport, place an Emerald in your luggage and ask Raphael to keep it safe. If you carry an Emerald Raphael can help control airplane turbulence, give you directions when you're lost or help you get your car safely to its destination.

EUDIALYTE
Self Worth / Appreciation / Love

Eudialyte is a stunningly beautiful crystal with an equally joyous energy. It is powerful in promoting self-love and opening you up to receiving love from others. When you see that you are of value to the world and worthy of love and acceptance, you allow loving new experiences to greet you around every corner. Eudialyte moves you towards this way of being.

Animal: Moose
Plant: Grapefruit
Astrological Correspondences: Venus and the constellation Andromeda
Power Day: Friday
Cleanse with: Water

Your Crystal Alignment Meditation

Go to the edge of a cliff where you can sit comfortably and safely. If there is not one nearby, visualise yourself there in your mind. What can you see surrounding you? Is it an ever-stretching forest with tall green trees continuing to the horizon? Perhaps you can see the ocean or fields of colourful flowers. Maybe you can also see your town or city, far off in the distance. Observe everything in the world below, all looking extremely small. Consider that within your view are hundreds, if not more, people, animals and plants all playing their role in the world. Contemplate how everyone's role is vital. You may not be the tallest, fastest or most academic, but you do have traits that make you special. Take some time to contemplate these now. Come up with at least three. What makes you special? Once you feel special, connect with your Eudialyte.

Self Worth

Eudialyte allows you to open your heart to yourself whilst grounding you to prevent an inflated sense of self-importance. It helps you develop a sense of appreciation for your individual gifts. It enables you to trust these gifts and find meaningful ways to use them, while also alleviating compulsive negative behaviours that no longer serve you. Low self-worth can display physically especially during times in life when your body is changing. Acne can be a physical manifestation of a lack of self-acceptance and the effects of menopause can heighten when you are feeling unwanted. Take some time to develop some self-worth affirmations and place them around the house. Each time you see one, take your Eudialyte in your receptive hand and repeat the affirmation three times. Using an affirmation and wearing Eudialyte over the heart each day can be extremely effective. Working with your Moose guide will also strengthen your self-worth.

Eudialyte gives you an appreciation for your body. Use it to support any work with body issues and related eating disorders. Wearing it against the skin will help to send its loving energies around the body. For a greater impact, stand in front of a large mirror naked and repeat the affirmation, "I love my body" several times while holding your Eudialyte. Consuming grapefruit and filling a space with the scent of grapefruit essential oil promotes the honouring of your body and acknowledgment of what your physical form allows you to do each day. By combining Eudialyte and grapefruit you will start to see that no amount of food will fill a hole in the heart — only love can, and that love must come from within.

Appreciation

As your self-worth increases, Eudialyte will also awaken your sense of value for things around you, reigniting your love for the finer things in life. By increasing alpha brain waves, Eudialyte provokes a greater appreciation for the arts, food, colour, stimulating conversation and other beautiful things that excite your heart and mind. Eudialyte will cause the things that you love the most to become part of your everyday experience, thus allowing for a more fulfilling life. Try listening to a beautiful piece of music or visiting an art gallery while holding your Eudialyte in your receptive hand. Add a piece of Eudialyte, a magenta candle and several items that signify what you appreciate in life to your altar as a sign of acknowledgement. Performers can grid Eudialyte around their theatre or performance space to increase audience responsiveness to their show.

Love

The more you love yourself, the more you are willing to allow love into your life. Eudialyte, through increasing your self-worth, helps you find soul mates or soul companions. A Eudialyte charged with your desire for love can increase occurrences of coincidence and synchronicity in your life so pay attention to chance meetings as these can be a sign. If you feel you are truly drawn to someone, Eudialyte can help you determine whether this chemistry is sexual or for another purpose. If you are unclear on the purpose for your attraction, sleep with Eudialyte in your pillowslip. Pay attention to your dreams as they may offer clues. When the time is right, the true reason will become apparent.

If you want a situation to change or a relationship to end, Eudialyte helps you to let go of the circumstances in a peaceful way. It teaches you to release feelings of hopelessness and accept a life full of joy, happiness and completeness. Take a piece of Eudialyte and fill it with all the remaining energy that keeps you emotionally connected to the relationship. Go to the water and throw the stone away. This is showing that you are willing to release the attachment.

Eudialyte nourishes friend and community relationships. It allows the rebuilding of families after tragedy as well as aiding reconciliation with anyone you feel has betrayed you. This crystal promotes on-going harmony in communities, dealing with jealousy in relationships and resolving anger issues with "God". With Eudialyte, you can forgive someone without having to see them. Hold the crystal in your receptive hand and look into the eyes of a photo of the person (or visualise them before you). Repeat the mantra, "I forgive you" several times until it starts to resonate true for you. Perform this practice several times to allow the healing to fully occur. If your issue is a family member, you may want to tune in to the energy of the constellation of Andromeda, which is most prominent during spring in the southern hemisphere and autumn evenings in the northern hemisphere. Andromeda allows you to understand the influences of your family's background and enables your liberation from it.

FLUORITE, RAINBOW

Study / Priorities / Pain / Bountiful Gardens

Fluorite grows in perfect little squares rather than points or rhomboids, often associated with crystals. This affects the energy of Fluorite making this beautiful rainbow crystal one of logic and common sense. Fluorite is ideal for helping you make the right choices. With so many crystals having a spiritual effect, Fluorite is a great crystal to get your head "out of the clouds". If you tend to be over emotional, this crystal will aid you to get a clearer perspective on what is really happening.

Animal: Skunk
Plant: Rosemary
Astrological Correspondence: Mercury
Power Day: Wednesday
Cleanse with: Air

Your Crystal Alignment Meditation

Go to a beautiful garden. Admire the play between the man-made structure of the garden and nature's chaotic order. As you sit in the garden practice two types of focus: closed focus and open focus.

First practice closed focus, which is narrowing your attention to just one thing. Start by focusing on nothing but your breath, allowing it to become slow and deep. As you breathe in count the number one, as you breathe out, the number two, in again and the number three and so on. If you get distracted or lose count, you must start from one again. Continue to do this activity and see how high you can get before you become side tracked. As you practice this activity more, you will improve your ability to concentrate on a single task or meditate without becoming distracted.

Secondly, practice open focus by shifting your focus from yourself to your surroundings. Pay attention to the sounds around you. How many can you hear? Relax and do not give any attention to your own mind. This practice enables you to free yourself from stressful thoughts and increases your awareness of what is happening around you.

Finally, pick up your Fluorite in your receptive hand and allow your focus to shift to connecting with your crystal.

Study

Rainbow Fluorite is the ideal study stone and should be kept nearby whenever you undertaking any learning or preparing for an exam. Also, diffuse rosemary essential oil, burn the incense or have the herb nearby so you can smell its scent. The crystal and plant will help to increase your aptitude and ability to remember information to recall later. Once you have finished studying take away the rosemary and place the crystal in a sacred place. When you need to recall the information, place the crystal near you again and bring back the rosemary scent. It will help you recall the information you previously studied.

Priorities

Fluorite can help you identify people, objects or activities that distract you from what your priorities are. Are you dedicating too much time or attention on a person, chore or activity? Take some time now to contemplate what distractions you need to remove from your life while holding your Fluorite in your receptive hand. Ask Fluorite to guide you on how you can make changes so you are giving your focus to that which is important to you. If you are not sure what to make a priority, consider what makes you feel good. How can you shift from doing feeling negative, lethargic or sad to feeling positive, vibrant and happy and enjoying your life? Simply pose this question to your crystal and allow insights to come to you.

Pain

Rainbow Fluorite is a great pain reliever. If you are experiencing any pain, hold the crystal against the site. Focus on the source of the pain and try to identify the exact point in your body it is coming from. Keep focusing on that point and with the power of your Rainbow Fluorite feel the pain slowly vanish.

Bountiful Gardens

If you want to give your garden a bit of a boost, collect eight small Rainbow Fluorite crystals. Opt for greener pieces if you'd like to attract butterflies into your garden. While meditating, share with your crystals your visualisation of the perfect, plentiful garden. See the colours, smell the scents, hear the sounds and infuse this into the crystal. Then bury them around the perimeter of the garden on the eight main directions i.e. north, north-west, west, etc. The same can be done with one crystal buried into the soil of a pot plant after your meditation.

GARNET, RED

Warmth / Base Chakra / Integrity

Red Garnets have been used for thousands of years, long being associated as a warrior stone. Soldiers wore Garnets when going into battle for two reasons: it protects and it speeds healing. Although few of us are soldiers, we are all warriors facing all kinds of adversity. Work with Garnet to allow you to overcome depression and melancholy, defeating thoughts, habits, positions and people that no longer serve you. Garnet brings a vibrancy that allows you to build upon the successes you've already had in life. There is a common misconception that all Garnets are red gems. They are found in a wide variety of other colours including purple, orange, yellow, green, brown, black and colourless. Each of these colours varies in its ability to help you in life. Here, let us explore how Red Garnet may bless you with optimum health and safety so that as you head along your path, nothing may deter you.

Animal: Jaguar
Plants: Guarana and Pomegranate
Astrological Correspondence: Vesta
Power Day: Tuesday
Cleanse with: Fire

Your Crystal Alignment Meditation

Go to a rainforest or jungle or visualise one in your mind. Take a walk and find a place away from other people. Quieten your mind and start to observe your surroundings. Tropical jungles and rainforests are home to more species of animals and plants than anywhere else in the world. Sense the buzz of life around you. Hear the finely tuned orchestra playing their part in the song of life. Realise that even in places that are overflowing with life (i.e. cities) everyone can play a vital role and live in harmony. When you feel ready, connect with your Garnet.

Warmth

Garnet keeps you warm in winter. Wear it as a bracelet or ring to improve your circulation. Keep Garnet in gloves when you're not wearing them for bring added warmth on a cool day. Let Garnet ignite your internal fires. Wear Garnet over your heart to increase your vitality and ability to create positive experiences in your life. Start each day by combining it with the magical fruit guarana known for its magical ability to remove problems from life. Obtain some guarana powder and make a smoothie, while visualising your problem vanishing. See life without the problem existing anymore. You may want to add strawberries (for love), banana (for fertility), coconut (for spirituality), citrus (for purification) and/or pineapple (for healing). As you drink the smoothie feel that energy start to emanate from you, awakening your Garnet. Soon you will attract what you need for your visualisation to come into fruition.

Wear Garnet near the site of any injury or sickness when you want to stimulate your body's ability to self-heal. Garnet is especially effective in speeding the healing of a cut or wound. Because of its fiery energy, it is not recommended for inflammation. In these cases, choose Amber or Amazonite to soothe the body.

Create a warm, close-knit home by placing a Garnet sphere in the centre of your house. To support your Garnet, add two red candles and invoke the energy of Vesta (the asteroid and the goddess) who is the ruler of the devotion, intimacy and a loving home. For the bedroom, six Garnets around the bed will work to spice up your lovemaking.

Base Chakra

Garnet works on stimulating your base chakra. Symptoms of an underactive base chakra include apathy, non-participation and lethargy. If your base chakra is under-functioning, you may tend to be severely disorganised or unstructured, even forgetting to complete simple daily tasks such as eat or pay bills. You may suffer from depression, chronic fatigue, daydreaming, delusions or an eating disorder. Take time each day to rest, placing your Garnet between your legs, close to your body. Visualise a vibrant red sphere of energy glowing from the base of your spine, stimulating the energy of your base chakra. Continue to carry your Garnet in your pocket throughout the day until you are feeling more balanced. Physical exercise such as yoga, eating red fruit and vegetables, enjoying a glass of red wine each evening, listening to music with deep beats such as Latin and including red into your wardrobe and décor will also help stimulating your base chakra. The sense governed by the base chakra is smell so you may notice an improved sense of smell as an indication that your chakra is returning to a balanced state.

Integrity

Garnet supports you in living life with integrity. A life of integrity requires you to act to the very best of your ability with whatever knowledge is available to you at any given moment. By living a life of integrity, you live life to the fullest and give every moment your total commitment. You treat people with honesty and fairness. Having integrity ensures you have no regrets and suffer no remorse. A life lived in this way is rich in joy and wonder, because there are no missed opportunities and no lost moments of pleasure. You can go to sleep each night knowing you have done the best you could have done. Take time to determine your definition of integrity. Your Jaguar guide can offer you guidance in meditating these ideals. Each morning as you don your Garnet, state your oath of integrity. Here's an example:

Today my word is my law.

Today I shall harm none, including myself.

Today I shall be honest, pleasant, helpful and respectful.

Today I acknowledge that I am no less, nor no more than any other.

Today I shall take responsibility for who I am, what I have and where I am.

I shall live today as if it is my last, so that I may make the world a better place.

Wearing Garnet will protect you from slander and situations that will compromise your integrity. It can help you foresee upcoming dangers or when keeping Garnet at work stops others stealing your ideas. Combine Garnet with Moonstone to reveal unknown enemies or the truth behind illusions. When faced with a situation challenging your integrity, summon Jaguar to devour your negative thoughts.

HELIODOR

Illumination / Success / Solar Plexus Chakra / Fairies

Heliodor comes from the Greek phrase meaning "gift from the sun", and just as a sunny day lifts both your mood and spirit, so can this crystal. Working with Heliodor brings balance to your life, especially when you are feeling stunted or become overly serious. The crystal's sunshiny nature helps you approach life with ease and start making decisions based on wisdom and experience rather than erupting emotions. Heliodor awakens confidence, sincerity, assertiveness, physical and mental strength, benevolence and initiative. It turns your skills and talents into practical realities. Working with Heliodor brings a sparkle back to a life that has lost its lustre.

Animals: Golden Pheasant and Hummingbird
Plant: Bergamot
Astrological Correspondence: Sun
Power Day: Sunday
Cleanse with: Sun

Your Crystal Alignment Meditation

Sit in the sunshine, or at least visualise yourself outside on a sunny day. Enjoy the feeling on your skin. Let this warmth fill your body. Allow happiness to rise from within you. Feel a smile on your face. You are ready to connect with your Heliodor.

Illumination

With Heliodor's strong connection to the sun, it is valuable at times a burst of solar influence is needed in your life. Bring the warmth of the sun into your home by placing a Heliodor on each windowsill. Add some bergamot essential oil and a yellow candle near an eastern window to induce warmth into the house on cold winter mornings. This technique can also counteract unwanted paranormal activity, ghosts or other dark energies, replacing them with a more angelic vibration. If you have animal companions from the tropics but live in a colder climate, grid their enclosure or keep some Heliodor near them to help them deal with the cold. In the winter draw the energy of Heliodor into your energy field to blast away sickness when those around you are coming down with colds or flus. You can also project this energy onto contaminated objects.

Meditate with Heliodor in the dark of night to illuminate your "inner sun". This is a spiritual light within you that gives you warmth and liveliness. Connecting with the teachings of the Golden Pheasant will encourage you to shine, sharing your inner beauty and vivacity with the world. Flirt with the world, be creative and fun and manifest good fortune each day. A particularly good time to work with the illuminating vibration of Heliodor is if you are unwell or dying. It will bring you strength and optimism, easing this difficult time.

Heliodor invokes the celestial Golden Ray of knowledge and learning, which stimulates the higher mind and enables you to think more efficiently. It is a crystal of true nobility and selfless leadership, encouraging you to carefully consider the consequences and likely outcomes of your actions rather than impulsively reacting to events. However, this crystal doesn't have a serious tone, rather it encourages you to adopt a sense of ease and confident when choosing which path to take. Hummingbird also teaches you to lighten up and so connecting with his energy can enhance your mental agility, your capacity to create mutually beneficial projects and inspire the determined warrior within.

Success

Heliodor improves your mental abilities allowing you to be more on-point in your interactions with others. Wearing Heliodor over the chest or throat enables you to win debates and persuade others to back you, either financially or with other resources. The crystal's vibration also has a tendency to bring out others' honesty.

This crystal can be used to regain what has been lost in terms of employment, prospects or money. If you have lost your job, start working with Heliodor to enable you to shine and encourage others to have faith in your abilities when seeking new sources of income. Those that are employed, especially if you are self-employed, can work with Heliodor to find balance devoting time between work commitments and spending quality time with loved ones. In the workplace, Heliodor boosts drive and determination to succeed if others have worn away your enthusiasm. In fact, its energy is so radiant it has a tendency to shed light over other's dark intentions of psychological and emotional manipulation.

In life, Heliodor promotes the will to succeed and follow through, even after setbacks. It reminds you that when times get tough, to be patient and remain open to a solution appearing over time. Heliodor teaches you that there is no obstacle that confidence, faith in the universe and conviction cannot resolve.

Solar Plexus Chakra

The solar plexus chakra is the energy centre that controls emotional stability and personal power. It is located at the bottom of your sternum, and you feel its energy when you get a sudden fright. When you have a balanced solar plexus chakra you are radiant, friendly and confident. You have complete control over your thoughts and emotions, and your ego has no unwanted influence over your actions. You have respect for others and the planet and are focused on working in collaboration with others to create a peaceful, harmonious world. Heliodor enables you to maintain balance in this chakra. Take time to rest with it each day against the solar plexus chakra, visualising a vibrant yellow ball of sunshine-yellow light radiating from this energy centre. Continue to wear Heliodor close to this chakra for support throughout the day.

Using Heliodor to maintain a balanced solar plexus chakra is especially powerful for those that have had their personal power stripped away in the past and are now working hard to regain it. It is especially helpful for survivors of any type of abuse. This crystal gives you a sense of self-trust that you have learned from the past and will not allow yourself to fall into the same traps again. It also helps those who avoid making decisions out of fear of doing the "wrong" thing, and increases mental fortitude in moving forward.

The solar plexus chakra also regulates the digestive system and thus, Heliodor is supportive of digestive health. It is especially useful in ensuring the effective absorption of nutrients and assisting your body to use these for optimum wellbeing.

Fairies

Fairies and sylphs are elemental creatures that are connected to the air and wind. You may simply see them as sparkly energy flashing and swirling around in the skies or as you develop your relationship with them, they may appear to you in a more visible form. They support us in our daily living by caring for a vital resource, the air we breathe. They also model snowflakes and gather clouds. Developing a relationship with them can help enhance inspiration, communication and mental clarity. If you need a miracle to happen, ask a fairy to bring it upon the winds. To attract these elementals into your life, build a fairy garden. Include fairy-attracting plants such as primrose, rose and thyme and make a circle with Heliodor for them to dance in. Ideally have hawthorn, ash and oak trees growing nearby. When you need to contact them, sit quietly and whisper your request while holding your Heliodor between your hands. Even though you may not see them you can close your eyes and feel their presence near you. They can offer you their wisdom without you having to lay eyes upon them. Simply listen with your heart and hear their words whisper within you. For this reason, Heliodor is an ideal naming day or christening gift for a child to ensure they don't lose their ability to see the magic in the world as they grow up.

HEMATITE

Grounding / Truth / Logic

This shiny Silver crystal when scratched or powdered displays red from its Iron content earning its name from the Greek word *haem* meaning blood. Hematite holds a very serious, grounding energy about it. It strongly guides you towards improving your life and averting distraction. Native American folklore states that war paint made from Hematite makes you invincible in battle while scientists of the Mars Exploration Rover Project believe that deposits of Hematite exist on Mars, the planet named after the warring god.

Animal: Aardvark
Plant: Fennel
Astrological Correspondences: Mars and Saturn
Power Days: Tuesday and Saturday
Cleanse with: Fire

Your Crystal Alignment Meditation

Go and sit in nature at night, ideally at midnight. Place your palms on the ground. Sense, feel and visualise all tension and anxiety flowing out of your body and mind and being swallowed up by the earth. You release all fear, sadness, anger, confusion and worry. Allow a sense of content relaxation to remain within you as you connect with your Hematite.

Grounding

Hematite is made up of the two elements Iron and oxygen. Metaphysically, Iron is a grounding metal, thus making Hematite a very settling and balancing crystal. Keep it in your pocket to enable you to stay committed to your own path and prevent being coerced by peer pressure, bullying or manipulative marketing. Strengthen Hematite's effect by adding the scent of fennel to your space as this essential oil helps you reconnect with your sense of power and responsibility for your life. Hematite works on the body to help it regain balance, especially by ensuring the blood is oxygenated. Wearing magnetised Hematite can have miraculous effects on arthritis. It is also useful for countering the negative effects of menstruation or any blood related ailment. When worn near the hands or as a ring it can improve manual dexterity.

Rest with Hematite at each end of your spine to balance and ground your thoughts. This is ideal if you are feeling spacey, especially when overwhelmed by exposure to too many crystals. Hematite is great for times when you are experiencing pain but not the recommended choice for animals or for people with pacemakers.

Wear Hematite over the heart when beginning a new relationship. It helps you maintain a level head and ensures you don't overreact to small "love wounds." It will also help ground all the love energies so that you don't get too carried away. It can be a saviour if you tend to rush into relationships head first and end up scaring away potential suitors.

Truth

Use Hematite in your pursuit for the truth. Its grounding qualities settle the mind and prevent you from getting distracted by trivialities and distractions. Use Hematite as a scrying crystal to unveil the truth of a situation. Sitting in a darkened room, light a red candle and hold your Hematite so that the candle's flame is reflected on it. Gaze at the reflection and state what you wish to know. Let your eyes to fall out of focus and as you relax, allow the answers to come. Diffusing fennel essential oil in your space will allow you to shed old restrictions and reach higher levels of consciousness, assisting your scrying session. If you are undertaking a large task to discover a great truth such as a research project, inventing or studying spirituality or philosophy, pair the use of Hematite with your Aardvark guide. This strong-willed animal can inspire you to remain determined and fearless in your pursuit for the truth. Meditate on the lessons of Aardvark and he will help you sniff out the answers you seek.

Logic

Not only will Hematite help you to feel grounded and dedicated to your path but it will aid you in solving any problems you face. It stimulates the rational, logical mind, allowing greater understanding of mathematics, science and law. When studying, create a triangle with three pieces of Hematite. Place two in your pockets and one above your books. When you need to recall this knowledge, create this triangle again by placing the two pieces back in your pockets and the third near your head.

HERKIMER DIAMOND

Transparency / Transformation / Spiritual Healing / Diamond Substitute

Herkimer Diamonds come from Herkimer County, NY, USA. The bedrock in which they are found started forming about half a billion years ago in a shallow Cambrian sea that once existed in the area. They are not actually true Diamonds but rather a form of double-terminated Quartz. Most Herkimer Diamonds are clear although some contain small black inclusions, a golden Iron covering, and a special few contain water inclusions, which enhance their ability to aid with emotional issues. Unlike true Diamonds that must be worked by machine to bring out their beauty, Herkimers have been prepared by Mother Nature, already naturally sparkling with light and rainbow. These have become a popular tool for any serious crystal worker because of their intense and transformational energy. Many find Herkimer Diamond to be one of the highest vibrations of Quartz on the earth, and often even the most inexperienced crystal worker can feel some energetic pulse while holding it. However due to Herkimer Diamond's intense spiritual energy, it is best to use it for special purposes at specific times. Prolonged exposure may cause disorientation in some people and may be too overwhelming for children, younger teenagers or animals.

Animal: Frog
Plant: Peppermint
Astrological Correspondence: Uranus
Power Days: Monday and Thursday
Cleanse with: Full Moon

Your Crystal Alignment Meditation

Go outside and sit with a seed in your hand. Connect with the seed and contemplate the potential within this tiny pod. A small seed has the potential to become a great tree, a beautiful flower or offer food for you and others. Ask yourself if this seed can become something great, ask what is possible for you to become. When ready, put down the seed and pick up the Herkimer Diamond to connect with it.

Transparency

Hold your Herkimer Diamond in your hand and allow its powerful vibration to shift you to a state of clarity and inspiration. Wearing Herkimer Diamond over your heart each day helps to bring buried issues to the surface and release them once and for all. The crystal helps to clear blocks and stagnation and bring new inspiration into your life. Meditating with a Herkimer Diamond can help you become clear on the natural gifts and talents you have to offer humanity. Furthermore, once programmed, it helps to amplify they skills so they are applied in a manner that serves everyone's highest good.

As you unveil a new-found direction, you may experience conflicts between your latest passions and previous roles and commitments. Herkimer Diamond helps you integrate all aspects of your life, whether that be to bring spiritual practices into everyday life or to merge conflicting responsibilities vying for your time and attention. Over time, Herkimer Diamond will continue to shine light on your true spiritual purpose so that you are constantly moving closer to fulfilling your life's mission. It will encourage you to surrender to the flow of the universe, trust the process and stop forcing things to unfold before their natural conclusion.

Herkimer Diamond unveils the truth in all matters. Hold one when dealing with someone new and if it vibrates in your hand, this person is not to be trusted. It will also help you to speak the truth, reminding you that even small lies cause damage and distort others reality. Herkimer Diamonds work best when your thoughts, words and actions are all in alignment. When these things are aligned the energy you output is the same, and Herkimer Diamond will project and amplify this to the world to draw you to that which matches this vibration.

As you work with your Herkimer Diamond you may start to experience a sense of grace or peace, as if you are constantly being guided by the universe. This blissful influence on your energy field attracts angelic support. Wear Herkimer Diamond high on your body to enhance your ability to detect and communicate with angels. On the night of the new moon, place your Herkimer Diamond near your bed to improve the frequency and clarity of guiding dreams. However Clear Quartzes, including Herkimer Diamond, sometimes keep certain individuals awake at night, especially as the moon becomes full. If this happens to you, try meditating with the crystal before bed, then leaving it in another room. If in the morning, the meaning of your dreams are vague, sit with your Herkimer Diamond and wait for clarity.

Transformation

Herkimer Diamond helps you move forward in your life. It allows you to heal past issues and strengthen your inner guidance and intuition. Wear a Herkimer over your heart to maximise its ability to bring about personal transformation. As you put it on each day, repeat nine times what you want to transform. Open yourself up to the call of your Frog guide when working with Herkimer Diamond. Frog is known as the rain bringer, often heard croaking before a rain shower. The rains wash away the old and bring new growth, and Frog will guide you through any transition towards more freedom in your life. Herkimer Diamond also harmonises with peppermint. Consuming peppermint and inhaling its scent can help restore health to the body, clarity to the mind and balance to the spirit, all of which are vital for transformation.

Herkimer Diamond is great for maintaining the strength of a relationship when it is transforming. Partners each wearing a matching Herkimer Diamond will find they will be able to smoothly evolve through the changing stages any long-term relationship experiences. Herkimer Diamond also supports the connection between two people when one is travelling or moving away. Obtain two similar Herkimer Diamond's and bind them together with a pink ribbon with the intention that they will form an energetic link. When it is time for your partner to depart, give them one of the two crystals while you keep the other near. It will enable you to both stay on the same page as well as aid telepathic and psychic communication.

Spiritual Healing

Herkimers are ideal for body layouts, Reiki, meditation and as energy tools. They have the ability of magnifying the frequency of other stones. If there is something you need to focus on, pair it with a crystal that can benefit this issue and allow the Herkimer Diamond to amplify the effect. If you have small crystals, use them with a Herkimer Diamond to get a worthwhile effect. Combining it with Mangano Calcite, Morganite or Rose Quartz will allow love to flow into the deep corners of your soul and flush out buried or unresolved issues, especially those associated with feeling neglected or uncared for. In meditation, place Moldavite on your heart chakra and Herkimer Diamond on your third eye to induce insightful realisations that will guide you along the right path.

Wear it whenever you are attending spirituality or meditation classes to help you retain knowledge. Herkimer Diamond is also good for teachers and healing practitioners as it will ensure clarity of thoughts, words and intentions. If you are hosting a group of people, place Herkimer Diamonds around the space as they will encourage spiritual connection between the people attending. Create a room spray with pure water, relevant essential oils and a Herkimer Diamond to spritz around before and after a session to lift the vibration of the area.

Herkimer Diamond can be used in earth healing. It can change the energy of any area from one of devastation to a more abundant and renewing energy. Combined with Aragonite or Lepidolite it settles the energy of the earth; with Lapis Lazuli or Kambaba Stone it cleanses the air; with Aquamarine it cleanses water; and with green crystals such as Emerald or Tree Agate it will enhance revegetation.

Diamond Substitute

Diamonds are powerful crystals with a multitude of helpful properties. However, acquiring a suitable Diamond for your purpose may be beyond your budget. Herkimer Diamond can be used as a substitute when you are doing healings, scrying, programming a crystal for unity or group cohesiveness or working with archangel Uriel.

HIDDENITE
Unconditional Love / Gratitude / Protecting Assets

Hiddenite is part of the Spodumene family along with the well-known pink Kunzite. This crystal comes in various shades of green including a deep green, lime green and a pale green that is almost yellow. Hiddenite guards the heart and prevents you from being hurt. You'll find it quickly dissolves grief or rage, allowing you dwell in a loving state of mind, constantly giving you a lively vigour.

Animal: Elephant
Plant: Gardenia
Astrological Correspondences: Moon and Venus
Power Days: Monday and Friday
Cleanse with: Moon

Your Crystal Alignment Meditation

Go outside and sit before a flower still attached to its plant. Study the beauty, structure and geometry of the flower. Close your eyes and take in the scent. Take the flower gently in your hands (don't pick it!) and tune in to its energy. Allow it to offer you any healing you may need. Once you are feeling balanced, connect with your Hiddenite.

Unconditional Love

Hiddenite is one of the highest vibration green crystals. It lifts the heart and connects you to a sense of universal love and oneness. Diffuse harmonising gardenia essential oil or burn the incense in your home to further enhance this connection. Hiddenite allows those moving to a new place alone or feel they must "put on a brave face" during hard times to feel supported. By wearing Hiddenite over your heart, you shift your whole approach to love, rather than the negatives of a situation or person. It compels you to love people simply for the sake of loving, allowing them to freely be themselves when they are with you.

Hiddenite can also be used help you decide whether you should get back with an ex-partner or move on. Infuse your crystal with all the love you still hold for your partner. Then go out to the garden and pick the first flower that catches your eye. Place the flower in some water and the Hiddenite next to the vase. If the flower is still looking vibrant in a week, the relationship has another shot.

Gratitude

Hiddenite promotes gratitude and abundance in your life. Each time you receive a compliment, your pay check or any kind of gift, hold your Hiddenite in your hand and say, "Thank you, thank you, thank you." Hold it in your hands each night and recall everything you are grateful for. By committing to these practises you will adjust your personal vibration to allow more to come to you, assuring you always have everything you need.

Placed by a family photo Hiddenite reminds all household members of the importance of family. Adding the image of an elephant will help to keep the family safe. Two pieces of Hiddenite, one carried or worn by each partner in a relationship, helps maintain a loving relationship and keeps communication honest and heartfelt.

Protecting Assets

Once you are grateful for what you have in your life, Hiddenite works to preserve it. Keep a piece of Hiddenite in safes to protect valuables and a piece in the wallet to prevent reckless spending. Gridded around the house ensures protection from theft, damage and geopathic stress. Place the crystal by photos of friends, family or a partner with a couple of candles (one green and one pink) and it will nurture harmonious relationships.

Hiddenite also works to protect our greatest asset, our planet Earth. Wearing Hiddenite will help you make environmentally conscious decisions. You can also grid them around national parks to protect them from illegal damage, or use it as the power crystal in power grids focusing on protecting nature.

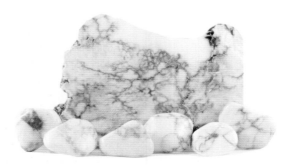

HOWLITE

Peace / Sleep / Spiritual Guidance

Howlite is named after Henry How, a geologist who discovered the crystal in Nova Scotia, Canada. Historically it has been a popular crystal with native North American tribes who could easily create carvings due to its softness. Energetically, Howlite is a crystal of peace and spirituality. The soft veins of black that run through this white crystal contribute a settling and grounding energy. Howlite calms the mind by reducing fretful thoughts, helping you to relax and remain composed throughout your day. It promotes healing and recovery in the body following a period of ill-health. Howlite's serene effect is also beneficial at bed time, counteracting insomnia and inducing a night of sweet dreams.

Animal: Sloth
Plant: Nutmeg
Astrological Correspondence: Moon
Power Day: Monday
Cleanse with: Full Moon

Your Crystal Alignment Meditation

Go to a place where a thick mist or fog covers the ground, or visualise this scene in your mind. As the mist surrounds you, feel its coolness on your skin. See how the mist hides the world from you. It takes away any vision of the past or future. When you sit and rest in the now, allow yourself to discover that there is nothing to regret and nothing to worry about in the present. This is a cleansing mist and it absorbs all the unwanted and unhelpful energies you no longer wish to carry. Once you feel cleansed, connect with your Howlite.

Peace

The soft vibration of Howlite brings peace and serenity to any area. Bury it around the perimeter of your house to ensure only harmonious energies dwell within your property. It will deter moles, raccoons, skunks or bandicoots from digging up your garden or aggressive cats from causing problems. Placing Howlite in house plants and/or at each door of the home blesses the space and creates a tranquil environment. Having it inside is also protection against unwanted ghosts and phantoms. When out and about, have Howlite in your car if you get frustrated by traffic jams, or on public transport or planes if you get overwhelmed by being in a confined space with a large number of people.

You can use Howlite to create a blessing spray. Place a candle in a bowl and then fill the bowl with snow or ice. Now place your Howlite on the ice as you say, "May light and love melt all barriers and obstacles of peace". Take some time to watch as the ice turns into water. The following day, place the water in a spritz bottle, add a couple of drops of nutmeg essential oil for protection and luck, and spray it around your home or space.

Howlite is great to wear near the throat if you tend to be confrontational in your communication. It will soften your communication and allow you to speak more kindly, openly, and with integrity. When conflict arises in your life, start working with Howlite to bring a peaceful energy to the space. If troubles arises at work, place a couple of pieces in your area. Continue to use Howlite after the issues subside as it promotes stability after turbulent times with friends, family or colleagues.

Howlite's calming effect is not limited to humans. It is a great crystal for animals, allowing them to feel safe and at peace at home. It can also be utilised to prevent them from straying. To help remedy this behaviour place a Howlite crystal on your pet's collar, in their bed, and also at the place where they normally escape from your property.

On a global scale, Howlite's energy promotes peace, understanding and humanitarian plights. During meditation visualise a place in the world you would like to send peaceful energy to. See the energy as a white mist surrounding everyone and taking away their hatred, ignorance and differences. See everyone in the area smiling and laughing. After your meditation, place the crystal with a picture or map of the place you are focusing on. Light a white candle and place it with the crystal and image. Be sure never to leave the candle unattended. Perform this activity weekly, ideally on a Monday.

As your sense of peace and security increases while using Howlite, this crystal can start to foster a thirst for knowledge and a desire to explore the world. Place it around the study to encourage yourself to stay engaged while studying or to help children focus on their homework. When placed in the classroom, not only does it work to reduce antisocial or disruptive behaviour, but it will help students to complete their work.

Sleep

Howlite helps to calm the mind by reducing fretful thoughts and by helping you to relax in preparation for sleep. If you or someone you know suffers from insomnia, caused by racing thoughts at bedtime, place a small tumbled stone in the pillowslip each night. You can also grid four pieces at the four corners of your bed to create a more relaxed and peaceful resting place. This technique is great for children who are afraid of the dark.

Most people experience more dreams when they place Howlite in their pillowslip. These dreams are more vivid, memorable and rarely nightmarish. Dreaming is a great way to get guidance from the deeper parts of our mind. When you sleep, your subconscious doesn't need to battle with your conscious mind and your emotional side is not challenged by logic. Therefore it is easier to access innate wisdom that exists within you without the interruption of exploring your dreams. When you have Howlite in the bedroom, keep a dream journal next to your bed and record patterns or trends in your dreams. To increase dreaming even more, drink a cup of warm milk and nutmeg before bed.

Spiritual Guidance

As you bring more peace to your life, both within and around you, Howlite will open you up to having more contact with your guides, angels and ancestors. As the stresses of everyday life affect you less, your attention will shift to what is happening around you. You'll be able to notice the synchronicities of life, and identify the divine guidance. Connecting with your Sloth guide can enhance your spiritual insights. Since he can move his head 270 degrees he shows you the advantage of broadening your view and considering other perspectives. By opening up our awareness, and becoming patient and peaceful yet deliberate in our conduct, you'll start to notice that which is not commonly perceived by others. By summoning Sloth's energy you can improve your psychic visions.

Meditating with Howlite against your third eye chakra can allow you to discover past hurts you've been carrying or repressing, even those you are not consciously aware of. Use the soft energy of Howlite to send peace to this pain, and combine it with emotional healing crystals such as Malachite, Chrysocolla, Quantum Quattro™ or Tinaksite to promote the healing of these past sufferings. This same technique can also be used for past life regression.

IOLITE

Guidance / Debt Reduction / Astral Travel

Iolite brings about change in your life that allows you to release the unnecessary and find both inner and outer balance. It grounds you in the now and allows you to then explore the multitude of lessons available within this beautiful universe. By choosing to work with Iolite you are acknowledging that you are on this planet to experience, learn and expand your understanding. A relationship with Iolite ensures a lifetime of wisdom.

> **Animal:** Wolf
> **Plant:** Myrrh
> **Astrological Correspondence:** Saturn
> **Power Day:** Saturday
> **Cleanse with:** Full Moon or Water

Your Crystal Alignment Meditation

Go for a walk, ideally in a natural setting. As you walk along focus purely on the present. Do not allow a conscious thought to enter you mind. If you feel you get distracted, bring your focus to your breath or the feel of your feet with each step. Whenever you come to a crossways or fork in your journey, tune in to yourself and follow the way you are drawn. Allow your higher self to guide you rather than logically deciding the most beautiful, logical or quickest path to take. This will help you tune in to your own inner guidance systems. When you feel ready, connect with your Iolite.

Guidance

You may have heard the expression that when the student is ready, the teacher appears. Iolite prepares the student more quickly. It takes your hand and guides you to see what actions are needed. When held in meditation, Iolite can show where your lack of discipline is holding you back, especially when Jupiter is retrograde. Wearing it around your neck enables you to understand why each person comes into your life and what lessons they can teach you. You will also build bonds with people more easily, regardless of whether you have just met them or known them a lifetime. Even people that are normally difficult to deal with will become more bearable as you develop greater levels of understanding. The Wolf guide is one of the strongest animal guides. Inviting him into your life will further allow you to receive spiritual guidance. Not only will he offer you his own wisdom but he has the ability to guide you towards other teachers.

Iolite can help you with any neck stiffness which is a physical manifestation of an unwillingness to look around at your current situation or behind and learn from past. Neck pain can also develop when you look at people as being a "pain in the neck" rather than opening yourself up to discover what they can teach you. Iolite can even help you deal with animals you find hard to love, whether a pet or a species of animal such as spiders or mice. Create massage oil with myrrh essential oil and use a tumbled Iolite or wand to give yourself a neck massage.

Debt Reduction

As Iolite gives you inner guidance, it is a useful stone for debt elimination. Iolite will help you to think outside the box and is excellent for brainstorming. First, write down your debts so that you are clear on your financial position. Then close your eyes while holding Iolite in your receptive hand and let your inner guidance offer you solutions. Filling your space with the scent of myrrh essential oil helps eliminate any fear of money, allows you to connect to divine guidance and encourages greater trust in your intuition.

Astral Travel

Astral travel is the ability for the astral body to leave the physical body and project or journey elsewhere. To enhance your ability to astral travel, sit amongst a circle of Iolite and burn myrrh incense. This will enable you to heighten your vibration and tune in to higher frequencies and more subtle energies where spiritual beings await you.

Further Crystal Connections – Starstone

Starstone is a combination of two crystals: Sunstone and Iolite. Sunstone can sometimes be found growing alongside Iolite, or as small crystals within the dark Iolite crystal creating a stone resembling the dark night sky filled with sparkling stars. Iolite helps you expand your horizons and find guidance, both within and around you. However, when it combines with Sunstone to create Starstone, the guidance allows you to remember what feels good and use this as the compass towards discovering happiness, bliss and comfort in your life.

When you are drawn to Starstone, its message is similar to the Star Tarot card. It reinstates your belief and faith in the world. It reminds you that good times are coming your way, to remain focused on your dreams and to reach for the stars. It inspires ambition and is a good crystal to have around when you are feeling despondent. Meditate with Starstone and ask it to help open you up to discover new opportunities.

The stone's vibration instils a sense of selflessness and service in its guardian as well as attracting other generous people into your life that will support you in your life's journey. Create grids or carry when networking to meet the right people for taking your career to the next level. Ongoing work with Starstone can also attract soul brothers and sisters into your life and can nurture the growth of these relationships.

Starstone, also called the Shaman's Sapphire, helps you merge light and darkness. It is ideal to use during past-life work, regressions, soul retrievals, working with shadow self and finding root causes of self-sabotage. Meditations can often take you back into a time in your life when you felt completely happy and at peace, often with loved ones. It reminds you of the optimum happiness you have experienced and encourages you to start seeking that level of contentment again. This stone also helps you to have more vivid drams, overcome blocks to create artistic masterpieces and to strengthen your intuitive abilities.

Starstone allows you to connect with the Divine Masculine as it melds the mighty warrior energy of Sunstone with the wise sage frequency of Iolite. Men can use it to discover their spiritual role in life as well as balance any traits that may be out of balance. Starstone will help men channel anger into passionate drive to make positive change or shift critical tendencies to greater understanding of situations. Women will benefit using Starstone to nurture their masculine side or resolve issues with men in their life.

Starstone reminds you of your divine perfection. Through meditation it will help you to see the universe reflected within you and fill you with a sense of oneness. Use Starstone to improve self-acceptance and to embrace who you truly are. It helps you enjoy your own company and feel okay with being by yourself. It helps you to develop a deep connection with your soul, increasing inner knowing of yourself. As you develop a relationship with Starstone you'll find an increase in confidence, enjoy social interactions more and uncover dormant leadership qualities. As Starstone is a stone that helps you cast of superficial facades, it is best worked with naked and in natural settings.

JADE, GREEN

Open Heart / Abundance / Dreams

Jade actually refers to two different crystals, Jadeite and Nephrite. However, both these crystals are so similar in energy that you can confidently interchange them. Jade is found in a variety of colours including black, blue, lavender, yellow, white but most commonly green. Green Jade promotes luck, growth and tranquility. It works to protect what you already have and help you maintain a sense of balance and harmony, both within and around. For these reasons Green Jade is one of the most popular crystals in countries throughout the East, where it is often carved into statues and power animal amulets as well as worn as jewellery. It is renowned for promoting the five traditional virtues associated with the sage Confucius: charity, courage, modesty, justice and wisdom.

Animal: Cow
Plants: The Seven Sacred Grains (barley, corn, millet, oats, rice, rye and wheat)
Astrological Correspondences: Venus and asteroid Hathor
Power Day: Friday
Cleanse with: Earth

Your Crystal Alignment Meditation

Go to a field nearby, ideally where grains are grown. Sink your hands deep into the soil. Contemplate that from soil just like this, all our food grows. This soil is the womb that births all our sustenance. Feel the energies and the nourishment from the ground flowing into your body energising you. Then send some love and gratitude back to the soil. Replenish it, repaying what you have taken. You are now ready to connect with your Green Jade.

Open Heart

Green Jade opens your heart to the world. It promotes the balancing of your needs with that of those around you. This lets you care for yourself and others simultaneously. It is ideal when you have a large family that spends a lot of time together. Green Jade promotes compassion, generosity and humility, allowing you to live a richer more fulfilling life as you are contributing not just to your own wellbeing but also that of your community. Wear Green Jade over your heart to nurture these aspects of yourself. Bring it into the bedroom to turn love-making into a spiritual experience. Team working with Green Jade with connecting to your Cow guide. She is one of the most giving animals on the planet, giving her meat and milk so that we may prosper. She will awaken your selflessness.

As you reignite your loving heart, you will notice a shift in your life and that which surrounds you. Green Jade surrounds you in loving support, while protecting you from hostile behaviour such as blackmail. As its peaceful influences surround you, it can have a beneficial effect on your health, especially your kidneys which can be affected my thoughts of anger, guilt, fear and ancient sadness. In fact, Nephrite gets its name from the word nephron which is Greek for kidney. For kidney or overall health, wear Green Jade against the skin for long periods of time or drink a Green Jade elixir each morning. Pets and animals will also benefit from being near Green Jade, as it brings them overall health, assists giving birth and promotes longevity.

To honour and nurture your compassionate aspect you may like to place a statue of Buddha or Quan Yin around your home surrounded by a circle of Green Jade. Always position the statue in a position of reverence. Don't put them in the bathroom, kitchen or near electronics. Looking down on the statue is also considered irreverent so position them at least at eye level.

Abundance

When you open your heart and give more, you open the gateways to allow abundance to flow towards you. As you strengthen your relationship with Green Jade, you will increase your abundance. Keep a piece in your wallet or with some coins to increase financial success. Green Jade is especially supportive for family businesses. Because of its open-hearted energy, Green Jade assures that leaders and people in positions of authority remain ethical and caring. It also helps those with these innate personality traits to succeed when vying for a promotion or leadership bid. If you resonate with deities of Egypt, call upon the cow-headed goddess Hathor, who blesses you with love, beauty and abundance.

Wearing Green Jade promotes friendship and helps young children make friends even if they are shy and helps teens suffering from puberty blues. If you are single and ready to find a partner, try the Chinese tradition of wearing Green Jade carved in the shape of a butterfly.

Green Jade promotes healthy plant and crop growth. Those working with plants or a love of the garden should wear Green Jade to develop their relationship with this aspect of nature. Bury it in the corners of your garden or field, in the soil of indoor plants and place a piece in a vase of cut flowers to increase their life-span. It has a reputation of being a rain-bringer, so take time to hold your Green Jade while you visualise rain falling around you as an anti-drought rite. In fact, use Green Jade in any creative visualisation, manifesting or magical work to ensure the results are for the highest good.

To increase overall abundance throughout your life, eat from Green Jade bowls. They will transfer their energy into your food. Another way is to add a piece of Green Jade into your water bottle to infuse the water with its energy. You can also create an abundance power grid. Place Green Jade, coins and statues in the centre and surround them with eight double-terminated Clear Quartz or Citrine. Add supporting crystals such as Turquoise for releasing energy blocks, Jet to promote wise spending and Charoite to help you be financially rewarded for fulfilling your passion.

You can also work with the seven sacred grains to promote abundance. Include them in your diet, reflecting on their gifts as you eat them, and add them to your power grid and altar. Here are their main attributes:
- Barley: fertility
- Corn: forever
- Millet: expansion
- Oats: clarity
- Rice: good luck and cooperation
- Rye: openness
- Wheat: continual bounty.

Dreams

If you would like to experience more vivid dreams that will offer you guidance, meditate with a piece of Green Jade on your forehead before going to bed and then place it in your pillowslip for the night. It will awaken inner knowledge, bringing it to the surface while you sleep. Green Jade also works to bring supressed emotions out in your dreams for you to face and deal with them. You can add other colours of Jade to further affect your dreamings. Lavender Jade promotes peaceful dreams that are easy to understand. If you place a piece of Yellow Jade in your pillowslip, it will attract an important spiritual teacher during your dream time. Black Jade can help lessen nightmares.

Furthermore, Green Jade is associated with your dreams when you are awake as well. It is a crystal that reminds you never to forget your dreams and when you are drawn to it, this may suggest you have lost your way in the demands of mundane life and are forgetting to listen to your soul's desires. If this is the case, take time to sit with your Green Jade and daydream, simply pondering what you'd love your life to become. Then use your crystal to give these dreams love, and nurture them into a fruitful reality.

JASPER, DALMATIAN
Contentment / Loyalty / Dogs

Dalmatian Jasper is a unique spotted variety of Jasper. Like other varieties of Jasper, it is a nurturing and grounding crystal. It leads you back to a sense of balance where you can connect with your true sense of happiness. It removes disillusionment and helps you understand your strengths and weakness so you can use them to your advantage. Dalmatian Jasper tends to work slowly so keep it with you all the time over an extended period.

Animal: Dog
Plant: Mandarin
Astrological Correspondence: Venus
Power Day: Friday
Cleanse with: Earth

Your Crystal Alignment Meditation

Go and spend time with a dog. You may like to sit with him and relax or take him for a walk in nature. Connect to his energy. Notice his loyalty and determination. What can you learn from this friend? When you are ready, connect with your crystal.

Contentment

Dalmatian Jasper has a playful, light energy about it, just like that of a puppy. If you are taking everything a bit too seriously, let Dalmatian Jasper help you lighten up. Carry it with you daily and each time you start to become overly serious take it out and roll it in your hands. If possible, look into a mirror and give yourself a big, goofy grin. Place it around the workplace to encourage teamwork rather than rivalry amongst competitive workers. Diffusing mandarin essential oil will further help create an atmosphere of harmony.

Loyalty

Use Dalmatian Jasper around the house to strengthen family ties by gridding it around the perimeter of the home or placing a sphere where the family spends time together. Wearing Dalmatian Jasper will help you attract loyal friends as well as ensure you always consider their best interests. It will also help you sense if someone is acting in an untrustworthy manner. Keep it near your computer or take it to meetings and seminars to help you see through financial scams.

As a crystal of loyalty, it helps you persevere with long-term goals. Cleanse and program the crystal to your goal and as you pick it up each morning to carry or wear, affirm what your goal is starting with words like, "Today I will..." If you smoke, Dalmatian Jasper helps you remain committed to your decision to quit. Carry it in your pocket and each time you feel stress or cravings, hold the crystal in your receptive hand and take eleven deep breaths.

Dogs

Dalmatian Jasper helps you connect with dogs. Working with Dalmatian Jasper will allow you to understand their behaviours as well as strengthen telepathic links. Anyone who has a fear of dogs should carry or wear the stone daily, especially when confronting the fear. It is undoubtedly the ultimate stone for dogs themselves, helping them feel happy and nurtured. Putting a small piece on their collar or in their bed will encourage a loyal and loving friend.

Dalmatian Jasper instils in others the ability to care for dogs as well as all other animals. If you are aware of an individual or establishment not caring properly for their animals gift them a piece of this Jasper, grid it around their perimeter and create a power grid using Dalmatian Jasper as the power crystal. Surround this by eight Clear Quartz points facing outwards and add supportive crystals like Rose Quartz for love, Black Tourmaline for trans-mutation and Amethyst or Royal Aura Quartz for deepened understanding.

JASPER, LEOPARDSKIN

Patience / Wellbeing / Shamanism / Cats

Leopardskin Jasper is a unique variety of Jasper found in a variety of reds, yellows and blues. It has distinct spots on it, similar to that of a leopard, hence its name. If life's complexity is becoming overwhelming, allow Leopardskin Jasper to get you back to basics. Leopardskin Jasper nurtures the base chakra and ignites within you the primitive survival instincts that have been part of humankind since the dawn of time. It improves perception and awakens dormant hunting instincts. This will enable you to remain focused on what is important and ignore unnecessary distractions. It will also rids you of preconceived ideas and allows you to see things as they truly are.

Animal: Leopard
Plant: Catnip
Astrological Correspondence: Saturn
Power Day: Saturday
Cleanse with: Earth or hold against a purring cat.

Your Crystal Alignment Meditation

Go and spend time with a cat. You may like to play a game or sit and stroke her. Connect to her energy. Tune in to the loving, wild, independent energy of the cat. If she starts purring and is agreeable, place her against your body to feel the healing vibrations. What can you learn from this friend? When you are ready, connect with your crystal.

Patience

Like a cat slowly and persistently stalking its prey, Leopardskin Jasper teaches patience. It has a magnetic energy and when programmed is able to attract things to your life. However, it has a tendency to draw to you what you actually need, not what you think you need or want. If you are seeking your soul mate, engage the power of Leopardskin Jasper. To strengthen your ties, hold some catnip in your hand to warm it and then hold your soul mate's hand. They will be yours as long as the catnip is kept in a safe place. If you need a career change, Leopardskin Jasper will make it happen. Tune in to your Leopard guide to teach you to listen to your heart's desire, how to patiently wait until it's time to strike and how to behave appropriately.

Wellbeing

If you are not at your peak health this crystal will draw into your life whatever you need for physical healing. If a pet is sick, placing Leopardskin Jasper nearby will help them heal. Wearing Leopardskin Jasper against the skin for a long period of time allows you to feel safe and comfortable in the skin you're in. This can have a follow-through effect of eliminating toxins, decreasing body odour and clearing the skin of anything from eczema to bites and stings leaving you looking vibrant and youthful. Leopardskin Jasper harmonises with any form of dance, tai chi or rhythmic practice so combine the two when you need grounding.

Leopardskin Jasper can help you deal with pain from the past. It allows you to overcome childhood trauma and breaks away mental conditioning of cults or dominating regimes. Take it with you to any therapy or healing session.

Shamanism

Leopardskin Jasper allows you to connect with the teaching of the shamans. It allows you to shift to altered states of consciousness and connect with the spirits of this world and others. Leopardskin Jasper also helps with all forms of shape shifting. If you need to become something you are not, such as take on a management role you're not comfortable with, keep Leopardskin Jasper in your pocket and ask it to guide you along the way.

Let Leopardskin Jasper introduce you to your animal guides. Put on some drumming music, hold Leopardskin Jasper in your receptive hand, close your eyes and relax. Visualise yourself standing in a wild and natural place such as a jungle. You hear a rustle and an animal comes towards you. Interact with this animal in whichever way feels appropriate. You may stay in the same location or accompany your guide elsewhere. Take note of the animal and where it takes you, as there are messages for you there. The animal will be a guide for you at this point in your life to offer you direction and support.

Cats

Cats are believed to be the most spiritually perceptive of all animals. Thus, Leopardskin Jasper, being so energetically close to cats, enhances your own spiritual perception. It allows you to intuitively connect and communicate with animals. Anyone working with animals should wear or carry a piece. Leopardskin Jasper will strengthen the bond between an animal and children. Give it to a child if they fear animals, especially due to a past bad experience. To deepen your personal connection with your cat, hold Leopardskin Jasper in one hand and stroke your cat with the other. Giving your cat catnip works to enhance your psychic bond with each other.

Leopardskin Jasper is a very powerful conservation stone especially for areas where the big cats live. If you care for the plains of Africa, the Amazon rainforest, or the domain of Tiger through Asia, create a power grid using Leopardskin Jasper as the power crystal. Suggested supporting crystals include Black Onyx for protection at night and Unakite for preservation and successful breeding. If you are fortunate to live or travel to one of these regions, charge a stone with your loving desires for the wellbeing of the big cats and bury it in the ground. You can also leave a stone near a zoo enclosure to resonate an energy motivating others to take proactive steps for big cat conversation.

JASPER, RED

Grounding / Base Chakra / Simplicity

Around the world, Jasper is found in a range of earthy colours. Due to its abundance, many civilizations have used Jasper for health, stability and fearlessness. Red Jasper is particularly popular as it guides you towards simplicity and improves your ability to ground yourself. It is a popular safety crystal as it allows you to remain sensible and avoid danger. It is also a crystal of justice, working to return everything back to a state of order.

Animal: Rhinoceros
Plant: Cedar
Astrological Correspondence: Mars
Power Day: Tuesday
Cleanse with: Earth, especially mud or clay

Your Crystal Alignment Meditation

Go and find some mud or clay. Immerse your hands or feet into its coolness. Rather than being concerned about getting dirty, consider the uses. Animals use mud for protection from the sun and eat it for its mineral content. Clay is used to make pottery and in beauty products. Connect with the clay and sense what it can offer you. When you are feeling grounded, connect with your Jasper.

Grounding

Red Jasper guides you to "keep your feet on solid ground" in an uplifting and positively energising way. Keep it in your pocket so it may settle your thoughts and emotions at times of distress. Make a grounding oil by placing a Red Jasper and a few drops of cedar essential oil in a carrier oil. Leave for an hour then anoint your feet, hands and forehead.

Red Jasper stops you getting flustered, ensuring you hold yourself with eloquence and grace. Its nurturing ability helps you feel secure and protected. It can assist in the healing of any adrenal or allergy issues that develop from feelings of being unsafe. Use Red Jasper as a "worry stone." Keep it outside, sit with it daily and tell it your worries, feeling your troubles vanish into the stone. Leave it outside on the earth to cleanse until the next day. You can use this same technique for sickness.

Base Chakra

Red Jasper nurtures a balanced base chakra. When your base chakra is balanced you feel grounded, settled and able to adapt within this changing world. You understand your place and purpose in the world and do not struggle with day-to-day living. You possess a sense that you have all you need in all areas of your life. Take time each day to rest with your Red Jasper between your legs, close to your body. Visualise a vibrant red sphere of energy glowing from the base of your spine. Carry a piece in your pocket and use as an elixir for continual balance each day.

Simplicity

Red Jasper allows you to understand to virtues of simplifying your life. It will prompt you to explore which responsibilities, activities or even material items do not aid your higher purpose. Anything that no longer makes you happy isn't serving you and can be removed to allow you to focus on what is important. Hold Red Jasper in your receptive hand and visualise a sword in the other. See yourself cutting away your bonds to these extraneous things. Give yourself permission to release your attachment to these things. Thank them for the roles they have played in your life, the lessons they have brought and let them go. Allow your attention to start shifting to its natural state of peaceful bliss. Allow Red Jasper to let you savour the experience of simplicity, where you are free from life's demands. With Red Jasper you can shed all the roles you play and simply be.

Red Jasper promotes the health of the essentials of all life. Heal the soil by burying a charged crystal in the earth. To bring rain, take a bowl of water outside and stir it clockwise using a Red Jasper while contemplating the abundance of the earth. When you are ready, call to the skies, "I call the rains to fall upon my head! Heavens, shed your tears so your children may be fed." As you do so, throw the water into the air above you and look up as if it is raining. Sense a feeling of gratitude for the universe and if your intentions are in earnest, rain will come soon.

Red Jasper helps you remain level-headed. As you work with Red Jasper, you'll start to obtain mental solidarity and a firm constitution, believing in equality and fairness. Call on your Rhinoceros guide to help you keep your feet planted firmly on the ground, allowing you to treat everyone as they deserve. When you witness injustice, work with Red Jasper. Place it on top of legal documents or gift it to an underdog to empower them to campaign for their rights. Use it in grids to empower timid animals to defend themselves and protect their territory. Be careful using it with young animals though, as they may get overly aggressive. Whenever you need support to return everything back to a state of order, call upon archangel Raguel, the guardian of justice. Hold your Red Jasper between your hands in prayer position and share with him your request.

JET

Unwanted Aspects / Stillness / Past Life Regression / Vibration Match

Jet has long been prized as a powerful amulet for protection and healing. It is used to protect from all evils, from physical illness and conditions such as depression, to spiritual challenges such as psychic attack, demons or any other form of negative energy. Jet will also help you deal with the grief of the death of a loved one, including pets. It plays a symbolic role in Wiccan traditions and High Priestesses will often wear necklaces of Jet with Amber, symbolising the dualities of life.

Animal: Okapi
Plant: Poppy
Astrological Correspondences: Ixion and Pluto
Power Day: Saturday
Cleanse with: Earth at night

Your Crystal Alignment Meditation

Go to a small island, where no one else can be seen or heard, or visualise yourself there. Consider what it would be like to be totally alone, isolated and still. Connect with this feeling of solitude. Does it bring up negative thoughts or feelings? How can you resolve these? Once you feel at peace being alone, connect with your Jet.

Unwanted Aspects

Jet helps to remove your own unwanted energies or urges. If you are having vengeful, angry or jealous thoughts, visualise them soaking into your Jet as you hold it in your projective hand. When dealing with grief from a death or loss, carry a Jet palm stone and rub it to bring you comfort. Keep it in your wallet to ensure you are wise with money. If you are focusing on saving, getting out of debt or are a self-confessed shopaholic, Jet will help to remind you of your financial goals each time reach for your credit card. This can also help with lower back pain that has manifested from a fear of financial support. As you work with Jet to become more financially responsible, you will feel more secure and your back issues should vanish. A lower back massage using a piece of Jet will also help dispel pain.

Jet is associated with the Pan; the wild Greek god with the legs and horns of a goat. Pan offers protection, guides you back to nature, sweeps away bad luck or bring back your confidence. Pan is the perfect consort when confronting any phobia. Clutch your Jet and invoke him by saying, "Pan, Pan, take my hand. Lead me to a safer land."

Stillness

When you are able to still yourself, you allow circumstances to play out before you without your influence. This ability can be rather insightful in revealing the true nature of others. Try this when you suspect someone is lying to you. Instead of replying immediately, pause. Often guilty people will feel the need to fill the void of silence. If you have a tendency to rush in to situations without examining the big picture, Jet can help you master stillness. Wear Jet over your chest and hold it while taking six breaths before acting.

Jet allows you to master the art of invisibility. This does not necessarily mean that you physically vanish so that no one sees you when you are standing right before them. Have you ever walked into a room, a party or a shop and gone unnoticed? This too is invisibility. It is simply the power to be present in a space but undetected. Hold Jet in your receptive hand and focus on each of your inhalations, drawing your aura in towards you. As you practise, you'll improve your ability to become invisible. When you are ready to release your aura again, breathe out quickly six times. An old technique uses poppies for invisibility. Soak poppy seeds in wine for fifteen days, and then drink the wine for five days while fasting. This tradition purports that you will then have the ability to turn invisible at will.

Past Life Regression

Use Jet to scry and awaken past life memories. Before starting to scry, state your intention that you wish to evoke past life memories, then gaze into the reflective black sheen and allow yourself to regress. If someone else is leading you in regression, hold a Jet in each hand. Taking a few drops of poppy flower essence can help facilitate journeying, as will burning poppy or opium incense.

Vibration Match

Okapi's quiet and illusive nature is the key to his survival. When you work with your Okapi guide in combination with Jet you can master the ability to release your desires and want for nothing. Learn to become still occasionally in your life and observe what happens. Don't contact anyone or book appointments, just take some time out. This opens you up to allowing the universe to provide you with a clear reflection of your true internal state. The behaviour of energy is that vibrations of the same frequency resonate with and draw towards each other, commonly expressed as "like attracts like" energy. In other words, you will draw towards you that which is a vibrational match to your current state of being. This is a powerful indication on where you are upon your path of spiritual growth. One simple example is the people who contact you first will be an indication of who is currently at a vibrational match to you. These are the people who most value what you contribute to their life. If you attract complaining, negative people this is a reflection of your own attitudes. If this is the case, you may want to look at what you can do to change your way of being so that you are attracting optimistic and pleasant people into your life. Meditate with Jet, asking it to dispel your own negative attitudes and help you progress along your spiritual path.

KUNZITE

Soul Love / Serenity / Optimism

Kunzite is possibly the highest vibrational and potent pink crystal currently available to humanity. The frequency of Kunzite is pure and strong and should be chosen only after you have "done your work" in relation to matters of the heart. In other words, ensure you have healed all past pains and let go of all hurt from previous relationships. Kunzite will open your heart to new levels, allowing you to take risks that make you feel extremely vulnerable. In return though you will feel an elated connection to a higher, unconditional, universal love. This will enable you to manifest mutually beneficial relationships in your life, including those that support your soul path.

Animal: Lovebird
Plant: Rose
Astrological Correspondences: Cupido, Juno, Psyche and Venus
Power Day: Friday
Cleanse with: Earth, especially placed near flowers.

Your Crystal Alignment Meditation

Go to a peaceful place in nature. Close your eyes, ensure your spine is straight and place your hands on your heart. Tune in to the beating of your own heart for a few minutes, allowing all other noises to slip away. Now start to see a glowing pink light, emanating from your heart centre. With each beat, it grows stronger and more radiant. Allow it to start to spread over your body. This pink light balances and heals your body, mind and spirit. Now start to spread this pink light beyond yourself offering healing to your surroundings. Spread this out further, affecting your whole country, then the whole planet and out to the universe. Finally connect with the healing, balancing nature of all that is. You are now ready to connect with your Kunzite.

Soul Love

If you are ready to attract your soul mate, Kunzite is the crystal for you. Take time to write down exactly what you are looking for to ensure you are clear on what you seek. Do not rush this process as the universe will provide you with what you ask for, but not always in the form you expect. Following this, wear Kunzite over your heart. It will connect with your heart's desire and draw a soul mate to you.

You can take other steps with Kunzite to prepare your life for the arrival of your soul mate. Organise your bedroom, making room for them on one side of the bed, clearing one of the bedside tables exclusively for their possessions. Place a Kunzite on each bedside table to compliment this action. You can also create a power grid with Kunzite as the power crystal. Add supporting crystals that symbolise traits you are looking for. Consider Citrine for happiness, Jade for generosity, Morganite for fairness, Thulite for sexuality, Watermelon Tourmaline for open-mindedness and Spurrite for a sense of humour. Include rose essential oil in your life, as it is one of the highest vibration oils available and will help lift you to where you need to be to attract a soul mate. Lovebirds are renowned for their devoted monogamous pairing and as a guide will help you align yourself to enjoy a truly fulfilling, long-term relationship.

Kunzite connects you with the joys of kissing. Ancients believed that a kiss connected two peoples' souls as the spirit was carried in the breath. Kunzite promotes this soul connection, encouraging you to savour the sensuality of kissing and maintains its importance as your relationship matures. It can also help make you a better kisser, especially if you are nervous about a first kiss. It soothes anxiety and increases your receptiveness to allow equivalent kissing styles.

Use Kunzite to reinforce bonds with your children, parents or spouse. Wear it and work with it regularly when Juno is retrograde as this is when relationships in your life are tested. Since it strengthens connection between parents and children, it is a beautiful baby shower gift. Initially it encourages the formation of healthy bonds and as the child grows older, it maintains mutual respect and communication. As the child becomes more independent, Kunzite will prevent parents being too restrictive or possessive, while ensuring the teenager respects their parents and is a harmonious contributor of the household.

Serenity

Kunzite has a calming energy, and making a gem elixir before interviews and exams will be beneficial. Use a Kunzite wand or tumbled stone in massage to help ease muscle tightness. Place Kunzite on your desk to prevent others bringing their personal life into the workplace. It is also works to keep yourself and others calm in traffic or crowds. If you are breeding animals, use Kunzite to maintain pregnancy in animals that are pregnant for the first time and ease their aggression towards offspring.

Optimism

Keep Kunzite close to maintain an optimistic outlook about life. It allows you to see the best in all people and situations. This enables you to treat others in a manner that encourages them to rise to their full potential. Kunzite is a good choice for a lost soul who no longer has any direction in life. Use it in prayer that they may find their way or gift it to them so its energy may allow them to discover their path again.

Kunzite is a balancing crystal that ensures you always look after your own wellbeing. If worn on your receptive side it lessens the likelihood of immoral temptations coming into your life and when worn on the projective side of the body, prevents you behaving in a self-destructive manner. Charge a Kunzite to remove lying, violence, bullying and gossip from your life and keep it by you at all times.

Kunzite allows you to embrace change. When you have moved to a new neighbourhood or country, grid it around your home to fill the air with feelings of acceptance and peace for your new location. Work with this crystal when you want to look for something new and exciting that will feed your true self. Wear it around your neck to get your mind ticking and allow you to make wise and progressive choices upon your path.

KYANITE, BLUE

Balance / Adaptability / Recall

Your natural state is one of equilibrium and harmony but daily interactions, events and experiences can cause you to lose this inner balance and either swing to an overly euphoric or depressed state. Kyanite works to counteract these unbalancing factors and allows us to remain centred. Kyanite is one of the few crystals that doesn't need cleansing as it neither accumulates nor retains energy that is not its own. This characteristic is passed on to you, leaving you feeling tranquil and poised.

Animals: Fox and Platypus
Plant: Strawberry
Astrological Correspondences: Neptune and Uranus
Power Day: Thursday
Cleansing: Does not need cleansing

Your Crystal Alignment Meditation

Go for a walk in the woods or visualise the trek in your mind. Find a sacred place to call your own here. Sit and take in the surroundings. Now practise your adaptability. Choose one thing in the woods. A single tree, a rock, maybe an insect. Change your energy so that you are like that object. Feel the power of the tree, the strength of the stone or the resolve of the insect. Once you feel a connection, try the same activity with another object. Eventually you want to sense an overall connectedness with everything in the woods, and then the entire Earth. Then you are ready to connect with your Kyanite.

Balance

Kyanite's energy balancing ability makes it the perfect all-round choice for forms of energy healing. It can be used to balance any of your chakras, your aura or energetic subtle bodies. Take time to rest, placing Kyanite on your base chakra and take a few moments to visualise the glowing red sphere of light that is this chakra. Repeat for all the other chakras, moving the Kyanite into position each time. For an overall auric healing, take a Kyanite wand or shard and slowly move it over your body keeping a distance of about 15 centimetres. When focusing on balancing work, you may like to work with your Platypus guide. Her lessons are complex but valuable. At first, she will often encourage you to take private time to get to know yourself and truly accept yourself and your quirks. Once you are confident with your identity, Platypus teaches you to balance your feminine side, regardless of your physical gender, and to nurture the gentle, caring side of your personality. This is a timely lesson in this masculine dominated world. Platypus can easily find her way through the realm of water, which governs emotions, and she can help you navigate through emotional troubles and find emotional balance. Your emotions are balanced once you are in touch with them but they do not control your behaviour.

Adaptability

As you develop your relationship with Kyanite, you will find your ability to remain balanced in all situations improves. Charge Kyanite and wear it near your throat. It dispels nervousness and fears associated with socialising, allowing you to remain relaxed and think clearly. It will improve your ability to adapt and integrate into different settings as well as converse with a diverse range of people on any subject. Kyanite helps you think on your feet and offer creative answers to tricky questions, making it a great crystal for presenters and public speakers. Invite your Fox guide to join you in these situations, for he is the master of adaptability, being able to prosper in any environment. If you don't want to wear Kyanite every day, keep pieces in your wardrobe. It will charge your clothes, allowing you to still take advantage of its energy. A lack of adaptability can manifest physically as problems with your elbows. If this is the case, tape or hold two pieces of Kyanite, one blue and one green, to the area.

Kyanite when combined with strawberries can help you adapt from single to coupled life. All relationships will require you to compromise and adapt. Place Kyanite near a strawberry scented candle in the centre of the home to promote loving harmony. Also regularly include strawberries in your diet and feel them open you up to these possibilities. Allow their energy to remind you of the fruitfulness of love and to abandon trivial habits that will hinder your opportunity to cherish these experiences.

Recall

Kyanite allows you to deflect distractions and focus the mind. Use Kyanite to jog your memory. If you are trying to recollect a word or a name hold Kyanite against your forehead. Place it with your childhood photos then hold it in your hand to bring back memories of your earlier years. Kyanite can be used to increase dream recall. Furthermore if you have a vivid dream that continues to play on your mind after waking, meditate with Blue Kyanite in your receptive hand or against your third eye chakra to help unveil the dream's message. When doing dream work you can invite Platypus to aid you. As an aquatic animal, she can teach you to delve deep into your subconscious to understand your dreams' hidden messages.

LABRADORITE

Independent Thought / Creativity / Adventure

Labradorite is a crystal for the seeker. Its luminescent shine inspires optimism within and shields you from negative naysayers who try to convince you that your dreams are not possible. Labradorite summons you to look within and ask yourself what you really want to do. The Inuit people tell the tale of a great warrior who once struck his spear into a Labradorite, releasing many of the lights to become the famed Northern Lights. Labradorite is here to help you shine your lights on the world.

Animal: Crow
Plant: Juniper
Astrological Correspondences: The star Arcturus and asteroid Lilith
Power Day: Monday
Cleanse by: Placing outside in nature on the new or dark moon or under the lights of Aurora Borealis or Aurora Australis.

Your Crystal Alignment Meditation

Go and sit beneath the dancing lights of Aurora Borealis or Aurora Australis. Watch the lights dance across the sky and as they do so allow them to enlighten your own inner light. Feel them brighten your disposition, allowing balance and harmony to dwell within you. Now you are ready to connect with your Labradorite.

Independent Thought

Labradorite encourages you to look within for answers rather than blindly believing what you are told by others. By querying and questioning commonly held beliefs, majority opinions or long standing norms you enable yourself to become a free thinker who can think outside the square. Wear Labradorite every day to embolden you to turn off the TV, visit places you've never been before and converse with others that respectfully disagree with your current beliefs. It will remind you to consider not just what someone is saying, but also their motivation for saying it. This increased awareness will quicken your personal growth. If you are starting a new venture that is creative, unique or designed to promote awareness, place a Labradorite sphere in the centre of the space to help encourage others to comprehend your message.

Creativity

As Labradorite encourages you to think outside the square it enables your creativity to expand. You'll experience original inspirations that resonate with humanity's heartbeat. Composers, playwrights and creative writers should harness Labradorite's powers. To birth a new idea, sit outside at night ideally on the night of the new moon. Hold your crystal in your receptive hand and start focusing on your breath. Once you feel centred and focused, allow ideas to start to flow. If you need to rush inside to start recording the ideas, keep the Labradorite with you. Place it on your desk, piano or wherever you do your creative work. As you sleep, put Labradorite in your pillowslip and pay attention to your dreams. Labradorite can encourage you to receive spiritual messages while you sleep since this is when you are least resistant to receiving guidance. Tuning into your Crow guide can also be advantageous. Crow teaches you how to create new things from nothingness.

Adventure

Working with Labradorite causes you to become more curious about the world. It incites a sense of adventure, as your desire to see, know and experience more is brought to life. This inquisitiveness can be heightened when the asteroid Lilith goes retrograde, so keep your Labradorite close by at this time. Labradorite resonates with the Fool card in the tarot and encourages you shake off perceived responsibilities and discover new options for your life. Labradorite inspires you if you are suffering from feelings of hopelessness and depression, replacing them with enthusiasm and confidence. Keep a Labradorite in your pocket and when you feel down, take it out and say, "Magical crystal, shimmering stone; bring me adventure I can call my own." In the next 24 hours accept any reasonable invite you receive as it can lead to an uplifting experience. A lack of love for life can manifest as warts. Combine traditional wart treatment with holding Labradorite and affirming "I love my life" can help lessen their occurrence.

Don't be surprised if Labradorite has you planning travel somewhere. Keep your Labradorite with you and surround yourself with the scent of juniper as you set off on your adventure. They both help you keep a clear mind and protect you against misfortune or injury. The energy of Arcturus, a bright golden red star situated in the constellation Boötes, harmonises with Labradorite. This star is connected to recognition and honour, especially through navigation or travel. Connect with it in the night sky and study its meaning in your astrology chart to unveil how you may uncover prosperous times upon your adventures.

LAPIS LAZULI

Third Eye Chakra / Vision / Honesty / Air Quality

Lapis Lazuli looks like an evening sky filled with sparkling stars. It is a stone containing primarily Lazurite (blue), Calcite (white) and Pyrite (Gold). Lapis Lazuli was being mined in Afghanistan as early as the 7th millennium BC. It was used for the eyebrows on the funeral mask of King Tutankhamun. In the middle ages it was exported to Europe and ground into ultramarine powder to be used the most important artists of the Renaissance and Baroque, and was often reserved for the clothing of the central figure of the painting, especially the Virgin Mary. If Lapis Lazuli were human, it would be a stern and powerful queen ruling her realm with complete control. This is the stone of royalty, leaders and the gods. It appears to have a unique attribute not characteristic of other stones. Whereas most crystals will help you alter your vibration to their level, lapis will not. Like the most commanding queen, Lapis Lazuli refuses to lower itself to your level. Rather she sits on her throne and waits patiently until you have aligned your energy with hers. Once you are at the same level, then Lapis Lazuli will reward you significantly, nurturing your intuition and strengthening your ability to control your life.

Animal: Cat
Plant: Sandalwood
Astrological Correspondences: Jupiter and Sirius
Power Day: Thursday
Cleanse with: Air or Starry Night; ideally place it outside on a starry night from the moment you see the first star until the final star vanishes the following morning.

Your Crystal Alignment Meditation

Go outside before sunrise. Face the east and relax, holding your crystal in your receptive hand. While it is dark and difficult to see, pay attention to your other senses. What can you smell and hear? As the sun starts to rise enjoy the colours spilling into the sky. Pay attention to how your body feels as the night fades making way for a new day. Feel the excitement and anticipation of new beginnings and opportunities. Share your desires with your crystal as you connect with it.

Third Eye Chakra

Lapis Lazuli nurtures a balanced third eye chakra. Signs that your third eye chakra is balanced include having a great memory, the ability to learn easily, a healthy imagination and good physical vision. A balanced third eye chakra also means you have accurate perception and inner vision. Lapis Lazuli stimulates this intuition, often choosing to bring you guidance in the form of images, rather than thoughts or sounds. During your meditations, place the Lapis Lazuli on your third eye. If holding it becomes bothersome, try putting it into a bandana or headscarf. Burn some sandalwood incense while doing intuitive or psychic work to enhance your ability to tune in to the vibrations of the spiritual realms. Once ready, breathe deeply and relax. Summon your guides and angels to aid and support you. You may want to sense an indigo blue lotus flower blooming from your third eye or a violet flame or light above your crown. Allow the veil of mystery to lift and reveal to you all the knowledge you seek. Now simply relax and allow any messages to flow to you.

You may start to feel pressure or tingling in the area of the third eye. Pay attention to your five senses. You may start to see a vision but can also hear a sound, even feel, taste or smell something that is not physically. Let go and don't strain to "see". Messages will happen when you when you are the most relaxed. To start with it may simply be a symbol, word or colour. Know that the third eye chakra and your psychic abilities are like a muscle. The more you practice and exercise this chakra with your Lapis Lazuli, the stronger your abilities will become.

Vision

Lapis Lazuli harmonises with your Cat guide. Working with both Cat and Lapis Lazuli will allow you to move towards independence so that you can take control of the success in your life, both professionally and personally. Lapis Lazuli heightens your awareness, increasing your ability to see opportunities and avoid problems. This newfound ability to see clearly can manifest physically, improving your eyesight, especially at night. To utilise this aspect of Lapis Lazuli's magic, wear it near your eyes or rest with it on your eyes each day. You can also place Lapis Lazuli in water for 24 hours and then combine one drop of the charged water for each eye with your eye cream in the morning.

Honesty

Being such an objective stone, Lapis Lazuli is used to reveal the truth. It can help you interpret the spoken and written word as well as spiritual messages you receive. If you need to find truth about a situation, meditate with a piece of Lapis Lazuli and anticipate a sense of knowingness to come to you. Lapis Lazuli is traditionally exchanged between partners as a sign of commitment and honesty in their relationships. If you need to have a "heart-to-heart" conversation with someone wear Lapis Lazuli over your chest and/or place it around the room where the talk will happen.

Air Quality

Lapis Lazuli works to promote the cleansing of air. Set up a grid to cleanse the air in your home or workspace. Find four indoor plants renowned for their air filtering skills such as aloe vera, spider plant, peace lily, Chinese evergreen or English ivy. Place them at the four sides of your house and place a lapis in the pots. Lapis Lazuli can also be used to strengthen any larger scale effort to reduce air pollution or repair the ozone layer.

LARIMAR
Ocean / Abundance / Communication / Atlantis

Larimar is a blue variety of Pectolite found exclusively in the Dominican Republic. Its beautiful colour resembles the crystal clear blue oceans surrounding the tropical Caribbean island from where it comes from. Larimar helps you find balance in your life and to ignore distractions that affect your inner peace and mission in life. Larimar reminds you of the lessons of the ocean. It teaches us that life is about the ebb and the flow, the give and the take. Larimar is also a strong protector of the truth and those that seek the truth.

Animals: Any ocean dwelling animal especially Dolphin and Seal
Plant: Seaweed
Astrological Correspondences: Earth and Neptune
Power Day: Friday
Cleanse with: Salt water ideally from the ocean

Your Crystal Alignment Meditation

Go to a tropical beach, or visualise yourself there in your mind. Feel the warmth of the sun on your skin and take a few deep breaths of the fresh, salty air. Take in the ocean as it expands before you to the horizon, enjoying the refreshing blue colour. You may like to take a cleansing swim to allow yourself to deepen your connection with the ocean. Consider the vastness of life teaming under the water's surface. Next, turn around and take in the profusion of animals and plants in the tropical forests that lay behind you. Once you're filled with a sense of abundance, connect with your crystal.

Ocean

The relationship between humans and the ocean is a deep one. It offers us the basic elements we need to survive. Ocean plants produce half of the world's oxygen, while the waters absorb nearly one third of human-caused carbon dioxide emissions. Oceans regulate our weather and form the clouds that gift us fresh water. Oceans are a source of food as well as recreation. They are the original source our ancestors evolved from millions of years ago. In many ways, we are like the ocean. A large portion of our body is water, and just as the moon affects the tides' ebb and flow, it also moves us.

When we reconnect with the ocean, we allow ourselves to receive life-giving healing. Larimar is the crystal to facilitate this healing. Hold Larimar against your chest and feel waves of healing relaxation wash over you. Scry with a thin slice, cabochon or pendant of Larimar held in front of a light or candle to reveal a mysterious underwater world. For a rejuvenating bath, take your Larimar into the tub and surround yourself with blue candles and sounds of the ocean and its creatures. Better still, swim in the ocean with your Larimar in hand to clear away all stress. You may find it helpful to connect with your Seal when using Larimar to heal. Seal teaches that when you feel drowned by emotions you need to come back to focusing on your breath.

Larimar is associated with the tides of the oceans and our ability to connect to these cycles. It also releases tension with its cooling energy. This makes it the perfect crystal for premenstrual syndrome (PMS). Simply rest with it upon the site of pain and wear it throughout the day to reduce irritability. You can also hold Larimar against a site of swelling to reduce inflammation, on your forehead for a fever, or against the skin for sunburn. You may find it helpful to connect with your Seal when using Larimar to heal. Seal teaches that when you feel drowned by your emotions you need to come back to focusing on your breath.

The wellbeing of our oceans is being challenged right now. Pollution and over fishing are having detrimental effects on oceanic ecosystems. Larimar fosters your connection to the spiritual aspect of the oceans, inspiring you to take action to ensure its livelihood. If you like to fish, carry Larimar to increase your sensitivity to the ocean, ensuring you only take what the ocean can provide and what you need. Take Larimar to the grocery store to encourage you to buy only sustainable seafood. Wear Larimar constantly to balance your feminine side, so that it makes you a caring and considerate individual, centred in the present and ready to make positive changes that benefit the ocean. Ask your Larimar to guide you on what actions you can take to ensure the ocean's future. Connect with any fish guide to receive guidance on what to do. Construct a power grid dedicated to the oceans with Larimar as the power crystal surrounded by six Clear Quartz points. Include supporting crystals such as Aquamarine or Malachite for detoxing pollution or Prehnite for removing rubbish.

Abundance

Larimar radiates tranquillity and constantly releases stress as if you are lying on a tropical beach soaking up the sunshine and listening to the sound of the waves. As you release hurt, fear, depression and pain, you open your life to exciting changes. Larimar washes away resistance and reminds you of the world's abundance, enabling you to allow goodness to come into your life.

Including seaweed in your diet will further facilitate healing and the allowance of abundance.

While holding your Larimar, contemplate an area of your life where you wish to see increased abundance. Visualise abundance flowing freely into this area of your life. What would it look like? How would it feel? Start to allow this picture of abundance to grow until it feels real. Let the Larimar work in harmony with you. It will dissolve any blockages that prevent the abundance you deserve coming to you.

The oceans are where life on Earth first appeared and thus the great Mother Ocean is the womb that births all new creations, all wishes, all desires that you request. Send your image of abundance out to the oceans. Know that here it will give your requests the energy they need and bring them back to you upon the tides of time. Know that your wish has been received and heard. Now, keep Larimar with you to ensure you act in a manner that will allow that abundance to come to you. Wear it over your heart if you wish to attract an abundance in lovers so that you may pick out your soul mate. Work with your Seal guide to give you a playful and flexible manner, increasing your ability to draw abundance.

Communication

The natural ebb and flow of Larimar's energy works to keep your throat chakra balanced. When this chakra needs soothing because you are too vocal, Larimar quietens you down. When the chakra needs stimulating so you can express yourself better, Larimar gives you waves of confidence. A balanced throat chakra will enable you to say things to others that may be slightly uncomfortable in some circumstances. It gives you guidance to phrase messages in a way that is more acceptable the listener. To meditate on maintaining a balanced throat chakra, rest with Larimar on your throat while visualising a blue sphere of light glowing in the area. Wearing it around your neck helps keep your throat chakra balanced throughout your day. Your Dolphin guide can also support you in listening more and speaking in a positive manner in order to manifest positive outcomes in your life.

Larimar encourages you to expand your knowledge about the world, enabling you to be able to converse with a wide variety of people of all ages, beliefs and backgrounds about a diverse range of topics. It will support you in exploring different viewpoints, beyond your current beliefs. As a strong protector of the truth, Larimar will always create opportunities for you to gain a better understanding of the world. It helps to break down old paradigms and restrictive attitudes in favour of new, more universal and harmonious ones. Not only can it strengthen communication with other people but it also facilitates communication with aquatic animals such as dolphins, seals and whales.

Atlantis

Psychic and prophet Edgar Cayce spoke of a soft blue crystal used in Atlantis as a powerful healing tool before he died in 1945. A crystal matching his description unveiled itself to the world in 1974. It was Larimar. Since its discovery many people have found that Larimar takes you back to the time of this ancient civilisation. Use it in meditation or past life regression to unveil Atlantean wisdom that you can use for healing and advancement in the current day. Larimar can help ensure our current society that we do not make the same errors as the Atlanteans. It helps ensure humanity lives in harmony with nature, rather than trying to manipulate it and thus Larimar can be used to support campaigns against genetic modification, altering weather cycles and so on. You can also use this crystal as a key to connect with other Atlantean beings such as the mer-people, centaurs and unicorns.

LEMURIAN SEED CRYSTAL

Lemuria / Oneness / Peace

In 1999 an unusual group of Quartz points were found lying separate in a bed of sand, rather than the natural form as grown in grouped clusters. Unusual as this is, the appearance of these crystals is even more striking. They are not clear and shiny, but rather have a frosted appearance and striations running across them. Legend has it that these crystals were broken from clusters during the time of Lemuria and programmed to hold their knowledge. It was anticipated that these Lemurian Seed Crystals and their knowledge would come to light at this time, in order for us to learn from their ways.

Animal: Turtle
Plant: Oak
Astrological Correspondence: Earth
Power Day: Monday
Cleansing: As these crystals have been programmed by the Lemurians, it is not recommended you cleanse them unless you want to remove the Lemurian wisdom held within. If you do feel the crystal has absorbed too much modern day energy or you simply want to use it like a regular Quartz point, place it outside on the earth.

Your Crystal Alignment Meditation

Go sit in nature, ideally in the southern hemisphere and allow your mind to drift back to the time of Lemuria. Place your hands on the ground and lift your head to the sky and invoke the wisdom of past cultures to come to you. Allow yourself to receive healing and guidance about the old ways of living in harmony with the Earth. When you are ready, connect with your crystal.

Lemuria

Lemuria was an ancient landmass believed to have existed in the Indian and Pacific Oceans, stretching to Madagascar in the west, South East Asia and Japan in the north, Hawaii and the Pacific Islands to the east as well as encompassing Australia and New Zealand. The Lemurians were highly evolved people, renowned for being caretakers of the Earth and living a very natural life in harmony with its cycles. They ate raw and fresh plant and seafoods, healed with crystals, and celebrated lunar and solar cycles. Lemurians lived in a peaceful and highly developed spiritual culture.

Wearing, carrying or gridding with a Lemurian Seed Crystal will aid you to reach your highest potential as a human, as well as aid the highest spiritual pursuits of humankind. This crystal gives you access to the ancient knowledge of how to live with nature giving your health the ultimate revamp, and leaving you feeling open-hearted and full of vitality.

Combine Lemurian Seed Crystal with guidance from your Turtle guide. In meditation, you'll be able to slow yourself down and access Lemurian wisdom. With practice, you will not only be able to obtain knowledge from the crystal but open yourself to contact with beings of other realms that existed on Earth in the Lemurian Age.

Oneness

Lemurian Seed Crystals teach us of the importance of unity. This Earth and all its inhabitants is one large macrocosmic organism, and what is done to one, affects all. The Lemurians taught that the key to advancement and evolution is love. This is not a conditional love to be shared with just those near to you, but rather each person upon the Earth must learn to love everyone simply for who they are. Wear a small Lemurian Seed Crystal over your heart to encourage you to open your heart to everyone you meet. Meditate and hold your crystal against your heart, breathing in its guidance and breathing out love to those you are yet to meet. Anyone doing healing of any kind should keep a Lemurian Seed Crystal close. It reminds you to look after yourself as well as others. As we are all connected, we all need to heal and evolve together, leaving no one behind.

Lemurian Seed Crystals prompt you to abandon thoughts of loneliness, neglect, isolation and separation. These crystals awaken your awareness of nature and remind you that in nature, nothing is alone. Everything is supported by the environment around it. Your Lemurian Seed Crystal will help reconnect you with nature. Wherever you are, you can find nature present and comforting, even if it is just a pot plant or bird passing by. To advance this connection further, take time to sit in nature with your crystal, running your fingers across the striations to activate it. Sit peacefully and eventually nature will start to speak to you.

Peace

Wherever there is love, there is peace, and Lemurian Seed Crystal brings both. The Lemurians lived in peace for a long time and gave us access to understanding how via these crystals. Substitute Lemurian Seed Crystals instead of Quartz points in your power grids devoted to peace or harmony to give an extra boost of harmonious energy. Charity and peace workers can receive guidance by holding the seed crystal against their forehead. When you are feeling defeated, overwhelmed, exhausted and that everything is hopeless, take a rest placing your Lemurian Seed Crystal over your solar plexus. Combine this with taking a few drops of oak flower essence or place an acorn next to the crystal and you will soon sprout new energy and determination.

Lemurian Seed Crystals are useful to bring peace to the sick. Use Lemurian Seed Crystals in healing, visualising a white laser coming from the crystal's point and cutting out disease. For those that are dying, a seed crystal by the bed can offer comfort to both the person dying and those caring for them.

LEPIDOLITE
Soothing / Crown Chakra / Wisdom

Lepidolite is a type of mica, consisting of many layers of hexagonal plates that look like the beautiful, sparkling scales of a fish. Often you may find yourself craving a crystal because of its properties, similar to when you crave a certain food due to its nutritional properties. Lepidolite is rich in lithium, which is what gives it the beautiful colour. Lithium is a stabilising element and is used to treat mood-swings in individuals who suffer from conditions such as bi-polar disorder. If you are feeling "all over the shop", you'll can benefit from the lithium energy within Lepidolite, as it will help calm and balance you.

Animal: Whale
Plant: Violet
Astrological Correspondences: Neptune and the constellation Cetus
Power Day: Thursday
Cleanse with: Water

Your Crystal Alignment Meditation

Go to the ocean or visualise yourself there in your mind. Watch the waves and breathe in the ocean's power. Notice the colours, the sounds, the smells. Feel the ebb and flow of the tides, similar to the ebb and flow of our lives, our energies and our life cycles. The strength of the water is something to observe with awe. The ocean is our primordial Mother. This is where all life originally came from and so much life still resides within her. Sit with the ocean until you feel as one. For the brave, take a swim and truly immerse yourself within the Mother. Once you are feeling cleansed and balanced, connect with your Lepidolite.

Soothing

Allow the soothing nature of Lepidolite to call you at times when you are feeling overwhelmed by pressure or stress. It allows smooth transitions during major life events such as moving house, career-changes, break-ups and death. Wear Lepidolite for extended times to quieten your mind and settle scattered energy. During times of extreme stress hold Lepidolite in your receptive hand and take seven deep breaths. Adding the scent of violets to your space or as a perfume will also allow you receive clear guidance on how to handle your stress as well as ease any healing process. A sachet of violet flowers carried with you can add luck to your life.

Lepidolite is renowned for reducing the negative impacts of pollution, radiation and X-rays on your health. Keep a piece in rooms that contain many electronic devices such as computers, microwaves and televisions. Tape a piece to your mobile phone or computer tablet. If going for an X-ray or working in health facilities that use X-rays, carry or wear Lepidolite. Take some time to use Lepidolite to purify areas around you that are suffering from the effects of pollution. You can either hold Lepidolite while visualising sending white light to the area, or charge the Lepidolite to help the Earth cleanse the area and then bury the crystals within the polluted ground.

Crown Chakra

Lepidolite soothes an overactive crown chakra. When this chakra is overactive you can feel disconnected from the physical world and struggle connecting with people. You may even have issues with your pineal gland, experienced unusual encounters in other realms or been prescribed psychiatric medication. Take time each day to rest with your Lepidolite placed by the crown of your head. Focus on your breathing and visualise a soft violet ball of energy radiating in the area. Continue to carry or wear Lepidolite with you throughout each day.

Wisdom

As your relationship with Lepidolite develops and you find yourself calmer overall, you will start to allow clear and honest spiritual experiences to enter your life. Lepidolite allows you to release old behaviours, habits and beliefs and embrace a new, more spiritually in-tune way of living. Program Lepidolite to attract new people that support your new way of life. It is a great stone for this reason, for city-dwellers, who are ready to start reconnecting with nature.

If you are beginning your spiritual journey, it will allow you to screen out any negativity and find trust in that which is of benefit for you. As your journey continues, Lepidolite will help facilitate astral travel, dream work, rebirthing and accessing akashic records. It will help you fall into deeper meditation and acquire ancient knowledge while releasing any negativity from your past that is creating blockages now. Listen to the call of your Whale guide and descend to the depths of knowledge long held upon this planet. Then rise again with your own song to sing to the world.

Lepidolite offers special guidance to those born around 14 March. At this time the Sun passes out of Pisces for less than 24 hours and passes close to the constellation Cetus (the sea monster or whale), which dips into the Piscean constellation. Some astrologers view this as a separate star sign that exhibits different traits than other Pisceans. Lepidolite resonates with the energy of Cetus and through connecting with the crystal you are able to align yourself with the influences of this constellation.

LIBYAN DESERT GLASS
Action / Fear / Silent Warrior

Libyan Desert Glass was created similarly to the well-known Moldavite. However, instead of a meteorite crashing in the Czech Republic, it landed in the sands of the Western Desert (also known as the Libyan Desert) of Egypt, hence its yellow colour. Libyan Desert Glass gets the ugly duckling treatment compared to the popular Moldavite but both these Tektite are energy packed in different ways. Whereas Moldavite works on the heart centre to bring love to your life, Libyan Desert Glass stimulates your solar plexus with a focus on empowerment and strength. It helps you to overcome fears and phobias and spring into action, seizing opportunities to progress along your path.

Animals: Caracal and White Tiger
Plants: African Canary wood, Banana and Manuka
Astrological Correspondence: Sun
Power Day: Sunday
Cleanse by: Placing outside in the sunlight during the day, ideally on sand or at night during a meteor shower.

Your Crystal Alignment Meditation

Go to the desert or visualise yourself there in your mind. This is one of the harshest environments in the world and only the strongest can survive here. Connect with this strength, feel the heat of the sun and the might buried within the sand. Allow this to awaken your inner strength. Once you are ready, connect with your Libyan Desert Glass.

Action

Libyan Desert Glass eliminates procrastination and arouses motivation. Resistance is futile as you become flooded with ideas of proactive actions to take and an accompanying energy burst to fulfil them. Place a piece in the couch if you have a tendency to sit down and then never get up or simply hold it in your receptive hand when you are feeling apathetic. Working with your White Tiger guide will show you how to uncover, raise and commit to what you are passionate about, that which nourishes your soul. Once you are clear on what excites you, allow White Tiger to feed your passion while helping you make wise decisions on when to act and when to stay still.

Use Libyan Desert Glass for absent healing in either a group or solo situation. It will give extra strength to the energy sent as well as speed the positive effects for the receiver. Place a piece in the centre of a circle of golden candles and use this as a point of focus to project your healing energy before it transports to the desired person, animal or place. Incorporating African canary wood in the practice will give extra vigour to both the sender and receiver. Include the scent of manuka in your space for an added boost. The essential oil of this native New Zealand shrub helps bring enthusiasm and colour back to your life.

Fear

Libyan Desert Glass allows you to summon the inner strength needed to overcome a fear or phobia. Clasp a piece in your hand when facing a fear or feeling anxiety due to a phobia. Allow it to summon your inner strength and move beyond anything that holds you back from a life of fulfilment. Meditating under a banana tree while visualising yourself confronting your fear will help you overcome the fear more quickly.

Many metaphysicians believe that a fear of the future or desire to avoid something feared can keep coma patients in a coma longer. Libyan Desert Glass works to overcome this type of fear. Simply place the Libyan Desert Glass as close to the patient as possible to allow its energy to interact with the patients.

Silent Warrior

Libyan Desert Glass teaches the virtues of the Quiet Warrior. It resonates with the energy of the Hermit card of the major arcana in the tarot; the wise teacher who looks within for answers of the universe and receives guidance in silence. Wear Libyan Desert Glass over your solar plexus chakra and it will give you inner strength to walk your path of service. It will inspire you to devote your time and energy to work that results in the upliftment of humanity. Combine Libyan Desert Glass with working with your Caracal guide when you are faced with great work. Caracal can teach you how to do the impossible with grace and effortlessness.

Through meditation and constant wearing, Libyan Desert Glass helps to connect with other realms, extra-terrestrials and advanced consciousness. Combine Libyan Desert Glass with Nuummite for past life and akashic records work. This combination will allow you to break free from restrictions placed on you in a past life and advance further in this lifetime. This is especially powerful for past lives lived in Egypt, Libya or other countries in that region.

MALACHITE

Letting Go / Transformation / Embrace Life

Green crystals work with the heart centre and love. They will open you up to readily love, and be loved. Of all the green crystals though, Malachite is the one to choose when ready to deal with any issues of the heart. Whether you are still holding on to a past hurt, don't understand the reasons behind a past relationship deterioration or anything else that stops you moving towards new, loving relationships, Malachite is a crystal for you. Don't place Malachite in water for elixirs as it has a high Copper content. Working with polished tumbled stones or jewellery is safer. Some people have found that Malachite gives them heart palpitations and if this happens to you, replace with Rose Quartz.

Animal: Butterfly
Plant: Pine
Astrological Correspondences: Polaris and Venus
Power Day: Friday
Cleanse with: Earth

Your Crystal Alignment Meditation

Go for a boat ride down a stream or river or visualise the journey in your mind. Relax and enjoy the ride in the boat, noticing how easy it is to go with the flow of life. In life we can often try to "go against the flow" and we end up exerting a lot of energy and don't get very far. Acknowledge that sometimes it is okay to let go and trust the universe will lead you in the right direction. As you gently float downstream, allow yourself to let go of any inner resistance you are holding. Once you are ready, connect with your Malachite.

Letting Go

Malachite is not a crystal for the faint hearted! Like a big hand, Malachite reaches into the depths of your heart and pulls any issue to the surface. With Malachite you can step into the darkness, face fears or secrets you have been repressing and rid yourself of distractions that have held you back once and for all. It helps you rid your life of trauma and emotional pain from the past. Wear Malachite over your heart to allow you to identify secrets, deception and sabotage and understand clearly what has happened in the past. It also forces you to face what role you played in the proceedings. Fill your space with the scent of pine to promote both cleansing and clarity. If you fear you may not be ready for such an abrupt confrontation with love issues, or feel ill-equipped to deal with anything that comes up, pair Malachite with Rose Quartz to soften the journey while still healing the hurt.

Malachite works powerfully with the mantra "this too will pass". Hold your Malachite and recite this mantra as emotional issues bubble to the surface. Surround an image of the Egyptian god Anubis, who rules over endings, with Malachite on your altar if you are working on something major you wish to release. Holding Malachite will help remove blockages both physically and energetically during massage and other forms of bodywork.

Malachite helps you resist the urge to control people or situations. It allows you to release deep-seated feelings of helplessness and encourages you to have trust in the universe. Malachite can be beneficial for sufferers of Parkinson's disease, which can manifest from fear and extreme desire to control everything. Malachite encourages our body and the environment to release plutonium or uranium radiation. Grid Malachite around the house if you live near a nuclear reactor or nuclear weapons development and testing sites. Malachite used for this purpose will need to be cleansed regularly.

Transformation

Is it time your life had a makeover? Then Malachite is the crystal you need. Malachite consists of Copper, the metal of conductivity and movement, making this green crystal a catalyst for change. To choose to work with Malachite means you are choosing to take responsibility for your own life. As you let go of old ways that no longer serve you, Malachite gives you strength and determination to adopt a better way of being. Each day, pick up your Malachite to carry or wear and state, "I am the creator of my destiny". Take time each day to sit quietly and creatively visualise the future you are creating while holding your crystal. Connect to your Butterfly guide to facilitate transformation and the star Polaris for extra guidance on your new path.

Embrace Life

As you further your connection with Malachite, you become more willing to embrace life. Any time you feel depressed or anxious, taking time to sit with Malachite and examining its unique flowing green lines and circles will uncover the reasons for your distress. Speak your worries aloud to your Malachite and leave it outside on the earth overnight so your worries are absorbed away.

Malachite ensures the health of your arms and hands. Pain or injured arms and hands can result from an unwillingness to embrace life. Wear Malachite on the affected arm(s) to speed healing. Prescribing yourself ten hugs each day will also help healing.

MOLDAVITE
Gratitude / Spiritual Growth / Extra-Terrestrial Connection

Moldavite is probably one of the most famed higher vibration crystals, created when a meteorite crashed to Earth in the Czech Republic 14 to 15 million years ago. This impactite is shrouded in myths including that it was part of the crown of Lucifer and that the Holy Grail was made of Moldavite. Some people, while holding Moldavite, experience great heat, sweating or energy surges often termed the "Moldavite flush". Use Moldavite to reopen your heart to the world and remember that life is a beautiful gift.

Animal: Dolphin
Plant: Frankincense
Astrological Correspondences: The constellation Orion as well as the entire universe
Power Day: Monday
Cleanse with: Fire, singing bowl or place outside during a full moon or meteor shower.

Your Crystal Alignment Meditation

Go and sit outside beneath the stars. Choose one bright star and fix your gaze upon it. Focus on your breath, starting by exhaling all of the air out of your lungs until they are empty. Then, begin to inhale to a slow count of five, hold the breath at the top for five counts, exhale for a count of five, and then hold the breath at the end of your exhale again for a count of five. Continue this same breath work to a count of six (inhale for six, hold for six, exhale for six, hold for six). On the next round, try for a count of seven. Keep increasing the number until you find it too challenging. All a while keep focusing and connecting with the star. Once you are feeling at one with the universe, connect with your Moldavite.

Gratitude

Moldavite allows you to feel reconnected to the world and love for all of life through stimulating the heart chakra. Wear it over the heart or meditate with it against your chest whenever you are feeling unloved, unworthy and unappreciated, or have a hard time trusting others or accepting love. If you are unwilling to take a risk in love or tell someone how you feel, have begrudgingly accepted that you have no choice but to remain single or you constantly fall for people who are not interested in you, then Moldavite will start to counteract your fears of love. It will awaken your sense of self value and give you the gusto to dive into the adventures of loving relationships with others.

Moldavite is perfect when you are feeling defeated, bored or pessimistic about the future. It can help to bring people back from suicidal thoughts. Its uniqueness makes it the perfect crystal if you are struggling to find your place in the world. Work with Moldavite and focus on what you are grateful for in life. Make it a daily practice to write down ten things that you are grateful for as you hold your Moldavite. Continue to add to this list each day until you have reconnected with the joy of living.

Spiritual Growth

Moldavite is a spiritual catalyst, speeding change necessary for spiritual growth. When Moldavite comes into your life, you may experience major shifts in your career, relationships and life path. Simply wearing or carrying Moldavite can bring about change but there are other techniques to enhance its effects. Make Moldavite massage or anointing oil by placing a piece in a bottle of sweet almond oil and adding some frankincense essential oil. Try meditating outside with Moldavite placed on your crown chakra while gazing at the constellation of the warrior Orion. This constellation has held much importance for many civilisations, especially the ancient Egyptians. Allow it to awaken the spiritual warrior within you.

For an exhilarating meditation, lie outside at night in the pentagram position (on your back with arms and legs stretched out) with a Moldavite or other Impactites/Tektites/Meteorites at each point of your body (hands, feet and head). Gaze at the stars and allow yourself to be guided on a journey through the universe. This practice will help you connect with the universe as a whole and may bring you some insightful guidance. Ideally spend the whole night outside, allowing yourself to fall asleep under the stars. Not only can this lead to power dreams but it will also have a healing effect on your body's circadian cycles and natural biorhythms as you tune back into the natural flow of the universe.

Note that working with Moldavite can leave you feeling "spaced out" so at first you may need to limit your contact time. Also make sure you ground yourself properly afterwards by switching to a grounding crystal such as Black Tourmaline or Smokey Quartz, having something to eat and drink or walking barefoot outside on the earth. It is not a good idea to drive when in contact with Moldavite.

Extra-Terrestrial Connection

Moldavite can facilitate connection and communication with extra-terrestrials or beings of different dimensions such as angels, guides or Ascended Masters. Place Moldavite on your third eye chakra during meditation to heighten your vibration, promote inspiration and open yourself up to higher forms of communication with other sentient beings of the universe. Working with your Dolphin guide while using Moldavite can allow you to discover alternative forms of communication not commonly known to humanity but used by animals and beings of other realms.

Moldavite allows you to have contact with aliens while remaining safe. Create a mighty extra-terrestrial attraction grid using Moldavite as the power crystal. Surround this by eight Clear Quartz Crystals and use other stones from outer space including Libyan Desert Glass, Thailandite, Darwinite, Pallasite as well as other Tektites and Meteors. Adding a carved crystal alien skull will enhance the grid's power further. If you experience an alien visitation, keep hold of your Moldavite to ensure safety.

MOOKAITE

Gentleness / Travel / Spiritual Exploration

Mookaite is a colourful stone only found at Mooka Creek, Kennedy Ranges in northern Western Australia, it was often used by Indigenous locals to make blades and spearheads because it was sharp when broken. The Aboriginal term *Mooka* means "running waters" and refers to the numerous springs that feed into this area. And just like the many springs of Mooka Creek, many stunning shades of red, ochre yellow, mauve and creams make up Mookaite. Each of these colours adds to the stone's vibration. Mookaite grounds while also prompting spiritual exploration, especially of Indigenous cultural beliefs. It gives you a sense of solidarity and confidence as well as encouraging you to explore the world and discover your full potential.

Animal: Wombat
Plant: Buddha Wood
Astrological Correspondence: Jupiter
Power Day: Thursday

Your Crystal Alignment Meditation

Go and sit outside. It doesn't have to be somewhere special. Just outside your door. Sit in silence observing the aspects of nature around you. It may be the clouds, the wind in the trees, the birds or whatever you notice around you. Then become aware of the ground beneath you. Tune into rhythms of nature and see if you can sense the energy of the land upon which you are resting. You may feel a pulsing, vibration or an emotion come across you. Perhaps the land has a message for you today. Just relax and allow your bond with the land to grow. Feel the energy reach out and kiss your body. Finally pick up your Mookaite and see if holding the stone in your receptive hand changes your experience.

Gentleness

The earthy red colours in Mookaite help ground you, while the ochre yellow support the solar plexus chakra giving you a sense of steady strength. This combination of colours is great for soothing anxiety and fears. Simply by standing or resting on the bare earth with your Mookaite will have you feeling more grounded. As you feel more stable and safe, you'll notice a renewed sense of independence. As your reliance on others reduces, so will your expectations upon them. Your approach will become gentler and your focus will be on nurturing their contentment. More importantly, Mookaite assists you to become gentler on yourself, reducing the tendency to be over critical of yourself. For full effect, wear Mookaite for an extended period.

While the red and yellow energies of Mookaite centre your physicality, the colour properties of the mauve and cream reach towards your spiritual side. Thus, Mookaite not only fosters a grounding connection to the earth but also allows you attune to the spiritual consciousness of the earth right beneath your feet, especially in Australia. Often there is a belief that we must travel to famous sacred sites to experience the magic of this planet. However Mookaite shows us that you can find the magic everywhere, as close as your own backyard. To connect with the earth, place your receptive hand upon the land and hold you Mookaite in your projective hand against your stomach. To continue this earthly spiritual connection throughout your day, inhale Buddha wood essential oil while outside and continue to diffuse it inside your home to constantly sense the link you experienced.

Regular connection with the land where you live can offer you two-folded guidance. Firstly, as you start to experience the vibrations, you can tune into the wisdoms and healing available for Mother Earth. Indigenous people would use Mookaite to magically heal wounds, so if you have a cut or injury, place Mookaite on the site while sitting on the earth. Hernias that manifest from strain, burden or ruptured relationships in your life can also be supported with wearing Mookaite or by consumption of a Mookaite elixir. This stone settles the mind and allows you to find peace amidst the turmoil in your life. Mookaite also brings awareness of the relationship between the body and mind. It reveals your beliefs about aging and degeneration to the conscious mind. Meditation and work with Mookaite can allow a positive attitude and a youthful spirit to reduce the effects of aging on the physical body.

The second benefit from Mookaite facilitated earth connection is a greater understanding of what you can do to heal the land. Allow yourself to be guided so you can walk more gently upon the earth, reducing any destructive behaviours that can damage the environment. Thus, use Mookaite to encourage behaviours such as recycling, reducing your carbon footprint and avoiding using toxic chemicals. If you are doing major earth works on your property, place Mookaite through the ground to heal and settle the energies following the disruption.

To progress your earthly connection, tune into the lessons of your Wombat guide. He teaches you the strength that comes from knowing your environment. Wombat shows you how to be resourceful and that a determination to dig will uncover what you seek. With Mookaite promoting gentleness, Wombat reminds you that this does not mean you become a "push-over" and that it is important to stand up for what you believe in.

Travel

As Mookaite nurtures secure feelings of comfort and connection to the land, it inspires you to journey beyond your residence, to explore, connect and heal other places around the world. If you have the "travel bug", keep Mookaite near to support you in channelling your restless energy into making actionable plans.

Once your journey begins, Mookaite is a worthy travel companion. It helps you remain grounded and helps you deal with different surroundings and energies. As soon as you arrive in a new place, find a quiet place to sit. Hold your Mookaite in your hands or sit it at the base of your spine. Close your eyes and visualise a large root growing from the base of your spine and delving deep into the earth. Sense and feel the energy of the area, understand it, connect with it and become one with it. It will make you feel at home wherever you are and can also help counteract jet lag.

As you explore new places not only will Mookaite continue to facilitate connection to the earth but it will also help you witness the beauty of what is around you. Often when something is different from what we are used to at home we become judgemental. However Mookaite encourages you to look for deeper meanings and knowledge available to you in each new experience. Furthermore, the inspiring qualities of Mookaite will encourage you to take well-calculated chances to discover hidden opportunities without fear or paranoia of negative consequences. Mookaite reminds you to consider the beneficial outcomes possible from stepping outside of your comfort zone.

Australians travelling or moving abroad would do well to have Mookaite with them when they are feeling homesick. In contrast, if you are holidaying or migrating to Australia, Mookaite can help you adjust and adapt to the lifestyle by aligning you with the energies of the land.

Spiritual Exploration

The drive Mookaite gives you is not only to travel and sight-see, but to partake in spiritual exploration. This applies both when abroad, as well as in your life at home. Mookaite promotes an ageless spirit willing to accept change and seek new experiences. It promotes open-mindedness and helps you unveil a multitude of possibilities. However its grounding nature supports you to make a wise choice from the options before you. Therefore if you are trying to choose a date, job, investment or life path, hold Mookaite against your stomach and follow your gut decision, even if external circumstances suggest otherwise.

Mookaite helps you find balance between the importance of being active and experiencing life, helping you make time to process, introspect and learn from those experiences. Walking meditation or becoming present while being active as you carry Mookaite can have profound results. Also take time at the end of a day to sit out in nature and contemplate the greater importance of what you've experienced. Ask yourself what you have learned and whether this can be used to contribute to the betterment of humanity. Also use this time to consider whether current worries and anxieties are of importance, or will they, in the passing of time, become irrelevant and forgotten. If so, place your Mookaite on your heart and your hands on the earth, and allow the stress to be absorbed and rebalanced in the dirt below.

MOONSTONE, RAINBOW

New Beginnings / Full Moon / Divine Feminine / Travel

Throughout history, civilisations have looked to the moon as a symbol of the Great Mother or Goddess. The soft light of the moon spreads a nurturing and magical energy across the Earth each night. It is only fitting that the crystal that shares the beauty of the moon, also shares its similar energy and attributes. Moonstone is found in a range of colours from dark browns, greys and black, through peach and green to the purist white. The most dazzling of the white crystals have a magical, bluish lustre or glow below the surface of the gemstone. This variety is known as Rainbow Moonstone and possesses an energy that induces calmness, relaxation, contentment and inspiration in its guardian.

Animal: Snow Leopard
Plants: Frangipani, Moonflower and Thyme
Astrological Correspondence: Moon
Power Day: Monday
Cleanse with: Full moon

Your Crystal Alignment Meditation

Go and sit beneath the moon. See the moonbeams stretching out toward you, wanting to connect with you. Reach out to her with your energy, forging a connection. Bathe in her light and feel her loving energies awakening great power and wisdom within you. Once you sense synergy with the moon, connect with your Rainbow Moonstone.

New Beginnings

Rainbow Moonstone, like a protective mother, watches over new ventures of all kinds. If you are starting a new job, business or relationship, wear or carry Rainbow Moonstone to feel relaxed, guided and safe. It promotes new growth and when placed around the garden encourages the conservation of native butterflies, dragonflies and moths. Use Rainbow Moonstone in meditation or power grids to project love and white light to assist war-torn areas to rebuild.

Rainbow Moonstone is associated with fertility and childbirth. If a couple is struggling to fall pregnant, Rainbow Moonstone can be used in a powerful triplet to aid their efforts. Use Rainbow Moonstone to strengthen the health of the woman's cycle and reproductive system while the man works with Carnelian to aid his virility and prowess. Adding Green Aventurine for overall fertility makes this an extremely effective combination. During pregnancy, take time out each day, especially on Mondays, to rest and connect with the baby. Place your Rainbow Moonstone upon your belly and sense the child's energy. This will encourage mother-child bonding as well as healthy growth for the child.

Full Moon

Different colours of Moonstone are best used at various times through the lunar cycle, with Rainbow Moonstone reserving the most magical time – the full moon. This is a time when our intuition is heightened and working with Rainbow Moonstone can improve your abilities. Wear it over the three-day span of the full moon and start to pay attention to your gut feelings. Rainbow Moonstone will help you trust the intuitive guidance you receive. Take a risk and allow yourself to be guided by your intuition and you'll feel it strengthening each month.

Often the full moon is a time when many people feel scattered, ungrounded and can quite literally become lunar-tics. At this time the moon's energy is at its strongest and is encouraging you to slow down, listen to your intuition, dream and introspect. However we often continue with our hectic lifestyles, regardless of the celestial energy, making this time a struggle. Rainbow Moonstone can help you work more harmoniously with the lunar energy. Wear it during the full moon time and even if you have a busy schedule, let Rainbow Moonstone encourage you to go about your day with an inner grace and awareness rather than a frenzied energy.

The movement of the moon and stars has a large impact on the systems of our body. Before the introduction of electrical lighting in our homes, women ovulated when the moon was full. This is because the pineal gland detects the amount of light while you are asleep and sends messages to the ovaries to release an egg. Ovulating at the full moon means bleeding at the new moon, the time when the energy is more inwardly focused anyway. The average menstrual cycle is naturally the same as the lunar cycle of 28 days.

If your body is feeling out of balance, place Rainbow Moonstone in your pillowslip for the night. It is ideal to sleep outside under the stars, to allow your body to realign itself with the universe, or at least sleep near a window where you can see the night's sky.

Divine Feminine

In many cultures, the moon represents the Divine Feminine and thus Rainbow Moonstone can be used to help connect with not only the moon, but all feminine energy sources. Sit in a circle of four Rainbow Moonstones and invoke the Divine Feminine energy to heal and guide you. You may call upon a particular lunar goddess such as Diana, Artemis, Astarte, Selene, Inanna, Ishtar, Change or simply use a name you are comfortable with such as Great Mother. Follow your intuition and allow the interaction to unfold organically. You may wish to ask a question, request help or simply connect with the energy. Simply relax and allow. If you are needing spiritual healing, a mouthful of maple syrup will support your aim. The night-blooming cereus is a lovely plant with enchanting white flowers and a hypnotising fragrance. A flower will open in the evening (or on overcast days) and stay open until sunrise, when it will wilt. Time your goddess circle with the flowering of your night-blooming cereus for a truly magical experience!

Moonstone encourages you to nurture your inner goddess, the feminine aspect within everyone. Wear the crystal over your heart to empower your gentle, caring and intuitive side and share it with the world. Understanding the wisdoms of Snow Leopard will show you how to be gentle without sacrificing your personal power. Moonstone helps heal breast-related health issues that can result from a refusal to allow nourishment in your life. Moonstone can be used in harmony with frangipani to make you irresistibly attractive. You'll perfect the ability to draw towards you what you need rather than actively seeking it. On the full moon, drop three drops of frangipani oil on a cottonwool ball and add it with a Moonstone into a medicine bag while stating clearly what you want to attract. Open yourself up to allow it to manifest in the next lunar cycle.

Travel

If you are travelling, keep a Rainbow Moonstone with you. So long as the moon looks over you, you shall be safe. Rainbow Moonstone's ability to awaken your intuition will keep you safe as well as ward off any thieves or pickpockets. Maple is a traveller's wood and is a wise choice to carry, especially if you have a full-on itinerary as it will help you feel right at home wherever you are. Pairing Rainbow Moonstone and maple wood allows you to focus on the choices in any situation, eliminating luck and chance, and ensuring you don't end up in a compromising position while in unfamiliar territory.

If you are travelling internationally and suffering from jetlag, keep Rainbow Moonstone close to help your body's circadian rhythms fall back into alignment with your new environment. Sleep where you can see the moon and stars as discussed earlier in this chapter. This can also be beneficial for shift workers or anyone finding it difficult to sleep through the whole night.

MORGANITE

Greater Love / Equal Rights / Balanced Relationships / Rites Of Passage

Although very similar in physical appearance, Morganite holds a deeper and wiser energy than the popular Rose Quartz. This high vibration love crystal induces positive change leading to a more harmonious and love-filled life. Morganite smooths out friction and works to create more equality in the world. Working with Morganite allows a joyous spirit to wash over you leaving you feeling happier, calmer and even a little giggly. Some refer to Morganite as pink Emerald, and like its green sister, it resonates universal love around the world. When combined with green Emerald, Morganite balances the force of the green crystal's energy with its softer vibration, creating a harmonious love-filled duo that are great to use together.

Animal: Dove
Plant: Ebony
Astrological Correspondences: Haumea, Juno and Venus
Power Day: Friday
Cleanse with: Water

Your Crystal Alignment Meditation

Go to a peaceful place in nature. Close your eyes, ensure your spine is straight and place your hands on your heart. Tune in to the beating of your own heart for a few minutes, allowing all other noises to slip away. Now place a hand on the earth in front of you. Sense the heartbeat of the planet, feel it resonate with your own, the two beating harmoniously as one. When you are ready, connect with your Morganite.

Greater Love

When you are feeling deflated or downtrodden reach for your Morganite. It opens you up to the limitless love of the universe which reaches further than the conditional love you can become reliant on from your friends and family.

Morganite invites you to hand over your wounds to Great Spirit, to take them far away where they shall no longer have an impact. As the sun, or better still the moon sets, hold your Morganite in prayer position against your heart. Pray to Great Spirit asking for any past pain or suffering you still hold to be transmitted out of your heart, through your fingertips, and out to the Sun or Moon to take it beyond the horizon into the unknown darkness.

Morganite reminds you of the marvel of life unfolding around you. It helps to open your inner eyes to the beauty in your life when you can't see it. To promote this, rest with your eyes closed and place a piece of Morganite over each eye. Furthermore it reminds you of your own brilliance. Developing a relationship with Morganite will help see the skills and traits you possess and how they are advantageous, even when others may mock or belittle you for being different. It helps you see your role within humanity and take responsibility for sharing your gifts for the betterment of all. In fact, Morganite awakens a joyous spirit within and an enthusiasm to be the creator of your life. Morganite energetically supports those with emphysema who have adopted an attitude that they are not worthy of living. Morganite will remind you it is your birthright to live fully and freely. Let Morganite help you to love yourself and the life you are creating for yourself.

Equal Rights

Working with Morganite allows you to realise that love is infinite and there is plenty to go around. Acknowledging love is abundant means selfishness and stinginess becomes irrelevant. Morganite works to bring equality to all life. Take a piece to legal, financial or business meetings to ensure fair treatment. Use Morganite in power grids and as a daily talisman to promote the rights of women, the LGBTIQ community, immigrants, asylum seekers, ethnic/religious minorities or endangered species. Meditate with it when dwarf planet Haumea goes into retrograde as this is when you are most likely to recognise where you are displaying prejudice in your own life

Morganite is great to use in group work as it helps align everyone's hearts to a common, unified purpose and fosters a harmonious bond. It ensures everyone considers the needs of others and the whole rather than just themselves. Place the crystal around an office or classroom to fill the space with an energy of cooperation and fairness.

Combine Morganite with ebony wood to further strengthen balance. Ebony encompasses the energy of all four elements (fire, air, earth and water) as well as being a feminine-masculine balanced tree. It works to break down social barriers, open the heart and give people the power to change.

Balanced Relationships

Morganite is a key crystal for this point in history as both men and women work to define their modern day roles in life and seek to find a new equilibrium. Men working with Morganite will be able to balance their masculine and feminine energies while retaining their innate masculinity. For women this loving crystal helps you to realise that you can be independent of men and still feel comfortable and in harmony with the male energy.

As your relationship with Morganite develops, you will be able to enjoy more balanced, romantic relationships. When worn over the chest, Morganite helps you be more receptive to your lover's loving words, actions and energy. It also helps you to be the best partner you can be, a common consideration during Juno retrograde. Call upon your Dove guide to give you guidance on how much to give in a relationship. Meditate with Morganite and ask Dove for direction before asking for more in a relationship if you feel you are giving more than receiving. When one partner in a relationship is dominating the other, affect the balance of power by placing Morganite around the home.

Morganite improves your ability to relate to others and understand their needs and desires. As a heart crystal it helps you not only speak from the heart, but more importantly, listen from the heart. Morganite helps quell judgment and criticism of others, reminding you that what you dislike in another is a part within yourself you are yet to learn how to love. To create an environment that fosters loving listening and understanding, pair Morganite with Angelite and a soft coloured candle, allowing the candles flame to transform judgemental behaviour into energies of love and peace, promoted by this crystal pair.

Rite of Passage

There are many milestones we pass in life including puberty, graduation, initiations, coming of age, marriage, menopause and death. A rite of passage is a ritual event that honours a person's transition from one status to another. A cornerstone of many cultures, rite of passage rituals have all but vanished in many Western cultures today. These rituals celebrate important parts of our life and help give everyone a greater sense of community support. They leave you feeling empowered and loved. If a rite of passage doesn't exist within your culture, design your own ritual and involve other people. Include Morganite in the ritual or as a gift, especially for girls. Morganite offers balance and support through puberty and during the transition into adulthood.

NUUMMITE

Manhood / Protection / Earth Star Chakra

Deep within its icy bed in Greenland, Nuummite waited patiently to be unveiled to humanity, until it was discovered in recent years. Nuummite is a crystal that connects you to the ancient wisdom that exists deep within the earth and reveals knowledge found in the dark, untouched caves and ravines. It allows you to hear the teachings of the great trees that have stretched towards the heavens over hundreds of years. Nuummite demands strength from its guardian and in return will move all that does not serve you to the side and allow you to stand in the centre of your personal power. Its deeply masculine energy allows you to honour the Divine Masculine and find peace with masculine influences and figures in your life.

Animal: Bear, especially Polar Bear
Plant: Pepper
Astrological Correspondences: Pluto and Quaoar
Power Day: Saturday
Cleanse with: Earth or drumming

Your Crystal Alignment Meditation

Go to the Arctic or visualise yourself there in your mind. Connect with this icy realm. While water cleanses, snow and ice can purify, for it brings everything back to a state of stillness and nothingness. Allow yourself to be still within. When you are ready, connect with your Nuummite.

Manhood

Nuummite allows you to resolve any issues with your father, grandfather, father-figure or men in general. Place a brown candle by a photo of the man with whom you want to mend the relationship. Gaze into his eyes and connect with his essence. Hold your Nuummite and ask what is needed to heal this relationship then wait for the answer. Keep the photo and candle in a special place and repeat this activity as often as needed. This activity is best done at times with Quaoar is in retrograde.

Nuummite can also balance your masculine side and help men understand their role within society. Wearing it over your heart to awaken the strength you desire while quelling any aggressive or dominating tendencies. Gaining wisdom from your Bear guide can help to know how to use your strength wisely. Bear will encourage you to take time to introspect, to discover for yourself what behaviours will nourish you. Once you know the path you wish to take, Nuummite will give you the energy you need to succeed. It's great when you need a sudden burst of energy. Hold it in your receptive hand or against your chest rather than reaching for a candy bar or soda—it has a lot less calories!

Protection

Generally two types of stones are best for protection. Black crystals absorb unwanted or unhelpful energies while shiny crystals (also referred to as chatoyancy) reflect negativity back to its source. Polished or tumbled Nuummite is black plus it contains golden flecks, making it powerfully protective. Charge Nuummite to protect you physically, emotionally and mentally. Nuummite is a powerful magician or shaman's crystal and can be used to protect you spiritually during magical work, psychic experiences, lower world journeying, hypnotherapy, shadow-work or simply during everyday living. Combine Nuummite with pepper for further protection. Black pepper sprinkled around the perimeter of a space absorbs low vibration energies while anointing yourself with black pepper essential oil, or spritzing or diffusing it inside, keeps you and your loved ones safe.

Earth Star Chakra

Believed to be one of the oldest crystals on the planet, Nuummite possesses great knowledge of the Earth. It helps its guardian to form a deep connection with the earth, one that extends beyond the flowers and trees and dwells deep in the corners of the world that are rarely explored, Nuummite will help your heart beat in time with that of the planet's, creating a rewarding relationship that leaves you feeling guided, protected and empowered. Combined with the wisdom of Polar Bear you'll recognise the guidance nature is giving you. This will give you strength during times of scarcity or emotional upheaval.

This relationship is nurtured through the awareness of your Earth star chakra. Nuummite balances this chakra, ensuring you are able to access the guidance from the collective consciousness of every animal, plant and mineral. Nurturing the Earth star chakra is vital to ensure spiritual advancement and to keep your soul star chakra balanced. These two chakras work in harmony and balance with each other. Like a tree, your spiritual branches can stretch no higher up into the universe than your spiritual roots descend into the Earth.

To connect with your Earth star chakra, find a quiet, dark place and lie down, positioning your Nuummite about 15 centimetres below your feet.

Visualise a dark brown or infrared ball of energy pulsing where the crystal rests and feel your earthly connection build. Playing drumming music or playing a drum can also be advantageous. Adding cayenne pepper to your diet or taking it as a flower essence can stimulate the Earth star chakra if you feel it is lagging a little. These practices can also work as a powerful healing technique for any foot ailment that has manifested from feelings of purposelessness or insignificance.

OBSIDIAN, BLACK

Inner Power / Protection / Mystery / Dragons

Black Obsidian is a naturally created glass formed from volcanic lava that cooled quickly, causing significant crystallization to occur. Black Obsidian stimulates personal growth on all levels by alleviating stress and promoting clarity, urging exploration of the unknown and opening new horizons. Working with Black Obsidian helps you to know who you truly are, enabling you to give more to the world with your newfound compassion and strength.

Animal: Komodo Dragon
Plant: Dragon's Blood
Astrological Correspondence: Pluto
Power Day: Saturday
Cleanse by: Ideally place near a volcano to allow it to cleanse and reconnect with its fiery place of origin. When this is not possible, use fire.

Your Crystal Alignment Meditation

Go to a volcano, as close as possible to its mouth. If it is not possible to do this physically visualise yourself there in your mind. Connect with the volcano before you, centring yourself and focusing on your breath. Sense a source of energy bubbling deep within you, around the area of your navel. This is a warm and loving energy and is like the lava that sleeps deep beneath the surface of the Earth. Just as the volcano erupts, sense that inner energy bursting forth through the centre of your body, emanating great warm energy around you. Like the volcano's hot, molten lava cascading down the slopes allow the energy within you to pour over your body, disintegrating any negativity within and around you, leaving new space for creation and fertility. Once you have cleansed yourself send the energy, still emitting from the top of your head, to others. It may be a person or group you'd like to focus on or you can blanket the entire world with this energy. Once feeling totally cleansed and prepared, connect with your Obsidian.

Inner Power

Obsidian helps you connect to the inner power and strength that lies within you. Just like a volcano erupting, it brings out hidden abilities that you are yet to share with the world. Being black it works to ground you and regain stability in your life. It removes negative talk and allows you to adopt a sense of gratitude and appreciation for the beauty of the world. Obsidian can deliver you whatever you need, whether it is leadership, vitality, mastery, insight, inspiration, longevity, happiness, beauty, majesty or strength. All these attributes are within you. Wear Obsidian on the centre of your body to summon what you need. As you put it on take three breaths. On each inhalation feel the power within you and as you exhale allow it to erupt out of you into your aura.

The Komodo Dragon has complete mastery over its environment. Nothing stands in its way and even the young must hide in trees for fear of being devoured by a determined adult. The teachings and energy of Komodo Dragon resonate with Obsidian and should be combined when you are ready to accept responsibility and take control of your life.

Dragon's blood incense harmonises with the energy of this crystal and burning it around your house works to attract what you desire. Take time to sit by a window at night and watch the incense smoke drift outside. Visualise in your mind's eye the smoke drawing your goal to you as you recite, "By the power of the dragon's wing, my desire shall you bring".

Protection

Black crystals such as Black Tourmaline, Black Onyx, Jet as well as Obsidian are renowned for being strong protective crystals. Just as dark clothes in the sun absorb heat, black crystals absorb low vibrational energies that may be unwanted or unhelpful in increasing your personal vibration. Subtly all black crystals are different in their creation and make-up so it is worth considering which one will serve you best. As Obsidian was created quicker than other black crystals and in a fiery environment, it is best for protection from aggression, anger or violence.

Arrowheads carved from Obsidian are powerful amulets to drive away threats. Carry one in your pocket, wear it around your neck or place one at an entrance. Face the point down if there is no immediate danger or upwards if you feel threatened. Place a piece of Obsidian in your car to avoid road rage and to prevent aggressive drivers from upsetting you. Place pieces around your house as well as sprinkling dragon's blood resin or powder to keep you safe from storms or intruders. If you desire some quiet at home, place a piece of Obsidian and some dragon's blood with some salt and sugar in a bottle. Seal it and hide it where it will not be discovered and you'll soon be enjoying the peaceful atmosphere.

Mystery

Black Obsidian slept deep within the earth until a volcanic eruption brought it to the surface and created this volcanic glass. For this reason Obsidian has a strong connection to deep, hidden mysteries. Often called the stone of truth, Black Obsidian can reveal boundless secrets and mysteries, both about the inner world of the person working with the Obsidian, as well as the inner workings of the cosmos at large. Use an Obsidian sphere or tumbled stone as a scrying tool. As you relax and gaze into its blackness allow answers to bubble into your mind.

Unless tumbled or polished, Obsidian is quite sharp. This sharpness is also expressed as a metaphysical property. This powerful stone can help cut through illusions, lies, fear and blockages. If you wish to break an emotional connection you have with someone or something slowly wave it before you while visualising it cutting the energetic cord that connects you and your attachment. Feel the change as you slice away the cord and free yourself from the bond. If you are struggling to find an answer to a question, slowly wave Obsidian through dragon's blood incense smoke. Let yourself relax and as you watch the smoke dance around the moving Obsidian, allowing the answers to come into your mind.

Dragons

Stories of dragons are found around the world in many different cultures. Obsidian and dragons have a close relationship. They are both associated with mystery and their fiery, transformative energy allows them to help bring you the changes you desire. Do you need to rid yourself of something old so that something new may grow? Combine the powers of your Obsidian and Dragon to assist you with this.

Find a quiet place, ideally in nature, and light two black candles (make sure you take precautions not to start a bush fire of course!). Place the Obsidian in the middle of the candles, close your eyes and summon your dragon to meet you. You can use the chant, "These two candles are the key, to draw my dragon here to me. Hear my call to be my friend, your fiery powers I ask you lend". You may choose to close your eyes and feel your dragon's presence by you even if you cannot see it. Allow your dragon to teach you how to burn away your doubts and show you how to awaken your hidden talents and abilities. Once you are finished thank your dragon for joining you and blow then blow out the two candles. Continue to keep your Obsidian near you as an amulet of your dragon's power.

OBSIDIAN, MAHOGANY

Overcoming Obstacles / Anger / Matriarchs

Mahogany Obsidian harnesses the energies of red and black crystals, offering you strength and protection. The crystal's black energy removes distractions and dangers while the red settles you so you can find solutions. The red colour, from quantities of Iron, also works to ground you, allowing you to feel safe and secure. It allows you to trust and follow your own inner guidance especially when faced with adversity or uncertainty.

Animal: Elephant
Plants: Cinnamon and Mahogany
Astrological Correspondence: Mars
Power Day: Tuesday
Cleanse by: Ideally placing near a volcano to allow it to cleanse and reconnect with its fiery place of origin. When this is not possible, use fire.

Your Crystal Alignment Meditation

Go and sit by a large rock, one larger than yourself. Tune in to the rock's energy. Feel its strength, stability and certainty. Once you are ready, connect with your Mahogany Obsidian.

Overcoming Obstacles

Mahogany Obsidian is an excellent stone for removing obstacles. It will allow you to see your own shortcomings and overcome them. Furthermore, its ability to promote a forgiving attitude lets you release ill feelings and grudges towards others that obstruct harmonious relationships.

Hold your Mahogany Obsidian in your receptive hand and in your mind's eye see this obstacle as a large symbol in front of you painted on a wall. It may be a shape, a word, an image or anything else that symbolises the obstacle stopping you going forth. Summon energy from the crystal and then visualise yourself demolishing the wall to find a solution on the other side.

You may want to call upon the guidance of the Hindu elephant-headed god Ganesh. He is known as the remover of obstacles and he works harmoniously with the vibration of Mahogany Obsidian. Chewing cinnamon flavoured gum or just smelling the scent of cinnamon, which also resonates with Mahogany Obsidian, can improve brain function and speed a solution to you faster.

Anger

Mahogany Obsidian releases anger and activates a positive sense of power. Whenever you are angry hold your crystal in your projective hand and visualise it absorbing your anger as you breathe deeply. If, hours later, you still feel frustrated by a situation, sit down before a black candle. Feel the candle's flame stretch towards you and burn away the negative thoughts and feelings, letting them collect inside the crystal. Cleanse the crystal afterwards. As you allow anger to leave your life, Mahogany Obsidian, when worn daily, will give you inner strength. You'll be able to see your path into the future and walk upon it with steadiness. You'll feel more in control of your life and feel secure in moving forward along your path of service.

Matriarchs

Mahogany Obsidian, when worn over the heart, offers support to the matriarch and any woman who is the head of a family or group. The crystal harmonises with your Elephant guide, which teaches women how to take the lead for the wellbeing of their family. Meditating with and carrying a small piece of mahogany wood with your crystal will help you if you need to strengthen relationships with family members, especially a son.

If you are experiencing menopause, keep Mahogany Obsidian in your pocket to help you find joys and celebrate this progression to the next stage of life. It helps the transition from the role as the nurturing mother to the respected wise sage, crone or grandmother. Mahogany Obsidian allows you to see your value in this new role. It also helps you feel more attractive, confident and at ease with your own sexuality. This confidence can help older woman find employment.

OBSIDIAN, SNOWFLAKE
Awareness / Introspection / Balance

Snowflake Obsidian is natural, black, volcanic glass containing the mineral Cristobalite in the shape of snowflake patterns. It is a great meditation stone, ideal for times of introspection. It will allow you to centre yourself and surrender to meditation while combating negative feelings of loneliness and isolation. Snowflake Obsidian allows you to find balance between spending time with others and allocating alone time. With this greater balance in your life, you establish a better understanding of your own personal needs as well as more fulfilling interactions with others.

Animal: Bear
Plant: Patchouli
Astrological Correspondence: Makemake
Power Day: Saturday
Cleanse with: Earth or snow

Your Crystal Alignment Meditation

Go and explore the dark depths of a cave, or visualise yourself there in your mind. The cave is a symbol of the Mother, the great womb from which we emerge. Tune in to the nothingness of the cavernous darkness around you. The universe began as a dark void. But within this void existed all the potential that has now become the world. All that is needed to begin creation is a spark, a simple thought. Know that within the darkness exists potential for you to create what you need. Connect to this potential. When you are ready, connect with your Snowflake Obsidian.

Awareness

There can be many demands for our time and attention each day and we end up spending our life in the fast lane, racing around from one task to another. If you look at your daily activities, you'll notice it is simply made up of identifying a desire and then taking action to achieve it. As soon as you fulfil that desire, you recognise another and start pursuing that. This could be as simple as getting breakfast to a long-term goal like building a dream home. This constant desire-action cycle rarely allows time for self-reflection. The danger in this is that life can become habitual, where you simply act upon the first impulse that comes to you without consideration. Then after a day, a week, a year or a lifetime you suddenly realise your life isn't where you thought it would be. Snowflake Obsidian encourages you to add another step to the desire-action cycle—a rest.

A rest can simply be a pause of a few seconds after completing an email, a few minutes after arriving home or an hour after achieving a milestone. Take these moments to hold your Snowflake Obsidian and become aware of the now and how you are truly feeling. These rests, or pauses, will allow for a moment of introspection. Pausing will give you the space and moment in time to evaluate that you are conducting yourself with integrity and allow you to enjoy your achievements. As you stop momentarily, it allows you to start noticing subtle things around you, from how others are feeling to what is happening in the natural environment. This increased awareness will help you remain in tune with yourself and others as well as keep you in line with your path of service.

Introspection

Use Snowflake Obsidian to help you go inward and get to know yourself better. Snowflake Obsidian is an ideal crystal to work with during the winter months. In winter, the nights are longer and nature slows down, with plants and animals being less active. Snowflake Obsidian will allow you to do the same. Sit by yourself with a black candle holding your crystal and ask yourself simple questions. What foods does your body desire? Does your body need more water, or more sleep? Are you happy? What makes you truly happy? What is your life's purpose? The answers to all these questions are inside you, and all you must do is give yourself the quiet time and space to hear them. If you cannot find the answers within, you will not find them without.

As the weather cools, Bear prepares herself for her winter slumber. Here, in a den or cave, she will take the time to go inward, consider the year's experiences and await the birth of her cubs which symbolise new opportunities that will emerge in the spring. By connecting with your Bear guide you will be able to do the same.

Scrying with Snowflake Obsidian can help you find solutions by accessing your innate inner wisdom. Keep your mind clear except for any question you may have need of answering. Snowflake Obsidian will allow you to recognise unhelpful thinking and patterns, allowing you to rid yourself of behaviours that hinder your path of service. This powerful crystal summons knowledge deep from within and brings it to the forefront of your mind, showing you what you need to change in order to advance in your life.

Balance

The black and white colour of Snowflake Obsidian makes it the crystal equivalent of yin and yang. Thus, Snowflake Obsidian is a great stone for establishing balance in life. It helps you appreciate time by yourself and enables you to use this time constructively. If you find yourself constantly interrupted by others, combine Snowflake Obsidian with patchouli. Magically, patchouli is used for its repelling power. Diffuse patchouli essential oil to detract others from contacting you, or place a few drops of the oil or patchouli leaves at each door and window to prevent uninvited guests. Wearing Snowflake Obsidian plus a perfume contain patchouli will offer protection against people who may take more from you than needed or deter you from your path of service.

Snowflake Obsidian ensures a fair and even distribution of finances, resources or responsibilities. Take a piece to custody battles or legal settlements. Keep the crystal in your office when working on budgets or agreements. Dwarf planet Makemake governs the equal sharing of world resources and when in retrograde brings awareness to where this is not happening. Create a power grid on top of a world map to encourage wealthy nations to give more assistance to poorer ones without placing overbearing financial pressures on them. Use Snowflake Obsidian as the power crystal and surround it by six Quartz points facing outwards towards chosen nations on your map. Add supportive crystals such as Blue Lace Agate or Angelite for peace and Red Jasper or Morganite for justice.

As Snowflake Obsidian allows you to find more awareness and balance in your life, you'll be able to advance along your path of service with more ease, while also noticing the beauty around you. Let Snowflake Obsidian guide you to see the splendour in a flower blossoming, the clouds passing by, or even beauty in those things usually considered ugly. It will also help you identify the synchronicities and coincidences that happen and make life so beautiful. As the months get colder, wear Snowflake Obsidian jewellery or grid it around your home. It guards you against harsh winters by ensuring you know how to work with the season, rather than against it.

ONYX, BLACK

Protection / Attraction / Nails

Black Onyx is a variety of Chalcedony coloured through the presence of Iron and Manganese. All black crystals have the ability to absorb low vibrational energies that cause unwanted or negative influences in your life, disrupting your inner balance. However, each crystal is best used for different dangers based on its make up and structure. Onyx flourishes in urban settings, helping to counteract the impact of pollution, noise and too many people. Those living in big cities can use Onyx every day to tackle the demands of dealing with the masses. This crystal works silently yet powerfully, also offering protection from dangers you are not aware of, from betrayal to toxin build up. In fact, Onyx doesn't just help us stay safe around people, it allows us to flourish by giving us the ability to tune into all around us when needed. Onyx allows you to perceive the connectedness between all things and understand that our actions affect everything.

Animal: Spider
Plant: Ivy
Astrological Correspondence: Pluto
Power Day: Saturday
Cleanse with: Earth. During times of extreme stress or pressure, cleanse daily.

Your Crystal Alignment Meditation

Go and find a spider's web. Study the intricacy of the weaving. Touch it gently and feel its tensile strength. Look to its perimeters and see how all threads connect to a central point. Let your mind drift to consider the web of life. Consider how your behaviour and actions makes a difference in others' lives. When you are happy, you can brighten other people's days. Smiling at strangers will quickly demonstrate this point. Knowing this simple truth gives you power to make a great difference in the world around you. Little things you do will have ripple effects and by acting in a positive, helpful, compassionate and friendly way each day you are contributing towards the world becoming a more loving place.

In nature all animals and plants are connected and play a role in the cycles of life. Consider how certain animals are pollinators and seed dispersers for plants, and plants supply nutrition for animals. Carnivores control the numbers of other animals, ensuring the strongest of these species survive and pass on their genes while also gaining their food source from these creatures. Everything has a vital role to play in maintaining balance in the world. Contemplate your role in the web of life. What is your special gift and how can you make positive ripples spread out through the world? Sense this connection and when you feel complete, connect with your Onyx.

Protection

Onyx offers protection from passive, secretive or psychic energies. It grounds and absorbs restrictions that prevent you from establishing balance of the body or mind. Wear Onyx daily for protection from the unforeseen and place it out on the earth or just the soil of a pot plant each night to allow it to cleanse. In turn, this gives you more strength, especially at times of high stress. It is a great stone for athletes or those who need to perform suddenly under pressure as it increases power, endurance, perseverance, and explosivity.

If there is something in particular you wish to banish from your life or protect yourself from, perform this powerful ritual. Set up a mirror with a purple candle in front of it. Lay nine pieces of Onyx in a semi-circle in front of the candle. Relax and visualise the Onyx absorbing the negativity you wish to remove from your life. Then light the candle and visualise the negativity being drawn from the nine crystals, towards the flame then through the mirror. The mirror is a doorway to the spiritual plane and will send this energy back to where it came from. This is extremely powerful for stopping gossip, cheating, betrayal, lying and theft.

To find out who might be working against you, place some ground ivy around the base of a yellow candle. Burn the candle on a Saturday and ask your Onyx to reveal any enemies to you. The person will become known to you. Ivy can also be kept in a pot at your front door with a charged Onyx in the soil for protection at home. Also place a symbol of good luck such as a white candle, Rose Quartz or deity statue at your front entrance to invite favourable energies into the home.

Onyx is associated with the night and thus allows us to safely navigate our way through the hours of darkness. Carry Onyx in your pocket to avoid falling or slipping on something you don't see. Have a piece in your car to avoid black ice. A Black Onyx in a dream catcher hung over the bed prevents bad dreams. It protects animals at night so place a piece in your pet's bed or sleeping area. Bury seven pieces around the habitat of a nocturnal animal you wish to help. If you cannot get to the animal's home, create a power grid with Onyx as the power crystal sitting with an image of the animal, four Clear Quartz pointing outwards and supporting crystals for successful breeding such as Green Aventurine or Unakite.

Onyx works to counteract the damaging effects of pollution, toxins and other poisons. If you live in a large city or near industrial areas, place an Onyx at each window. Placing Black Onyx at the site of chemical or oil spills will energetically help to reduce the negative impacts on the surrounding habitat.

Attraction

Onyx has a magnetic rather than electric energy, meaning it works to draw what you need to you so you do not have to forcibly pursue your desires. Work with Onyx to increase your personal magnetism. You can combine Onyx with the teachings of your Spider guide. Once Spider has woven her web, she shows great patience and faith until her prey is caught. However, Spider isn't an animal relying on luck. She creates her own luck. Spider takes control of her life and does everything she can to be successful. You don't need to frantically chase what you seek. Be clear on what you need, be properly prepared and Onyx will draw it to you so you may seize it when the time is right.

Work with Onyx and Spider to draw what you need. Sit down and write out exactly what you seek and place it in the centre of a power grid with your Onyx and a white candle. Surround this with eight Clear Quartz points facing inwards and add supporting crystals, depending on what you are trying to attract (for example Rose Quartz for friendship or Citrine for new income). Light the candle often and take a few moments to visualise what life will look and feel like once you have obtained it. Keep an eye out of opportunities each day and when the correct one comes, seize it without hesitation.

Nails

The name Onyx comes from the Greek word *onux*, meaning fingernail. Legend tells of how cheeky Eros (Cupid) cut off one of Aphrodite's (Venus) fingernails with an arrowhead while she was sleeping. He left the clippings scattered on the sand and the Fates turned them into stone so that no part of the heavenly body would ever perish. When we feel unsafe or unprotected this can physically manifest into weak or brittle nails. To counteract this wear Onyx near your hands until your nails regain full health. To avoid nail biting carry a tumbled Onyx in your pocket and each time you are tempted to bite your nails, pull out the Onyx and fiddle with it in your hands for a couple of minutes.

PIETERSITE

Devotion / Understanding / Spiritual Growth

Pietersite is a variety of chalcedony with embedded fibres of amphibole minerals with varying degrees of alteration creating a stunning variety of chatoyant blues, reds, browns and yellows. Pietersite was originally discovered on a farm in Namibia, by Sid Pieters and has since been found in China. Pietersite has earned names such as "Tempest Stone" or "Stone of the Storm" for its ability to help you during storms. This is both in the physical sense such as thunderstorms, as well as personal storms, when everything in your life is crazy. It lets you maintain a sense of inner balance and embrace what is happening around you. Pietersite facilitates understanding and acceptance as well as helping you progress along your spiritual path. This is crystal deserves a lot of attention considering its relevant attributes for modern life.

Animal: Scorpion
Plant: Basil
Astrological Correspondence: Saturn
Power Day: Saturday
Cleanse with: Air or placing outside during lightning or electrical storms

Your Crystal Alignment Meditation

Go and sit safely amongst a lightning storm. Alternatively, simply close your eyes, visualising yourself there. Feel the electricity pulse through the air and through your body. Lightning is precise and powerful, striking exactly where it desires. Harness this energy so you may achieve exactly what you need. Once you are feeling empowered, connect with your Pietersite.

Devotion

In times of personal chaos, Pietersite is a crystal to reach for. Remove yourself as best you can from a stressful situation for a few moments and take some deep breaths while holding your Pietersite in your receptive hand. Then perceive the chaos of your current situation whirling around you in a circular motion. See yourself and acknowledge that you sit in the eye of the storm where all is calm and quiet. Detach yourself from the emotions, stress and fear surrounding you. Allow feelings of joy and balance to fill your being so that you may devote your attentions to what you desire. This technique is perfect if you feel anxious in crowds.

In working with Pietersite you can also summon your Scorpion guide to direct you during rough times. Scorpion's sting has great power that can change both his destiny and those around him. However, he does not use this power recklessly. Scorpion teaches you that you have the power to dictate how your path unfolds. Remain centred, disciplined and devoted and only use your power for the greater good. Include the scent of basil in your life to connect to the Scorpion mindset and give you clarity of mind.

Turbulent times in our life can affect the wellbeing of our body's "control centre" gland, the pituitary. Blue Pietersite works well in correcting any imbalances of this gland as well as sex and growth hormone imbalances. The frenzied years of puberty can be made easier with Pietersite. Have teenagers wear Pietersite jewellery and place it around the family home. Add Rose Quartz to the combination to combat teen angst, giving them the best opportunity to thrive and flourish.

Understanding

As you develop your relationship with Pietersite, you'll notice your ability to simply allow and embrace what is happening around you. Wearing it over your heart will help you extend your boundaries of acceptance and tolerance of others and of life's events. Just as lightning clears the air and makes all things new, Pietersite discharges negative energies, confusion, fear and emotional turmoil, replacing them with a sense of love and ease. It assists you to resonate with compassion and connectedness to all of humanity while also promoting loyalty to your own life path. A strong relationship with Pietersite allows you to understand how the world works and gives you the ability to walk on to the "stage of life" and confidently present yourself and your gifts to others.

When confronted with a thunderstorm, hailstorm, flood, tsunami, cyclone, tornado, hurricane or other threatening weather phenomenon call on Pietersite to offer you protection. Pietersite allows you to understand the stormy tempered aspect of Earth's weather and make decisions that ensure your safety. It is interesting that this crystal was discovered just before the era when the climatic changes of global warming are causing more natural disasters around the world. Pietersite will calm nervous people and animals during storms, protect you when driving in bad weather and guard homes and businesses against storm damage. You can also summon a storm god such as Thor or Zeus to look over you, in conjunction with placing Pietersite on you, your car and your home. Furthermore, Pietersite will act as a shield against the adverse effects of technology, particularly if you work long hours in front of a computer or live near a mobile phone mast.

Spiritual Growth

As you start to remove extraneous stress and mental clutter from your life, Pietersite will allow you to grow spiritually. This crystal holds the keys to the kingdom of heaven by linking the spiritual realm with everyday living. Wearing Pietersite or adding a sphere to the centre of your home will ensure you remain centred and calm, supporting you as you devote yourself to your path of service regardless of what adversity you face.

Pietersite harmonises with the magical symbol of the pentagram, a five-pointed star (pictured below). This powerful symbol represents the balance of the human body (four limbs plus head), the five magical elements (fire, air, earth, water and spirit) and protection. For a meditation that is both balancing and empowering draw or visualise a pentagram on the earth of floor. Place a Pietersite at each point. Lie over the five points or sit in the centre. Feel the energy moving between your five extremities, realigning any imbalances and allowing your life force to grow.

a pentagram

PYRITE

Structure / Unity / Health

Pyrite heals through structure. This golden crystal, also known as fool's Gold, allows you to understand, value and heal what you have, and then builds upon it. Pyrite has a grounding vibration, giving you a sense of stability and confidence to influence the world. By striking Pyrite with metal or stone produces a spark, giving this crystal the ability to bring fire into your life.

Animals: Octopus and Quoll
Plant: Niaouli
Astrological Correspondence: Sun
Power Day: Sunday
Cleanse with: Fire

Your Crystal Alignment Meditation

Go to a beautiful garden. Admire the play between the man-made structure of the garden and nature's chaotic order. As you sit in the garden practice two types of focus, closed focus and open focus.

First practice closed focus, which is narrowing your attention to just one thing. Start by focusing on nothing but your breath, allowing it to become slow and deep. As you breathe in count the number one, as you breathe out, the number two, in again and the number three and so on. If you get distracted or lose count, you must start from one again. Continue to do this activity and see how high you can get before you become side-tracked. As you practise this activity more, you will improve your ability to concentrate on a single task or meditate without becoming distracted.

Secondly practise open focus by shifting your focus from yourself to your surroundings. Pay attention to the sounds around you. How many can you hear? Relax and do not give any attention to your own mind. This practice enables you to free yourself from stressful thoughts and increases your awareness of what is happening around you. Finally, pick up your Pyrite in your receptive hand and allow your focus to shift to connecting with your crystal.

Structure

Pyrite usually grows in perfect cubes, promoting an energy of structure and order. Working with Pyrite allows you to categorise and comprehend new knowledge, improving your learning, memory and overall intelligence. Keep Pyrite on your desk when studying or working especially when completing translations, spreadsheets, budgets or anything that requires logical thinking. While working with Pyrite diffuse niaouli essential oil. This fresh aroma from the Australian bush will help you stay relaxed yet focused as you work.

Pyrite's isometric structure translates to helping you finding physical perfection, both in yourself and in your surroundings. However Pyrite will not bring about perfection as you may believe it should be. Rather it will help you discover the true perfection of life that lays within the imperfection. Pyrite teaches that everything is aligned as it should be and shows you the order within the chaos. Sit outside with Pyrite and examine a tree. If you look and focus a single bent and rotting branch, you miss the beauty and perfection of the whole tree. Furthermore, Pyrite helps unveil the marvel of the Fibonacci sequence in nature. Another way to utilise Pyrite is scrying. It can bring unexpected results, enabling you to gain deeper access to the logical mind rather than the subconscious.

Unity

Once Pyrite has given you clarity and structure it allows you to pull all your ideas, learning or resources together to make the best decision. Anyone working in the medical profession can benefit from carrying Pyrite as it will help make the best decisions for their patients. On a grander scale, use Pyrite to promote the inception of clever ways to share the world's skills and resources so that all nations benefit, especially impoverished, third world countries. Create a grid over a map of the world, placing four Pyrites on the corners and add other crystals such as Red Jasper for justice and Purpurite to encourage leaders to compromise.

Pyrite allows you to generate wealth by using a variety of skills and networks. It helps you attract money from multiple sources rather than one job, making it a good crystal if you work as a sales representative, fund raiser or hold down several part-time roles. It helps you identify various avenues worth pursuing and enables you to influence others to see the benefits of supporting you. Your Octopus guide, who harmonises with Pyrite, will offer you wisdom on how to manage all these things at once. To increase your income place five green candles around the house, each with a Pyrite crystal. Sit in the centre of the house and visualise financial opportunities flying from all directions. Once prospects present themselves, use Pyrite in harmony with your Quoll guide who will spring you into action, seizing any opportunity. If you attract too many, meditate with Pyrite to organise your schedule.

Health

As Pyrite creates a more orderly life, your health will benefit. It will ensure you have a good work-life balance and don't become run down. Its golden lustre also gives it a protective quality, guarding you against sickness or disease. Wear Pyrite over the solar plexus chakra for overall health and increased energy. Pyrite helps with any bone problems that manifest from an unstructured life. If you break a bone, wear Pyrite near the area to assist with proper healing and regrowth. Combine niaouli with Pyrite when performing any healing. Niaouli essential oil will cleanse the body, removing unwanted and unhelpful energies as well as having an uplifting effect on the mind.

QUANTUM QUATTRO™

Liberation / Community / Hope

In 1996, a unique combination of crystals was discovered in Namibia. It is possible that this crystal was unveiled at a precise time to support light-workers and healers around the world in the preparation for the new millennium Quantum Quattro™ contains a swirl of colours contributed by Shattuckite (sky to royal blue), Chrysocolla (robin's egg blue), Dioptase (forest green), Malachite (light green) and Smokey Quartz. Each piece of Quantum Quattro™ is a unique combination of colours and will find the perfect human guardian with whom to align. Once you have met your Quantum Quattro™, may you break free from past restraints and begin your work to create an ideal world that is free from pain and suffering.

Animals: Lemur and Penguin
Plants: Coconut, Douglas Fir and Sturt Desert Pea
Astrological Correspondence: Chiron
Power Day: Friday
Cleanse with: Water

Your Crystal Alignment Meditation

Go and sit by a river or visualise one in your mind. Explore the edges of the river and see how slowly over time, the water has carved its way downstream and shaped its surrounding environment. This did not happen immediately but rather with continued, focused intention on a destination. Consider how you can apply the ways of the river to your own life. When you are ready, connect with your crystal.

Liberation

Quantum Quattro™ is a potent emotional healer that allows you to release old patterns, beliefs and pain that hold you back from your spiritual growth. When worn against the skin over the heart, each of the five individual crystals within the stone plays an individual role in the healing process, resulting allowing you to let go of the ill effects of your past:

Malachite – allows you to realise what pain you are carrying

Shattuckite – lets you comprehend what has happened and the impact it has had on you

Dioptase – awakens acceptance of the experience, honouring both the positive and the negative

Chrysocolla – facilitates release of the hurt and pain

Smokey Quartz – finally allows you to settle and ground yourself after healing

Quantum Quattro™ is highly in tune with the healing tools already present on Earth and works in harmony with any animal guide or plant. It strengthens the effectiveness of homeopathy, naturopathy, aromatherapy and herbalism. During times of personal healing, take note of the lessons from Penguin. With her ability to fly through the water (the element of emotions), she can show you how to endure great challenges and come out triumphant.

There are some key plants that work particularly well with Quantum Quattro™. Firstly, coconut allows for the safe release and purification of old energy as well as promoting fertile abundance and protection into the future. Start the day holding your Quantum Quattro™ in your receptive hand as you drink a glass of coconut water. As you ingest the water, feel its vibration removing unwanted energies and giving you a fresh start for the day.

Douglas Fir encourages the awareness and release of destructive patterns you've adopted from the past, especially family generational behaviours. It promotes awareness of who you truly are and releases any bonds that you feel placed upon you by your family. Its nurturing and protective qualities will help you transform family relationships into meaningful bonds. If your family history is a cause of suffering, meditate with Quantum Quattro™ under a Douglas Fir tree and diffuse its essential oil in your space while exploring these issues.

A course of Sturt Desert Pea flower essence can be used to combat any unwillingness to release deep hurt that have been carried over years or even through lifetimes. As healing occurs, Quantum Quattro™ will enable you to feel a new sense of joy and contentment. You will feel liberated from the past and charge eagerly into the future.

Community

Quantum Quattro™ has the potential to reunite the world. As we each heal the hurts of the past, we move forward towards a future where we embrace each other with unconditional love and acceptance. Quantum Quattro™ enables us to acknowledge past generations' mistakes, learn the lessons they offer and move forward as a cohesive whole.

Quantum Quattro™ resonates with the ancient ways of Lemuria where communities supported and empowered every individual to contribute. Lemurians lived in harmony with nature and in return lived lives of bountiful health and wellbeing. Let Quantum Quattro™ teach the people of today the beneficial wisdom of the past. Use Quantum Quattro™ to support community celebrations, environmental campaigns and world awareness movements by bestowing it to influential people, gridding it around relevant areas and including the crystal in power grids. When worn near the throat, Quantum Quattro™ enables inspirational speakers and protest leaders to inspire others with their authentically heartfelt words.

Ask Lemur, a guide with strong Lemurian energy, to guide you back to a connection with nature. He will show you how to rise above the chaos and corruption, the capitalism and consumerism of current-day life and tune in to the potential magnificence of the future that is currently unseen to most.

Hope

Quantum Quattro™ enables you to connect with higher forms of guidance such as angels, Ascended Masters and Great Spirit as well as spirit beings dwelling with us on Earth. Hold it to your third eye chakra to synergise your vibration with these higher beings. Through prayer and connection with the divine, you can find solace about the future of humanity and planet Earth, knowing that humanity is supported and loved. Quantum Quattro™ engenders a sense of hope, provided from spiritual guidance rather than mere wishful thinking. Wear or carry Quantum Quattro™ with you constantly as a reminder of your commitment to work towards the healing of the planet and the evolution of humankind to a more communal, supportive way of being. Start your day with an affirmation that supports the betterment of humanity as you don your crystal for the day. Each night light a candle and say a prayer for the world before you retire. Place your Quantum Quattro™ in your pillowslip overnight for peaceful sleep with pleasant dreams.

QUARTZ, ANGEL AURA

Beauty / Harmonious Relationships / Pregnancy and Birth / Angelic Connection

Angel Aura Quartz, sometimes called Opal Aura Quartz, is created via an alchemical process of bonding Clear Quartz with Platinum and/or Silver. This Quartz is an iridescent white or clear stone sparkling with a pearly rainbow shine. It is said that priests and priestesses of past civilisations such as Lemuria wore white robes that shone like Angel Aura Quartz. Angel Aura enables you to improve your meditation so you can open yourself to discover divine knowledge and enjoy deep spiritual experiences. Allow this crystal to aid in establishing a connection to your angels or guides, ensuring you always feel safe and guided. Angel Aura brings love and light into any situation, promoting kindness, compassion, peace and calming. It allows forgiveness of yourself and others and in turn works to mend broken relationships. This crystal truly heightens your ability to witness beauty in the world, even in the ugliest of situations or environments.

> **Animal:** White Dove
> **Plants:** Frangipani and White Rose
> **Astrological Correspondence:** Moon
> **Power Day:** Monday
> **Cleanse with:** Moon

Your Crystal Alignment Meditation

Go and sit with something in nature that is white. It may be fresh snow that has fallen or a fragrant white rose. Connect to the colour white. How does this colour make you feel? Can you feel any effect on your body? Once you feel you are connected to the healing of the white energy, connect with your Quartz.

Beauty

Angel Aura opens you up to the light of the world allowing you to tune in with all that is beautiful and bountiful. It helps you to let go of all that is in the past that may be holding you back. Are you happy today? If not, why not? Take fifteen minutes to sit outside, focusing on your breath while holding Angel Aura and feel that restriction dissolve into white light around you.

Wear Angel Aura anywhere on your body. Its powerful energy will fill your whole aura with light. As you put it on at the start of the day, state an affirmation such as, "Today the angels walk with me, and everything's true beauty is all I will see". Go about your day sensing this white light surrounding you and healing all those you interact with. Using Angel Aura in combination with taking frangipani flower essence can help you speak calmly and gracefully when in group situations.

Harmonious Relationships

With Angel Aura around, no issue or disagreement can remain unresolved for long. The soft energy of Angel Aura promotes love and romance. When disagreements do occur, Angel Aura guides you to talk with kindness and compassion. Place an Angel Aura near a photo of yourself and the other person in a prominent place. Add a white candle and light it daily. You may also like to add a vase of white roses or frangipanis on special occasions. This mini altar or shrine will send harmonious vibes around the space and act as a constant reminder or the sacredness of the relationship.

Pregnancy and Birth

Angel Aura offers support during all stages of pregnancy. If you are suffering from morning sickness or baby blues, carry or wear Angel Aura to boost your mood and remind you of the beauty of the miracle of birth. Place a piece in the baby's nursery before it is born. Take time each day to sit in the room, holding the crystal while listening to soothing music, feeling a sense of peace and ease. Leave the crystal in the room when you leave. This will start to create a soothing space for your newborn and will help them to settle and sleep peacefully. When placed near the crib Angel Aura also acts as a form of protection for the baby. Take a piece into the labour room to offer support to both the mother and newborn. Angel Aura is especially supportive to single mothers and can be worn every day to give them the strength and guidance of the angels.

Angelic Connection

The name Angel Aura comes from the likeness of the iridescent colours of angel wings as well as the connection these crystals have to the angelic realms. It is a powerful crystal for harmonising your vibration to a level that allows you to make angelic contact. Place your piece of Angel Aura in the centre of a power grid. Surround this with eleven Clear Quartz Crystals pointing inwards to encourage white light energy to move towards you and your space. If you are working on connecting with your guardian angel, start with using supporting crystals related to the angelic realms such as Angelite, Celestite and Seraphinite. If you would like to connect with an archangel use Ruby for Michael, Diamond (or Herkimer Diamond) for Uriel, Emerald for Raphael or Sapphire (or Iolite) for Gabriel as your supporting crystals. As your relationship with the angels strengthens, follow your guidance and change the supporting crystals accordingly. Angels can often use feathers as a sign to contact you at times when they wish you to pay attention. If you find a feather on the ground, add this to your grid. You may want to take a course of a white rose flower essence to enrich your connection. There are various ones to choose from but a little research will guide you to the one best for you.

QUARTZ, AQUA AURA

Throat Chakra / Healing Communication / Creating Opportunities / Telepathy

Aqua Aura Quartz is created via an alchemical process whereby Clear Quartz is fused with a layer of Gold. The result of this process is a Quartz with a distinctive, electric peacock blue colour. Aqua Aura Quartz is a powerful tool in clearing communication barriers and allowing healing to occur. It guides its guardian to speak with optimism and authenticity.

Animal: Blue-and-Gold Macaw
Plants: Blue Tansy and Olive
Astrological Correspondences: Mercury and Sedna
Power Day: Wednesday
Cleanse with: Water, ideally warmed or charged by the sun since Aqua Aura contains Gold, a solar metal.

Your Crystal Alignment Meditation

Go and sit with something in nature where you can see blue. You may want to go sit before the ocean or a vast lake. On a clear day, lie back and gaze at the sky. Connect to the colour blue. How does this colour make you feel? Can you feel any effect on your body? Once you feel you sense a connectedness to the healing of the blue energy, connect with your Quartz.

Throat Chakra

Aqua Aura is a powerful stimulator of your throat chakra. When your throat chakra is underactive you lack the ability to communicate clearly. You may find others cannot understand you or misinterpret what you are saying. People may find you unreliable and inconsistent. Telling the truth and even being honest with yourself may be a challenge and the unclear, hesitant messages that you give out may have caused you trouble in the past. You may find that dealing with people on a day-to-day basis is frustrating and feel misunderstood as an individual, leading to a tendency to keep to yourself more and more over time. Unless this is remedied you can end up becoming quite the hermit.

Take time to rest, with Aqua Aura upon your throat chakra. Cross your fingers on the inside of your hands, without the thumbs. Let the thumbs touch at the tops, creating a circle with your fingers and rest them in your lap. Breathe deeply focusing on your exhalation emptying your lungs. In this peaceful state you may start to feel words or thoughts come up. Verbalise them or write them down. You may want to share them with someone later. Continue to wear Aqua Aura near your throat each day for continual stimulation of the throat chakra.

To enhance this practice incorporate bright blue into your life by filling your home with blue decorations or burning blue candles and wearing blue. Keep your neck relaxed with neck-rolling exercises or a massage, and using an affirmation such as, "I lovingly express myself freely" that you repeat throughout your day. Olive oil facilitates the free flow of energy so add a healthy amount to your diet each day. All this will help stimulate your throat chakra.

Healing Communication

Sometimes we choose to withhold communicating something with someone that is important to us. You may not have the confidence yet, are waiting for the right time or you're not sure exactly how to put into the words how you feel. Perhaps you cannot get in touch with the person or it is inappropriate to talk to them about this matter. Maybe they have passed on.

Holding this inside can have ill effects on you. You may notice you're becoming restless, distracted or angry. When you are not able to express yourself freely, it can start to manifest physically in your body. A sore throat, laryngitis, tonsillitis, teeth or jaw problems, earaches, hearing problems, sinus infections, thyroid problems and sore neck or shoulders may all suggest you are facing a communication barrier somewhere in your life. If you are feeling suffocated, smothered or stifled this may manifest as asthma and unresolved sadness can manifest physically in the lungs. Aqua Aura can assist you as you take healing actions. Hold your Aqua Aura in your receptive hand and visualise the person in front of you. Sense their energy. Take a deep breath and in your own time, say what you need to say, either aloud or in your mind. Don't hold back and just let the words flow freely.

If you still feel it is important and possible to have this conversation in the physical world, let your Aqua Aura help you. Wear it near your throat chakra or on the receptive side of your body to give you the courage and the grace to say what needs to be said clearly and with love. In preparation, connect with your Blue-and-Gold Macaw guide who helps you think before you speak and deliver your message in a beautiful way that allows healing for everyone. When it is time to have the conversation, diffuse or inhale blue tansy essential oil as it dissolves anger and forcefulness to create a peaceful space, allowing clear communication to occur. All you must do if focus on expressing your truth, and do not allow the success of the conversation to be based purely on the other person's response. If you feel that you have reached the point where a communication breakdown has sapped all your energy, try a course of olive flower essence. It gives energy back if you feel you've given all and have no more to give.

Creating Opportunities

Once you have balanced your throat chakra, Aqua Aura can help you manifest your desires. The popular saying, "Watch your thoughts, they become words; watch your words, they become actions; watch your actions, they become habits; watch your habits, they become character; watch your character, for it becomes your destiny" definitely resonates with Aqua Aura. In other words, Aqua Aura adds power to your words bringing them into action and physical manifestation.

As well as wearing Aqua Aura, make a water elixir with the crystal and drink it daily. As you start to communicate freely and gracefully, your inner beauty will shine. It will break down closed doors, expanding opportunities and attracting like-minded people.

If you live in a household that has a severe case of emotional constipation, Aqua Aura can open up communication pathways again. Place a cluster and a light blue candle by a happy family photo in your living room. Its energy will start to increase affection and appreciation between family members. Using this cluster as the power stone in a power grid can help increase humanity's acknowledgement that we all have a responsibility for the wellbeing of this planet, empowering people to become involved in proactive initiatives.

Telepathy

Aqua Aura Quartz also strengthens higher forms of communication. It is great for inspired writing. You can also meditate with Aqua Aura Quartz and then start to write down what comes to mind while you are in the meditative state. Once you finish the meditation, re-read what you have written and see what messages are revealed.

Aqua Aura is renowned for aiding telepathy. While holding Aqua Aura in your receptive hand or against your third eye chakra, think of someone in your life you would like to send a telepathic message. See them before you, their eyes meeting yours. Tune in to how they are feeling now and empathise with them. Sense their energy until you feel a link between the two of you.

Now deliver that message to their mind. Keep the message clear and simple. See them receiving it, understanding it and reacting accordingly. Perhaps you may also get a message back. The more you practise this the more powerful it can become and Aqua Aura will support you in this practice. This is a great exercise to practise with a friend on a regular basis, ideally on a Wednesday. Each of you can hold a piece of Aqua Aura and agree who is the sender and who is the receiver. Start with a simple message such as a word or colour and as you improve, try messages that are more complex.

When you are not using your Aqua Aura, keep it in a box made of olive wood or with an olive leaf. Olive facilitates basic and higher forms of communication and will heighten your Aqua Aura's powers.

QUARTZ, CHAMPAGNE AURA

Celebration / Spontaneity / Sensibility

Champagne Aura Quartz is created through an alchemical process that fuses a mixture of all or some Gold, Iron, Indium and Platinum to Clear Quartz. This creates a crystal with a soft but sparkling golden brown colour, similar to that of the drink it's named after. Just like the celebratory drink, Champagne Aura picks you up and delivers fun-filled times. It can manifest impromptu events and pleasant surprises, all while keeping you level-headed and sensible.

Animals: Antelope and Canary
Plant: Mustard plant
Astrological Correspondence: Sun
Power Day: Sunday
Cleanse with: Sun

Your Crystal Alignment Meditation

Go and sit somewhere in nature where you can see brown. It may be a tree trunk or a large boulder. Perhaps you can just sit before some brown soil. Connect to the colour brown. How does this colour make you feel? Can you feel any effect on your body? Once you feel you've connected to the healing of the brown energy, connect with your Quartz.

Celebration

Champagne Aura will encourage guests to mingle and guard against gossiping and bitchiness. To ensure your party runs smoothly, sprinkle some mustard seeds at the entrance to ward of any danger or unwanted guests. Work with your Canary guide to ensure you keep conversation positive and upbeat. This beautiful songbird joyfully wishes for you to join her in song and speak of all the beautiful things that fill your heart. If you have a pet canary, place a piece of Champagne Aura near its cage. Their two energies will combine to make a cheerful environment at home.

Champagne Aura isn't purely a celebration crystal. It is powerful wherever groups of people gather. Place a piece with a gold candle in the home to promote harmony in busy households. At work, keep it on your desk or in meeting rooms to allow the resolution of conflict and complaints and create a haven of calm and contentment.

Spontaneity

The golden energy of Champagne Aura Quartz heals the body on all levels and opens you up to new abilities and experiences. It can also help you resolve inner conflicts between head and heart or instincts and morals. Wear Champagne Aura Quartz over the solar plexus for healing and new beginnings.

Once you have dealt with any issues, Champagne Aura will then inspire a sense of *carpe diem*. Keep it on you when you go travelling, start a new job or wanting to spice up a stale relationship. If you are a salary worker, working Monday to Friday, make this an everyday crystal if you fear your life is becoming mundane. You can connect with your Antelope guide who will show you how to rise above the petty and insignificant. She will teach you to have an up-beat approach to life, giving you the ability to attract fun experiences into your life, without neglecting your responsibilities.

Sensibility

Although Champagne Aura has a jovial energy, this crystal does prevent you getting drunk with excitement. Keep a piece in your pocket to keep you grounded when socialising. It promotes altruistic behaviour so when mixing with others it ensures you leave a good impression. If you are unsure whether to take a risk, hold Champagne Aura Quartz in your receptive hand for at least five minutes before committing.

Champagne Aura helps to ground and settle you when you feel anxious. It reduces stress by stimulating your survival instincts and giving more strength and focus. If you need to soothe an overactive solar plexus, chakra place or wear it over the energy centre. Hold Champagne Aura pointing away from the body to alleviate a panic attack or discourage a "healing crisis" during any kind of spiritual sessions. Champagne Aura attracts protective home guardians such as animal totems, guardian angels or spirit guides to protect the inhabitants physically and spiritually, especially from paranormal activity. Have Champagne Aura nearby during séances.

QUARTZ, CLEAR

Stamina / Health / Absent Healing

Clear Quartz, also known as Crystal Quartz or Rock Crystal, is the second most abundant mineral in the Earth's continental crust making it the "universal crystal". Clear Quartz is a strong energy transmitter and amplifies the energy of other crystals, hence why it is perfect in most power grids. It contains the essence of white light, which is made of all colours and thus is a great substitute for any crystal you require, but cannot find. Ultimately, Clear Quartz works to guide you towards a state of optimism and balance.

Animals: Camel, Horse, Kangaroo and Shark
Plant: Ginger
Astrological Correspondences: Sun and Moon
Power Days: Sunday and Monday
Cleanse by: Since Clear Quartz has such a diverse range of capabilities, it is also possible to cleanse it many ways. Choose a technique that matches your intent for the crystal. For example, if you want to work with it for endurance charge it by the sun or if you want help balancing emotions cleanse it by the element of water. Clear Quartz will cleanse just as well via the elements of fire, air, earth or by the moon. Other specialised ways to cleanse your crystal is by placing it in a crystal singing bowl, ideally one that is in the note of the chakras that matches your intent. Experienced healers can also cleanse Clear Quartz by visualising it being washed in white light. Whichever technique you decide, be sure to cleanse yourself at the same time.

Your Crystal Alignment Meditation

Go to the top of a mountain or visualise yourself there in your mind. Take a few deep breaths and inhale the fresh mountainous air. Observe everything around you and take in the diversity of the surroundings from every direction. Then become aware of the sky above you. See it stretching to the horizon. Consider that beyond the Earth's atmosphere expands a universe beyond measure. Tune in to the vastness of the world. Acknowledge the limitlessness of this place. Clear Quartz also encompasses these limitless possibilities and once you sense this, connect with your crystal.

Stamina

Clear Quartz lifts you on all levels. It boosts energy levels, shows you how to control your emotions, promotes optimistic thoughts and increases spiritual awareness. Due to its diverse nature, Clear Quartz can work well with the teaching of various powerful animal guides. Combine it with Shark for greater awareness, Camel for endurance or Kangaroo for control. Horse is a popular guide that can encourage strength and stamina. When feeling lethargic, Clear Quartz should be an immediate choice.

Wear a Clear Quartz pendant at times when you are burning the candle at both ends. Unless you are using Clear Quartz for a specific duty lower on your body, wear it as high as possible as it works largely with the crown and higher chakras. If you need a quick energy burst, rather than reaching for an unhealthy soda or energy drink, charge a glass of water by placing a Clear Quartz in it for thirty minutes before drinking.

If you have an old pet or work with aging animals that are starting to become weak and frail, Clear Quartz can help make their daily life easier. Place a piece in their water bowl, or four pieces at the corners of their playpen. You can add a pendant to your cat's or dog's collar too. However, you may need to remove this at night along with any other Quartz, especially close to the full moon if they can't settle or sleep.

Health

Illness and disease is a result of the body being out of balance. As Clear Quartz is a balancing crystal it works to guide you towards better health. It is a strong choice for healing any concussion, brain damage or brain tumours as this master crystal harmonises with the body's "master" organ.

Wear, carry or add a raw Quartz Crystal to your water for overall health. If you drink herbs in a liquid form, drink them out of a Clear Quartz cup to enhance their powers. In fact, any natural remedy can be amplified by combining it with Clear Quartz. Try adding ginger, Clear Quartz's harmonic plant, to your life to further enhance healing. Eating ginger before a healing or meditation increases the session's effectiveness as it encourages blood flow, increases body temperature and aids in the body's use and absorption of nutrients. Diffuse ginger essential oil or add it to carrier oil and then use in massage or as a perfume to take advantage of its stimulating properties. Some people do have an allergic reaction so a 24-hour test on a small patch of skin is recommended.

If you are feeling pain in a specific area, hold Clear Quartz on the site, close your eyes and with your mind's eye visualise the exact centre point of the pain. It may help to see it as a colour. The Clear Quartz will work to rebalance body systems and dissipate pain.

Clear Quartz is sometimes called the "milk crystal". It is reputed for initiating lactation and increasing milk flow. Simply keep a tumbled stone in your bra each day. While we are discussing newborns, a Clear Quartz is a perfect gift for a child. It can serve as a life talisman and will increase in power as they grow older.

Some people find it hard to sleep with Clear Quartz in the bedroom. If you want it in your room, give it a shot for a couple of nights and if you sleep restlessly, it may be best kept elsewhere.

Absent Healing

You don't have to be with a specific person or at a certain place you wish to heal. Clear Quartz allows you to perform absent or distance healing though its ability to project energy to an intended recipient. Relax and close your eyes, holding your Clear Quartz in your projective hand. Visualise and sense white light shooting forth from your crystal and travelling to the intended person. See them surrounded in white light and reacting positively to the healing. The same can be done to send healing to a place, spreading a mist of white light across an area.

Quartz will vary in vibration depending on the country it has come from as it absorbs the energy of the land. For example, you may find Tibetan Quartz to be quite peaceful while Brazilian quite uplifting and vibrant. Collect Quartz from around the word and use them to make a world-healing grid by placing them on a map then surrounding with peace and understanding crystals such as Angelite, Rose Quartz or Super Quartzes.

To enhance your ability as a healer, take a dose of ginger flower essence. This will help you align with the vibration of Clear Quartz when using it as well as remove your ego's selfish desire to be the cause of the change. Rather it increases your self-worth and allows you to humbly accept that you are merely a contributor to facilitating change in others.

QUARTZ, RAINBOW AURA

Adaptability / Turning Point / Success

Rainbow Aura Quartz, also known as Titanium or Flame Aura Quartz, displays an iridescent Titanium surface shimmering with multi-coloured rainbow reflections. Holding the vibration of all the colours of the spectrum, Rainbow Aura balances all your chakras and bodily systems. It is created by combining Titanium with Clear Quartz and sometimes includes Gold and Niobium. As Titanium is one of the highest vibration metals, Rainbow Aura enables you to reach new heights in perception and power, allowing you to rise above limits you thought impossible.

Animal: Gouldian Finch
Plant: Ash
Astrological Correspondence: Mercury
Power Day: Wednesday
Cleanse with: Air

Your Crystal Alignment Meditation

Go to a pyramid and sit within or by it. It can be one of your own construct if you like. Throughout history, many cultures have explored and honoured the power of the pyramid. Just like the Aura Quartzes, pyramids are a man-made construct created to maximise the power of natural energies. Sit quietly and tune in to the energies around you as well as any changes you sense in your body. Once you are feeling empowered, connect with your Quartz.

Adaptability

Rainbow Aura Quartz is the crystal of Hermes, the god of quick intelligence, communication and wit, and when worn, increases your energy, vitality and mental prowess. It gives you a zest for life and allows think on your feet, enabling you to adapt to any situation. For situations when you need to communicate effectively, carry it with you combined with an ash twig or leaf, as the ash tree further enhances communication skills. Wear it near the chest or head to counteract the effects of multiple sclerosis that have manifested from having a hard and inflexible mind and heart.

Turning Point

Rainbow Aura is the crystal to grab when you're faced with a "do-or-die" situation in life. It helps you face and overcome major life obstacles such as bankruptcy, life threatening sickness, partner separation, or starvation. Take some time to sit quietly and contemplate solutions to your challenge while holding your crystal. For a more formal practice, light seven candles (red, orange, yellow, green, blue, indigo and violet) and scry gazing into your Rainbow Aura. Connect with your higher self and allow guidance to come to you. It will allow you to become aware of all possible solutions to the challenges you are facing. Furthermore, Rainbow Aura will bring deep insight to your relationships and an understanding of the lessons to be learned from your present situation.

Success

Rainbow Aura enables you to find balance both within yourself and in your life. It ensures that you give attention to all areas of your life so that nothing goes unattended. Although we have one star (sun) sign, each of the zodiac constellations influences our life. A complete astrological birth chart looks at the placement of all planets amongst the constellations at our birth, not just the sun. Furthermore, the planets of our solar system are always passing through these constellations in their orbit and this energy can impact our life on Earth. Each of the twelve signs governs an aspect of our life. Take some time to sit down and set goals for all areas of your life using the twelve zodiac signs and the aspect they represent as a framework. The twelve areas of your life to set goals for are:

- Personal improvement (Aries)
- Financial matters and assets (Taurus)
- Social life (Gemini)
- Home and family (Cancer)
- Creativity and self-expression (Leo)
- Health and physical wellbeing (Virgo)
- Love life (Libra)
- Spiritual (Scorpio)
- New experiences and expansion such as learning or travel (Sagittarius)
- Career (Capricorn)
- Activism and community contribution (Aquarius)
- Sleep, dreams and mental health (Pisces)

Write them down or create a vision board and place this with your Rainbow Aura Quartz on your altar inside. Outside, charge twelve seeds, each with one of your twelve goals and plant them in a pot with a Rainbow Aura Quartz. You may like to invite the assistance of Hermes by repeating a wish such as, "Come to me Hermes upon the four winds. Help me design my destiny and colour my life." At least once a week take time to examine the progress of your seeds and your goals. You may like to work with your Gouldian Finch guide who shows you how to shift from one focus to another to ensure you are caring for all areas of your life.

Rainbow Aura will help you bring more colour and beauty into your life. Place a cluster in your home or workplace to increase positivity. Wear it as a pendant to enable you to see the beauty in all things. Each time you catch yourself talking negatively, clutch the pendant and say, "Show me the beauty within all things". Use Rainbow Aura Quartz in harmony with colour therapy to progress beyond unwanted personality traits.

QUARTZ, ROSE

Giving / Friends and Family / Forgiveness / Heart Chakra

Rose Quartz is the soft pink hued variety of Quartz found in various locations around the world, with much available on the market today, coming from Brazil. According to myth, Rose Quartz was created when Ares, god of war, jealous with Aphrodite's love for Adonis, turned himself into a wild boar and attacked the god of beauty and desire. As Aphrodite rushed to save Adonis, she caught herself on a briar bush and her blood spilt on white Quartz, turning it pink. Thus, Rose Quartz is known as the crystal of love. It enables you to see where love already exists in your life, opening your heart with gratitude and ensuring love continues to flow into your life.

Animal: Turkey
Plant: Rose
Astrological Correspondence: Venus
Power Day: Friday
Cleanse with: Water

Your Crystal Alignment Meditation

Go outside early in the morning. Find a single dew drop hanging upon a leaf. Observe it, notice the colours it reflects, how it makes the leaf bend. As you focus on it, feel the peace that comes with being in the moment. When you are feeling balanced, connect with your Quartz.

Giving

At first Turkey may seem like an unusual pairing with the stone of love, however, Rose Quartz doesn't teach you how to receive love. Rather, Rose Quartz teaches you the art of giving. When you give love, love will flow back to you in return. Turkey is one of the strongest guides for teaching you how to give.

Rose Quartz will shift your focus from the lack of love in your life to where love already exists and where you can give more love. As you fill your heart with gratitude for the love you already have, you willingly allow more love to gradually flow into your life. Keep a small Rose Quartz heart in your pocket each day and each time you remember it there, take a moment to recall where love already exists in your life. At night, take a few moments to relax, close your eyes and send loving thoughts back to the loving source.

When you are working towards finding a new lover, it is important to be clear on what you want. The more distinct your desire, the easier it is for the universe to deliver what you seek. Each night hold your Rose Quartz against your heart and visualise the type of person you wish to find. Look deep into their eyes and allow your souls to connect and speak. You can fill your space with the scent of roses to enhance the loving energies during this practice. Wear your Rose Quartz over your heart at all other times to enable it to lead you towards your heart's true aspiration.

Family and Friends

Rose Quartz understands the true essence of unconditional love, leading to more fulfilling relationships with family and friends. Wear, carry, grid and use Rose Quartz in elixirs to release your expectations of others. For when you expect anything from another, you set yourself up for disappointment and ill feelings any time they do not deliver. By placing your expectations and standards on another, whether it is a partner, child, friend, colleague or any other person you have a relationship with you hinder them from freely expressing who they truly are. Let Rose Quartz open your heart so that you see you have all you need and the loving gifts you receive from others are simply a bonus; the "icing on the cake"!

As you release these expectations, there can be a positive effect on your physical wellbeing. Rose Quartz is renowned as a bringer of youth, known for helping the body keep a clear, smooth complexion and preventing wrinkles. As part of your daily beauty routine take a tumbled Rose Quartz and gently massage it over your face to give you a more radiant glow. When held or worn as a bracelet or ring, Rose Quartz heals the hands and hand chakras, which are the gateways to giving and receiving. It eliminates any physical ailments, manifested from a tendency to hold on to a rigid ideal of how life should be. As you heal, you can improve your ability to paint, sculpt, massage or create things with your hands.

Use Rose Quartz to send loving energy to the rest of the world, your global family. Hold Rose Quartz in your receptive hand and connect to the Divine Feminine energy of peace and acceptance. Visualise a pink light encircling the people in another place in the world. Rose Quartz is especially useful for people affected by war and if a great support to any peace-worker. Give healing love back to Mother Earth by burying charged Rose Quartz in the ground, particularly in polluted areas to aid regeneration.

Forgiveness

Rose Quartz works to soften a hardened heart and allows you to give love to those you resent. It takes away pain and resentment held in the heart and allows you to freely love yourself and others for who they truly are. Hold your Rose Quartz in your receptive hand and place a pink candle by your projective hand. Visualise and feel the energy of the person (it may be yourself) or the event you'd like to forgive. Feel the loving energy of the Rose Quartz fill your being, surrounding your heart and all of your being. Then release the grudge and judgement into the flame of the candle. Let the fire burn away the hurt and pain. Continue this until you feel better.

Heart Chakra

Rose Quartz soothes an overactive heart chakra. If you find you give of yourself too much in relationships when it is not reciprocated, or wear your heart on your sleeve, resulting in getting hurt, you may have an overactive heart chakra. Other signs include greed, a tendency to dominate or control loved ones especially with emotional blackmail, or a tendency to be melodramatic or overly emotional with issues of the heart. Place your Rose Quartz on your chest and visualise a soft light healing this area. Repeat this daily until you sense your chakra has rebalanced.

QUARTZ, ROSE AURA

Kind Heartedness / Romance / Glamour

Rose and Ruby Aura Quartz is the fusion of Clear Quartz with Platinum, Gold and Silver. By varying the portions of these metals, two reddish pink Aura Quartz variations are created. For a youthful energy use fuchsia-coloured Rose Aura Quartz and for a more serious energy use Ruby aura, which is a deeper magenta red colour. Rose Aura Quartz is a crystal of good times. It fills your heart with joy and attracts what you desire into your life. It allows you to be kind natured and make a good impression on people around you.

Animal: Sugar Glider
Plant: Pink Rose
Astrological Correspondence: Venus
Power Day: Friday
Cleanse with: Water or by placing on rose petals

Your Crystal Alignment Meditation

Go and sit with something in nature that is pink. It may be the glowing sky at sunset or a fragrant pink rose. Connect to the colour pink. How does this colour make you feel? Can you feel any effect on your body? Once you feel connected to the healing of the pink energy, connect with your Quartz.

Kind Heartedness

Rose Aura imbues the whole body with love, restoring it to perfect balance while also removing limited beliefs and attitudes. It will help you release any ill effects of abuse on a physical, mental, emotional and spiritual level and forgive those who have hurt you in the past. When worn over the heart, Rose Aura awakens a sense of importance. However, it doesn't increase tendencies of selfishness or arrogance but rather allows you to realise your self-worth and understand the role you can fulfil within your community.

Rose Aura instils a sense of loving kindness in its guardian. Firstly this crystal encourages you to be kind to yourself. It is the perfect remedy if you work too hard or beat yourself up over failures. It enables you to treat yourself with loving kindness and open your heart to see the lessons from mistakes. This flows on to how you treat other people, making you considerate and accepting. It allows you to be tolerant of those who show ignorance, conceit, anger, jealousy or greed, understanding that this is symptomatic of a lost soul. If a challenging person upsets you, hold your Rose Aura between your hands and pray that they find guidance. Keeping Rose Aura with you will help you communicate tactfully in these awkward situations.

Romance

As Rose Aura lifts your mood, placing you in a state of tranquillity and peace, you will open yourself to attracting more love into your life. Singles looking for love should hold their crystal against their heart and repeat, "love, love descend from above, come near, come near and find me here". Once you find the perfect someone, your Sugar Glider guide can teach you how to successfully soar in love and openly embrace others with open arms and an open heart.

If you have a partner, work with Rose Aura on applying unconditional love in the relationship. This crystal harmonises perfectly with various rose flower essences. When combined they can help you connect with the knowledge that the universe provides you everything you need and that you don't need to demand anything from a lover.

Glamour

Rose Aura Quartz promotes good hair days and finding the perfect outfit. It enables you to put your best foot forward and stand out when you need to. It is especially helpful if you are interested in romance writing, hairdressing, fashion, fragrance, beauty products or modelling. It will allow you to combine your passion, knowledge, charisma and unique style to ensure success. Keep a Rose Aura point or cluster in your workspace, pairing it with fresh pink roses each Friday.

QUARTZ, ROYAL AURA

Water / Understanding / Integration

Royal Aura Quartz is an alchemical combination of the metal Cobalt, plus occasionally Platinum, with Quartz. Also known as Cobalt Aura Quartz, this crystal actualises creative pursuits, removes self-limiting blocks, and stimulates the imagination. It lifts the mood, and during contemplation helps to maintain a state of grace and inner peace. To work with Royal Aura is to choose to set out on a journey both physically and spiritually.

Animal: Blue Heron
Plants: Elder and Water Lily
Astrological Correspondences: Moon and Neptune
Power Day: Monday
Cleanse with: Water

Your Crystal Alignment Meditation

Go to a waterway at night. It can be a gentle stream, a gushing lake, a vast lake or the great ocean. Place your hands or feet in the water and feel its flow, both physically and energetically. Let the water wash away all stresses and tension. Slowly let relaxation flow within you, allowing the natural ebb and flow of the world return you to a state of balance. You are now ready to connect with your Quartz.

Water

Royal Aura Quartz has a strong resonance with water, so take a walk to a stream, river or beach and meditate with the crystal there. Not only will it help you calm down, it can aid you to learn more about the scientific, elemental, magical and metaphysical abilities of water. Royal Aura can also be used in combination with any therapy for phobias of water such as aquaphobia or cymophobia. Place Royal Aura on top of your water purifier to charge your water. Place it next to your water bottle and it will sing out to you, reminding you to keep drinking water. If you become dehydrated, hold it in your receptive hand to facilitate quicker rehydration. The same works for plants, so place the crystal on the soil until the plant picks up again. Place Royal Aura against the skin to soothe and cool sunburn. Royal Aura brings strong rains to drought-ridden areas. Place a piece in a small amount of water, pointing towards the sky to attract rain clouds.

Understanding

Use Royal Aura to stimulate your third eye chakra. This will strengthen your inner vision, intuition and grow your understanding and awareness of how the world works, especially during Neptune retrograde. Place Royal Aura upon your forehead during workings and wear it high on the body at other times. The scent of water lily during meditation will harmonise with your crystal, and help increase alternative states of consciousness. Royal Aura also resonates with the elder shrub's energy so wrap your Royal Aura in an elder leaf to amplify its energies. Place Royal Aura and some elderberries by your bedside to induce insightful dreams at night. You can make a room spray to eradicate mental and spiritual clutter from a space by placing elder flowers in boiling water at night. Add your Royal Aura once the water has cooled. In the morning strain the flowers and remove the Royal Aura and pour the water into a spray bottle. Spritz the solution around the house to spread the energy.

Integration

Once Royal Aura has allowed you to expand your spiritual knowledge, wearing it daily will allow you to assimilate your new learning into the practical and intellectual aspects of life. Working with your Blue Heron guide will enable you to stare into the waters of self-reflection and understand the relevance of knowledge for your personal circumstances. He can encourage you to gain new perspective by looking at the big picture to get a complete understanding of your life or a situation.

Due to its ability to encourage integration, Royal Aura assists each cell in the body to function correctly, ensuring all parts of the body are working at the optimum level. Place Royal Aura against the skin to assist in the treatment of cellular disorders. Place a piece of Royal Aura in the kitchen to guide you in the blending of foods and creative cooking. It will awaken insights within you to produce meals that thrill the tastebuds and enliven the whole body.

QUARTZ, SMOKEY

Grounding / Earth Star Chakra / Primal

Brown or Black Quartz is called Smokey Quartz, and is one of the most settling and nurturing crystals in the Quartz family. Smokey Quartz connects us with a sense of homeliness, both within our own space and out in nature. It allows us to pause, relax, reflect and feel good about the future and ourselves. It invokes a connection to plants and animals and guides us to learn from working in harmony with them. Smokey Quartz is great for "space cadets", bringing them back to the here and now. It combats flightiness, confusion and manic obsession by reactivating our primal self as the key controller of our actions, shifting our attention to the here and now.

Animal: Bison
Plant: Willow
Astrological Correspondence: Earth
Power Day: Friday
Cleanse with: Earth

Your Crystal Alignment Meditation

Go and sit on the earth. Become aware of the ground beneath you. Notice the parts of your body in contact with the earth. Tune in to rhythms of nature around you and see if you can sense the energy of the land upon which you are resting. You may feel a pulsing, vibration or an emotion come across you. Perhaps the land has a message for you today. Just relax and allow your bond with the land to grow. Feel the energy reach out and kiss you.

Then connect with the whole of planet Earth. Start to visualise large roots growing from the soles of your feet or the base of your spine. See the roots delve deeper and deeper into the ground, spreading in all directions to connect to all corners of the planet. These roots are an extension of your energetic self and act as a link between you and the Earth. Visualise and sense an exchange in energy with the planet, its heartbeat resonating with yours. With each out breath, send all unwanted feelings and energies into the earth to be dissolved. With each inhalation sense and feel the soothing, nurturing energies of the Mother Earth flowing into you. You are now ready to connect with your Quartz.

Grounding

Smokey Quartz is a powerful grounding stone. Hold Smokey Quartz in each hand to ground yourself after powerful spiritual work such as healing or astral travel. If you have a tendency to devote too much time to spiritual pursuits and struggle to meet daily demands such as remembering engagements and paying bills, wearing Smokey Quartz near the centre of your body will aid you to keep a better spiritual-physical balance. If you have a demanding lifestyle or an overactive mind, carry a Smokey Quartz in each pocket to centre yourself and allow you to give top priority to your key focuses. If you struggle to meditate, hold a Smokey Quartz point as you recite a prayer or mantra. You'll find it easier to clear the mind of extraneous clutter. When performing healing, if the crystal is terminated aim the point away from you to dispel negative energy and depression or towards you to revitalise yourself.

Smokey Quartz will help you relax and increase feelings of comfort, allowing you to fall asleep with ease. If you suffer from insomnia, place a tumbled stone in your pillowslip. Include Smokey Quartz in a dream catcher to stop nightmares or place with a crucifix and white candle to deter paranormal activity.

Smokey Quartz can help with healing the liver when ailments have developed as a physical manifestation of holding anger. Tape a small piece of Smokey Quartz onto the skin near the liver as you recite the affirmation, "all is well". Repeat the affirmation each night as you remove the crystal. Willow flower essence can help alleviate anger from feeling like a victim or being bitter at the world. If this is the case, combine the flower essence with the use of Smokey Quartz.

Earth Star Chakra

Smokey Quartz works to stimulate your Earth star chakra, allowing you to connect to all of the planet Earth and the knowledge it holds. When this chakra is functioning at its optimum you will be able to learn from the collective consciousness of every animal, plant and mineral. Developing the Earth star chakra is vital to ensure spiritual advancement and soul star chakra stimulation. These two chakras work in harmony and balance with each other. Like a tree, your spiritual branches can stretch no higher up into the universe than your spiritual roots descend into the Earth. An underactive Earth star chakra slows spiritual growth. Symptoms of your Earth star chakra being low in energy are a fear of spiritual exploration, a focus on demonic energies or you fail to find direction in life. Prepare yourself to stimulate your Earth star chakra by smudging yourself and your space with sage. Then lie down, positioning your

Smokey Quartz about 15 centimetres below your feet. Visualise a dark brown or infrared ball of energy pulsing where the crystal rests. Continue to keep Smokey Quartz with you throughout your day until you feel this chakra is balanced. These practices can also work as a powerful healing technique for any foot ailment that has manifested from feelings of purposelessness or insignificance.

Primal

Smokey Quartz awakens your primal self, the part of you that is connected to the basics and necessities of living. The primal self has no wants except to ensure the primary needs of survival such as food, water and shelter are met. Keep a raw, untreated piece of Smokey Quartz with you to connect with your primal self to help you distinguish wants versus needs and prevent over-spending or over-consumption.

As Smokey Quartz awakens the primal self, it strengthens the bond to the spiritual essence of Earth. Gaze at a candle through a piece of Smokey Quartz to unlock doorways to long-forgotten worlds and realms of the planet. Create an altar dedicated to the goddess Gaia including a pot plant and Smokey Quartz to honour this bond. Smokey Quartz from Australia can help you connect to the Rainbow Serpent and its teachings. Use a piece of Morion (black Smokey) Quartz from the Americas to connect with Pachamama. By working with your Bison guide, and regular prayer whilst holding Smokey Quartz, you can improve your ability to see signs and guidance offered by Mother Earth.

QUARTZ, TANZAN AURA

Inspired Guidance / Comprehension / Manifestation

Tanzan Aura Quartz is a combination of Niobium, Indium and Gold, fused upon Quartz, producing a gorgeous indigo colour similar to the crystal Tanzanite. This crystal resonates with the violet flame and brings you guidance on healing yourself and humanity. Tanzan Aura reveals to you the unknown and guides you in learning the great mysteries of life. It will awaken parts of you that lie dormant, increasing your ability to contribute to the world.

Animal: Hyacinth Macaw
Plant: Blueberry
Astrological Correspondence: Moon
Power Day: Monday
Cleanse with: Full Moon

Your Crystal Alignment Meditation

Go and sit with something in nature where you can see the colour of indigo. Look for an indigo flower or a feather lying on the ground. Connect to the colour indigo. How does this colour make you feel? Can you feel any effect on your body? Once you feel you sense a connectedness to the healing of this indigo energy, connect with your Quartz.

Inspired Guidance

Tanzan Aura is a crystal of the muse, allowing you to tackle any issue, find innovative solutions and generate creative ways to express your ideas. It encourages you to think before talking, giving you a sense of the right things to say in any situation. Also connect with your Hyacinth Macaw guide who will educate you how to beautify and colour your communication. Keeping a Tanzan Aura cluster on your desk helps you find the right words, whether you are drafting an email or penning a novel, attracting inspiration from all directions. Wearing or carrying a piece will allow you to access its inspirational guidance when needed. It is known to be especially beneficial for anyone with a disability as it enables them to comprehend their full potential. Due to Tanzan Aura's ability to stimulate the imaginative and creative mind, it is best to reduce its use to the hours before bed. Otherwise you may find yourself awake all night as ideas keep flowing into your head.

When placed near the third eye chakra or held in your receptive hand, Tanzan Aura facilitates channelling, spiritual guidance, psychic abilities and the gift of foresight. Combine this with eating some blueberries before undertaking any spiritual work to manifest a spiritual cloak of protection. Hold Tanzan Aura when leading group meditations or rituals. It will enable you to stay in tune with each individual and gain guidance on the best way to direct everyone for optimum results.

Archangel Raziel is the chief keeper of all earthly and celestial knowledge. He knows all the secrets of the universe and how it works. Dedicate a piece of Tanzan Aura to him and hold it in prayer when you wish to understand esoteric material, manifestation principles, sacred geometry and quantum physics. Raziel will help you with alchemy, clairvoyance and the ability to recognise divine guidance. You'll be able to uncover links between the spiritual and the scientific. Signs of Raziel's presence are flashes of rainbow light or sudden inspired guidance.

Comprehension

Tanzan Aura helps you comprehend your purpose. Whether you are questioning the significance of your job or struggling to understand your purpose in life, Tanzan Aura can help. Wear it around your neck and when feelings of confusion arise, hold the crystal and ask, "show me the purpose here". Each night meditate with Tanzan Aura, visualising a violet ray descending from above and entering your mind. This ray will give you guidance on how you can best be of service to the Earth and those around you. Tanzan Aura Quartz offers support to kidnap or hostage victims or if you have experienced a traumatic or near-death experience. It allows you to conceive the bigger picture as well as learn any valuable life lessons.

Tanzan Aura strengthens your connection to a soul group. This is a group of people that supports each other in learning from life's challenges. If you feel that you were with certain people in prior incarnations, Tanzan Aura will help you gain knowledge and understanding on what gifts you hold for each other. Meditate, gift to others in your soul group and wear or carry Tanzan Aura when with them to strengthen the bond.

Headaches and migraines can manifest from tension associated with resistance to be carried along by the natural flow of life. Place Tanzan Aura against your head where the pain is strongest and tune in to the site of the pain. Visualise it glowing as an indigo light and relax as you allow it to diminish. Tanzan Aura also promotes healthy masturbation to release built up tension. Furthermore, wearing this crystal and keeping it near skincare products is reputed to slow down the aging process.

Manifestation

Tanzan Aura brings together your ability to receive inspired guidance, understand its message and then communicate this to the world. As you deepen your connection with the spiritual, Tanzan Aura increases your magical ability to request back to the universe what you need and desire. Use a Tanzan Aura point, generator or obelisk as your power crystal in a power grid to enable clear communication with the universe about what you wish to manifest.

QUARTZ, TIBETAN

Balance / Eastern Philosophies / Abstinence

Tibetan Quartz is a variety of Clear Quartz found near the Himalayan Mountains of Tibet. It often has black carbon spots or inclusions in it, thus is also referred to as Black Quartz or Tibetan Black Quartz. Coming from Tibet, these crystals attune to the esoteric knowledge and peaceful energy that has existed in Tibet for so long. Work with Tibetan Quartz to access the wisdoms of the East and bring peace and balance to your life.

Animal: Panda
Plant: Bamboo
Astrological Correspondence: Moon
Power Day: Monday
Cleanse by: Placing with uncooked, organic rice or using the sound of a Tibetan singing bowl.

Your Crystal Alignment Meditation

Go to the Himalayan Mountains and find a peaceful place to sit. If you cannot visit them physically, visualise yourself there in your mind as you sit outside. Place your hands on the earth and tune in to the energy of the Earth from where your Tibetan Quartz came from. As a sense of peace washes over you, chant the mantra "OM" repeatedly, either aloud or in your mind. You may also like to play a Tibetan singing bowl. Once you are feeling balanced and grounded, connect with your Quartz.

Balance

As a clear crystal, Tibetan Quartz exudes a healing, white energy that places a bubble of light around you. This energy lifts your vibration, deterring disturbing dreams and paranormal activity. A pot of bamboo in your home will give further protection from these and other forms of negativity. If you need healing on a physical, mental, emotional or any other realm this crystal is great to work with. Place the crystal near an area of concern or simply wear it over your heart for overall upliftment. The black inclusions add to the crystal's energy, giving it a balancing yin-yang feel. Tibetan Quartz harmonises with your Panda guide, which offers guidance in finding balance in your life, and prompting to avoid stress or complacency. Carry Tibetan Quartz constantly with you or place a piece near anything that may cause you grief. If you get upset at work, place a crystal on your desk or if you feel nervous driving, keep a piece in your car. Place a Tibetan Quartz point in each pocket if you wish to improve your physical balance.

If you are serious about finding true balance in your life, meditate with Tibetan Quartz with a piece of paper and pen nearby. Think of a moment recently when you were criticised, put down, repressed or told you were no good. Then find how you were being lifted up, praised and put on a pedestal, at that exact same second. It may not be obvious at first, but as you search deeper, you'll find the answers. Write them both down and identify the balance. As you recognise these opposites you will start to experience and see the balance and harmony in all life. You will realise that life is neither good, nor bad, these are simply biased judgements of the human mind. Start scanning back over your entire life and equilibrate lopsided opinions of criticism and praise you can remember. As you find more balance, you leave states of dis-ease, discomfort, distress, sadness, anxiety, over-excitement or mania and shift towards a more centred and level-headed way of living.

Eastern Philosophies
Tibetan Quartz helps you attune to the wisdoms of the ancient cultures of the East, bringing you knowledge and information concerning healing and spirituality. It has a powerful OM vibration, written universally as (ॐ). Connecting with this vibration allows you to increase your awareness of the divine and the connectedness that exists between all things. After wearing Tibetan Quartz worn long enough you can start to attune and radiate this vibration. If you choose to follow their way of life, ask your crystal to help you remain balanced upon your path.

Abstinence
Tibetan Quartz supports you to eliminate unhelpful or unwanted aspects from your life. It offers resilience and strengthens willpower during fasting and abstinence. At times of weakness, hold your Tibetan Quartz and repeat a mantra—such as OM—to reconnect with your higher purpose and reaffirm your commitment. Tibetan Quartz will increase your spiritual vibration, giving you protection during any spiritual work. This also makes contact with spirit and animal guides easier. Ask your guides to remain by your side as you remove something unnecessary from your life or transition to a new lifestyle.

RHODOCHROSITE

Knowing Thyself / Play / Reunion

Rhodochrosite is called Inca rose by Native Americans, who believed it held the blood of their ancestral rulers. Within this crystal exists the ability to blend the physical and the spiritual, stimulating love and passion while energising the soul. Rhodochrosite opens the heart, lifts depression and encourages a positive and cheerful outlook while physically stabilising the heartbeat.

Animal: Pink Parrot
Plants: Marjoram and Orchid
Astrological Correspondence: Mars
Power Day: Tuesday
Cleanse with: Fire

Your Crystal Alignment Meditation

Go to a peaceful place in nature. Close your eyes, ensure your spine is straight and place your hands on your heart. Tune in to the beating of your own heart for a few minutes, allowing all other noises to slip away. Now start to see a glowing pink light, emanating from your heart centre. With each beat, it grows stronger and more radiant. Allow it to start to spread over your body. This pink light balances and heals your body, mind and spirit. Now start to spread this pink light beyond yourself, offering healing to your surroundings. Spread this out further, affecting your whole country, then the whole planet and out to the universe. Finally connect with the healing, balancing nature of all that is. You are now ready to connect with your Rhodochrosite.

Knowing Thyself

Rhodochrosite leads you to better understanding of strengths, weaknesses and needs. It promotes self-reflection in a healthy rather than vain manner. Wear Rhodochrosite over your heart each day and at night hold it in your receptive hand, taking at least ten minutes to reflect on the day. Consider what you enjoyed, and what you did not, questioning the reasons behind these reactions. Penning a memoir, a timeline of your life or your obituary can also prove helpful. Rhodochrosite will give you the energy and strength to answer the hard questions. As you learn to understand and love yourself, you'll be in a better position to know what you would like from your relationships with others.

Play

Rhodochrosite helps form strong bonds between you and a partner. It can be used to attract someone into your life with who you'll have a deep soul connection. Wear it while dating to help you develop trust and to open up to each other. The crystal's fiery energy also keeps the relationship fun and engaging. Here Rhodochrosite works divinely with marjoram as the plant is sacred to Venus, the goddess of love as well as her son Hymen, god of marriage. Therefore, use the herb in cooking and add marjoram essential oil to anointing oils, homemade perfumes and aromatic dressing and diffuser blends.

If you and a loved one have been growing apart or the relationship has lost its spark, Rhodochrosite helps you rediscover the art of play. Have yourself and your partner each carry a piece of Rhodochrosite, charged with the intentions you'd both like to see for your future together. Seize any opportunity you see to play and flirt like you did earlier in the relationship. Also carry a piece of Rhodochrosite in your pocket if you struggle to relate to children. To add happiness and fun to your other relationships, place a piece of Rhodochrosite by a photo of family and friends. Add an orchid and light a pink candle each morning, letting it burn for an hour as a sign you are ready to allow your relationships to grow deeper. Pink parrot guides such as the Galah, Major Mitchell Cockatoo or Bourke's Parrot are great for teaching us to be spontaneous and fearless in relationships. Connect with their teachings in addition to your workings with Rhodochrosite.

Reunion

If you wish to contact someone, whether it be a lost friend, a missing family member, or an old flame, place Rhodochrosite next to a photo of them. Whisper their name three times and ask the universe to bring them into contact with you. If a pet is missing, place it where the pet liked to spend time. Wearing or holding Rhodochrosite increases your empathetic and telepathic links with other people and animals. Hold it in your receptive hand while inhaling the scent of fresh marjoram or its essential oil when wanting to communicate with loved ones who have passed away. When you have misplaced something, hold Rhodochrosite in your receptive hand while searching to help you recall where you left the missing item.

Use Rhodochrosite if you are having difficulty falling pregnant. Since it helps you connect with those on the other side who are in your bloodline, it can be used to connect a spirit preparing to incarnate with you. Hold the crystal and allow yourself to sense the soul of your baby reaching out to you. Rhodochrosite's bonding ability can offer support if you are undergoing in vitro fertilisation (IVF). It facilitates the ovaries ability to accept fertile sperm. Once born, Rhodochrosite helps new parents understand what their newborn needs, especially when crying.

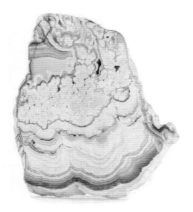

RHODONITE

Realistic Expectations / Moving On / Harmony

Often when you find yourself disappointed with someone it is because they have not lived up to your expectations. As Osho said, "If you love a flower, don't pick it up. Because if you pick it up it dies and ceases to be what you love. So if you love a flower, let it be. Love is not about possession. Love is about appreciation." Rhodonite resonates with these words. It helps you release the obsession with having others as you wish them to be, allowing you to love and accept them as they truly are. It also instils you with a sense of strength and independence so that you are never hindered or held back by others and their opinions.

Animal: Cassowary
Plant: Birch
Astrological Correspondence: Saturn
Power Day: Saturday
Cleanse with: Earth

Your Crystal Alignment Meditation

Sit by an open window and light a pink candle. Tune in to the air that flows in and out of the window. Feel it against your skin and see it cause the candle flame to flicker. Consider that to go through life like the wind is very powerful. The wind comes and goes as it freely desires. You cannot contain it with your hands. It can be gentle or forceful, changing direction with ease and travelling wherever it pleases. Feel this sense of freedom that the wind brings. Once you feel ready, connect with your Rhodonite.

Tolerance

Rhodonite combines loving pink energy with grounding black energy making it an ideal crystal for reminding us to hold realistic expectations of our romantic partner. Arguments, misunderstandings and general dissatisfaction with a partner often occur when they do not behave how you expect them to or they do not meet your expectations. Rhodonite helps you accept that your partner has the free will to act as they desire and helps you appreciate the person they choose to be. Place a Rhodonite crystal in each room and wear a piece near your heart to remind you. Singles can also benefit from working with Rhodonite, as it will ensure you hold sensible expectations when dating.

However Rhodonite isn't exclusively for the romance arena. It can also be used to defuse family or friendship conflicts. It promotes understanding and reconciliation, especially between people who have been hurting each other for a long time. Rhodonite brings the awareness that a perceived misdeed committed by another is not the real issue. Rather it is a lack of self-love for an aspect of yourself that the other is mirroring. Sitting in a circle of Rhodonites while meditating on the root of your upset will help bring spiritual maturity and encourage you to learn from your experiences to avoid them happening again.

It is a great crystal to have around the workplace when tensions are high. Working with people of different backgrounds, beliefs, habits and ethics can cause conflicts and divisions when another's work style contrasts yours. Major arguments can erupt from a dirty tea cup left in a sink or an overflowing rubbish bin. Rhodonite with help settle the need to have everything "your way" and remind you of the benefits of diversity in any group.

If you are working to invite more harmony into a space, it will involve getting a houseplant, a soft-coloured pot and a Rhodonite for each person in the home or workspace. If there are a large number of people, simply use four crystals as this is a balancing number. Still your mind and take some time to visualise your ideal, harmonious home or workspace. Once you can clearly see and feel this scene, keep this intent in mind as you replant the plant into the new pot and add the crystals to the soil. Keep this plant in the centre of this space and ensure you water and care for it. Diffusing birch essential oil, which heightens your tolerance of others, will also help.

At times of conflict, look to the wisdom of your Cassowary guide. He demands the respect and acceptance of other peoples' boundaries, as well as your own. He is a warrior bird who defends what is right and just. Cassowary also brings into focus paternal energy and the balance between masculinity and femininity. In particular, he strengthens a father's bond with his children, and brings his nurturing side to the surface without in any way compromising his sense of masculinity. These are all lessons supported by Rhodonite.

Moving On

Rhodonite offers you support after a break up. During your meditation, after you have asked your crystal for support, take some time to write down all the good and bad aspects of the relationship. Once you have finished the list, make sure that you have an equal number of positive and negative aspects. This will ensure you have a balanced perspective of the relationship. Consider what you have learnt from this relationship. Take your crystal in your projective hand now and fill it with all the memories, happiness, pain and other thoughts and feelings that remain. Once complete, bury the crystal and say, "By the powers of Saturn, I take control of my life and bid you farewell". As you do this, it is a sign that you have learnt your lessons and are letting go of the relationship. You are now on the road to a new, exciting relationship where you will not make the same mistakes again. You may like to symbolically sweep your space with a broom made of birch. This Winter Solstice tradition, can be used at any time when you want to sweep away old and stagnant energy.

Realistic Expectations

The grounding and assuring nature of Rhodonite allows you to feel comfortable regardless of other people's reactions to you. It allows you to have realistic expectations of yourself, encouraging not being overly critical of yourself. Keep Rhodonite with you at times when you are getting frustrated with an inability to complete a task. It helps you cope with aging, reminding you that you may not have the same physical abilities as when you were younger, while at the same time allowing you to honour the wisdom you've gained through your life. Rhodonite allows individuals with a disability to find peace in life. It offers support and promotes a positive, ambitious attitude while allowing a loving understanding of any limitations.

Rhodonite also allows you to tap into the support you have around you. It reminds you that when you are in conflict with others, to look where you are being supported. Maybe others "have your back" or you are learning how to stand up for yourself. Rhodonite helps you sense the support of your guides and ancestors. When feeling useless, undervalued or ostracised, combine Rhodonite with birch essential oil. The oil from this slender and magical tree purifies space while empowering you to ensure you do not get pushed around by those who are stronger willed. Drinking birch beer has a similar effect.

RUBY

Love / Warning / Archangel Michael / Lower Body

Ruby brings fire and success into your life. If you tend to live your life intensely, but often find it difficult to keep focus, Ruby can help bring clarity and wisdom to your world. Instead of flitting from idea to idea, it will very well help you choose your most productive path. Ruby will then fire your passions and keep you motivated, giving you strength to resist self-destructive patterns that have crippled you in the past. This crystal of nobility opens the way to remove any sense of limitation. It heightens courage, selfless work, all spiritual endeavours, joy and leadership qualities.

Animal: Lion
Plants: Carnation, Pimento Berry and Pomegranate
Astrological Correspondence: Mars
Power Day: Tuesday
Cleanse with: Fire

Your Crystal Alignment Meditation

Go and sit outside, taking time to gaze at the sky. Look beyond the clouds and tune in to its vastness, letting your mind disappear. Experience the beauty of the expansiveness. Know that as the sky is stretched out before you, so are the opportunities of life. As you gaze into the universe, connecting with all that is, notice the universe is connecting to you, resting upon the earth. Allow your spirits to rise to a level of blissful freedom. You are free, free to do all you desire. Eventually send some gratitude to the universe, even blow it a kiss if you're feeling adventurous and then connect with your Ruby.

Love

Ruby's deep red colour works to increase love in your life. Use it in love attracting spells or wear it over your heart to draw a passionate lover. Place five rubies around the bedroom to increase the frequency and duration of lovemaking, especially if you are trying to conceive. It helps to prevent the process becoming a means to an end and also helps eliminate impotence. Drink pomegranate juice to aid your efforts as it connects you to the wisdom and fertility of the goddess. An old method of divination to find out how fertile you are involves throwing a pomegranate on the ground with all your might. However many seeds spill out is the number of children you are destined to have. Bury these seeds with a Ruby and a Sapphire if you wish this divination to come true.

Ruby also helps increase love within a community. Hold it in your projective hand while visualising everyone coming together to work harmoniously. This crystal allows you to find new ways to contribute your skills and receive recognition for your contribution. Ruby harmonises with your Lion guide. Allow Lion to teach you about the power of communities and cooperation. He shows you that everyone has an important role to play in life.

Warning

Always pay close attention to the colour of your Ruby, especially if you wear a piece of Ruby jewellery. There is a long history of stories where Rubies have grown darker in the presence of an enemy, liar, or source of potential sickness. Catherine of Aragon wore an infamous Ruby, which turned dark and dull the day before Henry VIII announced he was divorcing her. Call on your Ruby to give you the strength and willpower to overcome any adversity. Diffusing or anointing your heart with pimento berry essential oil can further protect you against evil influences and boost your confidence in your ability to overcome anything trying to drag you down. Rubies can also assist trees to avoid damage or danger. Touch trees with your Ruby or plant one at its base to protect it from lightning strikes.

Archangel Michael

Ruby is a gem of the Archangel Michael. Hold your Ruby between your hands and pray to Michael when you need protection, courage, or integrity. You may see sparks of gold, blue or purple light when he's around or you may simply feel his presence. Ask him to use his flaming sword to slice away any toxins or disease, effects of others' negative attitude or any unwanted emotional attachment. He helps you meet impossible deadlines, eliminate addictions and increase energy levels. Michael helps lightworkers fulfil their life purpose. He keeps you motivated and on track as well as aiding protection and space clearing. If you have a battle ahead of you, dedicate a Ruby to him and summon his aid as you hold it. If you or a child is suffering from nightmares, place a statue or picture of Michael and a Ruby by your bed and ask him to help you sleep soundly.

Michael is the guardian of the element of fire. Call upon him when cleansing your crystals with fire. He also has a knack for helping electrical appliances work again. If an appliance isn't working or your car breaks down, call on Michael to help. Place a Ruby on top of the machine and return in half an hour.

Lower Body

Ruby and its harmonising plant pimento berry both stimulate and strengthen the base chakra. This leads to the strengthening of the lower parts of the body, especially the legs. If you are preparing for a marathon or your legs are wobbly after a long walk, mix a little pimento berry essential oil in a carrier oil and massage it in with a tumbled Ruby or wand.

If your legs are feeling weak or sore for no apparent reason, it may be a physical manifestation of a mental or emotional thought pattern. Your legs are concerned with moving forward and if you are feeling apprehensive or anxious about future events, leg problems may arise. Place your Ruby between your legs and close your eyes. Visualise red flames shooting from the crystal and surrounding your body. Feel the flames burn away your fear and replace them with a sense of courage and determination. See your legs glowing in bright red, healing light and know they can carry you wherever needed. Keep the Ruby in the pocket or worn as an anklet throughout your day.

RUTILE

Self Expression / Healing / Family / Employment

Rutile is a dazzling crystal that grows in long strands, and is often a sparkling golden colour. These sparkling threads have been connected to various ethereal beings throughout the ages. Some call Rutile angels' hair, the Romans named it the golden hair of Venus, while the Vikings believed it belonged to their Freyja. Rutile embodies the essence of a goddess or angel, gifting their guardian the ability to allow improvement in their life. Rutile gives you the confidence to speak up and share your gifts while bringing healing to yourself and your family.

Legend tells that when a goddess's hair was cut the earth spirits couldn't bear to see it be thrown away so they preserved it in stone, often Quartz. This Clear Quartz and Rutile combination commonly known as Rutilated Quartz, holds the properties of Rutile and is amplified with the energy of Clear Quartz. This is the most readily available form of Rutile and an acceptable substitute if you cannot obtain raw Rutile.

Animals: Peacock (Rutile) and Palomino Horse (Rutilated Quartz)
Plants: Aspen and Fragonia
Astrological Correspondence: Sun
Power Day: Sunday
Cleanse with: Sun

Your Crystal Alignment Meditation

Go and find a quiet place in nature where you can see the stars. Connect to the beautiful jewels that twinkle above us each night. Allow yourself to disappear into the darkness amongst the stars, becoming one. Once you feel linked to the heavens, connect with your Rutile.

Self Expression

Rutile allows you to find creative ways to express yourself. Wear it near your throat chakra to encourage you to speak words that heal and inspire those around you. Combine Rutile with wisdom of your Peacock guide. Peacock teaches you how to project an energy of confidence, stature and accomplishment. Be proud of your endeavours. However, Peacock also teaches to not let pride become arrogance. You must harness your ability to be noble, yet humble.

With Rutile, know that you are safe to say what you need to say. If your words motivate others to speak ill of you or work against you, allow the golden reflection of the Rutile to reflect that negativity back to them, leaving you unaffected. Peacock, with his many-eyed plumage, will ensure that in your quest for self-expression you observe the impact on others. Remember your ultimate aim should be contribute to the greater good, not just blow your own horn.

Healing

Feeling free to express yourself prevents you holding pent-up, unhelpful emotions inside, which can eventually start to manifest physically within the organs of your body. However, if sickness does develop, use the golden healing colour of Rutile to promote release and healing. Sweep Rutile across the aura to draw off any unhelpful energies that may be causing illness or blocking healing. If healing is sluggish, try wearing Rutilated Quartz over your solar plexus or near the site of illness. If possible, rest under an aspen and hear the leaves whisper as they carry your sickness away.

Fragonia is one of the newest and greatest essential oils available, coming from a shrub native to southern Western Australia. It has a high vibration and harmonises perfectly with Rutile. A few drops can be added to water and spritzed around the room or it can be placed neat on the skin. Fragonia cleanses and lifts the vibration of a space, allowing the body to rebalance, preventing problems from reoccurring. This makes it ideal to use at any time healing is needed.

Family

Rutile allows you to find harmony within the family. It helps you settle past rifts and let go of any old resentment you still carry. Furthermore, it can help you release old karma from past lives connected to family. Rutile can affect you down to your DNA so if family karma is engrained here, wearing Rutile will create a releasing transmutation, freeing you from the past. If there is tension in the air when you are spending time with your family, carry or wear Rutile. At home, set a piece near a family photo and light a gold candle to generate healing for the whole family. Add a leaf or twig from the aspen, for this is a tree of the spiritual warrior. However, this tree's strength is not in its ability to incite fear but rather in its ability to induce laughter. Any tense situation can be dissolved by one who can use wit and laughter to successfully lighten and diffuse a situation.

Employment

Rutilated Quartz is a supportive crystal for the unemployed. The Clear Quartz gives you the perseverance to find a source of income while Rutile allows you to be creative and clearly express yourself at job interviews, when applying for business start-up loans or engaging others in your new venture. Each Sunday visualise yourself succeeding as you sit before a gold candle and holding your Rutilated Quartz in your projective hand. Then carry your crystal for the whole week. Also summon your Palomino Horse guide along for the ride. He will show you how to go the distance and shine every stride of the way.

SAPPHIRE, BLUE

Loyalty / Wisdom / Archangel Gabriel

After Diamond, Corundum is the hardest crystal on Earth. Red Corundum is better known as Ruby, while all other colours, including yellow, green, purple, black, clear and the well-known blue are Sapphires. It is both the strength and beauty of Sapphires that has made it a popular gem among royalty leading to its deserved position in many legends and crowns. Sapphire is symbol of the heavens and guards innocence, delivers truth, promotes good health and preserves chastity. It allows you to discover ways to improve your life, enhancing fulfilment, joy, prosperity, inner peace and beauty.

Animal: Dog
Plant: Blue Lotus
Astrological Correspondences: Saturn and the asteroid Juno
Power Day: Saturday
Cleanse with: Water, especially rain.

Your Crystal Alignment Meditation

Go to a forest or woodlands that you have not visited before, either one nearby or if that is not possible, visualise one in your mind. Find a path and set along the way. As you come to forks along the path pause and listen to your inner guidance on which of the two options to take. Pay attention to what is affecting your decision. Does the path you prefer look easier or quicker? Maybe it looks more mysterious or beautiful? Then contemplate whether you always choose the easiest, quickest, mysterious or more beautiful way in life. Does this work for you or would it be worth trying another approach in your everyday life? Allow any realisations to arise. After walking for a while, find a place that feels special to you to sit and rest and, when ready, connect with your Sapphire.

Loyalty

Whenever loyalty is needed, Sapphire is perfect. Wear Sapphire for support in remaining dedicated to a course of study, an exercise regime, a goal or your path of service. Connect with man's best friend, your Dog guide, to teach you the virtues of loyalty. Grid Sapphires around the workplace if your company is losing employees to other organisations. This will improve employees' loyalty to their employer. Wear Sapphire when signing treaties, contracts or any other agreement to encourage all parties to keep their word.

Sapphire is the stone of fidelity and commitment and is perfect in betrothal rings. When moving in with your partner, place two tumbled Sapphires with a happy photo of you both somewhere prominent in the home. Add an extra Sapphire on each year's anniversary. This creates a monument of your love. If you have a wandering eye when in a relationship, wear Sapphire over your heart to remember the value of your current relationship. Connect with the energy of the asteroid Juno, named after the wife of the god Jupiter. She has a similar energy to Venus, but where Venus sparks initial attraction, Juno promotes commitment. Where you find Juno in your astrological chart is an indication of where the opportunity exists to meet someone that you will remain with for a long relationship.

Gum problems can arise as a physical manifestation of an inability to commit. To counteract this keep a Sapphire near your toothbrush to improve your loyalty. This is also a remedy to encourage children to always brush their teeth.

Wisdom

Around the world Sapphires have been used to promote wisdom. King Solomon's ring was said to be a Sapphire and people wore the gem when they consulted Apollo's Oracle at Delphi to help them understand the answer given. In parts of Asia, Saturday was the day to dress in blue and wear Blue Sapphire for wisdom and generous thinking. Wear a Sapphire to help you maintain wisdom during times of great change. Allow Sapphire to aid you in making wise life choices that will keep you loyal to your path of service. For guidance on deciding between two options, place a Sapphire by two different coloured candles, each representing one option. Light them at the same time and whichever lasts the longest is the recommended choice.

Sapphire can help you translate the meaning of messages received during meditation or other spiritual experiences. After meditation, hold your Sapphire in your receptive hand and allow interpretations to come to you. Inhale the scent of a blue lotus flower or diffuse its essential oil to lift your consciousness to higher levels of understanding and insight.

Archangel Gabriel

Gabriel is the archangel who delivers messages of guidance. His energy harmonises with Sapphire. Hold a Sapphire against your third eye chakra and ask Gabriel to awaken your spiritual vision, give you directional guidance, help you interpret dreams or visions and allow you to receive prophecy of changes ahead. If you're feeling lost, hold a Sapphire between your hands in prayer and ask Gabriel to give you signs of your path of service for this lifetime. Wear a Sapphire dedicated to Gabriel if your occupation involves the arts or communication. Gabriel will empower the Sapphire to help you in the fields of coaching, journalism, public speaking or art. If you are undertaking the process of adopting a child, place Sapphires near the family areas of the house and the new child's bedroom while asking Gabriel to make the process a smooth one.

Gabriel is associated with the element of water, the realm of love, emotions and cleansing. If you have been raped, abused or absorbed in someone else's problems, take a ritualistic swim, offering a Sapphire to the water and ask Gabriel to cleanse you, both emotionally and energetically. You can do this at home with a shower or bath and dark blue candles. Take a tumbled Sapphire and gentle slide it across your body, asking Gabriel to strip all the unwanted energy away.

SELENITE
Cleansing / Purity / Spirituality / Soul Star Chakra

Selenite gains its name from the moon goddess Selene who was honoured for her radiant beauty and harmonious nature. Selenite too has a peaceful, loving feel. Selenite forms as long sword like crystals, which could be called nature's fibre optics, for as you tilt the crystal back and forth white light bounces along it. Metaphysically this translates to Selenite bringing light to any individual or situation, cleansing body, mind, soul and space. Selenite can be permanently damaged if exposed to water, so do not cleanse or immerse it in water for any reason.

Animals: Polar Bear and Snowy Owl
Plants: Sage and White Lotus
Astrological Correspondence: Moon
Power Day: Monday
Cleansing: Doesn't need cleansing

Your Crystal Alignment Meditation

Go to the Arctic tundra on the night of the full moon or visualise yourself there in your mind. Sit and observe the stillness and scarcity of the environment. Feel the full moon bathing you and this barren landscape with loving lunar energy. This is a place of potential, where the icy temperatures have stripped away the weak. However life does exist here. Listen, connect and sense the life. This is a place where only the pure, determined and strong can prosper. Find these traits within yourself now. When you are ready, connect with your Selenite.

Cleansing

Selenite is the ultimate cleansing crystal as it remains pure and unaffected by other energies, thus not needing cleansing itself. Perform a cleansing ritual for your home and space whenever you feel you need to remove unwanted or unhelpful energies that are lingering there. This is recommended when moving into a new home, after a break up or simply after a bad day. Start by cleansing yourself with a white sage smudge stick, fanning the smoke over your body. Then hold your Selenite against your forehead. Feel it cleansing away all scattered and confused thoughts, bringing you clarity of mind. Move your Selenite to your feet and feel all physical pain and discomfort soak into the earth beneath you. Hold your Selenite to your heart and allow it to cleanse away all unwanted emotional instability. Finally place your Selenite above your head, feel it cleanse your aura and any unwanted spiritual effects, whether it be karma, a curse, fear or anything else that inhibits you from being your true self and living to your fullest potential.

Once you have cleansed yourself, start with your space. Open all window and doors then take your sage smudge stick and walk around your house three times, anti-clockwise. Fan the smoke into every space, seeing it cleanse and remove all negativity. Next, sit in the centre of your space and hold your Selenite in both hands. Feel its cleansing vibration within your body then send the energy throughout your surroundings. See the light around you expanding in all directions, purifying everything it touches, eliminating anything undesirable.

Once you have cleansed your space, it is vital to set your intention for what you would now like to have within the space. Choose a suitable incense such as lavender for peace, or lotus for purity, and complete three clockwise circles around the space while visualising and summoning your new desires into the house.

Once you have thoroughly cleansed your space, place four towers or pieces of Selenite in the four corners of the area. The Selenite will act as a constant filter, absorbing any disruptive energy and keeping your space feeling light and free. Include a piece of peach Selenite in each corner to encourage harmonious interactions within the space. At home this can encourage children to eat healthily, do their homework, help with chores and caring for pets. If your child is scared of the dark, give them a Selenite sphere to hold and explain that it holds the light of the moon that will shine on them and keep them safe as they sleep. Add Selenite to power grids to encourage the harmonious blending of other crystals' energies.

A Selenite wand is a great tool for healers. Activate your wand by gently squeezing it, then pointing it towards the problem area of a patient. Allow the Selenite to cleanse the auric field by moving it in an anti-clockwise direct around your patient. Then bring in light with clockwise circles.

Purity

Selenite promotes the ability to remain pure and true to yourself. As you meditate with your Selenite, sit before a white lotus flower and contemplate its unique ability to remain unaffected. If you were to pour liquid over it, it would simply roll off leaving the flower unaffected. Pour vinegar or the finest perfume on a lotus and it retains its own sweet smell. By bringing Selenite into your life each day, you can adopt the properties of this magical flower. When someone figuratively showers you in vinegar—in the form of abuse, insults or criticism—allow it to simply roll off. An even harder challenge is when someone showers you in a sweet perfume, or in other words, praise, compliments and embellishments, don't allow this to sway you from your course. Too easy is it to listen to one side or the other and end up with low self-esteem or an inflated ego. You can also start spending your life acting in a manner that earns you praise and avoids criticism. Remember that another's opinion is based on their perception and not necessarily the truth. The most reliable source of the truth comes from knowing yourself. You are the only person you should be trying to please. Through stillness and meditation with Selenite, you will develop the relationship with your true and authentic self. Ask your Snowy Owl guide to fly by your side to unveil the wisdom of your soul as you take time to fall quiet. Diffusing or wearing white lotus essential oil will further support your ability to remain authentic as well as align you with how you can best be of service to the Earth.

Spirituality

Wearing or carrying Selenite each day helps dissolve grudges, judgement and other negative feelings, removing erratic moods or behaviour. It will support you in acting more from a place of love rather than fear, anger or other ego-dictated reactions. In other words, Selenite will welcome peace both within and around you. This may help eliminate repetitive strain injury (RSI) or restless leg syndrome (RLS) that can manifest from feeling irritated or stuck in your current situation.

When working with Selenite, take time to explore the teachings of Polar Bear. He will show you how to follow your inner guidance and give your best, even when times are challenging. He is a symbol of purity of spirit, he has no time for fear and helps you dive into your emotional side of life. Polar Bear is a determined survivor and will encourage you never to give up.

As you become more peaceful, you'll be able to tune in to your psychic and animal telepathic abilities, contact guardian angels, guides and teachers and follow your higher purpose. Take some time each evening to enjoy some pleasant music as you hold your Selenite and open yourself up to your spiritual side. You may want to take a moment ask for guidance on a certain issue. Allow your intuition to give you answers or even a guide to communicate with you.

Soul Star Chakra

As you still your mind and soothe your energy, Selenite will allow the gentle flow of spiritual guidance and knowledge via your soul star chakra. Your crystal will give you the understanding that opportunities will come when you are ready, while ensuring you remain alert to recognise them. To connect with your soul star chakra lie down and place your Selenite about a hand's width above your head. Visualise a glowing white or ultra violet sphere of energy extracting knowledge from the universe above you and funnelling it towards your crown.

SERAPHINITE

Renewal / Wellbeing / Fulfilling Potential

Seraphinite is a variety of Clinochlore coming from the eastern-Siberian region of Russia. Its name comes from the word *seraph*, which are winged angelic beings in service of God and refers to glittering white feathered patterns emerging from the crystal's deep green colour. It is no wonder that Seraphinite aids spiritual enlightenment. This magical crystal works to guard your health and wellbeing, allowing you to find inner harmony and peace. As you remove all toxic influences in your life, Seraphinite helps you find connections that will benefit your spiritual development. It instils a sense of wonder at the world's beauty and allows you to soar through life without obstruction. This is a crystal to ensure you reach your full potential.

Animal: Eagle
Plant: Lemon
Astrological Correspondence: Venus
Power Day: Friday
Cleanse with: Earth for healing; Air for fulfilling potential.

Your Crystal Alignment Meditation

Go outside and watch the clouds, floating above you across the sky. Clouds drift high above our world, distanced from the hustle and bustle of life. They are unaffected by the frenzy below. Let the clouds remind you that this peace is available to you too. When difficulties stand before you, remember, like the clouds, this too will pass. Feel a sense of floating and freedom. You may want to simply enjoy watching them pass or you may want to look for messages to appear for you in the clouds' shapes. Now is the time to release thoughts of worry, stress, sadness, anger or anxiety. Let them drift away with the clouds. When you are ready, connect with your Seraphinite.

Renewal

When you are feeling flat find a peaceful place outside. Stand barefoot on the earth while wearing or placing your Seraphinite over your heart and open your arms out wide. Stand there for at least two minutes opening up your heart to the world. Your Seraphinite will help you. Feel the sun on your skin, the wind on your face and the earth below your feet. Allow a sense of peace and wellness to wash over you and feel your vibrancy and confidence growing.

Seraphinite is a guardian of the heart's temple and once this crystal is in your life it will work to guard you against any future hurt. Seraphinite works to lift you from the depths of sorrow and find love in life again. After a break up, divorce or death of a loved one, light a candle each night, hold your Seraphinite and ask for guidance and support. Place a piece of Seraphinite and a white candle in the home to bring harmony after a major disagreement. Use Seraphinite in harmony with the angel Seraphiel or Chamuel. Hold your Seraphinite between your hands and ask for guidance in removing guilt you hold about the past. On a global scale, ask for forgiveness for humanity's past mistakes so that the planet can heal and progress. Know help is on the way when you experience butterflies in your stomach or a pleasant tingling in your body.

Wellbeing

Once you have released the past, Seraphinite kicks into full gear as a powerful physical healer, creating fresh space for new patterns of wellbeing to form. It is part of the chlorite family, which works to remove toxins, weight or disease. Drink a freshly squeezed lemon in water then take Seraphinite into the shower. While holding it in your receptive hand, visualise the unwanted poisons, kilos or illness exiting your body and rinsing down the drain. Wear Seraphinite near problem areas of your body, allowing it to realign your body and all its systems. Take time each day to visualise a beautiful green light encompassing your whole body, returning you to your natural state of wellness.

Seraphinite promotes healthy living. Place it on the dining table to encourage children to eat healthily. The crystal supports vegetarianism, veganism or other conscious eating lifestyles. Restaurants and food suppliers promoting healthy eating and ethical food should place seven Seraphinite crystals along the front of their establishment to draw like-minded customers.

Fulfilling Potential

Seraphinite works to unfurl your own wings so that you may soar like Eagle and become closer to Great Spirit. If you are feeling limited or bound then this is a crystal for you. It will allow you to reach your highest potential by removing any previous restrictions and encouraging you to expand your realms of influence. Working with Seraphinite in connection with your Eagle guide will allow you to communicate with Great Spirit and receive divine guidance. Wear

Seraphinite over your heart each day to see what is true, enjoy the beauty of life and face challenges with an open heart and remarkable courage. It will allow you to step into chaos and return it to order. At night, place your Seraphinite on your upper back and sense your own pair of wings sprout from the point. Allow yourself to float off on great journeys. See yourself with total freedom, fulfilling your desires and dreams. This crystal placement also eases upper back pain that is a physical manifestation of feeling emotionally unsupported. Seraphinite will allow you to realise that the universe supports you and you don't have to rely on others when following your own path.

SERPENTINE

Healing Energy / Fear / Protection

The name Serpentine refers to a group of predominantly green minerals with a snakeskin appearance found all around the world. Certain types have become especially popular due to their attributes and have been given unique names such as Healerite™ from USA. and Infinite Stone™ from South Africa. The likeness to snakes isn't just in appearance, but also in its attributes. Serpentine is a crystal of healing and it encourages you to shed that which limits your growth, just as a snake sheds its skin in order to grow. The crystal has a fiery energy and challenges you to face the flames and confront your fears. It opens your heart to past lessons before it casts them far away where they no longer possess any hold on your life. Serpentine give you courage to pursue the life you were born to live, shielding you with its protective ability along the way. Used in meditation, Serpentine helps reduce both stress and pessimism while also awakening kundalini energies. Serpentine will help when working with the energies of mythical creatures, especially dragons, or when tapping into the energies of the Earth or ancient sites.

Animal: Snake
Plant: Palo Santo
Astrological Correspondences: Saturn and the constellation Ophiuchus
Power Day: Saturday
Cleanse with: Fire or palo santo smoke

Your Crystal Alignment Meditation

Go and sit before a fire. It may be a candle flame, fireplace or campfire. Sit close enough to feel the flames' warmth. Watch the flames dance and see them change whatever they touch. Connect with the essence of the fire and allow it to energetically burn away all stresses and tension. Allow all physical discomfort and mental disharmony to be replaced by a warm, comforting feeling. When ready, connect with your Serpentine.

Healing Energy

Serpentine arouses the body's spiritual energy centres and moves this energy along the meridians of the body. It works to stimulate any of the underactive chakras, especially the heart and below. Use Serpentine for stimulating the arousal of the kundalini energies. Place your Serpentine at the base of your spine. Tune in to the crystal and start to see and feel a spiralling energy arising from the base of your spine. Feel it growing stronger and rising as it starts to circle around your body. Visualise a green or white light or even a mighty serpent. Feel this energy strengthen and encompass your body. This energy empowers and protects you as well as improves your physical health, removing unwanted toxins and contaminants from the body. It can help bring awareness to the root cause of ill-health especially when the cause is currently unknown. It can also promote more fulfilling sexual relationships which is why Serpentine is renowned for helping women who are unable to reach orgasm due to tension.

Due to its ability to increase the shift of energy around the body, Serpentine is a valuable inclusion on any laying on of stones treatment. A knowledge of the meridians is beneficial as placing Serpentine along these energy channels will support the rebalancing of related issues. Use Infinite Stone™ during Reiki or energy healing sessions when the recipient is finding it hard to relax and allow the healing to occur. It lovingly helps to remove blockages and resistance preventing healing from occurring.

Serpentine helps you form a deep and loving connection with the earth, and to draw this into your own energy field. It is especially adept at allowing you to draw energy from the ground at sacred sites. Infinite Stone™ has a particular knack for keeping this energy within your auric field once you've left the area. Take time to sit on the earth, with your Serpentine against your heart. Sense and feel the energy moving up your spine and arms, around your body. Don't try to dictate what should happen but rather still yourself and observe what happens as you allow the interaction to occur. Allow yourself to get taken on a journey. Serpentine facilitates trance work so the more you can release resistance, the more insight you'll receive. Those working outside with Infinite Stone™ find it rouses your awareness of being one with creation and all life.

Fear

As you heal and raise your vibration, Serpentine allows you to tune in to your Snake guide, allowing you to symbolically shed your skin, cast away fear and start over. Sit quietly and reflect on a fear you wish to overcome. Connect with the fear, seeing it in front of you and sense how it makes you feel, physically and emotionally. Once the fear feels real, pick up your Serpentine in your left hand. Focus on your breath; each inhalation summoning strength from the crystal, and each exhalation releasing the grip of the fear. Finally visualise a sword in your right hand. Examine the sword, its blade and handle, notice materials, colour and weight. This is to be your personal sword for any spiritual work. Still seeing the fear in front of you, visualise a cord stretching from your body to your fear. This cord connects you and the fear. When you are ready, take the sword and with a big swing cut the cord. Look directly at the fear and say, "Fear, I banish you from my life, now and forever". Focus again on your body taking a moment to connect with this new sense of strength. If the fear has an emotional basis, Healerite™ has been found to be particularly potent.

To keep your fear at bay, carry your Serpentine in your pocket each day. This can also help reduce any disorder of the kidneys due to a physical manifestation of fear. Serpentine, when kept in the bra, can support healthy milk supply for breast-feeding mothers as it helps to counteract the fear of being an incapable mother. Connecting with the constellation Ophiuchus, the serpent bearer, will bring you added willpower to charm your fears and take control of them. Ophiuchus is especially influential for those born between 30 November and 17 December as this is when the sun passes by this constellation each year.

Being a crystal of reinvention, as you work with Serpentine to shed fears of expressing who you truly are, it will give you the confidence to start showing the world who you truly are. It also gives you the ability to establish healthy boundaries with others so as you open up more to the world, it'll guard that you don't overdo it, nor let others take advantage of you. If you feel you are needing a powerful transformation, combine it with a high vibration crystal such as Moldavite, Phenacite or Seraphinite, all which bring about huge shifts in your life. This can be beneficial for those with eczema which can manifest from a belief that you must hide or suppress parts of yourself from others. Serpentine, especially Infinite Stone™, can also help with claustrophobia or any sense of being imprisoned in life, giving you the capability to overcome the perceived restrictions.

Protection

As you step bravely out into life, Serpentine will help you trust your heart and improve your judgement of situations, ensuring your steer away from danger. This has given Serpentine a long history of being used for protection. "Fright stones" were created out of Serpentine in the Middle Ages, carving the crystal into the shape of ugly-faced amulets to scare away danger. In the past, Serpentine has been called upon to deter enemies, false friends, gossip, poisoning and propaganda. In modern times, Serpentine has developed a reputation for guarding you against fraud and con-artists when online, especially in chat groups or on dating websites and apps. Wear Serpentine over the heart whenever you are concerned about any of the abovementioned threats. Cleanse yourself and your space by smudging with palo santo wood or diffusing palo santo essential oil, which works in harmony with Serpentine. It will remove hindering energies that could have an adverse effect on you. This combination can also prevent disease or sickness. If a health problem is lingering, keep Serpentine near medicines, potions and remedies to increase their effectiveness. Due to its reptilian connection, Serpentine allows you to avoid snakebites by giving you better understanding of the snake's nature. Carry Serpentine when bushwalking and place at any entrance at home susceptible to snakes entering. It also has been used to guard against being attacked by spiders, bees, scorpions and other reptiles and insects. Use Serpentine to protect pets and other animals from fleas, ticks and mites as well as other irritations to the skin.

Serpentine can protect you from turbulent times in your life, especially when there seems to be excess struggle with others. As a green crystal, Serpentine connects with the heart chakra and thus, inspires the pursuit of establishing love and peace in the world. If there is conflict in your life, Serpentine will ignite your resolve to find peaceful resolutions. Just be aware, that at times, this crystal has been found to make you too eager to compromise for the sake of peace. You may want to call upon Wadjet, also known as Uadjet, a lesser known Egyptian goddess, depicted as half woman and half cobra. She was summoned to offer protection especially during childbirth as well as to aggressively defend both children and leaders. You can call upon her to offer you protection by holding your Serpentine to your heart and whispering a prayer.

Further Crystal Connections – Serpentine with Stichtite

Serpentine has been found in certain localities with veins of Stichtite growing throughout. When discovered in Tasmania, Australia, this combination was nicknamed Atlantisite™ however this name is generally applied to all stones of this combination. This is a powerful combination created by Mother Nature which has the ability to return us back to the levels of wisdom held in Atlantis.

Poor health can distract and hinder you from pursuing your spiritual growth. Thus a vital part of living a holistic life is to ensure your physical health and wellbeing is at an optimum state. Atlantisite™ helps you deal with the cause rather than just the symptoms of any illness. Stichtite will help you trust your intuition in finding the cause of your dis-ease and Serpentine will help you shed the cause and commence regeneration of a healthy body. Rest with Atlantisite™ on the site of illness and ask your body what it needs. Ask it to show the lost healing wisdoms and techniques of civilisations past to aid you in returning to your optimum state of being. Also take your Atlantisite™ with you when you visit your doctor, naturopath or other health care professional. Because Atlantisite™ has the addition of Stichtite to the Serpentine, when working with kundalini energy, this stone will help you to move the kundalini energies, up from the base of the spine, through the entire body via the spinal column to the crown chakra.

Once you are back to full health, Atlantisite™ then shifts to focus on the spiritual part of your life. Carry or wear Atlantisite™ with you daily to follow your intuition and eliminate any fears that prevent you from connecting with people who can offer you valuable guidance or lessons. Take Atlantisite™ into a bookstore or library and let it guide you to a book you need to read. Listen to your intuition rather than trying to logically determine what you "should" get. Once the book is at home, leave Atlantisite™ on top of it. When you are reading, sit the crystal by you and it will awaken insights that you can apply to everyday life. This stone can help you keep calm and prevents sudden outbursts when you realise you're not where you want to be. This can often happen during Uranus retrograde. Let Atlantisite™ guide you through the revelations and help get back on track.

Use Atlantisite™ to work from your higher self rather than being driven by the ego. Legend has it that the people of Atlantis created amazing technology, some that would surpass that of today. However, their hunger for power grew as they discovered new knowledge that allowed them to control life and the environment and eventually this led to the downfall of their civilisation. When we tune in to the Atlantean energy, we can awaken this wisdom and use it to guide us in appropriate uses of our own technology. Keep Atlantisite™ near your computer to avoid becoming over materialistic when shopping online and avoid fraudsters on dating and social networking sites.

Atlantisite™ offers support and strength to gay people, disabled people, or members of any race or religion that are a minority in their area. If you feel a sense of being outnumbered or marginalised, wear this crystal over your heart. Both Serpentine and Stichtite are protective crystals, with the added bonus that Stichtite also helps you to rise above the damaging effects of abuse and discrimination. Atlantisite™ creates a loving, peaceful environment wherever there is a diverse group of people. Place Atlantisite™ around your workplace or on a mantle place at home with purple candles to promote warmth and harmony.

SHUNGITE
Physical Health / Anchoring / Ancient Memory / Revival

Shungite is a two billion year old crystal shrouded in mystery, evoking the interest of both the scientific and New Age communities. It is a unique form of carbon, found primarily near Lake Onega of the village of Shunga in the Republic of Karelia, Russia. Most believe that Shungite originated in ancient oceans that were inhabited by a variety of microscopic organisms that died and became the carbon building blocks. Others have hypothesised that lighting or a meteorite may have also contributed to the formation of Shungite. Shungite is valued due to it containing fullerenes; complex carbon molecules in dome or soccer ball formations. This is an extremely positive crystal but not for the faint hearted, for when used in meditation it can initiate phenomenal journeys. It has the ability to remove toxic influences physically, mentally, emotionally and spiritually while making space for the birth of new growth and revolutions.

Not all Shungites are created the same as they have varying amounts of carbon, the element that makes this crystal so beneficial. Shungite can be categorised into three types. Type I is known as Silver, Elite or Noble Shungite. It has a silvery, metallic shine and contains up to 98% carbon. This accounts for a small percentage of available Shungite, but is the most potent of the types. Type II is Black Shungite and unlike Silver Shungite, can be carved and polished into shapes such as pyramids or spheres. It contains 50-70% organic carbon and is still considered viable for physical wellbeing and Shungite's spiritual properties. Type III is Grey Shungite, also called Shungite Rock, and only contains about 30-50% carbon along with a multitude of other elements. This variety, although still somewhat beneficial, lacks the potency of type I and II.

Animals: Pig and Boar
Plant: Petitgrain
Astrological Correspondence: Pluto
Power Day: Saturday
Cleanse with: Sun for health or earth for spiritual exploration

Your Crystal Alignment Meditation

Go to a large tree. Take a few moments to study the features of the tree. Notice its leaves as they dance in the wind. Does this tree have flowers? Can you smell any scent? Reach out and feel the bark. Each tree has its own energy and spirit. Allow yourself to connect to its beauty and magic. Now sit with your back against the tree. Nature is always seeking to regain balance so ask the tree to help you regain your own personal balance. Hear the tree creak as it absorbs your ills and hear its leaves flutter as it sends them far away upon the healing winds. Sense any tiredness, aching, pain, sickness, discomfort or disease leaving your body and being absorbed by the tree. Once you are ready, connect with your Shungite.

Physical Wellbeing

There are a multitude of ways that you can use Shungite to improve your health. The first recognised use of Shungite was the drinking of spring water from Lake Onega that had a profound physical and psychological effects on the locals. Unfortunately the water that comes out of our taps from the domestic water supply is "dead" due to the amount of chemicals used to disinfect it. In addition to this, the passing of the water through powerful electric pumps, which generate electromagnetic fields, destroy the living structure of the water. Place a piece of type I or II Shungite in purified water and leave it for about three days. It will help to reactivate and revitalise your water. Drink one glass a day when healthy or two to three when unwell. Children can have half a glass each day. You can also place Shungite in bath water or spritz Shungite water on your face to enjoy its revitalising effects on the skin.

Another major health concern as a result of modern day living is our constant exposure to electromagnetic radiation from mobile phones, computers, Wi-Fi and other electrical appliances. This radiation affects the subtle energies in and around your body and with constant exposure your body will struggle to maintain homeostatic balance physically, psychologically and spiritually. Shungite helps the body deal with exposure to electro-magnetic radiation by helping the body realign its energy centres as well as transform the harmful influences of the radiation without affecting the performance of your electrical appliances. To employ Shungite for this trait, either wear Shungite, place a piece of Shungite (pyramids are great!) near the appliance or have the appliance sit on a tile or slice of Shungite.

Free radicals are a type of molecule that are found in the body in relatively small amounts when we are living a healthy lifestyle in a clean environment. However excess exposure to X-rays, ozone, cigarette smoking, air pollutants and industrial chemicals can increase the amount of free radicals in your body. Free radicals have a damaging effect on our cells, weakening the systems of our body and increasing risks of heart attacks, neurodegenerative diseases and cancers. The fullerenes in Shungite act as an antioxidant, neutralising the harmful effects of free radicals. Therefore whenever you are unwell incorporate Shungite into your life. Research has shown support for the effectiveness of Shungite use for osteoarthritis, respiratory problems, digestive grievances, cardiovascular disease, skin complaints and more when used in conjunction with professional treatments. Also try placing or wearing Shungite over a bruise, cut or wound to accelerate healing.

A lot of your body's healing takes place while you sleep and so since you spend a large percentage of time in your bedroom, placing Shungite here can allow you to take advantage of both its protective and health promoting properties. In the bedroom egg and sphere shapes are ideal. However be aware that Shungite increases the energy of the body and some sensitive people may find Shungite keeps them awake. To counteract this try pairing your Shungite with a similar size Selenite.

Anchoring

Shungite has been found to stimulate all of the chakras, especially when paired with a crystal of the chakra's colour e.g. Shungite and an orange crystal stimulates the sacral chakra, Shungite and a yellow crystal stimulate the solar plexus chakra, and so on. However Shungite's biggest impact is on the base chakra. Meditate with a piece of Shungite, ideally in a cube shape as this is in resonance with the Earth and base chakra, at the base of your spine or carry a piece of Shungite in your pocket. Through increasing the energy of this chakra, Shungite allows you to forge a strong energetic connection with the Earth, nourishing your vital energy levels. This is known as anchoring, rootedness or grounding and helps you remain stable and balanced as you go about your everyday life. When you are properly anchored you are will find you are more resistant to external detrimental energies and recover quicker from physical illness or emotional shocks.

Once your energetic roots are firmly in the ground, you can then start to combine Shungite with other crystals that enable your energetic branches to reach out to the cosmos and draw in universal life force. Violet crystals such as Charoite are great and will help you to totally align your energies. Other Russian crystals are great to use too. Seraphinite and Shungite establish inner balance allowing you to bring in subtle information from the universe and angelic realms by heightening your extrasensory abilities. Nephrite (see Green Jade chapter) and Shungite purify and heal the body as well as restore your ability to integrate ancestral memory. Eudialyte and Shungite together open your receptivity to the love in the world, while Dianite and Shungite improve your ability to communicate and understand the world.

Harmonising rods are a tradition from ancient Egypt and are a great way to use Shungite. They are simply polished cylinders, one being Shungite which represents a yang energy and the other being a crystal of yin energy. Popular choices for your yin rod are White Jade, Karelian Steatite or any of the above-mentioned crystals. Sit with the Shungite rod in your projective hand and the other in your receptive hand, holding them vertically resting on your thighs. Then simply rest and enjoy the balancing effect.

Ancient Memory

Beyond Shungite's amazing physical and energetic benefits, it also possesses potent spiritual properties. Due to its age, Shungite has seen it all and stored wisdom from all past civilisations. Scry with a Shungite skull or sit holding a Shungite pyramid to access ancient soul wisdom and ancestral guidance. If you would like to connect with your ancestors, hold Shungite and invite past family members to join you. Sit quietly and allow guidance to come as a message, sensation or inspired thought. In-depth journeying with Shungite can reveal a re-remembering of the historical changes of the planet and understanding of the energetic formation of the planet.

Shungite supports Earth Workers, those individuals who feel they have lived many life times on this planet and have a stronger attachment to Earth than elsewhere in the universe such as Pleiades, Arcturus, Orion, Sirius or Vega. Earth Workers are drawn to working with the seasonal cycles of the planet as well as animals, plants and of course, crystals. Shungite nurtures this earthly connection. It supports Earth Workers in fulfilling their planetary role of returning Earth to its full glory. Shungite fosters honesty, builds faith between people, encourages charity, awakens courage and promotes, peace, joy and love. Summon the magic of Pig, or Boar, when working with Shungite. Pig shows you how to discover the mysteries and secrets of the Earth and the way to sniff out the abundance that exists around you.

Revival

Shungite supports ridding fears of loss, isolation or material harm as well as the release of old habits and destructive attitudes that hold you back. Wear Shungite each day to remind to let go of unhelpful ways of being and take time to meditate while holding your Shungite projecting anything unwanted into the crystal before leaving it on the earth to cleanse overnight. The added benefit of Shungite is that it ensures you keep the wisdom of the past in order to stop making the same mistakes continuously. Shungite then, through establishing a robust base, supports you in bringing your wishes into manifestation through encouraging you to develop a strong and practical plan and applying what you have learned from past experience. If you are lacking confidence in your ability to bring your dreams into reality, pair Shungite with Black Obsidian. Pairing the use of Shungite with the inhalation of petitgrain essential oil amplifies your work. Petitgrain is ideal for banishing unwanted energies and mental cobwebs in order to give you the sharpened mind and strong, joyous foundation needed to move forward.

Shungite is great for altering the energy of a space. It can be used to create a space for the sacred, sexual union of two lovers, especially when trying to conceive. Grid Shungite with crystals such as Rose Quartz, Red Garnet, Ruby, Rhodochrosite and Kunzite under the bed or around the space to promote a spiritually connecting sanctuary. Grid Shungite around rehabilitation spaces to improve the effectiveness of drug and psychological therapies. Hold a piece when smudging or bury it in the ground for Earth healing purposes, especially in places often subject to natural disasters. It will store the loving energies you charge the crystal with and emits them where most needed once it is buried.

Due to its purifying traits, Shungite promotes truth and when it is around, people will find it hard to speak or act falsely without feeling a deep sense of discomfort. Ask your Shungite to support you to always act with integrity or carry it with a Herkimer Diamond when dealing with anyone you find hard to trust to help you find their true motives.

Shungite can be used for spiritual protection, having a similar effect as Black Onyx, Jet, Smokey Quartz, Red Jasper or Red Garnet. By grounding you, Shungite prevent you from taking silly risks or doing anything that will endanger your wellbeing.

To find out more about the varieties of Shungite, the research conducted and to explore the many benefits of this crystal, please read Shungite – *Protection, Healing and Detoxification* by Regina Martino.

STAR RUBY

Open Heart / Self Appreciation / Overcome Adversity

Star Rubies are beautiful gemstones that display a six-ray star that glides magically across the crystal's surface as it's moved. The star effect is rare amongst rubies so these special crystals will often attract unique individuals who resonate with its glowing energy and have a exceptional gift to share with the world. In the past, it was believed that by gazing at the crystal's star, the mysteries of the entire universe were reflected back at you. Thus, these crystals offer guidance and awaken the hearts of those ready to preserve and protect the world's beauty and share its love with all they meet. Star rubies enable their guardian to shine in any situation and never let those with ulterior motives dull their glow.

Animal: Pegasus
Plants: Pimento Berry and Pomegranate
Astrological Correspondences: Mars and the Pegasus constellation
Power Day: Tuesday
Cleanse with: Fire or outside during a Red Moon

Your Crystal Alignment Meditation

Go and sit outside at night, taking time to gaze at the starry sky. Tune in to its vastness and let your mind disappear. Experience the beauty of the expansiveness. Know that as the sky is stretched out before you, so are the opportunities of life. As you gaze into the universe, connecting with all that is, notice the universe is connecting to you, resting upon the earth. Allow your spirits to rise to a level of blissful freedom. You are free, free to do all you desire. Eventually send some gratitude to the universe, even blow it a kiss if you're feeling adventurous and then connect with your Star Ruby.

Open Heart

Star Ruby promotes a pure and open heart. Unaffected by pain and sorrow and determined to shine love and light across the world. Wear your Star Ruby near your heart to nurture unconditional love for everyone in your life. It will awaken your true self to abandon judgement and fear, opting for a life full of authentic connections and uplifting experiences. This powerful crystal connects you to the magical guide Pegasus. He is an ascended horse whose heart centre has opened to its full potential giving him wings to fly. Whisper your desire to your Star Ruby and bring your Pegasus forth to meet you in meditation. After your initial contact, even if you cannot see him, you may feel his presence as your relationship strengthens.

To attract a twin soul, place your Star Ruby on a windowsill with a pomegranate and a dark-red candle on a Tuesday night. Sit by the open window and whisper your heart's desire out to the world. Wear the Star Ruby each day to draw the right person to you. It will help your inner spark shine outwards when the right person appears.

Star Ruby also supports the circulatory system, stimulating life force through the physical and spiritual bodies. It ensures a strong heart and healthy circulation. With Star Ruby you'll never get cold feet, physically or metaphorically! Star Ruby will promote a healthy sex life and helps eliminate fear or anxiety causing impotence or premature ejaculation.

Self Appreciation

As Star Ruby opens your heart to the world, it also ensures you embrace yourself with the same level of love and appreciation. Star Ruby is a powerful stone to heal tendencies of self-harm or self-neglect. Gaze into your own eyes in a mirror while holding your Star Ruby against your bare chest. Repeat the words, "I love you" until you feel the sensations of happiness and security. Allow Star Ruby to give you an inner sense of prosperity, knowing you have all you need to live the perfect life.

Overcome Adversity

As your light shines, so will those of the people around you. Any who are not ready to resonate with your heightened vibration or wish you harm will be deterred away. Like all other crystals with a strong shine, a Star Ruby is great for protection, not just physically but also emotionally, mentally and psychically. If you feel threatened, subtly shine the crystal outwards when you feel enemies around you. They are powerful talismans against others using magic to promote your downfall. If you can, diffuse pimento berry essential oil in your space to enhance your Star Ruby's power and disperse destructive or damaging energies. Like normal Rubies, a Star Ruby can change colour in the presence of someone who doesn't like you or is working against you. If you can acquire a decent size Star Ruby, use it to scry with to gain understanding of their disdain towards you.

STAR SAPPHIRE, BLUE

Intuition / Connection / Honourable Behaviour

Star Sapphires are a rare but invaluable find amongst Sapphires. They display a phenomenon known as asterism that is a shining rayed star that sashays across the crystal as it is moved in the light. Like normal Sapphires, Star Sapphires are associated with loyalty and service. However, when it comes to a Star Sapphire the focus is more on the spiritual arena. Star Sapphires allow you to devote your whole being to the spiritual betterment of yourself, your fellow people and the universe as a whole.

Animals: Narwhal and Unicorn
Plant: Holly
Astrological Correspondences: Saturn and the Monoceros/Unicorn constellation
Power Day: Saturday
Cleanse with: Water or outside during a Blue Moon

Your Crystal Alignment Meditation

Go and sit outside, taking time to gaze at the starry sky. Tune in to its vastness and let your mind disappear. Experience the beauty of the expansiveness. Know that as the sky is stretched out before you, so is all the universal wisdom. As you gaze into the far-off galaxies, connecting with all that is, notice the universe is connecting to you as you rest upon the earth. Allow yourself to connect with the knowledge sources of the cosmos. You are a student of the stars, and the night sky is your blackboard. When ready connect with your Star Sapphire.

Intuition

Star Sapphire enables you to constantly improve and heighten your psychic abilities. It helps you find guidance during moments of crisis or disaster. Firstly, it works to relax you at times of extreme physical or mental exertion so you can get to a point where you are open to divine guidance. Hold your Star

Sapphire against your third eye chakra and let it clear the mind of gibber and distraction as you focus on your breath. Once relaxed the crystal enables you to receive intuitive or psychic messages. Star Sapphire then helps shift this acquired knowledge to a denser reality for easy understanding. If you feel you need protection during spiritual or psychic work, keep a black Star Sapphire near you.

Star Sapphire helps you connect to Unicorn wisdom. To attract Unicorn sit outside with a lit white candle, an apple, a piece of holly and your Star Sapphire. Hold your Star Sapphire up to your mind and speak telepathically to the crystal, requesting it connect you with your Unicorn. Your Unicorn may then appear to you in a meditation or dream or you may sense its energy nearby. As your spiritual vibration increases, you may gain the ability to see your Unicorn. Unicorns grant soul wishes, those that satisfy you deeply and help you fulfil your path of service. Be clear and certain about what to request from your Unicorn.

Another way of working with Unicorn wisdom is by tuning into your Narwhal guide. Legend has it that at the fall of Atlantis, Unicorn passed his magical horns to Narwhal for safeguarding. Narwhal will guide you on how to intuitively access knowledge and magic that ensures you succeed in life.

Star Sapphire can be used for grounding great ideas into practical steps that enable you to make them a reality. They also offer extra determination to see plans through to completion. The grounding ability of Star Sapphires can assist those with Alzheimer's or dementia. Intuitive sources believe that the souls of these individuals are starting to separate from their physical body leading to disjointed thinking and confusion. Wearing a Star Sapphire can help the soul realign within the body and allow renewed clarity.

Connection

As Star Sapphire improves your intuition it enables you to anticipate the needs and intentions of others. Wear your Star Sapphire every day and it will allow you to fulfil the needs of those you love and care for before they ask. It also enables you to stay safe as you can foresee any harm someone is plotting. Working with Star Sapphire will allow you to gain a greater understanding of others' heart desires leading to an appreciation of their own personal drive for betterment. This crystal also helps form spiritual bonds between people. Two Star Sapphires charged together will allow twins to feel connected when they are apart and avoid separation anxiety. Similarly two crystals will help safely guide two people back together. You can also use Star Sapphire for contacting extra-terrestrial beings.

Honourable Behaviour

Star Sapphire empowers those that have committed to a spiritual path to remain loyal to its teachings. It strengthens faith and hope while enabling you to share your guidance when invited. When used in grids it encourages charitable acts and supports charities to succeed.

Star Sapphire also allows the integration of spiritual philosophy into modern life. Always take your Star Sapphire with you to any spiritual teachings and then carry it in the following days to remember what you learned and apply it when relevant. Star Sapphires when worn, especially as a ring, encourage a life of integrity. It strengthens your resolve and encourages you to find solutions to problems that benefit the greater good.

To create a blessing wand, to consecrate food, gifts, talismans, crystals or sacred spaces, combine a Star Sapphire with American hollywood, the whitest wood in the world. Fashion the wood into a shape that suits you and attach the crystal to the end. To give a blessing, lightly touch an object with the crystal end and say, "blessed be". You can also use this wand to direct energy during meditations for healing or cleansing.

STICHTITE

Spiritual Progression / Path Of Service / Homosexuality / Gentleness

Stichtite was first discovered in Tasmania, Australia in 1910 where it was named after the mine's manager Robert Carl Sticht. This crystal has since been found in other localities around the world occurring in a range of shades from a light pink, a medium hot pink, a deep purple colour, and quite a few shades in between. Stichtite is a calming crystal which facilitates gentle healing of any current issues in your life. It can also be used for earth healing to calm areas which have been severely disturbed. Its gentleness should not be mistaken for weakness as this is a crystal that powerfully helps you progress along your life path. It allows you to approach each day with a calm and attentive mindset, focusing you on what is important and serves your highest good. Stichtite reminds you that life is too short to waste your time on trivial matters or be held back by fear. It encourages you to seize life, explore and express who you are, and to leave a lasting positive legacy with the world.

Animal: Amazon River Dolphin
Plants: Hyacinth and Purpleheart
Astrological Correspondences: Antinous, Chiron, Jupiter and Uranus
Power Day: Monday
Cleanse with: Full Moon

Your Crystal Alignment Meditation

Take a walk through the forest or bush and after a while stop and examine one tree. Look at its crooks and bends, broken branches and contemplate why it has grown this way. Walk a little further and repeat this exercise. Continue to walk examining trees and plants, realising that none are perfect and all have blemishes and faults, but also seek understanding of why the tree has grown like that. Then sit with your Stichtite and meditate on the idea of perfection. Comprehend that each tree is perfect with its imperfections because it has grown like that to survive and do what a tree needs to do. Now as you leave the trees and start to see people over the next few days, treat them like the trees and try to understand why they have grown to be the way they are.

Spiritual Progression

As a violet crystal, Stichtite affects your crown chakra, stimulating it when it is underactive. This encourages you to explore the spiritual aspects of your life, and allows you to become clearer on your spiritual path and see the divine beauty and perfection, both around you and within you. It helps you to focus on the present, bringing to your awareness that living in the past is to live in depression and living in the future is to live in a state of anxiety. Stichtite will ease your worries from within, allowing you to focus more on the miracles of life unfolding before you at this very moment. If you are drawn to work with Stichtite, and find that you hold a view of the past or future as either better or worse than the present and this belief is negatively affecting your current life, then also work with hyacinth essential oil. Hyacinth essential oil helps to balance out fascinations, idolising and judgemental behaviours, and bring us towards a more balanced perspective. While wearing or carrying your Stichtite, make an anointing oil by mixing some hyacinth essential oil with carrier oil and then dab one drop behind each ear, one drop at the base of the neck, and one drop on the inside of each wrist. This spiritual combination will initiate you into a higher understanding of your past and future as well as about the people in it.

If the lopsided perceptions are more about yourself then Stichtite can support in reducing a tendency to be overly critical of yourself. Although being critical can be healthy as it is necessary for self-reflection and appraisal, overly negative self-talk deflates your understanding of your divine nature and gifts. If you are hard on yourself, Stichtite encourages you to ease off on the self-criticism and be more compassionate towards yourself. Furthermore, excessive and prolonged self-criticism can manifest kidney and renal disease in the body. In these cases, place Stichtite over the area and drink Stichtite elixir each day while exploring how to show yourself more self-love.

Stichtite enables you to have a broader view of the world and universe and to see the bigger picture regarding any issue. It increases your compassion and understanding for others and thus facilitates forgiveness, since it offers the understanding that each individual is doing their best and playing their role within the unfoldment of life's journey. It can help you to see that which you judge, despise or dislike in others acts as a mirror to show how we are repressing or denying that aspect within ourselves. As we discover this and can open ourselves up to loving this aspect of ourselves, we learn to embrace all our traits with love and kind-heartedness.

We often surround ourselves with people who share similar beliefs and views. Stichtite encourages you to seek out the company of those that are different as their alternative views can help to challenge your own wisdom, allowing you to contemplate and understand other perspectives, in turn giving you a greater knowledge of the world.

Once you have developed a relationship with Stichtite over time and have developed a more comprehensive and balanced view of yourself, others and the world, then this crystal can support you in higher spiritual pursuits. Stichtite helps you to become conscious of the presence of spiritual guides, angels and other spiritual beings in the higher realms. Team it with crystals such as Angelite, Angel Aura Quartz, Celestite, Danburite and/or Seraphinite to initiate a higher connection. These crystals will help the spiritual guides reach out to you and Stichtite will ensure you are mindful that they are there for you to reach out to if you wish to.

Working with Stichtite you may notice an increase in intuitive inspiration. Stichtite helps you in the early days of your spiritual journey to trust your intuition. It supports you on exploring your own path and facilitates the break away from a reliance on authority figures as your governing reference for guidance. To enhance the properties of your Stichtite, team it with Purpleheart wood. Purpleheart, is a flowering tree from the rainforests of Brazil, Guyana, and Suriname of Central and South America. This purple duo helps divination by stilling the mind from distractions to allow messages to come through. They are also both spiritually protective. Use them both for psychic protection and add Black Tourmaline or Black Onyx for an extra boost.

Path of Service

As Stichtite helps to balance the crown chakra, one of the results of this is that you gain clarity on your gifts and how to share them with the world. Sit quietly with your Stichtite and start to ponder what you are drawn to. Pay close attention to your feelings, as what feels good will be in alignment with your soul and should be explored further. As you develop your relationship with Stichtite, keeping it nearby each day, it acts to help you turn these desires into actions. Eventually these actions become habits and you are now living a life that will be spiritually fulfilling.

Stichtite will support you on your spiritual path especially when you have made a conscious decision to take a new turn in your journey. It helps us discover new opportunities and achieve new goals in alignment with what feels good. It is a crystal of the seeker, the hunter and the adventurer. As Stichtite helps, aligns you with your soul purpose, hold or carry it when heading into those big or testing moments of life such as an interview, presentation or performance. It'll help the outcome to be in alignment with your highest good. Due to its exploratory energy it is supportive of scientists and researchers, helping them to make new breakthroughs. Teaming it with a course of hyacinth flower essence can awaken the realisations of synchronicity in your life, recognising more clues to the correct path to take each day. If at any point you feel fear is holding you back, explore the use of Serpentine Stichtite, also known as Atlantisite™ (see the Serpentine chapter in this book).

However Stichtite extends beyond helping you discover and pursue your path of service, allowing you to also share your gifts with the world and make a worthwhile contribution to the world. It also supports you in assisting others to discover their gifts and individual ways to enrich society. In friendship, Stichtite promotes honesty and enhances spiritual connections, encouraging the relationships to become that which boosts the personal growth of you both. It shifts conversations from gossip and the past, to ideas and aspirations for the future. In dealing with people every day, it supports you in seeing the light in other people and knowing how to bring that light to the surface. It helps reinstate confidence in even the most evil of people. Stichtite is an essential tool for teachers, guides and healers. It encourages you to cease teaching from the egotistical approach that you know all the knowledge, shifting to an attitude that you are here to facilitate ways for others to find the answers themselves. Here, hyacinth teams magnificently with Stichtite as the aroma from the flowers or essential oil helps us to each reach deep inside and discover the light within so that we blossom and bloom.

Homosexuality

The challenges faced by homosexual, bisexual and transgender individuals are unique and specialised to this group in this day and age. In many places around the world, and even in the most forward thinking of countries, pockets of discrimination still occur. Generally, discrimination grows from a lack of understanding of another's unique gifts. Stichtite encourages a more open-minded approach to combat this kind of thinking. If you notice yourself finding it hard to understand another's way of life, meditate with Stichtite. If working to support those facing discrimination, Stichtite is great to add to grids.

This attitude to gay people has not always existed. In many cultures they were delegated a specialised role within a community, often of spiritual or shamanic importance. Some Native American tribes used terms such as two spirited, as these men often also has a strong feminine energy within them, while the women also possessed a masculine spirit. Possessing both yin and yang energies meant they were more balanced and able to support and guide heterosexual people. Stichtite, helps individuals understand and blossom their gifts to share these with those around them and thus helps gay or two spirited people understand their special and unique role in society. If you are gay, Stichtite has the ability for you to change your relationship with yourself, see your value in the world and develop self-love. It is relevant for those suffering from eating disorders brought on by extreme fear, self-hatred or rejection.

In finding your spiritual role within society, Stichtite also helps gay people find support from others. Gridded around the home. It can encourage more understanding views from other family members when someone is coming out. Meditate and program a Stichtite and wear it each day to attract friends who love and cherish you. Gay people should combine Stichtite with Kunzite when seeking to attract a romantic soul mate. Hold the two crystals against your heart while visualising the type of person you'd like to attract. It is important not to focus on a particular person as that is then directing energy that may be against their free will. Rather focus on how you will feel when the right person comes into your life. Now take a piece of paper and draw a circle. Dab a tiny amount of honey, just so there is enough to make the inside of the circle sticky. Then sprinkle cinnamon over the honey. Wrap the two crystals in the paper and place them in a piece of red cloth or bag. Carry the bag with you or place it on an altar for a full lunar cycle. This is best performed on the night of the new moon. You can also add drops of hyacinth, as well as laurel, cypress and rose to the cloth as well as diffuse it around your space. Once you have found your partner, Stichtite relieves shyness and inhibitions in showing affection.

Stichtite can be used to heal and protect gay people. It helps to clear hurts carried from the past, especially those from family members unable to understand them being gay. It also helps gay people release any guilt they feel for not fulfilling others expectations on them such as having a heterosexual partner and having children. It also acts as a protective amulet, navigating them out of dangerous situations. Dolphin has always been a protective totem of gay people, so visualise a pod of dolphins swimming around you when you are feeling threatened. The Amazon River Dolphin is an especially great guide to call into meditation when working with Stichtite to help you understand your divine purpose for this incarnation.

Simplicity

Although Stichtite is a crystal of advancement and progression, especially for the spiritual aspect of your life, it does not work to make your life more complex. In fact, it counteracts busyness, always ushering you back to ways of simplicity. Stichtite encourages you to find ways of going about your day remaining in a state of tranquillity. It supports mastery of the path of least resistance. Amidst the fast-paced environment, many of us dwell within. Stichtite coerces you to take some time out to luxuriate and pamper yourself. This is not for selfish or indulgent reasons but more so to ensure you are always at your optimum wellbeing so you can give your best to the world. Instead of trying to give yourself to the world 100% of the time, Stichtite suggests you give your best 75% of the time and recharge 25% of the time. This will ensure your longevity. Meditate with Stichtite to discover how to simplify life for better health and spirituality whenever you are feeling over-stretched or overwhelmed. When the demands of life become too overwhelming, angry feelings of hopelessness and helplessness can occur and manifest as Alzheimer's disease. Stichtite helps these individuals relax in knowing that they are safe, and to trust the process of life.

Stichtite is a great crystal to have around the family space to wash away petty bickering and bring back basic and simple good values in the home. Grid it around you home to create a more tranquil and spiritually conducive environment. Team it with Purpleheart wood, which works to remove destructive energies that cause strife. Stichtite helps to soften stubborn attitudes that are blocking the path to love and contentment between people. It is a support crystal for balancing those with ADHD. Be sure to place it in nurseries, play areas and children's bedrooms to encourage cooperation. It also can be used to alleviate nightmares when placed in the pillowslip. Make a spritz with pure water and nine drops of hyacinth essential oil to mist across the pillow for extra support.

SUGILITE
Universal Love / Community / Crown Chakra / Physical and Spiritual Balance

The recently discovered Sugilite is heralded as the crystal of universal love, needed to transform humanity. Sugilite leads you to understand that the universe will provide you with all of your needs, physically, mentally, emotionally and spiritually. This causes a transformation with all people in your life. You can now love unconditionally rather than with dependency and expectations on others. Sugilite leads you to embrace diversity and be part of the change towards a united humanity. Much confusion exists about the correct pronunciation of this crystal. Sugilite is named after the Japanese geologist Ken Sugi. Therefore, the correct pronunciation of Ken Sugi's name and thus the crystal is sue-gee (as in geese) – lite.

Animals: Beaver and Violet-backed Starling
Plant: Passionflower
Astrological Correspondence: Jupiter
Power Day: Thursday
Cleanse with: Water

Your Crystal Alignment Meditation

Go outside and sit in nature. Start by visualising a cord or root growing from the soles of your feet and into the earth, like the roots of a tree going deeper and deeper, heading towards the planet's centre. As the roots continue to forge deeper, sense the exchange of energy between yourself and the earth. Then send out a connection extending up above you like the branches of a tree. The branches are the most beautiful white light, sparking with every colour imaginable. The branches are reaching out and connecting with all that exists above and around you. Allow these branches to go as far as you wish, around the Earth, beyond the clouds, into space, to the Sun, connecting to the moon and the other planets, beyond our solar system and connecting you with all that exists beyond here. Feel this infinite wisdom and love flowing into you from all that is above.

Feel these two energies blending within you. Like a tree, you absorb energy from the ground below and the air above. Feel these energies slowly and gracefully spiral and circle around your body in a clockwise direction. In the world, everything spirals around a central axis. Electrons dance around a nucleus. The Earth rotates on its axis and we, along with the other planets in our solar system, revolve around the Sun. Feel that gentle circular drift, this spiral, this cosmic dance that drives all that is in the universe. Allow these two energies from above and below to dance around in circles within you and around you. You are now ready to connect with your Sugilite.

Universal Love

Sugilite has been touted as the love stone of this age. When it comes to love, set down your Rose Quartz and pick up your Sugilite. This crystal exists to teach you universal love that is not that which is felt for a partner or family but rather love for all of humankind. Universal love is an expression of the harmony of the totality. Everything that exists is included in an interrelated relationship, including yourself. Everything fits and functions as a togetherness, as a oneness. Wear Sugilite over your heart to awaken your understanding of universal love. Sugilite will increase your compassion for others and promote supportive, realistic love for those you are close to rather than over sentimentality and soppiness. It will allow you to see that what is done to one, affects all, empowering you to take every opportunity to act with consideration and kindness.

If you find that your relationships are highly volatile, overly emotional or sentimental then Sugilite can help you. Sugilite endows you with the wisdom to remain loving and balanced when those around you are not. Rather than getting affected by another's bad mood or misery, Sugilite will allow you to become a pillar of solidarity and understanding. This in turn will allow others to do the same, whether it is a child you refuse to argue with or a reckless driver attempting to rule the roads. At home, place a Sugilite sphere in the centre of the house or grid seven pieces around the edge of the house to generate a more harmonious home. A piece carried in the car spreads love wherever you travel. Wearing a Sugilite ring keeps the energy of universal love on your body and protects you from any negativity that may be attracted to your "light".

Sugilite can be especially helpful in certain situations. It is the ideal crystal to remind adopted children that they are still loved after tracking down their birth parents only to be rejected by them. It also offers support to those with schizophrenia, autism or Asperger's syndrome allowing them to ground more in the present and effectively share their emotions.

Archangel Zadkiel harmonises with Sugilite. He is the angel of mercy and compassion, giving you freedom from the past through learning to forgive others. Zadkiel also helps you to forgive yourself. He guides you to live a life of kindness, tolerance and integrity and rewards you with an abundance of what you desire. Zadkiel strengthens the memory and is a perfect companion for students. He is an angel of the violet flame and offers inspiration to scientists, engineers and architects, guiding them to design harmonious communities. To connect with Zadkiel, hold your Sugilite between your hands and pray. You will know he is reaching out to you if you see or sense a violet or indigo light or sense a strong feeling of gratitude.

Community

Grid Sugilite around spaces for parties, celebrations, conferences and negotiations. It will promote understanding and diminish hostility, ensuring every gathering is successful. Passionflower harmonises with Sugilite so place a small plant or part thereof in a space where a group is working together towards a common goal and allow it to aid transformation. The scent of passionfruit will create a soothing energy if there is the potential for disagreements or stress. Burn passionfruit incense or add the scent to the water when you wash the floors. Hold Sugilite and send positive thoughts whenever governments or organisations are meeting to support them to make decisions that benefit the greater good. When placed around playgrounds, Sugilite encourages children to play together and can be given to a shy child starting a new school to help them make new friends. Combine Sugilite with your work with your Beaver guide. This combination will help you make decisions and devise new ways that benefit the greater good each day.

Crown Chakra

Your crown chakra is the energy centre that governs your spiritual connection to the world and everything within it. Sugilite is a great crystal to help keep your crown chakra balanced. Signs that your crown chakra is balanced include having empathy for others, creativity, optimism, imagination, strong connection to Great Spirit and strong physical balance. To keep yourself at this optimum state simply carry or wear Sugilite with you each day, ideally on the upper part of your body. Take time to lie down and rest each day and place the Sugilite at the top of your head while visualise a perfect sphere of violet light at your crown. If you prefer a more active meditation, do some yoga. Stand in tree pose while holding your Sugilite above your head. A supported headstand can also be good for the crown chakra.

Physical and Spiritual Balance

Most pieces of Sugilite consist of two major colours: purple (spirituality) and black (grounding) making it another stone that is great for establishing balance between spirituality and physical life. Hold Sugilite when meditating, reading spiritual texts or attending spiritual gatherings to help you apply the knowledge you receive into your everyday life. Work with your Violet-backed Starling guide in unison with Sugilite. This beautiful bird teaches you how to share your spirituality with others appropriately. With such a buffet of religions and belief systems around the world, sometimes it can be hard to know the correct etiquette. Violet-backed Starling with help you share the messages of love and togetherness that underpin all our beliefs. Use him to help you bring people of difference together, so that no matter what spiritual path each person is on, we will all find how to live in harmony on this planet.

Sugilite is great for balancing compulsive behaviours such as out-of-control spending, gambling or partying, and assists in bringing you back to living as your true, authentic self. When a compulsion starts to take over, sit quietly with your Sugilite in your receptive hand and ask yourself, "What does my soul need right now?" Continue to wear Sugilite for constant support for your addictions. This purple treasure also teaches you how to keep a balance of work or study with fun in your life and when given to spiritually inclined children, can help them recall their past lives.

SUNSTONE

Sun / Dance / Family / Sacral Chakra

Sunstone is an orange variety of the Feldspar group that generally contains small Hematite crystals that give it an additional sparkle. Like the first warm, sunny days of spring, Sunstone brings refreshing joy to your life. It promotes optimism, self-empowerment, strength and playfulness. Even the most hardened pessimist is rendered helpless by the uplifting energy of Sunstone. Ancients believed it was actually a piece of the Sun and used it to attract power and wealth.

Animals: Otter and Scarab Beetle
Plant: Jasmine
Astrological Correspondence: Sun
Power Day: Sunday
Cleanse with: Sun

Your Crystal Alignment Meditation

Go and bathe in the radiant energy of the sun. Soak up its warmth and sense how it makes you feel. Does it elevate your mood? It is the sun that makes a seed want to burst from the soil and grow towards its highest potential. Rest in the sun with an awareness of the many blessings it brings to your life. Evoke a feeling of gratitude toward the sun. You may want to finish this practice by completing the yoga sequence, Sun Salutation, to increase the flow of energy around your body. When you are ready, connect with your Sunstone.

Sun

Sunstone enables you to connect with all levels of the sun's energy. When there is a lack of sunshine, Sunstone is a worthy substitute. Place it near some water in the daylight and create a solar charged elixir. When worn against the skin it helps counteract vitamin D deficiency and seasonal affective disorder (SAD). Place Sunstone in medicine bags to strengthen them just as the sun strengthens plants when they are growing. Grid Sunstone around solar panels to attract maximum energy collection or use the crystal in a power grid to encourage investment in renewable energy sources.

Sunstone enables you to connect with the Divine Masculine energy and associated solar gods such as Ra, Apollo, Khepri and Helios. Place orange candles around your home or on your altar and ask Him to help you shine in life. Carry your Sunstone when you are going for a promotion or leadership role or place near the computer to gain more interest if advertising online. You may be looking to spread your wings and travel or holiday, especially to sunnier places. If so, ask Sunstone to open up these opportunities.

Being a stone imbued with such masculine energy, Sunstone increases sexual energy, especially if worn or kept low on your body. Sunstone also helps to find and keep a beneficial sexual relationship. Combine it with the scent of jasmine to attract both physical and spiritual love. If you need to rebalance your masculine and feminine sides, meditate with a Sunstone in your projective hand and a Moonstone in your receptive hand. This powerful combo will balance you in no time.

Dance

Sunstone reminds you of the importance of joy and celebration. It brightens your life so that only good shall enter and you see the truth. Combine Sunstone with your Otter guide to remember the importance of play and fun. This can help with any muscular problems that arise as physical manifestations of an unwillingness to "dance through life". Sunstone can also be charged to support bodybuilding. If you find you are getting too serious and losing your sense of adventure take your Sunstone for a dance. Whether it be ballroom, folk, circle or nightclub dancing, allow yourself to get taken away with the music and reconnect with the movement of energy that swirls around the world.

Family

Sunstone works to ensure true, radiant happiness but this can come at a cost. Like a stern but loving father, Sunstone will not let you sweep issues under the rug to ignore. Sunstone resonates with the sacral chakra, which governs intimate relationships, such as those with your family. Meditate with Sunstone to awaken family issues you need to deal with. Then look at ways to resolve these issues through communication, reconciliation, counselling or spiritual healing. The scarab beetle rolls balls of dung across the ground, an act that the Egyptians saw as a symbol of the forces that move the sun across the sky. By working with your Scarab guide he will help you deal with your crap and lead you towards illumination.

Sacral Chakra

Sunstone is a perfect crystal for nurturing a balanced sacral chakra. When your sacral chakra is balanced, you feel comfortable forming close relationships with others, display intimacy appropriately, embrace your sexuality and honour your creative side. You have a great passion for life and embrace each day as an opportunity to grow. Meditate with Sunstone by placing it on the body at the point of the sacral chakra while visualising a vibrant, glowing orange sphere pulsating in the area. Feel feelings of arrogance, indifference and repression fading away. Feel your reproductive system shifting to a state of perfect functioning. Your sex drive is balanced and healthy. You are feeling sociable, connected and ready to share with others. You passionately welcome the pleasures of life. Keep a Sunstone in your pocket or wear as a belly ring to ensure this balancing energy is available to you every day.

SUPER QUARTZ
Spiritual Attunement / Family Harmony / World Unity

Around the world, amazing deposits of combination Quartzes are being discovered. These life-changing crystals can be any combination of Clear Quartz, Smokey Quartz, Citrine and Amethyst and are filled with a wonderment of phantoms and inclusions such as Rutile, Cacoxenite, Ajoite and Lepidocrocite. Some Super Quartzes are well known by other names such as Super Seven™ found in Espirito de Santos, Brazil, and Auralite-23™ from northern Canada. The combination of minerals plus the place of origin will affect each individual crystal's energy, however, as these crystals have such a powerful vibration, they will guide their guardian how to best work with them. As a combination stone, Super Quartz is a crystal of unification and balance. In meditation it will help you find solutions for life challenges and give you the energy to put these concepts into action. Working with Super Quartz leads to spiritual awakening, healing, clear communication, dedication and a sense of connection to universal love.

Animals: Ant and White Lion
Plant: Balsam of Peru (also known as Peru Balsam)
Astrological Correspondences: Haumea and Mercury
Power Day: Wednesday
Cleansing: Does not need cleansing but leave outside in nature to rebalance its energies if you feel it is needed.

Your Crystal Alignment Meditation

Sit outside in nature and focus your attention on one thing, such as a flower or a stone. Connect with this item, sensing its energy and essence. Once connected, shift your attention to a second item. While still acknowledging your connection to the first, also connect to the second item of focus. Continue this practice until eventually you are able to feel a connection to all things, like a web of energetic exchange. Finally, connect with your Super Quartz.

Spiritual Attunement

When looking for a Super Quartz for yourself, you'll know when you have found it. These crystals have a tendency to call out to their guardian and once united, will form a strong, lasting bond. It is best to keep your Super Quartz with you for long periods of time each day. Placing it by you at night will have you waking feeling a deep sense of peace, harmony and contentment.

Super Quartz helps you heal on all levels. If you are feeling out of sorts, blocked, and mentally clumsy, call on your Super Quartz and you'll likely find yourself refreshed, alert, and back in control. It alleviates the sense of the "ticking clock" or a need to rush in life, instilling a willingness to breathe and relax, creating space for serenity, peace and inner solitude. This gives the physical body a chance to repair and regenerate and thus, Super Quartz is beneficial for any ailment caused by the excesses or stresses of modern day living. As you slow down, Super Quartz will facilitate connection with your guides, totems and the angelic realms, especially if you pair your stone with Danburite. Combine it with Tanzanite to enhance all types of psychic abilities and skills including telepathy, clairvoyance, clairaudience, clairgustance, clairalience (sometimes also called clairscent), channelling and psychometry.

A great aspect of Super Quartz is its ability to connect you to the higher realms while keeping you physically grounded. This can be done through an awareness of the soul star and Earth star chakras. These two chakras work in harmony and balance each other. Just as a tree's roots must grow as deep as the branches stretch high, your connection with the Earth must be as strong as your connection with the rest of the universe. Certain Super Quartzes have the ability to stimulate both these chakras if they contain both Smokey Quartz plus either Amethyst or Clear Quartz. Smokey Quartz resonates with the Earth star while Amethyst and Clear Quartz resonate with the soul star chakra. Lie down, placing a piece 15 centimetres below your feet and another 15 centimetres above your head. Visualise these two spheres are energy harmonising and facilitating your connection to the Earth, universe and universal love. Once they feel balanced, switch your working to using Achroite (Clear Tourmaline) or Goshenite.

Super Quartz helps to dispel imbalanced perspectives you hold, bringing insight to how a person or event both served you and caused you to suffer. When you hold a lopsided view, failing to see both sides of the situation, it can lead to feelings of desperation, anger, anxiety, resentment, judgement, depression and defeat. Mediate or sit with your Super Quartz and ponder or journal how a good situation did not serve you or a bad situation benefited you. Keep working with your Super Quartz until you can see the balance of the situation and start to sense a feeling of gratitude wash over you. Combining Super Quartz with Moldavite will allow your heart to embrace past happenings for what they truthfully are. As you develop your relationship with your stone, you'll continue to see core belief systems that have been created in this lifetime (or possibly other incarnations) that are now holding you back from fully embracing your life purpose, and most importantly how to transform this pain into a higher frequency to facilitate growth.

As you continue to balance your perceptions of past events, a renewing sense of upliftment will start to infuse into your being. Your Super Quartz will help you approach new situations with a balanced attitude, preventing out of control emotional or mental breakdowns. This crystal induces a rise in optimism and new hope, and as your awe of life grows, you'll experience euphoric excitement about the possibilities of the future.

Once you have found balance physically, mentally, emotionally and spiritually, Super Quartz accelerates your spiritual evolution. It opens the doorway to re-remember why you are here, what your role is, and how you can live that purpose to its highest degree. Super Quartz as a relentless energy and will constantly create situations for you to gain insight into your magnificence and full potential. It will push you to keep expanding your life and play a role in awakening humanity to an enlightened way of being. In this pursuit, summon the guidance of White Lion, who helps you understand the important spiritual role you have to play in humanity's growth, as well as the best way to expend your energy to fulfilling this purpose.

You will benefit from combining Super Quartz with other high vibration crystals. With Phenacite you'll speed up your spiritual growth, while combining it with Natrolite or Petalite will fill your life with light and joy. Super Quartz with violet crystals awakens your awareness of the interconnectedness of all things in the universe. Try Violet Sugilite to access universal love, Purpurite to discover ways for humanity to work together or Tiffany Stone to ensure you enjoy your spiritual progression. Combining Super Quartz with Prasiolite, a green variety of Quartz, helps you make a deep spiritual connection with the Earth and its magic. If this is an attribute you feel a strong pull to, you may want to work with Emerald Auralite™, a variety of Super Quartz recently discovered in Northern Canada near the site for Auralite-23™. Emerald Auralite™ contains Prasiolite as well as up to 23 other different crystals and is a powerhouse for reuniting your bond with our planet.

Family Harmony

Just as Super Quartz brings together a variety of mighty crystals to work together, it works to bring people together. When used at home, Super Quartz creates peace and harmony between family members, especially when blending families. Create a centrepiece using Super Quartz crystals, candles and plants in your home or on the dining table to bless the space. A crystal point acts as a great talking stick at family meetings. When worn, it allows step-parents and step-children to understand their new family members' point of view. Take a piece with you when you're meeting the in-laws for the first time.

When family troubles arise in your life, take time to meditate with Super Quartz. These stones help to bring awareness to why you have incarnated into this family group, or attracted in-laws to support you on this life journey.

Super Quartz can also help you to deal with hereditary diseases, giving you an understanding of generational patterns that are being passed on, and how to handle them in your life.

Super Quartz is effective without being overwhelming for use with children. In fact, for guidance on how you should use your Super Quartz ask children to show you. Younger children, without their preconceived ideas, will be able to tune into the unique attributes and energy of your crystal. Let children choose their own Super Quartz to wear or carry to support them to grow into well-adjusted adults. Super Quartz is great for children who are struggling to deal with the world or have experienced severe trauma.

World Unity

Super Quartz is a crystal of global awareness, encouraging you to be aware of what is happening around the world. Keep a piece nearby when reading the newspaper or surfing news websites to expand your knowledge and understanding of the world. A piece of Super Quartz can be charged to help you raise funds and resources to travel overseas, especially if it is for altruistic, educational or charitable reasons. Super Quartz supports the internet for its ability to share information around the world. Place a piece of Super Quartz near your modem to avoid connection issues and a piece near your computer to help you gain exposure on the internet.

Super Quartz brings together communities, whether it is your local community or the global community. It helps you, and everyone else understand that we each play an important, co-dependent role in the circle of life. This stone tones down anger and cools hot tempers and can help to remove prejudice and unnecessary judgment. It brings an awareness that any trait we dislike in another, also exists within us, and that we are yet to accept and love it. Work with Super Quartz to unveil the source of your judgemental behaviours and learn how to love a part of yourself that you have been repressing. This can be amplified if you combine Super Quartz with Eudialyte, Naujaite or Dioptase.

Use Super Quartz in harmony with the scent of Balsam of Peru, by either burning the resin or diffusing the essential oil. This balsam from Central and Southern America penetrates deep into the spaces that have remained cold, untouchable, and unreachable, allowing the heart to open and trust. Balsam of Peru facilitates the bringing up of anger in yourself which is now manifesting and being mirrored by others around you and causing you to be overly critical of others.

Use Super Quartz for healings and meditations aiming to improve harmony amongst groups and for counteracting the effects of terrorism or racial unrest. Super Quartz can protect embassy workers and buildings threatened by terrorist attack. Create a worldwide peace grid by sending pieces of Super Quartz to other spiritual people in other countries. At a chosen time all mediate, visualising a global grid of tolerance, compassion and love encompassing the globe.

Wearing Super Quartz over the heart can ignite feelings of hope and optimism, allowing you to see the positive effects of the awakening spiritual awareness of humanity. It allows you to see the divine spark in every person and shifts your attention to the beauty of nature and the kindness of people. Super Quartz awakens the global citizen within you, filling you with energy and determination to contribute towards the greater good, whether it is shifting to a greener lifestyle, organising community events or campaigning for human rights. It will attract opportunities and resources into your life that are necessary to accomplish your goals. In attuning with your Super Quartz you'll start to be surrounded by people who can support you in aiding the planet, especially people who possess an inner drive similar to your own. In your efforts to unite humanity, do not feel despondent when you're confronted with a setback. Your Ant guide, who also harmonises with Super Quartz, will give you the strength to understand that each small step in the right direction will eventually achieve great things.

TANZANITE

Clarity / Awakening / Spiritual Exploration

Tanzanite was kept hidden from the world until 1967. It is believed that a powerful lightning storm set surrounding grasslands on fire and unveiled these brilliant indigo-violet crystals to local Masai cattlemen in the region of the Merelani Hills near Mount Kilimanjaro, Tanzania. This dazzling crystal soon gained popularity. In faceted form it is stunning, celebrated as the gemstone of the 20th century and first promoted by the New York jewellers, Tiffany & Co. It is interesting that it was not discovered until late last century as the busyness of everyday life started to take its toll on our wellbeing. Tanzanite is the crystal of today's magician, enabling you to master balance in your life and direct your will towards your own spiritual path rather than being influenced by others or trying to conform to the norm. It creates a space to allow alternative aspects of your personality to come to the surface, helping practical people become creative and inventive while free spirited individuals may find new ways to channel their efforts. Those that are quite serious, may discover their playful streak. Tanzanite strengthens your intuition and helps you make choices that will keep you safe and benefit the greater good.

Animal: Cat
Plants: Amyris and Sandalwood
Astrological Correspondences: Moon, Uranus and Neptune
Power Day: Monday
Cleanse with: Full Moon or Lightning Storm

Your Crystal Alignment Meditation

Sit out under the full moon with your Tanzanite, bathing in her lunar beams. Visualise a cape around you, shimmering in the most beautiful silver colour. Silver is a colour that enhances connection with your higher self. In Islam, Silver is synonymous with being soft spoken, eloquent and fluent. Allow your greater self to awaken, the aspect of yourself that is in complete alignment with your soul's purpose and able to execute it with precision in the physical world. Tune into that energy, share it with your Tanzanite and draw it into your being. Share this feeling with your Tanzanite and following your meditation, continue to carry your crystal to bring this way of being into your everyday life.

Clarity

Tanzanite is a part of the Zoisite family, a group of crystals found in a variety of colours including pink, brown, green, yellow, clear and grey. All Zoisites bring a playful energy into your life. Orange-pink Zoisite, better known as Thulite, encourages you to engage your flirtatious self while the readily available Green Zoisite fosters a playful heart. When it comes to indigo-violet Tanzanite, it encourages you to not take your life too seriously. It helps you see things for what they truly are, bringing greater clarity and to see the truth in situations. Tanzanite helps you see the "bigger picture" and keeps you on track with your life purpose, preventing you getting caught up in the trivialities and mundane demands that can fight for your attention and energy.

For this reason, Tanzanite's initial effect slows you down and forces you to relax. This has aptly earned it the nickname of the "workaholic's crystal". It should be worn or kept at the desk if you tend to put in too many working hours each week, neglecting your health or loved ones. As Tanzanite decelerates your pace, it restores harmony and balance to all areas of your life, preventing you from focusing on one aspect at the detriment of others. Tanzanite is pleotropic, meaning the indigo, grey, blue and violet tones within the crystal vary depending on the angle the stone is viewed from. This translates metaphysically to Tanzanite aiding you to comprehend a situation from different angles or understand others' points of view.

Take time each night to sit holding your Tanzanite and it will encourage you to take a holistic view of your life. Diffuse or inhale amyris essential oil, as its relaxing scent helps to focus and centre the mind on what importantly nourishes your soul to bring you inner peace and a compassionate approach to life. As the scent of the essential oil enhances your Tanzanite's vibration you'll be able to look at where your life is out of balance and how each aspect can all be harmoniously united to contribute to your life mission. If you are looking to learn what truly makes your heart sing, combine Tanzanite with Moldavite. Call upon your Cat guide or the feline goddess Bast to remind you of the importance of home, family and pleasure.

As you start to experience more clarity in your life thanks to Tanzanite, you'll remain focused on the task at hand if you have many jobs to complete or keep getting distracted. This crystal is great for you if you feel there is never enough time to get everything done.

Tanzanite's ability to induce clarity also translates to the physical body. It supports detoxification, especially after medical procedures that drain the body such as radiotherapy or chemotherapy. Wear Tanzanite against the skin for lengthy periods to support the immune system to perform at optimum levels. If medications or treatments are generating unwanted side-effects, work with Tanzanite to reduce their impact on your daily life and improve your sense of wellbeing. Tanzanite can support the healing of stress related problems such as nervous tension, excess sweating, migraine headaches, and in conjunction with counselling, psychological disorders and substance abuse.

In love, Tanzanite can guide you to understand the feelings of others. If a new potential love has caught your eye, keep Tanzanite nearby to help you effectively interpret signs and know how to put your best foot forward. If you are in a committed relationship, Tanzanite will help you to gain deeper understanding of your partner and their needs, creating an opportunity for a deeper connection.

As a workplace crystal, Tanzanite is calming and soothing. Even a tiny piece is beneficial for overcoming communication difficulties. It is also practical in providing a solution to problems when there seems to be none. It is an especially good crystal for those in fields such as counselling or any role requiring the intellectual interpretation of emotional experiences as Tanzanite aids in sharing spiritual information and knowledge from a heart-centred perspective, an attribute which is intensified when used with Moldavite. It is a good crystal for career change or finding new sources of support or income. Tanzanite can help with learning other languages by improving your ability to think and understand what is being communicated.

Awakening

This is an ideal crystal for those who have spent much of their life "asleep", simply following the path society has dictated to them. Something in their life may have triggered a re-evaluation of direction and priorities. At this point a crystal such as Amethyst is ideal to start pondering new avenues and then Tanzanite will ensure they continue this exploration rather than going "back to sleep".

Because of its unique indigo-violet colour, Tanzanite works to balance two chakras, the third eye and crown. These two chakras tend to be underactive in the section of our community who blindly follow authority with an inability to think for themselves, fail to consider the spiritual aspects of life and mock others who have spiritual endeavours, and fail to consider the greater meaning to their life. If you are beginning your spiritual journey focusing on these two chakras can be beneficial. Take time each day to lie down and rest with your Tanzanite near your head. Visualise an indigo orb of light at your forehead and a violet sphere at your crown. Feel your mind clearing and allow the veil of mystery to lift and reveal all the knowledge you seek. Let deep-seated doubts and disbeliefs that weaken your intuition be released. Give yourself permission to think for yourself and release reliance on authority figures. Continue to keep your Tanzanite with you every day until these energy centres feel more balanced. You can also use a pendulum to monitor how balanced these chakras are. Other beneficial activates for these two chakras are include adding more purple into your life through foods, clothes and decorations as well as practicing yoga positions such as Eagle, Dolphin, Warrior III, Thunderbolt, Lotus, Tree and Child's pose. Increasing your water intake will help these chakras and open your reception to spiritual messages.

Another effective meditation to start with when using Tanzanite is candle gazing. Sit outside at night or in a low-lit room and place a candle in front of you. The flame should be at the level of the eyes so that it can be seen straight without being uncomfortable. Take some deep breaths and allow your awareness to come to the flame of the candle. Keep gazing at it. If thoughts arise, do not fight them just simply let them be. Gradually they will disappear, or add Purple Fluorite to your meditation if it's an ongoing challenge. Your eyes may water from time to time, blink and even close. When they close, concentrate on the after image, and hold it for as long as possible. Open your eyes and follow the process again. Continue as long as you can and gradually increase the time. This helps to improve the function of the eyes, increases awareness, focus and concentration. It activates the third eye and crown chakras, develops psychic abilities and stimulates the pineal gland.

Working with your Tanzanite need not be complex. A beautiful way to enjoy your Tanzanite is to lay somewhere comfortable with your crystal, put on beautiful music, close your eyes and allow the crystal to take you on a journey. If you're out and about, especially in nature, you can sit quietly with your Tanzanite and a journal and just jot down the pondering that comes to mind. Writing out your thoughts can help to bring clarification on where your mindset is currently at.

As Tanzanite starts to strip away distractions and restrictions from your life and allows you to include spiritual pursuits into your lifestyle, you'll experience renewed levels of vitality. Those working with Tanzanite have experienced a renewal of their skin and hair as well as a sparkle in their eyes. This is the awakening of your spirit. You may even find working with your Tanzanite starts to slow down the ageing process.

Tanzanite is a good crystal to be worn as jewellery to keep its spiritual properties constantly in your energy field. Wearing it in a manner where others can see it is beneficial as this promotes the awakening of those you interact with too. You may find when wearing your Tanzanite interactions change, with conversations shifting from small talk to discussions of higher ideals. Your Tanzanite will help you to remain present and loving in these conversations too.

Although one of the most powerful crystals available for spiritual awareness, novices need not be worried. Tanzanite has a protective quality and will remove unhelpful energies during spiritual workings. As your spiritual skills develop Tanzanite will prevent psychic impressions from becoming overwhelming. If you start to feel spacey and light-headed, hold a Black Tourmaline, Hematite, Red Jasper, Shungite or Smokey Quartz for a while. It may be best to avoid working with your Tanzanite for the last couple of hours before you go to bed, as you may find yourself kept awake by new thoughts flooding your mind.

Spiritual Exploration

Once you have learned to slow down and balance yourself, Tanzanite becomes a premier stone for spiritual exploration. It allows you to release any unwanted or unhelpful aspects of your life that are holding you back, especially when used with Azurite, as well as aid you to heal karmic-related problems. Once ready to move forward, use Tanzanite in your meditations with creative visualisation to begin manifesting changes and improvements you wish to make. If doing group meditations, have each participant hold a Tanzanite while you all visualise a common goal.

Tanzanite opens you up to infinite realms of spiritual exploration. It awakens awareness of dimensions beyond the construct of your third dimensional reality and the nonmaterial and transcendent aspects of your existence. This can bring on deep existential reflection, an enhancement of meaning, recognition of a transcendent self, and mastery of spiritual states. This is amplified if you combine Tanzanite with White Selenite or Golden Selenite. Tanzanite with Petrified Wood, Shungite, Isua Stone or Nuummite can help you access the knowledge of Akashic Records.

Place Tanzanite near your forehead (by holding it or using a headband) to strengthen your psychic and intuitive abilities during meditation or consider drinking a Tanzanite elixir each day. Meditate outside with Tanzanite to connect psychically with the ancient wisdom of the land upon which you are meditating. It also helps you understand the knowledge of local Indigenous cultures. For this reason, Tanzanite facilitates clear communication with Indigenous and tribal people still living on the land. Use Tanzanite in grids to protect their knowledge and future. If you are performing healing on animals, pass the crystal over their body to heal and energise their aura.

Tanzanite can help you find your true purpose on this planet and connect you with guides, both on Earth and the spirit realms to support you. It has a resonance with angelic energies and when combined with Angelite, can open up your ability to hear the whisperings of the angels. Tanzanite, used with Rhodochrosite or Hackmanite, can help you connect with deceased love ones the following 28 days after their death. Connecting with the spiritual realms can be enhanced by burning sandalwood incense or diffusing the essential oil while working with your Tanzanite. Once you start using Tanzanite, prepare for your spiritual growth to move to a new level. Enjoy it, live with it and move forward with it. If you desire to experience major transformation in your life, you have to begin at some point. Using Tanzanite may be where it all begins.

THULITE

Showmanship / Seduction / Fidelity

One of the greatest expressions of love is sex and if that's what you're seeking, Thulite is the crystal for you! Thulite is a crystal with only one thing on its mind and that is attracting love, so hold on to it tightly with an embrace of passionate devotion. Think of the lover Romeo and you capture the essence of Thulite perfectly. Once love has arrived, Thulite works to preserve and maintain the relationship, allowing naught to stop a lovers' union.

Animal: Robin
Plant: Apricot
Astrological Correspondence: The asteroid Cupido
Power Day: Tuesday
Cleanse with: Hot breeze or incense smoke

Your Crystal Alignment Meditation

Go to a peaceful place in nature. If you have a lover, take them with you. Sit facing your lover, or if you are alone visualise them before you. Close your eyes, ensure your spine is straight and place your hands on your heart. Both tune in to the beating of your own heart for a few minutes, allowing all other noises to slip away. Then reach out and place a hand on your lover's chest, with them doing the same to you. Now tune in to the energy of your two hearts beating together. Feel the flow of energy between you. When you are ready, connect with your Thulite.

Showmanship

If you were born to be on stage, Thulite will help you shine once you're in the spotlight. Thulite is a crystal that allows you to connect with your own creativity and express it in a way that captivates others. Wear Thulite on the centre of your body to promote eloquence, articulation and flair. Thulite resonates well with all performers, especially jugglers and buskers who should place a Thulite in their hat on the ground to draw money. Children who are nervous about appearing on stage or giving an oral exam should keep a Thulite in their pocket and hold it when they feel anxious.

The fiery nature of Thulite gives its guardian added stamina. Marathon runners or artists performing long pieces should keep a crystal on them to ensure they don't wane. Thulite also reduces aimlessness and increases focus on your life purpose. Charge a Thulite to ensure devotion to a long-term goal such as saving for a house, creating a global charity or enterprise or obtaining worldwide fame and recognition.

Seduction

Thulite turns the shyest individual into a Don Juan or femme fatale. It gives you the ability to attract, flirt and woo the object of your eye. Keep a Thulite in your wardrobe to help the perfect outfit stand out. When out on a date, wear Thulite near your throat to invoke flirtatious banter and allow you to read signals from your companion. Combine it with Thulite's harmonising plant by eating an apricot, to ensure you speak smoothly and sweetly. Then carry its pit in your pocket to draw your lover closer.

If you struggle to attract new lovers, create a 'Ring of Eros' meal. Invite four friends for dinner and have them each bring a friend you don't know. Subtly include romantic themes around your home such as red candles and seductive music while placing a ring of Thulite around the dining area. Serve aphrodisiac foods such as seafood, strawberries, chilli, avocado, banana, fruit, chocolate and red wine. This dinner will extend your circle of friends and set the tone for love. Do not despair if you don't meet someone that night. One of these four people could be the link to your next lover.

To attract a sexually compatible partner place a Thulite against your skin, near the pubic area and visualise a scarlet beam of light drawing a suitable lover to you. You may want to share your intentions with the god Eros who awakens love and desire. But in your efforts to bring love into your life you must never do anything to jeopardise another's free will. A lover must be drawn to you on their terms and if manipulated, the relationship is doomed. Keep this crystal in your pocket to help you express your sexuality.

In the bedroom, create a passionate massage oil by placing a tumbled Thulite in massage oil allowing it to infuse the oil with its seductive energy. Thulite teaches you that lust, sexuality and sensuality are a normal part of life. If you or your partner is shy in the bedroom, meditate with Thulite while naked, summoning your inner goddess or god to awaken your sexy side. Exploring the sign position of the asteroid Eros in your birth chart can also unveil some of your erotic turn-ons, as well as the level of your erotic nature. If you struggle to ask for what you want from a partner, especially in the bedroom, ask Robin to help you vocalise. Combine a Robin feather (must be found on the ground) or the image of the bird with a Thulite crystal on the bedside table to incite lovemaking that pleases you both.

Fidelity

Thulite is a guardian of love. Wear it to maintain your passion and loyalty to your partner. Place a piece with a red candle and a happy photo of you both in the centre of the home to help maintain the romance. When worn, Thulite also protects you and your partner from rival suitors.

TIGER'S EYE

Protection / Upliftment / Success / Tiger Conservation

Tiger's Eye, like all crystals that have a "sheen", is protective and wards off danger. The advantage it has over black crystals, which protect by absorbing and removing negativity, is that Tiger's Eye will send unhelpful energies back to their source or sender, emanating the threefold karmic law. Furthermore, this crystal lifts your vibration, giving you energy and confidence, and enhancing your opportunities in life. Tiger's Eye will help you rise above and leave negative situations behind you. It is great for all addictions as it both diverts unbeneficial energies from around you and empowers you to overcome destructive tendencies or behaviours. Tiger's Eye most commonly refers to the golden-yellow variety of this crystal. However it is also found in blue, better known as Falcon's Eye or red, known as Ox's Eye.

Animal: Tiger
Plants: Cumin and Ginseng
Astrological Correspondences: Sun
Power Day: Sunday
Cleanse with: Sun; place it on desert sand to give it an extra resilient boost.

Your Crystal Alignment Meditation

Sit in the sun and feel its warmth on your skin. Move your attention around your body and feel the sun's effects on your different parts. Close your eyes and see the golden glow through your eyelids. Contemplate how the sun makes you feel. Can you feel the sun reinvigorating you, urging you to grow, expand and explore life? Do you feel more buoyant and optimistic? Once you've finished connecting with the sun, hold your crystal in your receptive hand or against your solar plexus chakra and sense its energy.

Protection

Tiger's Eye has long been used for protection. Roman soldiers wore Tiger's Eye engraved with protective symbols, and during the Middle Ages it was used as a protective amulet against spells, demons and the evil eye. By wearing or carrying Tiger's Eye it can offer you the same protection as your ancestors. Tiger's Eye surrounds you in a golden light that creates an encasement of protection. Like a mirror, this golden light will simply rebound anything that is harmful or unwanted back to where it came from. All wanted energies that serve your highest good will still easily pass through this golden light of protection. Whenever possible in meditation take a few minutes to connect with this golden light. Sense it and make it strong. Then fuse your Tiger's Eye crystal with this protective energy. You may also want to summon the strength of your Tiger guide for added protection.

For personal protection, wear the crystal over your chest each day. If you are unsure about trusting someone, carry a Tiger's Eye with you all day. Tradition states that by sunset any deception or ill-intent will be revealed or dissolved. To protect your home or work space, charge four crystals and then place one at each direction at the perimeter of the building or space. Add a mixture of cumin seeds, sea salt and frankincense resin to amplify the crystals' protective potency. You can also place Tiger's Eye around your space to prevent "prying eyes" or near surveillance cameras to reduce intrusive or unwarranted monitoring of your actions from others.

Due to its ability divert energies, if you are experiencing problems with the flow of energy in your body, wearing Tiger's Eye excessively may bring on numbness in your limbs. If this happens, limit your exposure to the crystal to seven days at a time, having at least a week's rest in between.

Upliftment

The more you are empowered the less likely you are to need protection. If you give your attention to positivity you're less likely to be bothered by hindrances. How can you shift your attention to focus on higher ideals and more positive pursuits? What can you do to walk away from negative situations and towards helping yourself and others? Contemplate this during meditation asking Tiger's Eye to lift you above negativity. During the day, pay attention to your thoughts and words, stopping yourself whenever you are negative. Wear Tiger's Eye near your throat to enhance positive talk. Burning ginseng incense or taking ginseng flower essence can enhance your positivity further.

As you continue to work with Tiger's Eye, your view of life can lift. It is great during challenging times to reignite your belief in the goodness of others and the world. Some people experience a heightened sense of smell or colours appear more vivid, when working with Tiger's Eye. These are signs that their vibration is lifting.

Tiger's Eye prepares and supports you to take wise action. It allows you to make grounded and calculated decisions and then act on them with certainty. It stimulates the solar plexus chakra, allowing you to be more confident, courageous and friendly in your interactions with others. You can also use this with any pets who try to dominate others in the household. Gridding it around the home should start to dissolve these power struggles. Since the solar plexus chakra regulates the digestive system, Tiger's Eye's stimulating effect can also be energetically beneficial for digestive problems, especially with ulcers and the gallbladder.

As you feel more balanced and confident in life, you'll notice an improvement in your spiritual abilities. Use your Tiger's Eye to support your work in channelling information from past worlds. A great technique to induce this is scrying, gazing at the sun's or candlelight's reflection in the crystal to still the conscious mind and allow other information to come through.

Success

As the unwanted falls to the wayside and your attention focuses on the favourable side of life, Tiger's Eye, with its golden energy of growth, luck and fortune will help bring success into your life. It's great to meditate with before an important meting or presentation to get you prepared and focused. For an added boost, listen to the song "Eye of the Tiger" by Survivor. It is great for generating confidence and promoting success for young people, especially when their youth or lack of experience may be perceived as a disadvantage. Young men can definitely benefit from this crystal's solar influence as it helps them connect with the Divine Masculine within them. It will help them to shine without becoming overbearing or arrogant.

You can program Tiger's Eye to attract wealth into your life. Hold the crystal and visualise your wish, then leave it by a green candle to add fire's spark and transformational qualities to your desire. Once charged carry it with you where you place your purse or wallet i.e. in your pocket or handbag. Cumin essential oil can be used to contemplate the laws of manifestation (especially with regards to money) and to meditate on the balance of give and take and so can be inhaled while visualising your wish.

Tiger's Eye can also be used to attract someone you are sexually compatible with. Visualise or write down exactly what you are looking for then hold that vision in your mind as you hold two Tiger's Eyes, Black Onyxes and either two Red Garnets or Rubies. Then take two red candles, placing one on either side of your bed. As you light them recite something such as, "Twin flames bring me the passion I desire, I summon my equal to share my sexual fire". Carry one set of the crystals with you each day, leaving the other set in your bedroom. This trio of crystals in the bedroom also helps to promote mutually enjoyable love making. Using cumin essential oil during this rite will help to attract a long term, loyal partner.

Tiger Conservation

Tiger's Eye has a strong connection to Tiger allowing you to make an energetic link to him. Just as Tiger can help you as you observe his lessons and his wisdom, his species needs your help for its survival upon this planet. During meditation, visualise a place in the world where tigers live and see them surrounded in a golden healing light, keeping them protected and healthy. After your meditation, place the crystal with a golden candle and an image of a tiger. You may like to create a full power grid adding other crystals such as Unakite for successful breeding, Green Jade for promoting human compassion for animals and Moss Agate for protecting tiger habitats. This technique can also be applied to any of the big cats in the wild or in zoos or conservation parks. Combine this with taking any other steps you can to help the plight of tigers by staying informed with conservation efforts and supporting wildlife organisations.

TOPAZ, IMPERIAL

Glow / Clairsentience / Soul Path

Imperial Topaz is a sought after crystal worth adding to your collection. Most natural Topaz is clear or blue and harmonises with the moon's lunar vibration, but the rarer red, yellow, violet, brown or imperial orange hold the empowering energy of the sun. In fact, an Egyptian myth states that it was the sun god Ra who gave Imperial Topaz its colour. This makes Imperial Topaz a crystal of action. It removes distractions from your life and enables you to focus on what is important to you. Working with Imperial Topaz leaves you feeling balanced and leads you towards a life full of happy adventures, pleasurable success and a sense of connectedness to all around you.

Animal: Golden Lion Tamarin
Plant: Marigold
Astrological Correspondence: Sun
Power Day: Sunday
Cleanse with: Sun

Your Crystal Alignment Meditation

Go and sit out in the sunlight. Connect to the Sun and draw from its energy. Visualise its golden light reaching out to you, burning away all unwanted and unhelpful energies. Breathe the golden light into your body. Let it soften any tightness and dissolve any disruptive thoughts. Let it release all tension and tightness in your muscles. Allow the golden light soak through every cell of your body, rejuvenating it and allowing it to fulfil its function completely. Once you feel strengthened and radiant, connect with your Topaz.

Glow

Working with Imperial Topaz allows your inner light to shine, making you more radiant and alluring. Wearing your crystal against the skin can increase your metabolism. Imperial Topaz is great to wear when you are starting a new exercise regime aimed at moving to a healthier weight. Take your crystal off at night if you need to allow your body to slow down or repair itself. Try combining the radiant energy of Imperial Topaz with marigolds (calendula). Look for skincare with calendula to give your skin a natural glow. Overall, by working with Imperial Topaz you will increase the flow of life force around your body, ensuring that you have a youthful glow that has everyone noticing. As you increase your personal energy, you can then direct this into manifesting your dreams. Start by leaving your crystal in the afternoon sun to cleanse. That night as the sun sets, sit with your crystal in your projective hand and visualise your desire, using all of your senses to raise energy until your visualisation feels real. Then project this image into the crystal. Leave the crystal by some marigolds, which will add their radiance to your wish. Collect your Topaz as the sun rises the next morning and start carrying the crystal everywhere with you while looking for opportunities to move towards your desired outcome. You can also place marigolds with Imperial Topaz around your space to create a more radiant atmosphere and encouraging yourself and others to open up to the world and engage in meaningful interactions with others.

Clairsentience

You have probably heard of clairvoyance and maybe even clairaudience but have you heard of clairsentience? Rather than seeing or hearing divine communication or messages, with clairsentience you get a "gut feeling". Keep Imperial Topaz near your belly or when you start to sense something, place it against your skin. If you are developing your skill of clairsentience you may find you feel over-emotional around certain people or in certain places, especially around crowds. Wearing Imperial Topaz over the centre of your body in these instances will help you regain your balance.

You will want to protect your belly as you fine tune your clairsentient ability so pay attention to the colour of your Imperial Topaz. It is believed to change colour when in the presence of poisoned food or drink. If you do fall sick from food poisoning, massage your belly in a clockwise direction with your Imperial Topaz to bring relief.

Soul Path

Constant work with Imperial Topaz can allow you to unveil your soul path or what lessons your true self needs to learn in this lifetime. Imperial Topaz is connected to Rahu, a shadow planet in Vedic astrology named after a Hindu deity. It is not actually an astrological body, but rather a calculated point, also known as the north node. It is considered a vital point on your astrological birth chart as it indicates the lessons your true self desires to learn and experience in this life. Once you are aware of your north node, work with Imperial Topaz to help attract what you need, in a safe manner, to learn these lessons. Imperial Topaz works with you to bring only like-minded and helpful people into your life, keeping time-wasters away. Keep a piece by your front door to start drawing welcome visitors or carry with you when socialising or networking.

Working with the teachings of the Golden Lion Tamarin will enhance your connection with Imperial Topaz. Golden Lion Tamarin lives in small family groups and can guide you on how to work cooperatively and harmoniously with others you are close to. As Golden Lion Tamarin lives in small family groups, depending on them for his wellbeing, he can guide you on how to work cooperatively and harmoniously with others you are close to so that everyone benefits.

TOURMALINE, BLACK

Transformation / Balance / Mindfulness / Base Chakra
Animal Connection

Black Tourmaline, also called Schorl, acts as your personal guardian along your life path. Its protective nature removes distractions and dangers that could lead you astray. It allows you to find inner balance and discipline to keep you focused on what it truly important to you. It improves your perception allowing you to see spiritual messages that are guiding you to fulfil your spiritual role for this lifetime. As you align with Black Tourmaline, your troubles will fall by the wayside as the beauty and perfection of life presents itself before you.

Animal: Chimpanzee
Plant: Ravensara
Astrological Correspondence: Saturn
Power Day: Saturday
Cleanse with: Earth

Your Crystal Alignment Meditation

Go to a jungle or visualise yourself there in your mind. Centre yourself, taking deep breaths to inhale the scents around you. Connect with the large amount of life around you, even if you cannot see it all, feel it around you. Notice the sun shining above you and feel the sunlight upon your body. The great power of the sun will bless you with creativity and energy to help bring your intention into manifestation. Draw its power into your being now and then connect with your Tourmaline.

Transformation

Black Tourmaline takes that which no longer serves you and changes it into that which allows you to progress. It helps you find the Silver lining of every cloud and focus on the opportunity rather than the challenge. It turns the weary pessimist into the empowered optimist. Wear Tourmaline each day when you are ready to make change in your life. Keep it nearby when you write New Year's resolutions or doing any form of goal setting. Once you have clearly written down your aims, hold the Tourmaline and visualise yourself achieving the goals. As you put the Tourmaline on each morning, recite, "I know the changes I am to make, show me the steps that I should take". The Tourmaline will increase your ability to seize positive opportunities towards your goals and remember why you first set them.

Do you ever arrive home feeling stressed, agitated or tired from a chaotic day? Create a magical doorway of cleansing by placing nine pieces of Black Tourmaline around your front door. As you arrive home slowly walk through the door and become aware of all the stresses and upsets of the day being absorbed and transformed, leaving you balanced and relaxed. Placing Black Tourmaline near electronic devices such as microwaves and modems will reduce the negative impacts of electro-magnetic radiation or WiFi. Be sure to cleanse these crystals often.

All Tourmaline encourages the flow of energy and Black Tourmaline is especially suited for counteracting stubbornness. Include it in power grids if you are finding a desire taking longer than expected or you are met with unexpected obstacles. If you tend to be stubborn, carry Black Tourmaline as a reminder to become more flexible and open-minded. Stubbornness can manifest as ringing in the ears (tinnitus) from an unwillingness to hear what others are saying. Black Tourmaline earrings can help relieve this.

Balance

Black Tourmaline balances energies between two parties. It is great to place in negotiation rooms where there are power struggles or in play areas to stop bickering siblings. Place it near a family photo with a white, pink or purple candle to encourage the fair settlement of family feuds to do with inheritance or distribution of assets.

Black Tourmaline stimulates a proper balance between the left and right sides of the brain. It helps logical people be more creative and artistic people behave more rationally. It also works to counteract dyslexia. For this use, keep Black Tourmaline close to the head, ideally with the striations of the crystal running horizontal.

Mindfulness

Black Tourmaline guides you to be present, often referred to as mindfulness in Buddhism. Staying present allows you to remain totally aware of what is happening before you without letting the sorrow of the past or anxiety of the future affect you. Apply it to every practice. As you wash the dishes feel the warmth of the water, hear the clink of the cutlery and crockery, smell the scent of the detergent and watch your hands move the cloth. Apply the same principles to when you walk, shower, drive or interact with others. Wearing Black Tourmaline or having it near you supports this practice and day by day it'll become easier. Soon you'll start to notice the benefits as you become more aware of your own body and feelings as well as gaining a clearer perspective of the people you're interacting with and what is happening around you. Keep a piece of Black Tourmaline at your desk if you tend to get easily distracted. It will help you concentrate and bring inspirational new ideas. Combine Black Tourmaline and ravensara during creative visualisation or manifestation meditations and spells, as ravensara further strengthens focus. Furthermore as it helps you be more sensitive to those you work with, it will help you avoid accidentally upsetting or offending work colleagues.

As you become more disciplined and present in your everyday life, this can lead to new spiritual discoveries and paradigm shifts. This is the perfect time to invite the direction of your Chimpanzee guide into your life. He can teach you to use the tools and gifts around you, whether physical or non-physical, to evolve and improve your life. Chimpanzee when used in harmony with Black Tourmaline awakens both your intuition and intelligence to solve challenges and allow you to prosper.

Base Chakra

Black Tourmaline can be used to quell an overactive base chakra. Constant aggressiveness and reckless, overly impulsive or belligerent behaviour are signs that your base chakra needs to be soothed. If the base chakra remains unbalanced, it can start to manifest in the body. Bladder issues may arise when you're constantly feeling "pissed off". Taking time to rest and placing Black Tourmaline by the base chakra will help to remove these unsociable behaviours. Carry your crystal in your pocket daily for constant centring. You may find cutting down on food such as red meat, animal fats, caffeine, peppers and hot spices as well as spinach (because of its Iron content) will aid the effects of the Tourmaline. So will diffusing, inhaling or anointing with ravensara essential oil.

Animal Connection

One key use for Black Tourmaline that should not be overlooked is to facilitate connecting and communicating with animals. It enables you to shift your vibration to resonate with theirs. Wearing Black Tourmaline around your neck will allow you to receive messages from them and understand what they are trying to say. Don't expect animals to start opening their mouth and talking to you. Often these messages come telepathically, where you will hear or feel a message coming to you from an animal. Sometimes their message can be delivered in your dreams. You may also find it easier to interpret their sounds and body language. If you are working with a hyperactive animal, Black Tourmaline can also help them to calm down. Place a piece on their collar or in their sleeping area will help them settle.

TOURMALINE, BLUE

Commitment / Language / Nervous System

Blue Tourmaline, or Indicolite, is a beautiful crystal coveted by collectors and crystal guardians. It has a strong yet peaceful energy that encourages an open-minded attitude and the ability to treat others who are different or show weakness with tolerance and compassion. It will also give you courage to speak passionately from the heart about what inspires you. Through developing a relationship with your Blue Tourmaline, you can become a persuasive speaker, able to seduce anyone with your words.

Animal: Gorilla
Plant: Vanilla
Astrological Correspondences: Mercury and Sedna
Power Day: Wednesday
Cleanse by: Often in spring and autumn, the transitional months between extreme heat and cold, dry and wet, there will be days when a little rain falls while the sun still shines. Naturally, this often produces a rainbow. The vacillating energy of these days harmonises with Tourmaline so whenever you see a rainbow place your Tourmaline outside to cleanse. If you need to cleanse prior to seeing a rainbow, cleanse Blue Tourmaline with the element of water.

Your Crystal Alignment Meditation

Go to where you can see a rainbow stretching above you or sit outside and visualise one arcing above you. Start focusing on the red part of the rainbow. Draw it inside you with each inhalation. Then exhale the colour red. Your whole body becomes the colour red. Feel yourself resonating with the colour and sending it around world. Repeat this with orange, yellow, green, blue, indigo and violet. Then allow the colours to combine to the most vibrant white light you can conceptualise. Allow this white light to cleanse you and the rest of the world. You are now prepared to connect with your Tourmaline.

Commitment

Blue Tourmaline is a stone of commitment making it a great choice for a wedding or anniversary gift. It can also help you and others escalate your passion and dedication to work or career. Charity workers and volunteers benefit from Blue Tourmaline as it helps them to continue to understand the significant contribution they are making (and receiving). A Blue Tourmaline ring is an ideal sign of commitment, but a raw or tumbled piece worn regularly has the same effect.

Blue Tourmaline helps you discover how you can be of service to others and encourages ethics, tolerance and a love of the truth. It inspires you to dedicate time to the betterment of humanity and planet Earth. Place Blue Tourmaline on your altar as a reminder to always act for the benefit of the greater good. The deep blue or indigo coloured Blue Tourmalines, when placed by the bed or in your pillowslip, helps foster vivid and prophetic dreams and gives you further spiritual guidance for your path.

Language

Blue Tourmaline gives you the ability to change the way you communicate. Use Blue Tourmaline when you can't find the right words to express yourself when you are talking or writing. If there is something you need to say that you have been keeping pent up, hold Blue Tourmaline in your receptive hand and allow it to lend you the strength to communicate what you have to say in a harmless way.

Revolutionists and inspirational speakers may wish to use Blue Tourmaline in harmony with the dwarf planet Sedna that was discovered in 2003 and governs shifting values of humanity. When preparing to talk to a large group, hold your crystal against your mouth and tune in to Sedna's energy flowing to you from the cosmos. Feel the crystal and dwarf planet's energies merge, gifting you with eloquence, elocution and authenticity.

Singers and musicians should keep Blue Tourmaline during rehearsals and performance to help with challenging key changes. Actors working to master a new accent can hold it in their receptive hand during rehearsals and then hide it in their costume when on stage. A daily elixir with Blue Tourmaline will also help.

If you are learning a foreign language, wear Blue Tourmaline around your neck. It will help you translate words quickly and accurately. When studying the language also burn or anoint your pulse points with vanilla essential oil. When you get a chance to practice with a natural speaker, do the same. Vanilla will stimulate learned memories from your studies as well as making your delivery more passionate and authentic.

Nervous System

Blue Tourmaline encourages communication not only between us, but also within us by nurturing a healthy nervous system. When you feel unable to communicate, this can manifest as issues for your nervous system until the point when you feel that you can no longer communicate with the world and have a nervous breakdown. When you feel overwhelmed, take a few moments to hold your Tourmaline against your chest, focus on your breath and remind yourself to simply do one thing at a time. You may like to work with your Gorilla guide who can teach you how to balance strength and gentleness effectively.

TOURMALINE, GREEN

Compassion Renewal / Herbalism / Income Change

Green Tourmaline, also called Verdelite, was often confused with the Emerald until the 18th century. This enchanting green crystal is an earth energy stone. It connects you to the earth and attunes you to the vibration of Mother Gaia. It has a strong healing capacity and is especially helpful for Earth healing and aiding the nature kingdom. As a Tourmaline, it promotes healthy growth and change on all levels. Connected to the heart chakra, Green Tourmaline allows you to realise exactly what makes your heart sing and communicate this to the hearts of others. Don't be surprised if when meditating with Green Tourmaline, your mind leaps back in time, reminding you of lost goals or ideas that got buried under the rubble of responsibilities. Green Tourmaline will show you how to resurrect these plans and bring them to fruition.

Animal: Orangutan
Plant: Geranium
Astrological Correspondences: Earth and Venus
Power Day: Friday
Cleanse by: Often in spring and autumn, the transitional months between extreme heat and cold, dry and wet, there will be days when a little rain falls while the sun still shines. Naturally, this often produces a rainbow. The vacillating energy of these days harmonises with Tourmaline so whenever you see a rainbow place your Tourmaline outside to cleanse. If you need to cleanse prior to seeing a rainbow, cleanse Green Tourmaline with the element of earth.

Your Crystal Alignment Meditation

Go to where you can see a rainbow stretching above you or sit outside and visualise one arcing above you. Start focusing on the red part of the rainbow. Draw it inside you with each inhalation. Then exhale as you give out the colour red. Your whole body becomes the colour red. Feel yourself resonating with the colour and sending it around world. Repeat this with orange, yellow, green, blue, indigo and violet. Then allow the colours to combine to the most vibrant white light you can conceptualise. Allow this white light to cleanse you and the rest of the world. Once you feel balanced, connect with your Green Tourmaline.

Renewal

Green Tourmaline has a tender and gentle energy that encourages you to nurture both yourself and those around you. It works well on the heart chakra and is great for those who feel they are exhausted and tired from their love life. Wear Green Tourmaline over your heart and it will renew your faith that love exists for you in the world. It allows you to rejoice in the experiences you've had in the past along with their accompanying lessons. Diffusing, inhaling or anointing the chest with geranium essential oil furthers assists with issues of the heart. It helps heal a broken heart and restore confidence in the innate goodness of others when you've lost faith due to tough past events, especially with your parents.

Green Tourmaline is reputed to help your heart make an electro-magnetic connection with the Earth itself, and help to improve the health of the physical heart. It is great for giving athletes increased stamina. Place a piece of Green Tourmaline half in the ground and place your hand on top to experience the healing energy transfer. If you're seeking to bolster your relationship with nature, take Green Tourmaline in one hand, and Orangutan by the other. Step into the forest and never look back for here you will find happiness like never before. Your Orangutan guide teaches you how you can tread more lightly on this Earth. Green Tourmaline and Orangutan can also support you shifting to a more vegetarian or vegan diet.

Herbalism

Green Tourmaline is an excellent aid to those who are studying herbalism. Herbalists should keep it by them as they work to gain a greater understanding of the flow of energy within the plant kingdom. Green Tourmaline's vibration will both heal plants and aid the herbalist to choose the correct herbal remedies required for individual clients. If kept on the body, Green Tourmaline works to increase the effectiveness of herbal remedies.

Income Change

Tourmaline is a crystal that brings you changes in life. When you desire to change jobs or seek a promotion or raise at your current work, place a piece of Green Tourmaline in your purse or wallet. Placing a crystal in a pot plant at a reception desk or cash register will ease customers getting upset by price increases. Green Tourmaline will also nurture your innovation and creativity. Use it to assist with inspiration and luck when turning a passion into a source of income. It is a great amulet if you are wanting to transition from your current job into a new career that you are more passionate about.

TOURMALINE, PINK

Heart Chakra / Romance / Love / Pleasure

Pink Tourmaline ranges from the softest pink, with a gentle, nurturing energy to an intense and vibrant hot pink, which possesses a far more lustful vibration. This crystal has you surrender to love, making you more tolerant and compassionate. Pink Tourmaline works to make all relationships in your life more joyous and fulfilling, facilitating forgiveness and humanitarianism, and removing the grudges and hatred that keep people apart. It encourages you to embrace the pleasures of life, beckoning you to pause and enjoy the flowers in your garden, the meal before you or the hug of a child. This crystal encourages you to take a risk and discover new joys you are yet to unveil. Whether it be a new book, a varied routine or a foreign lover, take an alternate path and see where Pink Tourmaline leads you.

Animal: Bonobo
Plant: Ylang Ylang
Astrological Correspondence: Venus
Power Day: Friday
Cleanse by: Often in spring and autumn, the transitional months between extreme heat and cold, dry and wet, there will be days when a little rain falls while the sun still shines. Naturally, this often produces a rainbow. The vacillating energy of these days harmonises with Tourmaline so whenever you see a rainbow place your Tourmaline outside to cleanse. If you need to cleanse prior to seeing a rainbow, cleanse Pink Tourmaline with the element of water.

Your Crystal Alignment Meditation

Go to where you can see a rainbow stretching above you or sit outside and visualise one arcing above you. Start focusing on the red part of the rainbow. Draw it inside you with each inhalation. Then exhale as you give out the colour red. Your whole body becomes the colour red. Feel yourself resonating with the colour and sending it around world. Repeat this with orange, yellow, green, blue, indigo and violet. Then allow the colours to combine to the most vibrant white light you can conceptualise. Allow this white light to cleanse you and the rest of the world. Once you feel balanced, connect with your Pink Tourmaline.

Heart Chakra

Both Green Tourmaline and Pink Tourmaline can be used to maintain balance in the heart chakra. However Green Tourmaline is best used to do with issues of abundance and value, whereas Pink Tourmaline is more appropriate when the emotions are involved. When you are called to use Pink Tourmaline for this chakra, wear it over the heart as much as possible. Take time each day to visualise a pink sphere of energy in the centre of your heart. Gradually grow the pink ball to encompass all of your body and then send it further out into the world, sharing your love with others. Surrounding yourself in the colour pink, diffusing or wearing ylang ylang essential oil and practicing Camel, Cat, Cow and Cobra yoga positions and drinking green teas especially with rose petals, rosehip and vanilla pods will also help maintain a balanced heart chakra.

Romance

Pink Tourmaline is a crystal to transform your love life. However, it should never be used to try to change a partner and their behaviour as this is against their free will. Rather use Pink Tourmaline to change how you are in romantic relationships. As you change you will notice you bring about change in others. Kindness attracts kindness, honesty promotes honesty and so on.

Work with Pink Tourmaline to change any negative attitudes you have towards love. Create an altar with Pink Tourmaline, candles and a mirror. On the mirror write an affirmation such as, "I allow love to flow into my life". Each day look into the mirror and recite the affirmation several times.

Charge a Pink Tourmaline to attract an exotic new lover or partner from a foreign country. Hold it and recite three times, "Over sea, through the air, from another land bring me a new flame". Then close your eyes and sense them in front of you. Focus more on their energy and what they will like, rather than physical attributes. You want to avoid focusing on a particular person and what they look like, rather how they make you feel when they are around. The universe, in conjunction with your Pink Tourmaline, will work to attract someone who matches this feeling.

Pink Tourmaline attracts passionate love while ensuring you are in a position where it is safe to love. Do not be concerned that it will simply draw you a one-night stand or frivolous liaisons. Pink Tourmaline also brings a spiritual side to these new relationships. If you are ready to attract your life's soul mate, combine Pink Tourmaline with Kunzite in your workings.

Love

Pink Tourmaline reminds you that loving is limitless and that you are free to give love without it ever running out. This crystal showers you in the loving pink light of the universe and encourages you to show loving kindness to everyone who you meet along your life journey. Pink Tourmaline reminds you that until love is given and received freely it is simply an emotion. However when love becomes unconditional, it is the most powerful healing tool in the world, both for yourself and others.

For this reason, Pink Tourmaline can be used for more than just attracting a lover. It also invites loving friends and family to step into your life. It initially works to improve your sense of self-value and worth, which shifts your mentality to one that believes you are worthy and deserving of love. The universe will then respond by delivering loving relationships into your life. Carry Pink Tourmaline for this reason when you are moving to a new place or are somewhere unfamiliar. This crystal can also help children make friends at a new school. This can be supported with ylang ylang flower essence, which helps you feel comfortable in new or unusual places.

Pink Tourmaline ensures that the loving relationship between you and others are balanced and two-way. If you have a tendency to be ruthless, uncaring or cold-hearted at times, Pink Tourmaline will assist you to be more empathetic. Meditate with the crystal when you have to make a tough decision or deliver bad news with compassion. However if you tend to always give your time and energy to others, usually at the expense of your own needs and desires, Pink Tourmaline shows you how to give a bit of tough love.

Pink Tourmaline soothes the heart, reminding you that grudges and hatred poison your own soul more so than punish another. It aids the healing process of those who have been abused, especially children. Hold Pink Tourmaline against your heart while looking at an image or visualising a person with whom you have a grievance and repeat "I am loving and compassionate. I forgive you". This can also been done when you need to forgive yourself. To choose to work with Pink Tourmaline and embrace forgiveness, invites healing into your life. If you are still feeling very angry or emotional about an issue use Pink Tourmaline in conjunction with Lepidolite, sometimes found growing together. Other crystals that work well with Pink Tourmaline for forgiveness are Mangano Calcite, Cobaltocalcite and Zircon.

Furthermore, when you develop an in-depth relationship with Pink Tourmaline, it brings awareness that in the end, you are the creator of your reality and perceptions. It reminds you that humans are "meaning-making machines", constantly deciding what is good and bad, when in truth, events are just unfolding. Depending on what meaning you attach will determine how you approach each situation. For example, it's terrible when a beautiful deer dies, but when it's feeding a starving wolf and her pups, it's also beneficial. It's just the circle of life.

When you choose to attach a good or bad judgement to any situation, you are creating a lopsided perception, you are being narrow minded. An unloving parent is serving you, while one who means the best is detrimental...can you see how? If not, sit with your Pink Tourmaline and contemplate how. As you work with your Pink Tourmaline, you can learn to see the two sides of any scenario in complete balance, you'll understand that everything doesn't happen for just one reason, it happens for many reasons, and all are part of the unity and balance of the universe. This is the unfolding of universal love.

Bonobo has great lessons that resonate powerfully with Pink Tourmaline. This great ape uses its sexuality to sooth tension and increase bonds with all members of its troop. He is the epitome of "make love not war" and encourages you to find peaceful resolutions to conflict. Bonobo teaches the value of taking time to form close bonds with loved ones. He inspires you to embrace your own sexuality. Working with your Bonobo guide in synergy with Pink Tourmaline can allow you to relate to others more intimately.

Beyond, personal relationships, Pink Tourmaline helps you love your life. If undertaking any form of learning, Pink Tourmaline can help maintain your loving interest in the field of study, when the course becomes challenging. It helps you embrace the changes in their body through a lifetime. Both boys and girls should wear Pink Tourmaline against the skin as they approach puberty. Pink Tourmaline will also assist in the balancing of any gynaecological issues as well as supporting conception.

Pleasure

This lovely pink crystal is high in lithium, which is known to stabilise emotional, and mood-related problems. Therefore, if you have been feeling emotionally numb, dejected, stressed or lacking interest in life, wearing Pink Tourmaline over your heart will help bring back your passion for living. It can reduce the risk of heart attacks as a physical manifestation of a lack of joy in life. Hold the crystal as you meditate by a ylang ylang plant can inspire new ways to experience pleasure. Don't like the way the world is today? Meditate with Pink Tourmaline to reconcile these ill feelings and discover the beauty and positive changes people are making. Do not allow the media to deceive you. There are many people, around the world, working to make this world a happier, greener, safer, fairer more harmonious place. Pink Tourmaline will allow you to discover these people.

Pink Tourmaline opens the door for you to enjoy physical pleasure. It has a reputation for strengthening your sense of smell, and thus, can also enhance the perception of pheromones which produces an aphrodisiac effect. Keep it in your pocket to awaken your libido. Placed in the bedroom Pink Tourmaline makes your sex life more satisfying. Fill the space with scent of ylang ylang to harmonise with your crystal, awaken the lover within and stimulate sensitivity to touch. This essential oil and crystal will also work well together to reawaken the playful heart which embraces opportunities to connect deeply with others. Massage therapists and healers can get clients who find it hard to relax to hold a Pink Tourmaline in each hand. Pink Tourmaline can also help the healer, allowing them to heal their own pain, evolving their healing abilities to be more potent and fulfilling.

TOURMALINE, WATERMELON

Sharing / Heart Chakra / Wishes / Balance

Watermelon Tourmaline is a remarkable duo of green encasing a vibrant pink. These are the two colours of love, the heart chakra and giving and receiving. This crystal works to bring balance to all areas of your life, especially with spouses, lovers and friends. With balance, comes stability, which allows you to cooperate with others to achieve great outcomes.

Animal: Fruit Dove
Plant: Watermelon
Astrological Correspondences: Juno and Venus
Power Day: Friday
Cleanse by: Often in spring and autumn, the transitional months between extreme heat and cold, dry and wet, there will be days when a little rain falls while the sun still shines. Naturally, this often produces a rainbow. The vacillating energy of these days harmonises with Tourmaline so whenever you see a rainbow place your Tourmaline outside to cleanse. If you need to cleanse prior to seeing a rainbow, cleanse Watermelon Tourmaline with the element of water.

Your Crystal Alignment Meditation

Go to where you can see a rainbow stretching above you or sit outside and visualise one arcing above you. Start focusing on the red part of the rainbow. Draw it inside you with each inhalation. Then exhale as you give out the colour red. Your whole body becomes the colour red. Feel yourself resonating with the colour and sending it around the world. Repeat this with orange, yellow, green, blue, indigo and violet. Then allow the colours to combine to the most vibrant white light you can conceptualise. Allow this white light to cleanse you and the rest of the world. Once you feel balanced, connect with your Tourmaline.

Sharing

As Watermelon Tourmaline encompasses both the coloured energies of love in green and pink, it is a powerful crystal for supporting the strong exchange of loving energy between individuals. Both partners should wear this crystal during all stages of the pregnancy process. It supports a connection between the man and woman when they are trying to conceive, an understanding of each other's needs during pregnancy and birth plus balancing responsibilities with the newborn. It also allows the mother and father to connect with the baby before and after birth. Watermelon flower essence and watermelon juice will offer further support through the whole process as well as increase male virility and female fertility. This will help balance the emotions and attitudes of everyone, filling this exciting time of life with compassion and appreciation.

Tune into the teaching of your Fruit Dove guide, who harmonises with Watermelon Tourmaline. She will teach you how to be gentle and nurturing with those you love. During times of friction between lovers, she will guide you how to make amends and not keep making the same mistake repeatedly. A beautiful photo of a pair of fruit doves in the house acts as a reminder to be considerate and works towards constantly improving your relationship.

Watermelon Tourmaline fosters sharing and cooperation in all aspects of life. Placed in the playground or gamesroom, it encourages children to play together. Keep it nearby to encourage workers or sports players to unite rather than compete against each other. To cultivate a more compassionate vibration within yourself, meditate while holding your Watermelon Tourmaline against your heart. Visualise a small flame in your chest coloured pink on the inside and surrounded with green. This is the divine flame of compassion. Feel that flame transforming any hardened or uncaring thoughts and feelings you hold and as you breathe deeper, then expand the flame to encompass your whole body. Then extend it into the world, transmuting everything it touches into a more compassionate way of being.

When worn over the solar plexus, Watermelon Tourmaline promotes the easing of hardened beliefs. It shows you your beliefs are nothing but opinions you refuse to reconsider. The stronger your beliefs are, the less open you are to questioning yourself, possibly finding more truthful answers and allowing yourself to expand your wisdom. Hold your Watermelon Tourmaline in your hand when listening to others who have ideas that differ from yours to see if you have anything to learn from the interchange. Use this crystal in grids to encourage cooperative efforts between people, governments or nations towards the greater good.

Heart Chakra

The regulation of loving energy flowing into and out of your being is controlled by your heart chakra. Watermelon Tourmaline nurtures this chakra, creating an even ebb and flow of love in your life. When your heart chakra is balanced you feel completely at ease with yourself and others in your life. You form healthy relationships as well as feeling comfortable on your own. You are generous and caring and gratefully accept what comes your way. You disregard judgement, choosing to show compassion and acceptance for all Earth's people and creatures. Wearing your Tourmaline over your heart will help you keep this loving equilibrium. To reinforce this balance, meditate on your heart chakra seeing loving energy flowing from the centre as you exhale, and rolling back in as you inhale.

Wishes

Watermelon Tourmaline brings lightness into your life and allows you find joy in any situation. During times you feel downtrodden, hold your watermelon and jump up and down again, shaking away negative energy. By keeping an upbeat approach to life, you will have the ability to attract desirable experiences into your life. Perform the following ritual over four nights to make a wish come true. Each night hold the crystal and visualise your wish, whispering it to the crystal. Then do the following in order:

Night 1: Place it by a flowering plant and say, "By earth I give my wish its might."
Night 2: Place it by a white candle and say, "By fire I bring my wish to light."
Night 3: Place it by water and say, "By water my wish flows tonight."
Night 4: Place it outside with an incense stick and say, "By air now my wish takes flight."

Balance

Watermelon Tourmaline helps you find balance in many situations. Holding it releases feelings of low self-worth, especially after being rejected or in cases of unrequited love. In relationships, it ensures you treat your partner as an equal when placed in the centre of the house. Place near photos of friends to foster strong friendships, creating equivalent give and take. It allows you to balance work and pleasure and stops you from doing something you regret at a work social function when you carry it with you. After tough times, meditate with Watermelon Tourmaline to see the benefits and humour in your situation.

TUGTUPITE

Heart's Desire / Rapture / Resilience / Miracles

The Inuit people tell the story of Tutu, the reindeer girl. She went to the mountains to give birth to her first child and as she did, her miraculous life-giving blood seeped into the mountain stones and created Tugtupite. Here tucked within its icy bed, Tugtupite, also called reindeer stone or reindeer blood, has patiently waited to be awoken. Once this crystal sees the light of day and is exposed to sunlight, its soft pink hue turns a rich magenta, only to fade again when put back into the cold darkness. Tugtupite is a stone that radiates passion. Legend says that the desiring thirst a new couple have for each other can ignite the stone's colour if their love is true.

Animal: Reindeer
Plant: Hawthorn
Astrological Correspondence: Makemake
Power Day: Monday
Cleanse with: Fire

Your Crystal Alignment Meditation

Go and sit before a lit candle. If the winds are still, sit outside. Connect with the candle's flame and sense that you are breathing the light of the candle in and out with each breath. Feel a sense of warmth and purity throughout your body and mind as you absorb yourself in this meditation. When you feel cleansed, connect with your Tugtupite.

Heart's Desire

Tugtupite awakens the love residing within your heart and radiates it out to the world around you. When working with Tugtupite, you may physically feel a pushing through your chest or a sensation of blissful connectedness. If you have been hurt in the past or lost faith in others, allow Tugtupite to resurrect your hope and melt your hardened heart. Wear Tugtupite over your heart to bring an optimistic attitude back into your life.

As you open your heart to others, Tugtupite rewards you by allowing pleasant experiences to come into your life. Tugtupite will help you win friends, attract lovers and gain admiration. When you have programmed another crystal to attract something in your life, team it with Tugtupite to ensure you manifest something that you'll love. Tugtupite will ensure you always have what you desire. It even ensures a good catch when fishing if worn with hawthorn in a medicine bag, providing you honour nature and only take what you need. If you are unsure about what you want in life, meditate with Tugtupite, asking it to show you your destiny. Put some music on and allow it to take you on a journey of imagination and dreams. When you feel your heart skip a beat, you've found where you need to point your attention.

Rapture

Tugtupite creates enchanting romances. Wear it over your heart to attract a lover who will support you to grow as a person. Increase connectedness in a relationship by gazing into each other's eyes while holding Tugtupite between your hands. It will cause passions to flame and increases sexual exploration. Make a seductive massage oil by leaving your Tugtupite in the oil to infuse it with its energy. Use this oil to anoint the points on your body to awaken chakras. To use Tugtupite to promote long-term commitment and a fertile future, plant a hawthorn tree in a prominent place in your new home and bury a Tugtupite underneath as a guardian of the relationship. If your relationship is facing challenging times, place Tugtupite with a red candle on a sunlit windowsill. It will fill your home with loving energies and bring back feelings that instigated the romance when you first met. It will also give you the strength to face events or issues you have been ignoring or avoiding.

Tugtupite can arouse passion, even if you are not seeking a lover. By opening your heart Tugtupite fully nurtures your own self-love and self-esteem. It releases the belief you need another person to be complete, developing your emotional independence. Tugtupite engenders a deep love for Mother Earth and inspires you to live a life that protects her beauty. Use Tugtupite in a power grid to spread your will for the protection of the planet. Include eight Clear Quartz points and supporting crystals such as Angel Aura for appreciation of beauty, Hiddenite for Earth protection and Shungite for Earth healing.

A word of warning, Tugtupite has the ability to lift you to euphoric and ecstatic states. If you find yourself overwhelmed, try switching to Sugilite for a while.

Resilience

Once Tugtupite has woken your heart's desire and filled you with passion, nothing can stop you. It eradicates fear and self-doubt. When combined with the teachings you receive from your Reindeer guide, it gives endurance over the long haul. Tugtupite allows you to ignore critics and pessimists who do not support your actions purely because it counters their own beliefs. Hold your Tugtupite when watching the news or receiving information portraying the world's progress as failing. It will guard your passion to carry on supporting the betterment of this world.

Tugtupite harmonises with the dwarf planet Makemake, which was discovered in 2005, and started to have an impact on human consciousness immediately from that point. Makemake's influence helps ensure that every living thing receives the bounty of the planet and brings reckoning to anyone, from yourself to large corporations, who are motivated by greed and use manipulative and diversionary antics to interrupt the fair distribution of resources. These behaviours tend to come into the spotlight when the dwarf planet falls into retrograde. However use Tugtupite here to inspire sustainable manifestation behaviours that benefit all of humanity. Makemake has a particular influence over finding solutions for climate change.

Miracles

The world is currently at a turning point and it is hard to predict what is around the corner. If humanity is to raise its awareness and take strong, decisive actions to improve the wellbeing of the natural world and less fortunate people in third world countries, Tugtupite can be a catalyst. When enough people are driven by a passion to contribute to the greater good, and an unfailing determination, positive change will emerge. Use Tugtupite regularly and allow miraculous changes to flood your reality. Each change may simply be a small daily miracle such as bringing a near dead plant back to life, proactive legislation passing in government, or finding the inspiration to write a poem that touches the heart. Nevertheless, each of these will amount to drops within the ocean of change.

TURQUOISE

Health / Wealth / Self Expression

Turquoise has been associated with the gods for thousands of years in many civilisations around the world. Some Native American tribes called it "sky stone" or "stone of heaven" as Turquoise can build a spiritual bridge between worlds and give strong psychic powers to its guardian. Wear or carry Turquoise to bring you closer to the gods and bring you god-like traits such as luck, success, fame, creativity and articulate speech. Turquoise surrounds you in a healing bubble of protection and lets only beneficial and prosperous energies to flow into your existence. It eliminates blockages and encourages the free flow of chi around the body.

Animal: Bluebird
Plant: Lime
Astrological Correspondence: Venus
Power Day: Friday
Cleanse with: Water

Your Crystal Alignment Meditation

Go to a place where you can sit and observe birds. Notice how freely they take off and land, the smaller birds flit from tree to tree while the great birds soar high above. They are not bound by anything. They freely go wherever they choose. Connect with this sense of freedom and draw it into your being. When you feel free, connect with your Turquoise.

Health

Turquoise helps to reduce energy blocks that cause illness and prevent the flow of healing energy around the body. It powerfully treats any ailment related to constriction such as blood clots, blocked blood vessels, knee pain or stiff joints. Turquoise resonates with the thymus and ensures its proper functioning. Wearing Turquoise will help your body return to a state of wellbeing and attract to you what your body needs. Thus, when you are working with Turquoise, pay attention to cravings as this may be a sign of a nutrient you are lacking.

Turquoise stabilises the emotions, uplifting you when you are down or calming you when you are stressed. It is great for settling panic attacks or inducing restful, restorative sleep. Place Turquoise near light blue candles to create a relaxing mood. Alternatively, use it in conjunction with lime juice or lime essential oil for a zesty boost.

Wealth

Money is simply another form of energy flowing from one person to another. Sometime we give too much away, sometimes we bottle it up and sometimes we do not allow money to freely flow to us. Work with Turquoise to increase the free flow of money in and out of your life. Sit quietly with Turquoise and focus on your breath. With each inhalation feel money coming into your life and as you breathe out release any fear of lack or spending money. Start to visualise yourself as wealthy. What does this look like? What do you do to earn income? Is it following a passion? Are there multiple streams of income? See your bank balance. How much is there? How do you spend your money? What does it allow you to do? Maybe you travel. Maybe there is one thing you've always wanted to gift to yourself as a reward for your hard work. See yourself purchasing this gift. Where are you shopping? Where do you live? What does your day look like when you are in control of your money rather than money in charge of you? Visualise this life. Fill in every detail. The more precise you are, the clearer you are in your mind of what you seek, the better. Carry Turquoise in your purse or coin pocket each day thereafter to keep you in tune with this vision. It will also inspire creative ways to earn money. Creating a vision board and placing Turquoise near it will further enhance your prosperity.

If you notice anxiety about lack of money or a tendency to become so wrapped up in earning money, sing out to your Bluebird guide. He teaches you to return to a state of blissful freedom. Bluebird reminds you to take time to enjoy yourself and when he appears, it is often a sign that better times are around the corner.

Turquoise supports the accumulation of money to support the greater good. You may be saving for your education, to help family or friends or to donate to a charity. Turquoise reminds you that every dollar you spend dictates what kind of world you want to live in. By buying from ethical and green companies, you empower this kind of conduct for the future. Wear Turquoise over the heart to keep you conscious of how and where you spend your money.

Place Turquoise near valuables and assets to protect them. A piece on a pet's collar or in a zoo animal's enclosure deters theft or the animal straying. Turquoise offers protection to horse riders when placed by the saddle. Keep five pieces of Turquoise on you or around the home to turn away the evil eye. Combine it with the aroma of lime essential oil as according to Malay folklore evil spirits hate it.

Self Expression

Turquoise aids the free flow of ideas. It balances and combines both the heart and throat chakras, allowing you to speak from a position of love and truthfulness. Turquoise allows you to express yourself fully and appropriately as well as supporting group decision-making or therapy sessions. This crystal allows you to contribute more in conversations and realise your ideas have merit and validity. It is an especially good crystal for campaigners involved in environmental or human rights movements. It will give you the ability to make decisions that truly serve the greater good and affect the most people, animals and environments in a positive way. When preparing yourself for an important speech or conversation, surround yourself with the scent of lime essential oil as it strengthens spiritual warriors in their work to improving the world. Also summon your Bluebird guide, a guardian of the throat chakra, to enable you to share your ideals in a creative and captivating manner.

UNAKITE

Self Esteem / New Relationships / Preservation

The combination of the green epidote and orange orthoclase Feldspar makes Unakite a beautiful stone with unique energy. Unakite's rare combination of green and orange stimulates two chakras. Firstly, it engages your sacral chakra that is the centre of creativity, sensuality and harmonious interaction. The green resonates with the heart chakra, the centre of love and abundance. Hence, Unakite helps us develop new ideas and relationships and give them the love they need to grow.

Animal: Moose
Plant: Yarrow
Astrological Correspondences: Mars and Venus
Power Days: Tuesday and Friday
Cleanse with: Earth

Your Crystal Alignment Meditation

Go to the edge of a cliff where you can sit comfortably and safely. If you cannot go there physically, visualise being there in your mind. What can you see surrounding you? Is it an ever-stretching forest with tall green trees continuing to the horizon? Perhaps you can see the ocean or fields of colourful flowers. Maybe you can also see your town or city, far off in the distance. Observe everything in the world below, all looking extremely small. Consider that within your view are hundreds, if not more, people, animals and plants all playing their role in the world. Contemplate how everyone's role is vital. You may not be the tallest, fastest or most academic, but you do have traits that make you special. Take some time to contemplate these now. Come up with at least three. What makes you special? How are your unique traits of value to the world? Once you have acknowledged your self-worth, you are ready to connect with your Unakite.

Self Esteem

Unakite is great for your self-esteem. It gives you courage to take control of all aspects of your life without feeling you need to tighten your grip over them. Rather, Unakite gives you confidence that things will turn out as they should and you have the tools and skills to deal with any situation as it unfolds. Develop a personalised set of affirmations that promote self-esteem. Each morning repeat them while holding your Unakite. Wear or carry your stone with you to keep this uplifting energy surrounding you for the rest of the day. Your Moose guide will be a powerful teacher, showing you how to be proud of who you are. Align with him while working with Unakite. Keep your Unakite in a pocket to guard against a sexually transmitted infections (STI), which you may be susceptible to from a physical manifestation of not accepting your sexuality.

Work with Unakite to deal with any past issues or habits that still affect your confidence. Light a green candle and sit before it holding your Unakite. As you breathe out, visualise yourself sending the unwanted characteristic into the candle flame. As you inhale, draw in the flame's radiance and see it surround your body. Keep your Unakite with you at least 28 days after this successful ritual to help you remain powerful in situations where you may be more likely to become a victim and slip back into old, unfavourable habits.

New Relationships

As your self-esteem grows you'll feel more comfortable mixing with others. Once you feel good about yourself, use Unakite to attract new friends or a partner. Meditate holding Unakite and visualise your ideal friend or lover while chanting the mantra, "I am loved". Just keep an ear out for the front door as soon opportunities will come knocking!

Preservation

Unakite's ability to improve self-esteem can be applied on a larger scale to aid the planet. As humankind improves their self-esteem, they will listen to their higher self rather than the self-fulfilling ego. People will no longer feel the need to dominate and desecrate the natural environment due to greed and a fear of lack. This is one side of the coin of protecting endangered species.

On the flipside, Unakite offers protection and promotes new life to endangered species. The orange orthoclase Feldspar nurtures manifestation of new life and encourages animals to find suitable mates. The green epidote promotes vitality and abundant growth ensuring successful reproduction. If you are breeding animals or plants in captivity, place Unakite safely nearby where they can benefit from its vibration. For wild animals and plants, bury Unakite around their habitat. You can also create a grid dedicated to the future success of an endangered species. Place a Unakite and image of the species in the centre of the grid and surround it in a ring of rose and Smokey

Quartz. Add supporting crystals such as Azurite for animal protection and Green Aventurine for new plant growth.

Unakite preserves a happy family at home. Mothers-to-be should wear Unakite over their belly to stimulate healthy growth of the baby. Unakite, possessing the energies of both Mars and Venus, creates a happy and harmonious union between long-term lovers or partners. It is an appropriate stone for handfastings or weddings, especially when bound with yarrow, a herb of magic. Another technique to promote a happy, long-lasting relationship, is to fill a small red cloth bag with yarrow and Unakite and keep it in the bedroom or near a happy photo of the two of you. On the anniversary of meeting or marriage throw the yarrow and crystal into running water and replace. Repeat this every year. Unakite is an effective guardian to heritages, cultures or languages that are at risk of becoming

ANIMAL GUIDE

Aardvark – Hematite
Alpaca – Amazonite
Ant – Super Quartz
Antelope – Champagne Aura Quartz
Bat – Azurite
Bear – Nuummite, Snowflake Obsidian
Beaver – Sugilite
Bison – Smokey Quartz
Blue Heron – Royal Aura Quartz
Blue–and–Gold Macaw – Aqua Aura Quartz
Bluebird – Turquoise
Blue Heron – Cobalt Aura Quartz
Boar – Shungite
Bonobo – Pink Tourmaline
Bourke's Parrot – Rhodochrosite
Butterfly – Malachite
Camel – Clear Quartz
Canary – Champagne Aura Quartz
Caracal – Libyan Desert Glass
Cassowary – Rhodonite
Cat – Lapis Lazuli, Tanzanite
Chimpanzee – Black Tourmaline
Cow – Green Jade
Crocodile – Amber
Crow – Labradorite
Deer – Blue Lace Agate
Dog – Blue Sapphire, Charoite, Dalmatian
    Jasper
Dolphin – Larimar, Moldavite
Dolphin, Amazon River – Stichtite
Dove – Morganite
Dove, white – Angel Aura Quartz
Eagle – Seraphinite
Elephant – Hiddenite, Mahogany Obsidian
Fish – Aquamarine, Larimar
Flamingo – Mangano Calcite
Fox – Blue Kyanite
Frog – Herkimer Diamond
Fruit Dove – Watermelon Tourmaline
Galah – Rhodochrosite
Giraffe – Blue Apatite
Golden Lion Tamarin – Imperial Topaz
Golden Pheasant – Heliodor
Gorilla – Blue Tourmaline
Gouldian Finch – Rainbow Aura Quartz
Green Parrot – Emerald
Hawk – Angelite
Horse – Clear Quartz
Horse, palomino – Rutilated Quartz (Rutile)
Howler Monkey – Covellite
Hummingbird – Ametrine, Citrine, Heliodor
Hyacinth Macaw – Tanzan Aura Quartz
Ibis – Aventurine
Jaguar – Red Garnet
Kangaroo – Clear Quartz
Koala – Bloodstone
Komodo Dragon – Black Obsidian
Lemur – Quantum Quattro™
Leopard – Leopardskin Jasper
Lion – Ruby

Lion, White – Super Quartz
Lizard – Howlite
Llama – Amazonite
Lovebird – Kunzite
Macaw, Blue-and-Gold – Aqua Aura Quartz
Macaw, Hyacinth – Tanzan Aura Quartz
Major Mitchell Cockatoo – Rhodochrosite
Manatee – Blue Calcite
Meerkat – Dumortierite
Monkey – Dumortierite
Moose – Eudialyte, Unakite
Mouse – Dumortierite
Narwhal – Larimar, Star Sapphire
Octopus – Pyrite
Okapi – Jet
Orangutan – Green Tourmaline
Ostrich – Emerald
Otter – Sunstone
Owl – Amethyst, Ametrine
Owl, Snowy – Selenite
Panda – Tibetan Quartz
Parrot, pink – Rhodochrosite
Peacock – Rutile
Pegasus – Star Ruby
Penguin – Apache Tear, Quantum Quattro™
Pig – Shungite
Platypus – Blue Kyanite
Polar Bear – Selenite
Quoll – Pyrite
Quokka – Chrysoprase
Rabbit – Carnelian
Reindeer – Tugtupite
Rhinoceros – Red Jasper
Robin – Thulite
Salamander – Fire Agate
Scarab Beetle – Sunstone
Scorpion – Pietersite
Seahorse – Bronzite
Seal – Larimar
Shark – Clear Quartz, Larimar
Skunk – Rainbow Fluorite
Sloth – Howlite
Snake – Serpentine
Snow Leopard – Moonstone
Spider – Black Onyx
Squirrel – Chrysocolla
Sugar Glider – Rose Aura Quartz
Swan – Celestite
Tiger – Tiger's Eye
Tiger, White – Libyan Desert Glass
Tortoise – Moss Agate
Turkey – Rose Quartz
Turtle – Lemurian Seed Crystal
Unicorn – Star Sapphire
Violet–backed Starling – Sugilite
Warthog – Botswana Agate
Whale – Larimar, Lepidolite
Wolf – Iolite
Wombat – Mookaite

PLANT GUIDE

acacia – Blue Apatite
African canary wood – Libyan Desert Glass
alder – Mangano Calcite
almond – Dumortierite
amyris – Tanzanite
apple – Azurite
apricot – Thulite
arborvitae – Green Aventurine
ash – Aventurine, Rainbow Aura Quartz
aspen – Rutile
bamboo – Tibetan Quartz
banana – Libyan Desert Glass
barley – Green Jade
basil – Pietersite
bergamot – Citrine, Heliodor
birch – Rhodonite
bluebell – Blue Calcite
blueberry – Tanzan Aura Quartz
blue tansy – Aqua Aura Quartz
Buddha wood – Mookaite
cacao – Carnelian
cajeput – Amazonite
calendula – Imperial Topaz
carnation – Ruby
carrot – Carnelian
cassia – Botswana Agate
catnip – Leopardskin Jasper
cedar – Red Jasper
chamomile – Blue Lace Agate
cherry – Celestite
cherry blossom– Celestite
cinnamon – Mahogany Obsidian
coconut – Apache Tear, Quantum Quattro™
corn – Green Jade
cumin – Tiger's Eye
cypress – Apache Tear
date palm – Emerald
dill – Emerald
Douglas fir – Quantum Quattro™
dragon's blood – Black Obsidian
ebony – Morganite
elder – Royal Aura Quartz
eucalyptus – Bloodstone
eucalyptus, lemon scented gum – Chrysoprase
fennel – Hematite
fragonia – Rutile
frangipani – Angel Aura Quartz, Moonstone
frankincense – Moldavite
gardenia – Hiddenite
geranium – Green Tourmaline
ginger – Clear Quartz, Diamond
ginseng – Tiger's Eye
grape – Chrysocolla
grapefruit – Eudialyte
guarana – Red Garnet
hawthorn – Tugtupite
hazel – Aventurine
holly – Star Sapphire
hyacinth – Stichtite
ivy – Black Onyx

jasmine – Sunstone
juniper – Labradorite
lavender – Amethyst
lemon – Angelite, Seraphinite
lemon scented gum – Chrysoprase
lime – Turquoise
lotus, blue – Blue Sapphire
lotus, white – Selenite
mahogany – Mahogany Obsidian
mandarin – Charoite, Dalmatian Jasper
marigold – Imperial Topaz
marjoram – Rhodochrosite
millet – Green Jade
moonflower – Moonstone
mulberry – Amethyst
mustard – Champagne Aura Quartz
myrrh – Iolite
nettle – Fire Agate
niaouli – Pyrite
nutmeg – Howlite
oak – Lemurian Seed Crystal
oak moss – Moss Agate
oats – Green Jade
olive – Aqua Aura Quartz
orange – Amber
orchid – Rhodochrosite
palo santo – Serpentine
passionflower/fruit – Sugilite
patchouli – Snowflake Obsidian
pepper – Nuummite
peppermint – Herkimer Diamond
petitgrain – Shungite
pimento berry – Ruby, Star Ruby
pine – Malachite
plum – Ametrine
pomegranate – Ruby, Star Ruby
poppy – Jet
purpleheart – Stichtite
ravensara – Black Tourmaline
raspberry – Mangano Calcite
rice – Jade
rose – Kunzite, Rose Quartz
rose, pink – Rose Aura Quartz
rose, white – Angel Aura Quartz
rosemary – Rainbow Fluorite
rye – Green Jade
sage – Selenite
sandalwood – Lapis Lazuli, Tanzanite
seaweed – Aquamarine, Larimar
star anise – Covellite
strawberry – Blue Kyanite, Bronzite
Sturt Desert pea – Quantum Quattro™
vanilla – Blue Tourmaline
violet – Lepidolite
water lily – Royal Aura Quartz
watermelon – Watermelon Tourmaline
wheat – Green Jade
willow – Smokey Quartz
yarrow – Unakite
ylang ylang – Pink Tourmaline

INDEX

animals, protecting – Azurite (pg 59-61), Black Onyx (pg 193-195), Dalmatian Jasper (pg 134-135), Leopardskin Jasper (pg 136-138), Unakite (pg 327-329)

animals, relocating – Azurite (pg 59-61)

antiaging – Mookaite (pg 172-175), Tanzan Aura Quartz (pg 231-233)

antioxidants – Shungite (pg 262-266)

Anubis – Malachite (pg 167-168)

anxiety – Champagne Aura Quartz (pg 212-213)

Aphrodite/Venus – Celestite (pg 77-79), Rutile (pg 245-247)

Apollo – Sunstone (pg 282-284)

appreciation – Eudialyte (pg 105-107)

aquaphobia – Royal Aura Quartz (pg 226-227)

Aragonite – Herkimer Diamond (pg 118-121)

archangels –Angelite (pg 44-46), Blue Sapphire (pg 248-250), Diamond (pg 97-99), Emerald (pg 102-104), Ruby (pg 242-244)

architects – Sugilite (pg 278-281)

arguments – Blue Lace Agate (pg 24-25), Howlite (pg 124-126), Rhodonite (pg 239-241), Seraphinite (pg 254-256)

arms – Malachite (pg 167-168)

aromatherapy – Quantum Quattro™ (pg 202-204)

Artemis – Rainbow Moonstone (pg 176-178)

arthritis – Hematite (pg 116-117)

artist – Blue Sapphire (pg 248-250), Covellite (pg 94-96), Thulite (pg 296-297)

arts – Azurite-Malachite (pg 62-63)

Ascended Masters – Moldavite (pg 169-171), Quantum Quattro™ (pg 202-204)

Asia – Leopardskin Jasper (pg 136-138)

Asperger's syndrome– Sugilite (pg 278-281)

Astarte – Rainbow Moonstone (pg 176-178)

astral travel – Iolite (pg 127-128), Lepidolite (pg 162-164), Smokey Quartz (pg 228-230)

Atlantis – Serpentine with Stichtite (pg 260-261), Larimar (pg 155-158)

attention to detail – Dumortierite (pg 100-101)

attracting – Leopardskin Jasper (pg 136-138), Rainbow Moonstone (pg 176-178)

aura – Blue Kyanite (pg 147-149)

Auralite-23™ - Super Quartz (pg 285-289)

Australia – Mookaite (pg 172-175)

authority – Tanzanite (pg 290-295)

autism – Sugilite (pg 278-281)

awareness – Clear Quartz (pg 214-217), Quantum Quattro™ (pg 202-204), Royal Aura Quartz (pg 226-227)

B

baby, sleeping – Angel Aura Quartz (pg 205-207)

back pain – Amazonite (pg 32-35), Mangano Calcite (pg 72-73), Seraphinite (pg 254-256)

bad luck – Jet (pg 141-143)

balance – Ametrine (pg 42-43), Black Tourmaline (pg 305-307), Blue Kyanite (pg 147-149), Snowflake Obsidian (pg 190-192), Tibetan Quartz (pg 234-235), Watermelon Tourmaline (pg 318-320)

balancing power – Morganite (pg 179-181)

bankruptcy – Rainbow Aura Quartz (pg 218-220)

base chakra, nurturing – Leopardskin Jasper (pg 136-138), Red Jasper (pg 139-140)

base chakra, soothing – Black Tourmaline (pg 305-307)

base chakra, stimulating – Red Garnet (pg 110-112), Shungite (pg 262-266)

Bast – Tanzanite (pg 290-295)

beauty – Celestite (pg 77-79), Imperial Topaz (pg 302-304), Rose Quartz (pg 221-223)

beauty, inner, awakening – Aqua Aura Quartz (pg 208-211)

beauty, seeing – Angel Aura Quartz (pg 205-207), Chrysoprase (pg 88-90), Morganite (pg 179-181), Snowflake Obsidian (pg 190-192), Super Quartz (pg 285-289)

beginnings, new – Chrysoprase (pg 88-90), Rainbow Moonstone (pg 176-178), Moss Agate (pg 30-31)

beliefs – Watermelon Tourmaline (pg 318-320)

betrayal – Black Onyx (pg 193-195), Eudialyte (pg 105-107)

birth, animals – Green Jade (pg 130-133)
bisexual - Stichtite (pg 272-277)
Black Jade – Green Jade (pg 130-133)
bladder – Black Tourmaline (pg 305-307)
blended family – Super Quartz (pg 285-289)
blessings – Blue Star Sapphire (pg 269-271)
bliss – Amethyst (pg 39-41)
blockages – Herkimer Diamond (pg 118-121)
blood – Bloodstone (pg 64-67), Hematite (pg 116-117)
blood clots – Turquoise (pg 324-326)
blood vessels – Bloodstone (pg 64-67), Turquoise (pg 324-326)
body issues – Blue Apatite (pg 50-53), Emerald (pg 102-104), Stichtite (pg 272-277)
body odour – Leopardskin Jasper (pg 136-138)
bodybuilding – Sunstone (pg 282-284)
bones – Pyrite (pg 199-201)
botany – Moss Agate (pg 30-31)
brainwashing – Leopardskin Jasper (pg 136-138)
breaking up – Eudialyte (pg 105-107), Lepidolite (pg 162-164), Malachite (pg 167-168), Rhodonite (pg 239-241), Seraphinite (pg 254-256)
breast feeding, trouble - Serpentine (pg 257-260)
breasts – Rainbow Moonstone (pg 176-178)
breeding – Unakite (pg 327-329)
bride – Blue Calcite (pg 70-71)
broken heart – Chrysoprase (pg 88-90), Green Tourmaline (pg 311-312)
Buddha – Green Jade (pg 130-133)
Buddhism – Tibetan Quartz (pg 234-235)
budgets – Pyrite (pg 199-201), Snowflake Obsidian (pg 190-192)
bullying – Bloodstone (pg 64-67), Kunzite (pg 144-146)
bushfire – Fire Agate (pg 28-29)
business, family – Green Jade (pg 130-133)
busker – Thulite (pg 296-297)

C

Cacoxenite – Super Quartz (pg 285-289)
cancer – Covellite (pg 94-96)
capitalism – Celestite (pg 77-79), Quantum Quattro™ (pg 202-204)
career, changing – Moldavite (pg 169-171)
carers – Charoite (pg 80-82)
celebrations – Champagne Aura Quartz (pg 212-213)
cells – Royal Aura Quartz (pg 226-227)
centring – Botswana Agate (pg 26-27)
Cetus – Lepidolite (pg 162-164)
chakras, balancing – Blue Kyanite (pg 147-149)
Chalcopyrite (pg 199-201) – Green Aventurine (pg 56-58)
Chamuel – Seraphinite (pg 254-256)
Chang'e – Rainbow Moonstone (pg 176-178)
change – Dumortierite (pg 100-101), Herkimer Diamond (pg 118-121), Kunzite (pg 144-146), Moldavite (pg 169-171), Tugtupite (pg 321-323)
change, dealing with – Azurite (pg 59-61), Lepidolite (pg 162-164)
channelling – Tanzan Aura Quartz (pg 231-233)
chaos – Pietersite (pg 196-198)
charity – Blue Star Sapphire (pg 269-271), Blue Tourmaline (pg 308-310), Charoite (pg 80-82), Green Jade (pg 130-133), Lemurian Seed Crystal (pg 159-161), Turquoise (pg 324-326)
chastity – Blue Sapphire (pg 248-250)
chemotherapy – Tanzanite (pg 290-295)
chi – Turquoise (pg 324-326)
child birth – Angel Aura Quartz (pg 205-207), Bloodstone (pg 64-67), Clear Quartz (pg 214-217), Moss Agate (pg 30-31), Watermelon Tourmaline (pg 318-320)
Child, inner – Chrysocolla (pg 83-86), Chrysoprase (pg 88-90)
childhood memories, recall – Blue Kyanite (pg 147-149)

childhood trauma – Chrysoprase (pg 88-90), Leopardskin Jasper (pg 136-138)

children – Amazonite (pg 32-35), Blue Calcite (pg 70-71), Chrysoprase (pg 88-90), Moss Agate (pg 30-31), Sugilite (pg 278-281), Watermelon Tourmaline (pg 318-320)

chores, help with – Amazonite (pg 32-35), Kunzite (pg 144-146), Selenite (pg 251-253)

Christ – Bloodstone (pg 64-67)

christening - Heliodor (pg 113-115)

Christmas parties – Watermelon Tourmaline (pg 318-320)

circadian rhythms – Amethyst (pg 39-41), Rainbow Moonstone (pg 176-178)

circulatory system – Bloodstone (pg 64-67), Hematite (pg 116-117), Red Garnet (pg 110-112), Star Ruby (pg 267-268)

city life – Black Onyx (pg 193-195), Pietersite (pg 196-198)

clairaudience –Angelite (pg 44-46)

clairsentience – Imperial Topaz (pg 302-304)

clairvoyance – Azurite (pg 59-61), Azurite-Malachite (pg 62-63)

clarity – Diamond (pg 97-99), Herkimer Diamond (pg 118-121)

claustrophobia - Serpentine (pg 257-260)

cleansing – Blue Sapphire (pg 248-250), Blue Star Sapphire (pg 269-271), Selenite (pg 251-253)

climate change – Pietersite (pg 196-198), Tugtupite (pg 321-323)

clothing – Blue Kyanite (pg 147-149)

clumsiness – Sugilite (pg 278-281)

coaching – Blue Sapphire (pg 248-250)

Cobaltocalcite – Pink Tourmaline (pg 313-317)

cold – Bloodstone (pg 64-67)

cold weather, handling – Chrysoprase (pg 88-90)

colon – Citrine (pg 91-93)

colour therapy – Rainbow Aura Quartz (pg 218-220)

coma – Libyan Desert Glass (pg 165-166)

commitment – Blue Sapphire (pg 248-250), Blue Tourmaline (pg 308-310)

communication – Blue Tourmaline (pg 308-310), Celestite (pg 77-79), Chrysocolla (pg 83-86), Howlite (pg 124-126), Larimar (pg 155-158), Rainbow Aura Quartz (pg 218-220)

communication, animal – Black Tourmaline (pg 305-307), Dalmatian Jasper (pg 134-135), Larimar (pg 155-158), Leopardskin Jasper (pg 136-138), Rutile (pg 245-247)

communication, breakdown – Aqua Aura Quartz (pg 208-211), Celestite (pg 77-79)

community – Quantum Quattro™ (pg 202-204), Sugilite (pg 278-281), Super Quartz (pg 285-289)

compassion – Celestite (pg 77-79), Green Jade (pg 130-133), Sugilite (pg 278-281), Super Quartz (pg 285-289), Tanzanite (pg 290-295)

competitiveness – Dalmatian Jasper (pg 134-135), Watermelon Tourmaline (pg 318-320)

compliments – Selenite (pg 251-253)

composer – Labradorite (pg 150-151)

compromise – Chrysocolla (pg 83-86)

computers – Pietersite (pg 196-198)

conceiving – Carnelian (pg 74-76), Rainbow Moonstone (pg 176-178)

concentration – Black Tourmaline (pg 305-307)

concierge – Bronzite (pg 68-69)

confidence – Amazonite (pg 32-35), Jet (pg 141-143), Mookaite (pg 172-175), Pietersite (pg 196-198), Unakite (pg 327-329)

conflict, inner – Azurite-Malachite (pg 62-63)

Confucius – Green Jade (pg 130-133)

connectedness – Black Onyx (pg 193-195), Blue Star Sapphire (pg 269-271)

conservation - Amazonite (pg 32-35)

constipation – Citrine (pg 91-93)

consumerism – Celestite (pg 77-79), Quantum Quattro™ (pg 202-204)

contact, reinstating lost – Rhodochrosite (pg 236-238)

contentment – Quantum Quattro™ (pg 202-204)

control – Amazonite (pg 32-35), Clear Quartz (pg 214-217), Malachite (pg 167-168), Tanzanite (pg 290-295)

cooking – Royal Aura Quartz (pg 226-227)

cooperation – Sugilite (pg 278-281), Watermelon Tourmaline (pg 318-320)

coordination – Sugilite (pg 278-281)

counselling - Tanzanite (pg 290-295)

courage – Azurite-Malachite (pg 62-63), Bloodstone (pg 64-67), Green Jade (pg 130-133), Tiger's Eye (pg 298-301)

cravings – Turquoise (pg 324-326)

creating, new things – Green Aventurine (pg 56-58)

creative visualisation – Tanzanite (pg 290-295)

creativity – Labradorite (pg 150-151), Sunstone (pg 282-284), Thulite (pg 296-297), Turquoise (pg 324-326)

crisis – Champagne Aura Quartz (pg 212-213), Dumortierite (pg 100-101)

criticism – Mookaite (pg 172-175)

crowds – Pietersite (pg 196-198)

crown chakra, nurturing – Sugilite (pg 278-281), Tanzanite (pg 290-295)

crown chakra, soothing – Lepidolite (pg 162-164)

crown chakra, stimulating – Amethyst (pg 39-41), Stichtite (pg 272-277)

crying – Apache Tear (pg 47-49), Blue Lace Agate (pg 24-25)

cult – Leopardskin Jasper (pg 136-138)

curiosity – Chrysoprase (pg 88-90), Dumortierite (pg 100-101)

current affairs – Super Quartz (pg 285-289)

custody battles – Snowflake Obsidian (pg 190-192)

customer service –Angelite (pg 44-46)

cuts – Red Garnet (pg 110-112), Shungite (pg 262-266)

cyclone – Diamond (pg 97-99), Pietersite (pg 196-198)

cymophobia – Royal Aura Quartz (pg 226-227)

D

Danburite – Stichtite (pg 272-277), Super Quartz (pg 285-289)

dance – Azurite-Malachite (pg 62-63), Sunstone (pg 282-284), Leopardskin Jasper (pg 136-138)

danger – Ruby (pg 242-244)

dating – Rhodochrosite (pg 236-238), Rhodonite (pg 239-241), Tanzanite (pg 290-295), Thulite (pg 296-297)

death – Apache Tear (pg 47-49), Jet (pg 141-143), Lemurian Seed Crystal (pg 159-161), Morganite (pg 179-181), Seraphinite (pg 254-256)

death, pet –Angelite (pg 44-46)

debates – Heliodor (pg 113-115)

debt reduction – Iolite (pg 127-128)

decisions – Blue Sapphire (pg 248-250), Bronzite (pg 68-69), Champagne Aura Quartz (pg 212-213), Charoite (pg 80-82)

decisiveness – Bronzite (pg 68-69)

dehydration – Aquamarine (pg 54-55), Royal Aura Quartz (pg 226-227)

dementia – Blue Star Sapphire (pg 269-271)

deportment – Amazonite (pg 32-35)

depression – Dumortierite (pg 100-101), Labradorite (pg 150-151), Pink Tourmaline (pg 313-317), Red Garnet (pg 110-112), Smokey Quartz (pg 228-230)

determination – Tugtupite (pg 321-323)

detox – Amber (pg 36-38), Aquamarine (pg 54-55)

devotion – Blue Sapphire (pg 248-250), Red Garnet (pg 110-112)

devotion, spiritual – Blue Star Sapphire (pg 269-271)

Diamond (pg 97-99) substitute – Herkimer Diamond (pg 118-121)

Diana – Rainbow Moonstone (pg 176-178)

Dianite – Shungite (pg 262-266)

diet – Green Tourmaline (pg 311-312)

digestion – Citrine (pg 91-93), Heliodor (pg 113-115), Shungite (pg 262-266)

Dioptase – Quantum Quattro™ (pg 202-204), Super Quartz (pg 285-289)

disabilities – Rhodonite (pg 239-241)

disagreement – Seraphinite (pg 254-256)

discipline – Dumortierite (pg 100-101), Tibetan Quartz (pg 234-235)

discrimination - Amazonite (pg 32-35)

disease, life threatening – Rainbow Aura Quartz (pg 218-220)

dishonesty – Black Onyx (pg 193-195)

distraction, avoiding – Dumortierite (pg 100-101), Tanzanite (pg 290-295) diversity – Serpentine with Stichtite (pg 260-261), Sugilite (pg 278-281)

divination – Amethyst (pg 39-41), Covellite (pg 94-96)

Divine Feminine – Chrysocolla (pg 83-86), Rainbow Moonstone (pg 176-178)

Divine Masculine – Starstone (pg 128-129), Sunstone (pg 282-284)

divorce – Lepidolite (pg 162-164), Rhodonite (pg 239-241), Ruby (pg 242-244), Seraphinite (pg 254-256)

doctors – Emerald (pg 102-104)

dogs – Dalmatian Jasper (pg 134-135)

dogs, settling – Dumortierite (pg 100-101)

dragons – Black Obsidian (pg 185-187), Serpentine (pg 257-260)

dreams – Blue Sapphire (pg 248-250), Green Jade (pg 130-133), Howlite (pg 124-126), Lepidolite (pg 162-164), Quantum Quattro™ (pg 202-204)

dreams, interpretation – Blue Kyanite (pg 147-149)

dreams, preventing bad – Black Onyx (pg 193-195), Green Jade (pg 130-133)

dreams, prophetic – Blue Tourmaline (pg 308-310), Green Jade (pg 130-133), Labradorite (pg 150-151), Royal Aura Quartz (pg 226-227)

dreams, recall – Blue Kyanite (pg 147-149)

dreams, vivid - Starstone (pg 128-129)

driving – Tibetan Quartz (pg 234-235)

drought – Moss Agate (pg 30-31), Royal Aura Quartz (pg 226-227)

drug addiction – Botswana Agate (pg 26-27)

dying – Heliodor (pg 113-115)

dyslexia – Black Tourmaline (pg 305-307)

E

ears – Aquamarine (pg 54-55), Angelite (pg 44-46)

ears, ringing – Black Tourmaline (pg 305-307)

Earth connection – Serpentine (pg 257-260), Shungite (pg 262-266)

Earth healing – Azurite-Malachite (pg 62-63), Herkimer Diamond (pg 118-121), Larimar (pg 155-158), Mookaite (pg 172-175), Shungite (pg 262-266), Stichtite (pg 272-277)

earth spirits – Quantum Quattro™ (pg 202-204)

Earth star chakra, nurturing – Nuummite (pg 182-184)

Earth star chakra, soothing using Honey Calcite – Blue Calcite (pg 70-71)

Earth star chakra, stimulating – Smokey Quartz (pg 228-230), Super Quartz (pg 285-289)

Earth Workers - Shungite (pg 262-266)

earthquakes – Diamond (pg 97-99)

Eastern philosophy – Tibetan Quartz (pg 234-235)

eating disorder – Botswana Agate (pg 26-27)

eating, healthy – Blue Apatite (pg 50-53), Selenite (pg 251-253), Seraphinite (pg 254-256)

eczema – Leopardskin Jasper (pg 136-138), Serpentine (pg 257-260), Shungite (pg 262-266)

ego – Selenite (pg 251-253)

Egypt – Libyan Desert Glass (pg 165-166)

electricians – Fire Agate (pg 28-29)

elves – Chrysoprase (pg 88-90)

embassy workers – Super Quartz (pg 285-289)

emergencies – Dumortierite (pg 100-101)

emotional connections, breaking – Black Obsidian (pg 185-187), Red Jasper (pg 139-140)

empathy – Tanzanite (pg 290-295)

emphysema - Morganite (pg 179-181)

employees, retaining – Blue Sapphire (pg 248-250)

employment, finding – Heliodor (pg 113-115), Rutile (pg 245-247)

endangered species – Morganite (pg 179-181)

endurance – Clear Quartz (pg 214-217)

enemies – Red Garnet (pg 110-112), Serpentine (pg 257-260)

energy – Clear Quartz (pg 214-217), Nuummite (pg 182-184)

energy blocks – Turquoise (pg 324-326)

engineers – Sugilite (pg 278-281)

environment, returning to balance – Ametrine (pg 42-43)

environmental campaigns – Amazonite (pg 32-35), Quantum Quattro™ (pg 202-204), Turquoise (pg 324-326)

equality – Blue Calcite (pg 70-71), Morganite (pg 179-181), Watermelon Tourmaline (pg 318-320)
Eros – Thulite (pg 296-297)
etiquette – Bronzite (pg 68-69)
exams – Kunzite (pg 144-146)
exercise – Imperial Topaz (pg 302-304)
ex-partner – Hiddenite (pg 122-123)
extra-terrestrials – Blue Star Sapphire (pg 269-271), Moldavite (pg 169-171)
eyes – Lapis Lazuli (pg 152-154), Tanzanite (pg 290-295)

F
face – Rose Quartz (pg 221-223)
fairies – Chrysoprase (pg 88-90), Heliodor (pg 113-115)
fairness – Blue Calcite (pg 70-71), Morganite (pg 179-181), Red Jasper (pg 139-140)
Falcon's Eye – Tiger's Eye (pg 298-301)
fame – Thulite (pg 296-297)
family – Dalmatian Jasper (pg 134-135), Eudialyte (pg 105-107), Green Jade (pg 130-133), Pink
     Tourmaline (pg 313-317), Rose Quartz (pg 221-223), Tanzanite (pg 290-295)
family, harmony – Amazonite (pg 32-35), Ametrine (pg 42-43), Champagne Aura Quartz (pg
     212-213), Howlite (pg 124-126), Pink Tourmaline (pg 313-317), Seraphinite (pg 254-256)
family, inherited patterns – Rutile (pg 245-247)
family, resolving issues – Howlite (pg 124-126), Rhodonite (pg 239-241), Rutile (pg 245-247),
     Sunstone (pg 282-284)
farming – Green Aventurine (pg 56-58), Moss Agate (pg 30-31), Red Jasper (pg 139-140)
fashion – Rose Aura Quartz (pg 224-225)
fasting – Tibetan Quartz (pg 234-235)
father – Nuummite (pg 182-184)
fear – Amazonite (pg 32-35), Dumortierite (pg 100-101), Libyan Desert Glass (pg 165-166),
     Serpentine (pg 257-260)
fear, of water – Royal Aura Quartz (pg 226-227)
feet – Nuummite (pg 182-184)
feminine side – Larimar (pg 155-158), Rainbow Moonstone (pg 176-178), Morganite (pg 179-181)
fertility –Carnelian (pg 74-76), Green Aventurine (pg 56-58), Moss Agate (pg 30-31), Rainbow
     Moonstone (pg 176-178), Watermelon Tourmaline (pg 318-320)
fever – Larimar (pg 155-158)
Fibonacci sequence – Pyrite (pg 199-201)
fidelity – Thulite (pg 296-297), Tugtupite (pg 321-323)
financial scams – Dalmatian Jasper (pg 134-135)
fire – Fire Agate (pg 28-29)
fire fighters – Fire Agate (pg 28-29)
first impressions – Rose Aura Quartz (pg 224-225)
fishing – Larimar (pg 155-158), Tugtupite (pg 321-323)
flirting – Rainbow Aura Quartz (pg 218-220), Thulite (pg 296-297)
floods – Pietersite (pg 196-198)
flu – Bloodstone (pg 64-67)
focus – Leopardskin Jasper (pg 136-138)
food poisoning – Imperial Topaz (pg 302-304)
forests - Amazonite (pg 32-35)
forgetfulness – Blue Kyanite (pg 147-149)
forgiveness – Bloodstone (pg 64-67), Eudialyte (pg 105-107), Pink Tourmaline (pg 313-317)
fragrance – Rose Aura Quartz (pg 224-225)
fraud – Serpentine (pg 257-260)
free radicals - Shungite (pg 262-266)
free thinking – Labradorite (pg 150-151)
Freyja – Rutile (pg 245-247)
friends – Dalmatian Jasper (pg 134-135), Howlite (pg 124-126), Pink Tourmaline (pg 313-317), Rose
     Quartz (pg 221-223), Watermelon Tourmaline (pg 318-320)
friends, new – Unakite (pg 327-329)
fundraising – Pyrite (pg 199-201)
funeral – Jet (pg 141-143)
future – Blue Apatite (pg 50-53)

future generations – Blue Calcite (pg 70-71)

G

Gabriel - Blue Sapphire (pg 248-250), Gem Silica (pg 86-87)
Gaia – Moss Agate (pg 30-31), Smokey Quartz (pg 228-230)
gambling – Sugilite (pg 278-281)
gardening – Green Aventurine (pg 56-58), Green Jade (pg 130-133), Heliodor (pg 113-115), Moss
   Agate (pg 30-31), Rainbow Fluorite (pg 108-109), Royal Aura Quartz (pg 226-227)
gay – Stichtite (pg 272-277)
gay marriage – Stichtite (pg 272-277), Super Quartz (pg 285-289)
gay rights – Morganite (pg 179-181), Stichtite (pg 272-277)
generosity – Green Jade (pg 130-133)
gentleness - Mookaite (pg 172-175)
geopathic stress – Hiddenite (pg 122-123)
ghosts – Heliodor (pg 113-115), Howlite (pg 124-126)
gifting – Diamond (pg 97-99)
glamour – Rose Aura Quartz (pg 224-225)
global awareness – Super Quartz (pg 285-289)
global healing – Gem Silica (pg 86-87), Seraphinite (pg 254-256), Tugtupite (pg 321-323)
global warming – Pietersite (pg 196-198), Tugtupite (pg 321-323)
GMO foods – Moss Agate (pg 30-31)
gnomes – Chrysoprase (pg 88-90), Emerald (pg 102-104)
goal setting – Black Tourmaline (pg 305-307), Rainbow Aura Quartz (pg 218-220)
goals, long term – Dalmatian Jasper (pg 134-135), Thulite (pg 296-297)
God – Sunstone (pg 282-284)
Goddess – Amazonite (pg 32-35), Chrysocolla (pg 83-86), Rainbow Moonstone (pg 176-178)
Golden Selenite (pg 251-253) – Tanzanite (pg 290-295)
Goshenite – Super Quartz (pg 285-289)
gossip – Kunzite (pg 144-146), Serpentine (pg 257-260)
governments – Sugilite (pg 278-281), Watermelon Tourmaline (pg 318-320)
grace – Celestite (pg 77-79)
graduation – Morganite (pg 179-181)
grandfather – Nuummite (pg 182-184)
grandmother – Celestite (pg 77-79), Rainbow Moonstone (pg 176-178)
gratitude – Hiddenite (pg 122-123), Moldavite (pg 169-171)
greater good – Blue Tourmaline (pg 308-310), Sugilite (pg 278-281), Watermelon Tourmaline (pg
   318-320)
greed – Celestite (pg 77-79), Tugtupite (pg 321-323)
green living – Super Quartz (pg 285-289), Turquoise (pg 324-326)
Green man – Moss Agate (pg 30-31)
grief – Apache Tear (pg 47-49), Jet (pg 141-143)
grounding – Fire Agate (pg 28-29), Hematite (pg 116-117), Leopardskin Jasper (pg 136-138),
   Mookaite (pg 172-175), Red Jasper (pg 139-140), Shungite (pg 262-266), Smokey Quartz (pg
   228-230)
group therapy – Turquoise (pg 324-326)
groups – Diamond (pg 97-99), Morganite (pg 179-181), Turquoise (pg 324-326)
growth – Emerald (pg 102-104), Unakite (pg 327-329)
grudge – Pink Tourmaline (pg 313-317)
guidance – Blue Sapphire (pg 248-250), Iolite (pg 127-128)
guidance, divine – Seraphinite (pg 254-256), Tanzan Aura Quartz (pg 231-233)
guilt – Mangano Calcite (pg 72-73), Seraphinite (pg 254-256)
gums – Blue Sapphire (pg 248-250)

H

habit, breaking – Botswana Agate (pg 26-27)
haemorrhoids - Bloodstone (pg 64-67)
hail storms – Pietersite (pg 196-198)
hair - Tanzanite (pg 290-295)
hairdressing – Rose Aura Quartz (pg 224-225)
hand chakras – Rose Quartz (pg 221-223)

hands – Malachite (pg 167-168), Rose Quartz (pg 221-223)

happiness – Citrine (pg 91-93)

harmony, workplace – Black Tourmaline (pg 305-307), Champagne Aura Quartz (pg 212-213), Howlite (pg 124-126), Kunzite (pg 144-146), Rhodonite (pg 239-241), Watermelon Tourmaline (pg 318-320)

hate – Pink Tourmaline (pg 313-317)

Hathor – Green Jade (pg 130-133)

hay fever – Aquamarine (pg 54-55)

headache – Dumortierite (pg 100-101), Tanzan Aura Quartz (pg 231-233), Tanzanite (pg 290-295)

Healerite™ - Serpentine (pg 257-260)

healers – Charoite (pg 80-82), Emerald (pg 102-104), Pink Tourmaline (pg 313-317), Selenite (pg 251-253)

healing – Blue Star Sapphire (pg 269-271), Chrysoprase (pg 88-90), Emerald (pg 102-104), Heliodor (pg 113-115), Lemurian Seed Crystal (pg 159-161), Mookaite (pg 172-175), Selenite (pg 251-253), Seraphinite (pg 254-256), Smokey Quartz (pg 228-230)

healing, absent/distance – Blue Star Sapphire (pg 269-271), Clear Quartz (pg 214-217), Libyan Desert Glass (pg 165-166)

healing, emotional – Chrysocolla (pg 83-86), Chrysoprase (pg 88-90), Mangano Calcite (pg 72-73), Quantum Quattro™ (pg 202-204), Seraphinite (pg 254-256)

health – Amazonite (pg 32-35), Bloodstone (pg 64-67), Clear Quartz (pg 214-217), Red Garnet (pg 110-112), Serpentine (pg 257-260), Shungite (pg 262-266), Turquoise (pg 324-326)

healthy eating – Blue Apatite (pg 50-53), Selenite (pg 251-253), Seraphinite (pg 254-256)

hearing – Covellite (pg 94-96)

heart attack – Pink Tourmaline (pg 313-317), Shungite (pg 262-266)

heart chakra, nurturing – Pink Tourmaline (pg 313-317), Turquoise (pg 324-326), Watermelon Tourmaline (pg 318-320)

heart chakra, soothing – Rose Quartz (pg 221-223)

heart chakra, stimulate – Moldavite (pg 169-171)

heart, open – Green Jade (pg 130-133), Lemurian Seed Crystal (pg 159-161), Star Ruby (pg 267-268)

heart, physical – Bloodstone (pg 64-67), Green Tourmaline (pg 311-312), Star Ruby (pg 267-268)

heartbeat – Rhodochrosite (pg 236-238)

Helios – Sunstone (pg 282-284)

Hemimorphite – Bloodstone (pg 64-67)

Hephaestus – Fire Agate (pg 28-29)

herbalism – Green Tourmaline (pg 311-312), Quantum Quattro™ (pg 202-204)

herbs, enhancing – Clear Quartz (pg 214-217)

Hermes - Rainbow Aura Quartz (pg 218-220)

hermit - Libyan Desert Glass (pg 165-166)

hidden abilities, awakening – Black Obsidian (pg 185-187)

Hinduism - Tibetan Quartz (pg 234-235)

hoarding – Black Tourmaline (pg 305-307)

holiday – Sunstone (pg 282-284)

holistic – Tanzanite (pg 290-295)

home – Smokey Quartz (pg 228-230), Tanzanite (pg 290-295)

homeopathy – Quantum Quattro™ (pg 202-204)

homework, children – Howlite (pg 124-126), Selenite (pg 251-253)

homosexuality - Stichtite (pg 272-277)

honesty – Chrysocolla (pg 83-86), Heliodor (pg 113-115), Lapis Lazuli (pg 152-154)

Honey Calcite – Blue Calcite (pg 70-71)

hope – Quantum Quattro™ (pg 202-204), Starstone (pg 128-129), Tugtupite (pg 321-323)

hormones, balance - Bloodstone (pg 64-67)

horticulture – Moss Agate (pg 30-31)

hostage – Tanzan Aura Quartz (pg 231-233)

housemate – Angel Aura Quartz (pg 205-207)

housework, help with – Amazonite (pg 32-35)

human rights – Morganite (pg 179-181), Super Quartz (pg 285-289), Turquoise (pg 324-326)

humanitarianism – Pink Tourmaline (pg 313-317)

humanity – Blue Tourmaline (pg 308-310)

humility – Green Jade (pg 130-133)

hurricane – Diamond (pg 97-99), Pietersite (pg 196-198)
hydration – Royal Aura Quartz (pg 226-227)

I

illness, life threatening – Rainbow Aura Quartz (pg 218-220)
illness, soothing – Amazonite (pg 32-35), Amber (pg 36-38)
illness, understanding cause – Serpentine with Stichtite (pg 260-261)
immigrants – Morganite (pg 179-181)
immune system – Tanzanite (pg 290-295)
impotence – Carnelian (pg 74-76), Fire Agate (pg 28-29), Star Ruby (pg 267-268)
impressions, good – Rose Aura Quartz (pg 224-225)
improvement – Diamond (pg 97-99)
impulsiveness – Black Tourmaline (pg 305-307)
in vitro fertilisation - Rhodochrosite (pg 236-238)
Inanna – Rainbow Moonstone (pg 176-178)
income – Carnelian (pg 74-76), Green Aventurine (pg 56-58)
independence – Rhodonite (pg 239-241), Tugtupite (pg 321-323)
indigenous people – Tanzanite (pg 290-295)
Indigo Children – Azurite (pg 59-61)
Infinite Stone™ - Serpentine (pg 257-260)
inflammation – Larimar (pg 155-158)
influence – Pyrite (pg 199-201)
influenza- Bloodstone (pg 64-67)
initiation – Morganite (pg 179-181)
injury – Red Garnet (pg 110-112)
injustice – Red Jasper (pg 139-140)
in-laws – Super Quartz (pg 285-289)
inner conflict – Azurite-Malachite (pg 62-63)
inner goddess – Carnelian (pg 74-76), Rainbow Moonstone (pg 176-178)
inner peace – Dumortierite (pg 100-101), Herkimer Diamond (pg 118-121), Howlite (pg 124-126)
inner power, summoning – Black Obsidian (pg 185-187), Mahogany Obsidian (pg 188-189)
inner radiance – Imperial Topaz (pg 302-304)
inner strength, summoning – Black Obsidian (pg 185-187)
innovation – Chrysoprase (pg 88-90)
insect bites/stings – Bloodstone (pg 64-67), Leopardskin Jasper (pg 136-138)
insomnia – Dumortierite (pg 100-101), Howlite (pg 124-126), Smokey Quartz (pg 228-230)
inspiration – Celestite (pg 77-79), Chrysoprase (pg 88-90)
inspirational speaking – Blue Tourmaline (pg 308-310), Quantum Quattro™ (pg 202-204)
inspired guidance – Tanzan Aura Quartz (pg 231-233)
instincts – Leopardskin Jasper (pg 136-138), Smokey Quartz (pg 228-230)
insults – Selenite (pg 251-253)
integration – Royal Aura Quartz (pg 226-227)
integrity – Blue Star Sapphire (pg 269-271), Red Garnet (pg 110-112), Sugilite (pg 278-281)
intellect – Heliodor (pg 113-115)
intelligence – Rainbow Aura Quartz (pg 218-220)
international travel – Rainbow Moonstone (pg 176-178), Super Quartz (pg 285-289)
internet – Sunstone (pg 282-284), Super Quartz (pg 285-289)
intersex - Stichtite (pg 272-277)
interviews – Kunzite (pg 144-146), Rainbow Aura Quartz (pg 218-220), Rutile (pg 245-247)
intimacy – Red Garnet (pg 110-112)
introspection – Rainbow Moonstone (pg 176-178), Snowflake Obsidian (pg 190-192),
intuition – Blue Sapphire (pg 248-250), Blue Star Sapphire (pg 269-271), Covellite (pg 94-96), Lapis Lazuli (pg 152-154), Rainbow Moonstone (pg 176-178), Royal Aura Quartz (pg 226-227), Stichtite (pg 272-277), Tanzanite (pg 290-295)
inventing – Hematite (pg 116-117)
invincibility – Diamond (pg 97-99)
Invisibility – Apache Tear (pg 47-49), Jet (pg 141-143)
involvement, attracting – Fire Agate (pg 28-29)
irritability – Larimar (pg 155-158)
Ishtar – Rainbow Moonstone (pg 176-178)

likeminded people, attracting – Aqua Aura Quartz (pg 208-211), Imperial Topaz (pg 302-304), Star Ruby (pg 267-268)

listening –Angelite (pg 44-46), Morganite (pg 179-181)

liver – Chrysoprase (pg 88-90), Smokey Quartz (pg 228-230)

loan, applying – Rutile (pg 245-247)

locavores – Moss Agate (pg 30-31), Seraphinite (pg 254-256)

logic – Pyrite (pg 199-201)

loneliness – Chrysocolla (pg 83-86), Lemurian Seed Crystal (pg 159-161)

lost souls – Kunzite (pg 144-146)

lost, item, person, love or pet – Rhodochrosite (pg 236-238)

lotto – Green Aventurine (pg 56-58)

love – Diamond (pg 97-99), Emerald (pg 102-104), Eudialyte (pg 105-107), Moldavite (pg 169-171), Pink Tourmaline (pg 313-317), Rose Aura Quartz (pg 224-225), Rose Quartz (pg 221-223), Ruby (pg 242-244), Tugtupite (pg 321-323)

love, accepting – Morganite (pg 179-181), Rose Aura Quartz (pg 224-225)

love, attracting – Bronzite (pg 68-69), Mangano Calcite (pg 72-73), Rose Aura Quartz (pg 224-225), Rose Quartz (pg 221-223), Sunstone (pg 282-284), Tugtupite (pg 321-323), Unakite (pg 327-329)

love, rekindling – Rhodochrosite (pg 236-238)

love, unrequited – Watermelon Tourmaline (pg 318-320)

lovemaking – Green Jade (pg 130-133), Red Garnet (pg 110-112), Ruby (pg 242-244)

loyalty – Blue Sapphire (pg 248-250)

loyalty, spiritual – Blue Star Sapphire (pg 269-271)

luck – Amazonite (pg 32-35), Carnelian (pg 74-76), Green Aventurine (pg 56-58), Green Jade (pg 130-133)

lunar cycles – Rainbow Moonstone (pg 176-178)

lungs – Aquamarine (pg 54-55)

lying – Black Onyx (pg 193-195), Kunzite (pg 144-146)

lymphatic system – Chrysocolla (pg 83-86)

M

Ma'at – Emerald (pg 102-104)

magnetism – Black Onyx (pg 193-195), Rainbow Moonstone (pg 176-178)

manhood – Nuummite (pg 182-184)

manifesting – Aqua Aura Quartz (pg 208-211), Green Aventurine (pg 56-58), Rainbow Moonstone (pg 176-178), Tanzan Aura Quartz (pg 231-233)

manners – Bronzite (pg 68-69)

manual dexterity – Hematite (pg 116-117)

marathon – Ruby (pg 242-244), Thulite (pg 296-297)

marine biology – Aquamarine (pg 54-55)

marriage – Blue Tourmaline (pg 308-310), Chrysoprase (pg 88-90), Diamond (pg 97-99), Morganite (pg 179-181)

masculinity – Morganite (pg 179-181), Nuummite (pg 182-184)

massage – Kunzite (pg 144-146), Pink Tourmaline (pg 313-317), Rose Quartz (pg 221-223)

masturbation – Tanzan Aura Quartz (pg 231-233)

materialism – Black Tourmaline (pg 305-307), Smokey Quartz (pg 228-230)

mathematics – Hematite (pg 116-117)

matriarch – Mahogany Obsidian (pg 188-189)

mediation – Blue Calcite (pg 70-71)

medical staff – Pyrite (pg 199-201)

medicine – Serpentine (pg 257-260)

meditation, leading – Herkimer Diamond (pg 118-121), Tanzan Aura Quartz (pg 231-233)

melancholy – Red Garnet (pg 110-112)

memory – Tanzanite (pg 290-295)

men – Nuummite (pg 182-184), Starstone (pg 128-129)

menopause – Bloodstone (pg 64-67), Emerald (pg 102-104), Eudialyte (pg 105-107), Mahogany Obsidian (pg 188-189), Morganite (pg 179-181)

menstruation – Bloodstone (pg 64-67), Hematite (pg 116-117), Rainbow Moonstone (pg 176-178)

mental agility – Rainbow Aura Quartz (pg 218-220)

mental disease – Dumortierite (pg 100-101)

Mercury retrograde – Botswana Agate (pg 26-27), Green Aventurine (pg 56-58)

mermaids – Aquamarine (pg 54-55)
metabolism – Imperial Topaz (pg 302-304)
Michael (archangel) – Ruby (pg 242-244)
midwife – Moss Agate (pg 30-31)
migraine – Tanzan Aura Quartz (pg 231-233), Tanzanite (pg 290-295)
mindfulness – Black Tourmaline (pg 305-307), Chrysoprase (pg 88-90)
miracles – Tugtupite (pg 321-323)
missing, person or pet – Rhodochrosite (pg 236-238)
mistakes, learning from - Shungite (pg 262-266)
mobile phone – Shungite (pg 262-266)
modelling – Rose Aura Quartz (pg 224-225)
modesty – Green Jade (pg 130-133)
money – Citrine (pg 91-93), Green Jade (pg 130-133), Jet (pg 141-143), Pyrite (pg 199-201), Turquoise
    (pg 324-326)
moodiness – Selenite (pg 251-253)
Moon – Rainbow Moonstone (pg 176-178)
mother – Blue Lace Agate (pg 24-25), Celestite (pg 77-79), Mahogany Obsidian (pg 188-189),
    Rainbow Moonstone (pg 176-178)
Mother Earth – Chrysocolla (pg 83-86), Mookaite (pg 172-175), Smokey Quartz (pg 228-230)
Mother Nature - Chrysocolla (pg 83-86)
motivation – Azurite-Malachite (pg 62-63), Libyan Desert Glass (pg 165-166)
mouth – Aquamarine (pg 54-55), Aqua Aura Quartz (pg 208-211)
moving house – Kunzite (pg 144-146), Lepidolite (pg 162-164), Pink Tourmaline (pg 313-317)
multiple incomes – Pyrite (pg 199-201)
multiple sclerosis – Rainbow Aura Quartz (pg 218-220)
muscles – Kunzite (pg 144-146), Sunstone (pg 282-284)
muse – Tanzan Aura Quartz (pg 231-233)
music – Chrysocolla (pg 83-86), Eudialyte (pg 105-107)
music, classical - Gem Silica (pg 86-87)
music, sacred/spiritual - Gem Silica (pg 86-87)
musician – Azurite-Malachite (pg 62-63), Blue Tourmaline (pg 308-310), Chrysocolla (pg 83-86),
    Covellite (pg 94-96), Eudialyte (pg 105-107)
mysteries, uncovering – Black Obsidian (pg 185-187)

N
nails – Black Onyx (pg 193-195)
naming day – Heliodor (pg 113-115)
Natrolite – Super Quartz (pg 285-289)
nature spirits/sprites – Chrysocolla (pg 83-86), Chrysoprase (pg 88-90)
nature, connection – Chrysocolla (pg 83-86), Jet (pg 141-143), Super Quartz (pg 285-289)
naturopathy – Quantum Quattro™ (pg 202-204)
Naujaite – Super Quartz (pg 285-289)
near-death experience – Tanzan Aura Quartz (pg 231-233)
neck – Aqua Aura Quartz (pg 208-211)
needs, understanding others' – Blue Star Sapphire (pg 269-271)
negativity, avoiding – Tugtupite (pg 321-323)
neglect – Lemurian Seed Crystal (pg 159-161)
negotiations – Black Tourmaline (pg 305-307), Chrysocolla (pg 83-86)
Neptune – Aquamarine (pg 54-55)
nervous breakdown – Amazonite (pg 32-35)
nervous system – Amazonite (pg 32-35), Blue Tourmaline (pg 308-310)
nervous tension - Amazonite (pg 32-35)
networking – Pyrite (pg 199-201)
new business – Chrysoprase (pg 88-90), Green Tourmaline (pg 311-312), Rutile (pg 245-247)
new school – Moss Agate (pg 30-31), Pink Tourmaline (pg 313-317)
new venture – Apache Tear (pg 47-49), Chrysoprase (pg 88-90), Rutile (pg 245-247)
New Year's resolutions – Black Tourmaline (pg 305-307)
newborns – Angel Aura Quartz (pg 205-207)
news – Tugtupite (pg 321-323)
nightmares – Chrysoprase (pg 88-90), Green Jade (pg 130-133), Smokey Quartz (pg 228-230)

north node – Imperial Topaz (pg 302-304)
nose bleed - Bloodstone (pg 64-67)
nurses – Emerald (pg 102-104)
nurturing – Rainbow Moonstone (pg 176-178)
nutrients – Heliodor (pg 113-115), Turquoise (pg 324-326)

O

obstacles – Amazonite (pg 32-35), Mahogany Obsidian (pg 188-189), Red Garnet (pg 110-112)
OCD (obsessive-compulsive disorder) – Ametrine (pg 42-43)
ocean – Larimar (pg 155-158)
old patterns – Blue Apatite (pg 50-53), Celestite (pg 77-79), Quantum Quattro™ (pg 202-204)
OM – Tibetan Quartz (pg 234-235)
oneness – Lemurian Seed Crystal (pg 159-161), Serpentine (pg 257-260), Starstone (pg 128-129)
online dating – Serpentine with Stichtite (pg 260-261)
online shopping, protection – Serpentine with Stichtite (pg 260-261)
Ophiuchus – Serpentine (pg 257-260)
opportunities, creating – Aqua Aura Quartz (pg 208-211), Pyrite (pg 199-201), Starstone (pg 128-129)
optimism – Kunzite (pg 144-146)
oral exams – Thulite (pg 296-297)
Orange Calcite – Blue Calcite (pg 70-71)
organic food – Moss Agate (pg 30-31), Seraphinite (pg 254-256)
organisation – Dumortierite (pg 100-101), Pyrite (pg 199-201)
orgasm – Serpentine (pg 257-260)
originality – Labradorite (pg 150-151)
ovaries – Rhodochrosite (pg 236-238)
overconsumption – Smokey Quartz (pg 228-230)
oversensitivity – Botswana Agate (pg 26-27)
overspending, preventing – Amber (pg 36-38), Jet (pg 141-143), Smokey Quartz (pg 228-230),
    Sugilite (pg 278-281)
ovulation - Rainbow Moonstone (pg 176-178)
Ox's Eye – Tiger's Eye (pg 298-301)
ozone layer – Lapis Lazuli (pg 152-154)

P

Pachamama – Moss Agate (pg 30-31), Smokey Quartz (pg 228-230)
pain – Clear Quartz (pg 214-217), Rainbow Fluorite (pg 108-109)
painting – Rose Quartz (pg 221-223)
Pan – Jet (pg 141-143), Moss Agate (pg 30-31)
panic – Dumortierite (pg 100-101)
panic attack – Champagne Aura Quartz (pg 212-213), Turquoise (pg 324-326)
paranormal activity – Champagne Aura Quartz (pg 212-213), Heliodor (pg 113-115), Smokey Quartz
    (pg 228-230), Tibetan Quartz (pg 234-235)
parent-child bond – Kunzite (pg 144-146), Mangano Calcite (pg 72-73), Rainbow Moonstone (pg
    176-178)
parenting – Carnelian (pg 74-76), Kunzite (pg 144-146), Rhodochrosite (pg 236-238)
Parkinson's disease – Malachite (pg 167-168)
part-time work – Pyrite (pg 199-201)
party – Champagne Aura Quartz (pg 212-213)
partying – Sugilite (pg 278-281)
passion – Pink Tourmaline (pg 313-317), Tugtupite (pg 321-323)
past – Covellite (pg 94-96), Howlite (pg 124-126), Libyan Desert Glass (pg 165-166)
past lives – Howlite (pg 124-126), Jet (pg 141-143), Libyan Desert Glass (pg 165-166), Shungite (pg
    262-266), Starstone (pg 128-129), Sugilite (pg 278-281)
path of service – Blue Sapphire (pg 248-250), Blue Star Sapphire (pg 269-271), Charoite (pg
    80-82), Pietersite (pg 196-198), Snowflake Obsidian (pg 190-192), Stichtite (pg 272-277),
    Tugtupite (pg 321-323)
patience – Chrysoprase (pg 88-90), Jet (pg 141-143), Leopardskin Jasper (pg 136-138)
pausing – Snowflake Obsidian (pg 190-192)
pay rise – Carnelian (pg 74-76), Green Tourmaline (pg 311-312)
peace –Angelite (pg 44-46), Blue Lace Agate (pg 24-25), Gem Silica (pg 86-87), Herkimer Diamond
    (pg 118-121), Howlite (pg 124-126), Lemurian Seed Crystal (pg 159-161), Rose Quartz (pg 221-223)

peace workers – Lemurian Seed Crystal (pg 159-161)

Pegasus – Star Ruby (pg 267-268)

penis – Carnelian (pg 74-76)

perfection – Pyrite (pg 199-201)

performing – Blue Calcite (pg 70-71), Blue Tourmaline (pg 308-310), Eudialyte (pg 105-107), Thulite (pg 296-297)

personal needs, understanding – Snowflake Obsidian (pg 190-192)

personal obstacles, overcoming – Charoite (pg 80-82)

persuasion – Blue Tourmaline (pg 308-310)

pessimism – Moldavite (pg 169-171), Pink Tourmaline (pg 313-317), Serpentine (pg 257-260)

pet, health – Green Jade (pg 130-133)

pet, lost - Rhodochrosite (pg 236-238)

pet, straying - Howlite (pg 124-126)

Petalite – Super Quartz (pg 285-289)

Petrified Wood – Tanzanite (pg 290-295)

Phenacite – Serpentine (pg 257-260), Super Quartz (pg 285-289)

philosophy – Hematite (pg 116-117)

phobias – Dumortierite (pg 100-101), Jet (pg 141-143), Libyan Desert Glass (pg 165-166)

physical-spiritual balance – Sugilite (pg 278-281)

pickpockets – Rainbow Moonstone (pg 176-178)

pineal gland – Amethyst (pg 39-41), Lepidolite (pg 162-164), Rainbow Moonstone (pg 176-178)

pituitary gland – Lapis Lazuli (pg 152-154), Pietersite (pg 196-198)

planes - Howlite (pg 124-126)

planetary healing – Aqua Aura Quartz (pg 208-211)

plants – Green Aventurine (pg 56-58), Green Jade (pg 130-133), Moss Agate (pg 30-31), Royal Aura Quartz (pg 226-227), Sunstone (pg 282-284), Tugtupite (pg 321-323)

play – Rhodochrosite (pg 236-238), Sunstone (pg 282-284)

playfulness – Chrysoprase (pg 88-90), Dalmatian Jasper (pg 134-135), Tanzanite (pg 290-295)

playwright – Labradorite (pg 150-151)

pleasure – Carnelian (pg 74-76), Mangano Calcite (pg 72-73), Pink Tourmaline (pg 313-317), Tanzanite (pg 290-295)

Pleiades – Celestite (pg 77-79)

PMS (premenstrual syndrome) – Bloodstone (pg 64-67), Larimar (pg 155-158)

poetry – Tugtupite (pg 321-323)

poise – Celestite (pg 77-79)

police – Blue Calcite (pg 70-71)

politics – Tugtupite (pg 321-323)

pollution – Black Onyx (pg 193-195), Lepidolite (pg 162-164), Rose Quartz (pg 221-223)

pollution, air – Lapis Lazuli (pg 152-154)

pollution, ocean – Larimar (pg 155-158)

Poseidon – Aquamarine (pg 54-55)

positivity – Rainbow Aura Quartz (pg 218-220), Tiger's Eye (pg 298-301)

postnatal depression – Mangano Calcite (pg 72-73)

potential, fulfilling – Lemurian Seed Crystal (pg 159-161), Seraphinite (pg 254-256)

poverty – Pyrite (pg 199-201)

power struggles – Black Tourmaline (pg 305-307)

praise – Selenite (pg 251-253)

Prasiolite (pg 127-128) – Super Quartz (pg 285-289)

prayer – Quantum Quattro™ (pg 202-204)

pregnancy – Angel Aura Quartz (pg 205-207), Bloodstone (pg 64-67), Rainbow Moonstone (pg 176-178), Unakite (pg 327-329), Watermelon Tourmaline (pg 318-320)

premature ejaculation – Star Ruby (pg 267-268)

present, staying – Black Tourmaline (pg 305-307), Chrysoprase (pg 88-90)

presenter – Blue Kyanite (pg 147-149)

preservation, of animals, plants, heritage, languages and culture – Leopardskin Jasper (pg 136-138), Unakite (pg 327-329)

primal self – Leopardskin Jasper (pg 136-138), Smokey Quartz (pg 228-230)

priorities – Herkimer Diamond (pg 118-121), Rainbow Fluorite (pg 108-109), Tanzanite (pg 290-295)

problem solving – Mahogany Obsidian (pg 188-189)

procrastination – Libyan Desert Glass (pg 165-166)
progress – Rainbow Aura Quartz (pg 218-220)
promotion, job – Carnelian (pg 74-76), Diamond (pg 97-99), Green Tourmaline (pg 311-312), Sunstone (pg 282-284)
prophecy – Blue Sapphire (pg 248-250)
prosperity – Amber (pg 36-38), Citrine (pg 91-93), Green Jade (pg 130-133)
protection – Diamond (pg 97-99), Fire Agate (pg 28-29), Nuummite (pg 182-184), Rainbow Moonstone (pg 176-178), Tiger's Eye (pg 298-301)
protection, assets – Hiddenite (pg 122-123)
protection, at night – Apache Tear (pg 47-49), Black Onyx (pg 193-195)
protection, Earth – Hiddenite (pg 122-123)
protection, emotional – Black Onyx (pg 193-195), Nuummite (pg 182-184), Star Ruby (pg 267-268)
protection, for animals – Black Onyx (pg 193-195), Leopardskin Jasper (pg 136-138), Red Jasper (pg 139-140), Unakite (pg 327-329)
protection, for gay people – Stichtite (pg 272-277)
protection, for minorities – Serpentine with Stichtite (pg 260-261)
protection, from fire – Fire Agate (pg 28-29)
protection, habitats – Hiddenite (pg 122-123), Unakite (pg 327-329)
protection, home – Apache Tear (pg 47-49), Black Obsidian (pg 185-187), Black Onyx (pg 193-195), Tiger's Eye (pg 298-301)
protection, illness or disease – Pyrite (pg 199-201)
protection, mental – Black Onyx (pg 193-195), Nuummite (pg 182-184), Star Ruby (pg 267-268), Tiger's Eye (pg 298-301)
protection, physical – Black Obsidian (pg 185-187), Nuummite (pg 182-184), Star Ruby (pg 267-268)
protection, sacred or ancient sites – Carnelian (pg 74-76)
protection, self – Black Obsidian (pg 185-187), Black Onyx (pg 193-195), Nuummite (pg 182-184), Star Ruby (pg 267-268)
protection, spiritual – Nuummite (pg 182-184), Star Ruby (pg 267-268), Stichtite (pg 272-277), Tibetan Quartz (pg 234-235)
protection, unloving energies – Pink Tourmaline (pg 313-317)
protests – Quantum Quattro™ (pg 202-204)
psychiatric health – Lepidolite (pg 162-164)
psychic attack – Apache Tear (pg 47-49), Stichtite (pg 272-277)
psychic awareness – Azurite (pg 59-61), Blue Star Sapphire (pg 269-271), Stichtite (pg 272-277), Tanzanite (pg 290-295)
psychologists – Emerald (pg 102-104)
puberty – Emerald (pg 102-104), Eudialyte (pg 105-107), Morganite (pg 179-181)
public speaking – Blue Calcite (pg 70-71), Blue Kyanite (pg 147-149), Blue Tourmaline (pg 308-310)
public transport - Howlite (pg 124-126)
purification – Shungite (pg 262-266)
purity – Selenite (pg 251-253)
Purple Fluorite - Tanzanite (pg 290-295)
Purpurite –Angelite (pg 44-46), Pyrite (pg 199-201)
Purpurite – Super Quartz (pg 285-289)
pyramid – Rainbow Aura Quartz (pg 218-220)

Q
qi – Turquoise (pg 324-326)
Quan Yin – Green Jade (pg 130-133)

R
Ra – Sunstone (pg 282-284)
racism – Morganite (pg 179-181), Super Quartz (pg 285-289)
radiation – Black Tourmaline (pg 305-307), Lepidolite (pg 162-164), Shungite (pg 262-266)
radiation, electromagnetic – Black Tourmaline (pg 305-307), Shungite (pg 262-266)
radiation, nuclear – Malachite (pg 167-168)
radiation, plutonium – Malachite (pg 167-168)
radiation, uranium – Malachite (pg 167-168)
radiotherapy – Tanzanite (pg 290-295)
Raguel – Red Jasper (pg 139-140)

Rahu – Imperial Topaz (pg 302-304)

rain – Bloodstone (pg 64-67), Red Jasper (pg 139-140)

Rainbow Serpent – Smokey Quartz (pg 228-230)

rape – Blue Sapphire (pg 248-250)

Raphael – Emerald (pg 102-104), Gem Silica (pg 86-87)

rashes – Leopardskin Jasper (pg 136-138)

Raziel – Tanzan Aura Quartz (pg 231-233)

rebirth – Azurite (pg 59-61), Lepidolite (pg 162-164)

recluse – Smokey Quartz (pg 228-230)

recognition – Snowflake Obsidian (pg 190-192)

reconciliation – Blue Calcite (pg 70-71), Rhodonite (pg 239-241)

recovery – Howlite (pg 124-126), Red Garnet (pg 110-112)

recycling – Amazonite (pg 32-35), Amber (pg 36-38)

Red Calcite – Blue Calcite (pg 70-71)

rehabilitation – Shungite (pg 262-266)

rehydration – Royal Aura Quartz (pg 226-227)

Reiki – Herkimer Diamond (pg 118-121), Mangano Calcite (pg 72-73), Serpentine (pg 257-260)

rejection – Watermelon Tourmaline (pg 318-320)

relationships, harmony – Angel Aura Quartz (pg 205-207)

relationships, improving – Rhodochrosite (pg 236-238), Rhodonite (pg 239-241), Tanzanite (pg 290-295)

relationships, interracial, interreligious, gay – Ametrine (pg 42-43), Stichtite (pg 272-277)

relationships, long-distance – Herkimer Diamond (pg 118-121)

relationships, realistic expectations – Mookaite (pg 172-175), Rhodonite (pg 239-241)

relaxation – Amethyst (pg 39-41), Blue Lace Agate (pg 24-25), Larimar (pg 155-158)

relocating home – Pink Tourmaline (pg 313-317)

remembering – Blue Kyanite (pg 147-149)

renewable energy – Sunstone (pg 282-284)

renewal – Green Tourmaline (pg 311-312)

repressed thoughts and emotions – Covellite (pg 94-96)

repression - Amazonite (pg 32-35)

reptiles – Chrysoprase (pg 88-90)

research – Hematite (pg 116-117)

resilience – Tibetan Quartz (pg 234-235), Tugtupite (pg 321-323)

resourcefulness – Amber (pg 36-38)

resources, fair distribution – Pyrite (pg 199-201), Snowflake Obsidian (pg 190-192)

responsibility, taking - Morganite (pg 179-181)

rest – Snowflake Obsidian (pg 190-192)

restaurants – Seraphinite (pg 254-256)

revenge – Chrysocolla (pg 83-86), Jet (pg 141-143)

revolution – Tugtupite (pg 321-323)

rites of passage – Morganite (pg 179-181)

ritual – Tanzan Aura Quartz (pg 231-233)

rivals, in love – Thulite (pg 296-297)

road rage, avoiding – Black Obsidian (pg 185-187)

robbery – Mangano Calcite (pg 72-73)

romance – Rose Aura Quartz (pg 224-225), Tugtupite (pg 321-323)

RSI – Selenite (pg 251-253)

RSL – Selenite (pg 251-253)

runes – Covellite (pg 94-96)

running – Ruby (pg 242-244)

S

sacral chakra, nurturing – Sunstone (pg 282-284)

sacral chakra, soothing – Amber (pg 36-38)

sacral chakra, stimulating – Carnelian (pg 74-76)

sacred geometry – Tanzan Aura Quartz (pg 231-233)

sacred sites - Serpentine (pg 257-260)

SAD (seasonal affective disorder. – Sunstone (pg 282-284)

sadness – Amber (pg 36-38), Citrine (pg 91-93)

safety, workplace – Carnelian (pg 74-76)
sailing – Aquamarine (pg 54-55)
sales representative – Pyrite (pg 199-201)
scheduling – Pyrite (pg 199-201)
schizophrenia – Sugilite (pg 278-281)
school, success – Green Aventurine (pg 56-58), Howlite (pg 124-126), Pink Tourmaline (pg 313-317)
science – Hematite (pg 116-117), Tanzan Aura Quartz (pg 231-233)
scientists – Emerald (pg 102-104), Sugilite (pg 278-281), Tanzan Aura Quartz (pg 231-233)
scrying –Angelite (pg 44-46), Black Obsidian (pg 185-187), Covellite (pg 94-96), Diamond (pg 97-99), Hematite (pg 116-117), Herkimer Diamond (pg 118-121), Jet (pg 141-143), Larimar (pg 155-158), Pyrite (pg 199-201), Rainbow Aura Quartz (pg 218-220), Snowflake Obsidian (pg 190-192), Star Ruby (pg 267-268)
sculpting – Rose Quartz (pg 221-223)
sea – Larimar (pg 155-158)
séance – Champagne Aura Quartz (pg 212-213)
security – Mangano Calcite (pg 72-73)
seduction – Thulite (pg 296-297)
Seichim – Mangano Calcite (pg 72-73)
Selene – Rainbow Moonstone (pg 176-178)
self-expression – Chrysocolla (pg 83-86), Rutile (pg 245-247)
self-harm – Kunzite (pg 144-146), Star Ruby (pg 267-268)
self-neglect – Kunzite (pg 144-146), Star Ruby (pg 267-268)
self-destructive behaviour – Kunzite (pg 144-146)
self-employment – Ametrine (pg 42-43), Heliodor (pg 113-115), Rutile (pg 245-247)
self-esteem – Emerald (pg 102-104), Eudialyte (pg 105-107), Rose Aura Quartz (pg 224-225), Star Ruby (pg 267-268), Tugtupite (pg 321-323), Unakite (pg 327-329)
self-knowledge – Rhodochrosite (pg 236-238)
selflessness – Green Jade (pg 130-133), Starstone (pg 128-129)
self-worth – Eudialyte (pg 105-107), Pink Tourmaline (pg 313-317), Rose Aura Quartz (pg 224-225), Star Ruby (pg 267-268), Tugtupite (pg 321-323)
selling house – Carnelian (pg 74-76)
sensuality – Carnelian (pg 74-76), Mangano Calcite (pg 72-73), Pink Tourmaline (pg 313-317)
separation – Lepidolite (pg 162-164), Rainbow Aura Quartz (pg 218-220), Rhodonite (pg 239-241)
Seraphiel – Seraphinite (pg 254-256)
serious, overly – Dalmatian Jasper (pg 134-135)
sex – Carnelian (pg 74-76), Green Jade (pg 130-133), Pink Tourmaline (pg 313-317), Red Garnet (pg 110-112), Star Ruby (pg 267-268), Sunstone (pg 282-284), Thulite (pg 296-297)
sex hormones – Pietersite (pg 196-198)
sexism - Amazonite (pg 32-35)
sexuality – Fire Agate (pg 28-29), Star Ruby (pg 267-268), Sunstone (pg 282-284), Thulite (pg 296-297)
shadow self – Covellite (pg 94-96)
shadow work – Nuummite (pg 182-184)
shamanism – Leopardskin Jasper (pg 136-138)
shapeshifting – Leopardskin Jasper (pg 136-138)
sharing – Pink Tourmaline (pg 313-317), Watermelon Tourmaline (pg 318-320)
Shattuckite – Quantum Quattro™ (pg 202-204)
shift work – Rainbow Moonstone (pg 176-178)
shopaholic – Jet (pg 141-143)
shopping – Celestite (pg 77-79)
shopping, grocery – Larimar (pg 155-158)
shoulders – Aqua Aura Quartz (pg 208-211)
showmanship – Thulite (pg 296-297)
shyness – Dumortierite (pg 100-101), Fire Agate (pg 28-29), Moss Agate (pg 30-31)
siblings, playing happily – Black Tourmaline (pg 305-307)
sight – Covellite (pg 94-96)
Silent Warrior – Libyan Desert Glass (pg 165-166)
simplicity – Red Jasper (pg 139-140), Stichtite (pg 272-277)
singing – Blue Tourmaline (pg 308-310), Celestite (pg 77-79), Covellite (pg 94-96)
skeleton – Pyrite (pg 199-201)

skin – Chrysoprase (pg 88-90), Leopardskin Jasper (pg 136-138), Tanzanite (pg 290-295)

skin care – Chrysoprase (pg 88-90)

skin disorders – Shungite (pg 262-266)

slander – Red Garnet (pg 110-112)

sleep – Amethyst (pg 39-41), Celestite (pg 77-79), Howlite (pg 124-126), Rainbow Moonstone (pg 176-178), Quantum Quattro™ (pg 202-204)

smell – Covellite (pg 94-96), Red Garnet (pg 110-112)

smog – Lapis Lazuli (pg 152-154)

smoking, quitting – Botswana Agate (pg 26-27), Dalmatian Jasper (pg 134-135)

smudging – Shungite (pg 262-266)

snakebites – Serpentine (pg 257-260)

snoring – Blue Lace Agate (pg 24-25)

sobriety – Amethyst (pg 39-41)

socialising – Blue Kyanite (pg 147-149), Diamond (pg 97-99), Sunstone (pg 282-284)

solar plexus chakra, nurturing – Heliodor (pg 113-115)

solar plexus chakra, soothing – Champagne Aura Quartz (pg 212-213)

solar plexus chakra, stimulating – Citrine (pg 91-93)

solar power ¬– Sunstone (pg 282-284)

solidarity – Red Jasper (pg 139-140)

soppiness – Sugilite (pg 278-281)

sorrow – Seraphinite (pg 254-256)

soul groups – Starstone (pg 128-129), Tanzan Aura Quartz (pg 231-233)

soul mate – Eudialyte (pg 105-107), Kunzite (pg 144-146), Larimar (pg 155-158), Star Ruby (pg 267-268), Stichtite (pg 272-277)

soul path – Herkimer Diamond (pg 118-121), Imperial Topaz (pg 302-304)

soul star chakra, nurturing with Achroite or Goshenite – Super Quartz (pg 285-289)

soul star chakra, soothing – Selenite (pg 251-253)

soul star chakra, stimulating – Super Quartz (pg 285-289)

sound healing - Chrysocolla (pg 83-86)

south node – Blue Apatite (pg 50-53)

special needs - Rhodonite (pg 239-241)

spirit guides – Herkimer Diamond (pg 118-121), Moldavite (pg 169-171), Quantum Quattro™ (pg 202-204), Rhodonite (pg 239-241), Stichtite (pg 272-277), Tanzan Aura Quartz (pg 231-233)

spiritual awakening – Super Quartz (pg 285-289)

spiritual growth – Serpentine with Stichtite (pg 260-261), Jet (pg 141-143), Lepidolite (pg 162-164), Moldavite (pg 169-171), Mookaite (pg 172-175), Pietersite (pg 196-198), Quantum Quattro™ (pg 202-204), Stichtite (pg 272-277)

spiritual messages, interpreting – Blue Star Sapphire (pg 269-271)

spirituality, studying – Hematite (pg 116-117)

spontaneity – Champagne Aura Quartz (pg 212-213)

sports – Watermelon Tourmaline (pg 318-320)

spreadsheet – Pyrite (pg 199-201)

stage work – Thulite (pg 296-297)

stage fright – Dumortierite (pg 100-101)

stamina – Clear Quartz (pg 214-217), Nuummite (pg 182-184)

starvation – Rainbow Aura Quartz (pg 218-220)

staying present – Black Tourmaline (pg 305-307), Stichtite (pg 272-277)

Steatite – Shungite (pg 262-266)

stepfamily – Super Quartz (pg 285-289)

stillness – Jet (pg 141-143)

STIs (sexually transmitted infections – Unakite (pg 327-329)

storms – Bloodstone (pg 64-67), Diamond (pg 97-99), Pietersite (pg 196-198)

storytelling – Covellite (pg 94-96)

stress – Black Onyx (pg 193-195), Black Tourmaline (pg 305-307), Dumortierite (pg 100-101), Larimar (pg 155-158), Lepidolite (pg 162-164)

stress, at work – Blue Lace Agate (pg 24-25)

structure – Pyrite (pg 199-201)

stubbornness – Black Tourmaline (pg 305-307)

stuck – Heliodor (pg 113-115). Mahogany Obsidian (pg 188-189) studying – Ametrine (pg 42-43), Dumortierite (pg 100-101), Howlite (pg 124-126), Pink Tourmaline (pg 313-317), Rainbow Fluorite (pg 108-109)

success – Diamond (pg 97-99), Tiger's Eye (pg 298-301)

suffering - Morganite (pg 179-181)

suicide – Moldavite (pg 169-171)

suitors, other – Thulite (pg 296-297)

sun – Sunstone (pg 282-284)

sunburn – Larimar (pg 155-158), Royal Aura Quartz (pg 226-227)

Super Seven™ - Super Quartz (pg 285-289)

support – Rhodonite (pg 239-241)

supporting others - Stichtite (pg 272-277)

surgeons – Emerald (pg 102-104)

surveillance – Tiger's Eye (pg 298-301)

sweating, excess - Tanzanite (pg 290-295)

swimming pool, safety – Aquamarine (pg 54-55)

sylphs/sylphides – Heliodor (pg 113-115)

T

table manners – Bronzite (pg 68-69)

Tai Chi – Leopardskin Jasper (pg 136-138)

tarot – Covellite (pg 94-96), Starstone (pg 128-129)

taste – Covellite (pg 94-96)

teaching – Herkimer Diamond (pg 118-121)

teamwork – Dalmatian Jasper (pg 134-135), Watermelon Tourmaline (pg 318-320)

teenagers – Kunzite (pg 144-146)

teeth – Aquamarine (pg 54-55)

teeth, brushing – Blue Sapphire (pg 248-250)

teething – Amber (pg 36-38)

telepathy –Angelite (pg 44-46), Aqua Aura Quartz (pg 208-211)

terrorism - Gem Silica (pg 86-87), Super Quartz (pg 285-289)

theft – Black Onyx (pg 193-195)

third eye chakra, nurturing – Covellite (pg 94-96), Lapis Lazuli (pg 152-154), Tanzanite (pg 290-295)

third eye chakra, soothing – Dumortierite (pg 100-101)

third eye chakra, stimulating – Blue Sapphire (pg 248-250), Royal Aura Quartz (pg 226-227), Tanzanite (pg 290-295)

Thor – Pietersite (pg 196-198)

Thoth – Green Aventurine (pg 56-58)

throat – Aquamarine (pg 54-55), Aqua Aura Quartz (pg 208-211)

throat chakra, balancing – Blue Apatite (pg 50-53), Larimar (pg 155-158), Turquoise (pg 324-326)

throat chakra, soothing – Blue Lace Agate (pg 24-25)

throat chakra, stimulating – Aqua Aura Quartz (pg 208-211)

thunderstorms – Pietersite (pg 196-198)

thymus – Chrysocolla (pg 83-86), Turquoise (pg 324-326)

thyroid – Aquamarine (pg 54-55), Aqua Aura Quartz (pg 208-211)

Tibetan singing bowl – Tibetan Quartz (pg 234-235)

tidiness – Amazonite (pg 32-35), Dumortierite (pg 100-101)

Tiffany Stone – Super Quartz (pg 285-289)

tiger conservation – Tiger's Eye (pg 298-301)

timewasters – Imperial Topaz (pg 302-304)

Tinaksite – Charoite (pg 80-82), Howlite (pg 124-126)

tinnitus – Black Tourmaline (pg 305-307)

toes – Nuummite (pg 182-184)

togetherness – Sugilite (pg 278-281)

tolerance – Chrysocolla (pg 83-86), Pietersite (pg 196-198), Rose Aura Quartz (pg 224-225), Super Quartz (pg 285-289)

tongue – Aquamarine (pg 54-55), Aqua Aura Quartz (pg 208-211)

tonsillitis – Aqua Aura Quartz (pg 208-211)

tornado – Diamond (pg 97-99), Pietersite (pg 196-198)

touch – Covellite (pg 94-96), Pink Tourmaline (pg 313-317)

Tourmaline, Clear – Super Quartz (pg 285-289)

toxins – Leopardskin Jasper (pg 136-138), Seraphinite (pg 254-256), Serpentine (pg 257-260)

transformation – Black Tourmaline (pg 305-307), Herkimer Diamond (pg 118-121), Malachite (pg 167-168), Serpentine (pg 257-260), Tanzanite (pg 290-295)

transgender – Stichtite (pg 272-277)

transition – Lepidolite (pg 162-164), Pyrite (pg 199-201)

trauma – Dumortierite (pg 100-101), Tanzan Aura Quartz (pg 231-233)

travel – Bronzite (pg 68-69), Champagne Aura Quartz (pg 212-213), Emerald (pg 102-104), Mookaite (pg 172-175), Rainbow Moonstone (pg 176-178), Sunstone (pg 282-284), Super Quartz (pg 285-289)

Tree Agate – Herkimer Diamond (pg 118-121)

trees – Moss Agate (pg 30-31)

tropical pets – Heliodor (pg 113-115)

trust – Herkimer Diamond (pg 118-121)

truth – Blue Calcite (pg 70-71), Chrysocolla (pg 83-86), Hematite (pg 116-117), Herkimer Diamond (pg 118-121), Larimar (pg 155-158), Shungite (pg 262-266), Tanzanite (pg 290-295)

tsunami – Diamond (pg 97-99), Pietersite (pg 196-198)

turning point – Rainbow Aura Quartz (pg 218-220)

twin soul – Star Ruby (pg 267-268)

twins – Blue Star Sapphire (pg 269-271)

two spirited - Stichtite (pg 272-277)

typing, improving skills – Green Aventurine (pg 56-58)

U

Uadjet (pg 141-143) - Serpentine (pg 257-260)

uncle – Nuummite (pg 182-184)

unconditional love – Hiddenite (pg 122-123), Pink Tourmaline (pg 313-317), Rose Aura Quartz (pg 224-225), Rose Quartz (pg 221-223), Star Ruby (pg 267-268), Sugilite (pg 278-281)

underdog – Red Jasper (pg 139-140)

Unicorn – Blue Star Sapphire (pg 269-271)

unity – Diamond (pg 97-99), Lemurian Seed Crystal (pg 159-161), Pyrite (pg 199-201), Super Quartz (pg 285-289)

Universal Love – Sugilite (pg 278-281), Super Quartz (pg 285-289)

unknown illness - Serpentine (pg 257-260)

Uriel – Diamond (pg 97-99), Herkimer Diamond (pg 118-121)

V

vagina – Carnelian (pg 74-76)

vandalism – Mangano Calcite (pg 72-73)

vanity – Covellite (pg 94-96)

vegan – Green Tourmaline (pg 311-312), Seraphinite (pg 254-256)

vegetarian – Green Tourmaline (pg 311-312), Seraphinite (pg 254-256)

veins, varicose – Bloodstone (pg 64-67)

Vesta – Red Garnet (pg 110-112)

Vibration, raising – Tiger's Eye (pg 298-301)

vibrational match - Jet (pg 141-143)

victim mentality – Amazonite (pg 32-35)

victory – Bloodstone (pg 64-67)

violence – Kunzite (pg 144-146)

vision – Blue Apatite (pg 50-53), Blue Calcite (pg 70-71), Covellite (pg 94-96), Lapis Lazuli (pg 152-154)

vitamin D – Sunstone (pg 282-284)

volunteering – Blue Tourmaline (pg 308-310), Charoite (pg 80-82)

W

Wadjet (pg 141-143) – Serpentine (pg 257-260)

walking – Ruby (pg 242-244)

war – Blue Lace Agate (pg 24-25), Gem Silica (pg 86-87), Rose Quartz (pg 221-223)

warmth, during winter – Heliodor (pg 113-115)

warnings – Ruby (pg 242-244)

warts – Labradorite (pg 150-151)

RECOMMENDED READING

Cassandra Eason, *The New Crystal Bible*, Carlton, London, 2012

Dr. John F. Demartini, *The Breakthrough Experience*, Hayhouse, USA, 2002

Fred Hageneder and Anne Heng, *The Tree Angel Oracle*, Earthdancer Books, Scotland, 2008

Greg Travena, **www.essentiallyaustralia.com.au**, information retrieved 2014

Gritman Essential Oils, **www.gritman.com**, information retrieved 2014

Gurudas, *Flower Essences and Vibrational Healing*, Cassandra Press, USA, 1983

Henry M. Mason, *The Seven Secrets of Crystal Talismans*, Llewellyn, USA, 2008

Inna Segal, *The Secret Language of your Body*, Blue Angel, Australia, 2014

Jamie Sams and David Carson, *Medicine Cards*, St Martin's Press, USA, 1999

Jolyon Ralph and Ida Chau, **www.mindat.org**, information retrieved 2013–2014

Louise L. Hay, *You Can Heal Your Life*, Hayhouse, USA, 2004

Regina Martino, Shungite – Protection, Healing and Detoxification, Healing Arts Press, Canada, 2014

Rev. Annette Young, **www.angelfocus.com**, information retrieved 2014

Scott Alexander King, *Animal Messenger*, New Holland Publishing, Australia, 2007 (revised and republished as *World Animal Dreaming*, Animal Dreaming Publishing, Australia, 2014)

Scott Cunningham, *Cunningham's Encyclopaedia of Crystal, Gem & Metal Magic*, Llewellyn, USA, 1996

Scott Cunningham, *Cunningham's Encyclopaedia of Magical Herbs*, Llewellyn, USA, 1994

Susan Gregg, *The Complete Illustrated Encyclopaedia of Magical Plants*, Fairwind, USA, 2014

Ted Andrews, *Animal-wise*, Dragonhawk, USA, 2009

www.psychic-revelation.com, information retrieved 2013–2014

OTHER WORKS BY THE AUTHOR

CRYSTAL REFLECTIONS – ANNUAL DIARY

Following the seasons of the Southern Hemisphere, this beautiful full-colour diary is so much more than just an organiser. Each week offers the opportunity to learn more about a popular crystal aligned with the changing seasons of the year. The diary offers space for you to reflect and be grateful for the beauty in your life. Also included are simple crystal meditations and practices for each full moon, star sign, Mercury and other planetary retrogrades and significant seasonal events. The perfect tool for reconnecting with the magic of Mother Nature.

CRYSTAL CONNECTIONS MESSAGE CARDS

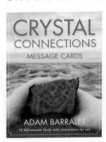

Mother Nature communicates to us in many ways, lovingly guiding us through our lives. The messages from crystals can help us to finding our way towards a path of love, peace and harmony. The *Crystal Wisdom Message Cards* are a set of 70 cards of beautifully photographed crystals accompanied by messages from that crystal just for you. These cards are ideal for instant guidance or to set you up for your day ahead.

CRYSTAL KEEPERS ORACLE CARDS

Around the globe, in realms beyond our world, exist the guardians of the crystal world. Beings that manifest as a recognisable personifications to guide and support us all on our path towards the greater good. You have been invited to step into their worlds and learn their teachings and wisdoms. Allow each guardian to meet you upon the threshold of change and teach you how to unlock the powers of their crystals as well as plants, animals and more so that you may harness their power today. This unique oracle of 45 original artworks, gives you access to a new level of working with your favourite crystals. Allow the *Crystal Keeper Oracle* to offer you guidance and direction as they answer your deepest life questions in clear and profound ways.

CRYSTAL CONNECTIONS – GUIDED MEDITATIONS

 The Crystal Connections meditation range offer the ultimate way to connect with the crystals that have come into your life. Allow yourself to be gently guided to feel, hear and connect with your crystal, so you can begin to experience its true magic. Allow *Crystal Connections Meditations* to take you on an amazing journey to a happier, healthier, loving, safe, free and powerful you! Each album contains four individual guided meditations inspirationally designed to include elements of the natural world that harmonise with each crystal's energy, and further enhance the aim of the meditation. The accompanying music includes various components, including planetary frequency and chakra keys, allowing you to harmonise your own energy with that of your crystal.

NOTES

NOTES

ABOUT ADAM BARRALET

 The true *Rock Star* of the crystal community, Adam Barralet has been observing and living in tune with nature since childhood. Growing up amongst the bushland and wildlife of the hills in Western Australia, and residing in various locations around the world has presented Adam with diverse opportunities to access extensive and eclectic teachings about the secrets of Mother Earth. All this knowledge he takes back to nature, with a crystal in hand and the moon as his consort, to rediscover the ways of old and how they can again be used to help us in this New Age. He has now established himself as one of Australia's premier spiritual teachers, adept at working with crystals, along with essential oils, animal guides, tarot and astrology. Adam's passionate, engaging and relatable style of sharing the magic of nature has helped people all around the world change their lives and reconnect with the blessing of nature's gifts. Let him help you discover the secret messages that the universe eagerly wants you to hear.